Rebuilding Societies After Civil War

Critical Roles for International Assistance

edited by Krishna Kumar

LYNNE
RIENNER
PUBLISHERS

BOULDER
LONDON

Published in the United States of America in 1997 by
Lynne Rienner Publishers, Inc.
1800 30th Street, Boulder, Colorado 80301

and in the United Kingdom by
Lynne Rienner Publishers, Inc.
3 Henrietta Street, Covent Garden, London WC2E 8LU

Library of Congress Cataloging-in-Publication Data
Rebuilding societies after civil war : critical roles for
    international assistance / edited by Krishna Kumar.
        p.   cm.
    Includes bibliographical references and index.
    ISBN 1-55587-642-0 (alk. paper)
    ISBN 1-55587-652-8 (pbk. alk. paper)
    1. International relief.   2. Revolutions.   3. Economic assistance.
4. Technical assistance.   I. Kumar, Krishna.
HV553.R359   1996
361.2'6—DC20   96-25508
                                                                        CIP

British Cataloguing in Publication Data
A Cataloguing in Publication record for this book
is available from the British Library.

This book was typeset by Letra Libre,
1705 14th Street, Suite 341, Boulder, Colorado 80304.

Printed and bound in the United States of America

    The paper used in this publication meets the
(∞) requirements of the American National Standard for
    Permanence of Paper for Printed Library Materials Z39.48-1984.

5 4 3 2 1

Contents

Part 3
Assistance for Economic Rehabilitation

Illustrations

Tables

Figures

Sidebars

Foreword

Rebuilding Societies After Civil War is a particularly timely publication, and Krishna Kumar deserves considerable credit for his skill in organizing and editing the book.

The issues addressed reflect the increasingly complex challenges the international community faces in the post–Cold War era. The end of the Cold War brought with it rising expectations that a new world order was imminent. The old security threats, which consumed inordinately large national expenditures and preoccupied the global community for forty-five years, diminished with astounding rapidity.

But the world has not turned out the way many of our leaders had envisioned or hoped. For better or worse, the international community (because of the threat of mutually destructive nuclear warfare) was much more focused and much more proactive during the Cold War. Crises could be more easily managed because there existed international rules of the game that the superpowers, for the most part, observed. This tacit understanding produced relative stability and global prosperity for nearly forty years. The superpowers could and did exercise control over their clients or surrogates. This was a reality born of necessity to avoid direct superpower confrontation.

The end to the Cold War brought with it the unraveling of some nation-states, where the leadership no longer had resources lavished on them by their patrons, or the ability to maintain themselves in power. In other cases, such as the former Yugoslavia, forces were unleashed that had been frozen in time for nearly forty-five years. This is one of the legacies of the Cold War for which we are now paying the price. The global management challenges we face today are very different from those of the Cold War era; the new challenges require us to rethink our traditional understanding of national security.

Instability breeds greater instability. If it could be contained just to the countries experiencing the upheavals, then the consequences might be tolerable for the global community. However, the consequences are rarely contained, and often they sow the seeds of larger conflict. This century's early history bears witness. After all, few people recognized at the time that the Balkans would be the tinderbox that would plunge the world into the twentieth century's first global war, sparked by the assassination of an Austrian archduke in an obscure city called Sarajevo.

Just as institutions were created to help manage the global economy and prevent a repeat of the 1920s and 1930s, precursor to World War II—just as institutions were created or restructured to contain the Cold War—so now are we compelled to restructure our mechanisms and tools to deal with the world as it is today. Our ability to manage these new challenges and dangers for the benefit of the American people (including their continued security) will depend on whether we possess the wisdom that comes with an understanding of, and appreciation for, these lessons of history.

Krishna Kumar's book presents us with a series of case studies that gives us insight into what went wrong and what went right—and why. Most important, he challenges us to reassess where we have been and where we are going. It is must reading.

J. Brian Atwood
Administrator,
United States Agency for
International Development

Acknowledgments

In preparing this volume, I received invaluable help from scholars, humanitarian experts, officials of international donor agencies, and senior managers of the Agency for International Development. While it is not possible here to acknowledge them all, each has my heartfelt gratitude. I single out a few for special mention:

The idea of a volume on rebuilding war-torn societies occurred to me while I was directing the rehabilitation, reconstruction, and repatriation component of the *Joint Evaluation of International Assistance to Rwanda.* I discussed the idea with Niels Dabelstein, chairman of the steering committee for the evaluation, who not only strongly encouraged me to pursue it, but also indicated that DANIDA (Danish International Development Assistance) would purchase copies of the book for wider distribution in developing countries. But for his enthusiastic support, I would not have undertaken this time-consuming endeavor.

Within the Agency for International Development, I would like to express my gratitude to Brian Atwood, the administrator. Many senior officials also encouraged me. Richard McCall, the chief of the staff, was very supportive. So was Larry Garber, the senior deputy assistant administrator of the Bureau of Policy and Program Coordination, who read and commented on the manuscript. Michael Calavan, director of the Program Operations Division in the Center for Development Information and Evaluation, freed me of many managerial responsibilities during the Rwanda evaluation, enabling me to work on this volume as well. Finally, Gerald Britan, director of the Center, was very generous with his time and support.

Among experts who commented on the initial proposal or on the manuscript were Nicole Ball of the Overseas Development Council; Jeff Drumtra of the U.S. Committee for Refugees; Dennis Gallagher of the Refugee Policy Group; John Eriksson, a World Bank consultant and former USAID official; Ted Kliest of the Netherlands Ministry of Foreign Affairs; and Mattias Stiefel of the UN Research Institute for Social Development.

I would not have completed this volume without the efficient and gracious assistance of Carolyn Knapp. She was involved in every phase of the enterprise from conceptualization through reviewing and editing articles, and proved to be a superb researcher and coordinator. Gia Hamilton at Lynne Rienner Publishers very ably supervised production of the book.

I dare not thank individual contributors who authored different chapters, for this volume is as much their's as mine.

Krishna Kumar
United States Agency for
International Development

Rebuilding Societies After Civil War

1

The Nature and Focus of International Assistance for Rebuilding War-Torn Societies

Krishna Kumar

The end of the Cold War, vigorous international mediation, growing war fatigue among the suffering people, and the realization on the part of warring parties that their objectives cannot be achieved through war have led to the cessation of intrastate conflict in many parts of the world. In other cases, one warring party has clearly emerged victorious, thereby ending the conflict. Consequently, countries such as Angola, Cambodia, El Salvador, Ethiopia, Haiti, Mozambique, Nicaragua, Rwanda, and Uganda are now breathing a respite from civil wars.

The cessation of civil wars presents an unprecedented opportunity for these countries to rebuild their societies, polities, and economies and to embrace reforms that have been elusive in the past. There are many successful examples of this: The war-shattered countries of Europe rebuilt themselves into powerful democracies. Japan emerged from the ashes of war as a leading world economic power. South Korea became known as an Asian tiger after a devastating war. However, all these societies required substantial and sustained economic and technical assistance to recover and grow.

This chapter gives an overview of the nature and focus of international assistance for the rehabilitation of war-torn societies in order to provide context for the articles and case studies that follow. It focuses on the political, social, and economic sectors in which the international community has designed and implemented a vast array of projects and programs. It examines the nature of these international interventions, their problems and achievements, and issues that deserve further discussion in each sector.

The discussion in this chapter is illustrative and not comprehensive; the scope is limited in two respects.[1] First, the role of international diplomacy—including the UN peacekeeping operations, which is critical for promoting peace accords, monitoring cease-fires, and resolving thorny political and military issues during transition—is not examined, because of constraints of time and space. Second, the primary focus is on developing countries, where the perennial problems of poverty, political instability and underdevelopment are compounded by violent conflicts that devastate political and economic institutions and erode the social fabric.

This chapter is organized as follows: A brief clarification of the key concepts is presented in the first section. The second section focuses on political rehabilitation; the third concentrates on the rehabilitation of social services and institutions. Economic reform and reconstruction are discussed in the fourth section. Finally, the fifth section discusses a few crosscutting issues underlying international assistance programs.

Conceptual Clarification

A number of concepts used in the following pages need clarification. *Civil war* refers to violent conflicts between two or more parties for control of political authority in a state or part of it. Such conflicts can take the form of conventional battles or prolonged guerrilla warfare.

The concept of *rehabilitation* is problematic.[2] In the literature on physical disasters, it means restoring physical and institutional structures to their predisaster levels. Sometimes a distinction is also made between rehabilitation and reconstruction; the former refers to the rehabilitation of crisis-affected households, the latter to physical and social infrastructures. Such a narrow conceptualization of rehabilitation is inappropriate in the case of war-torn societies for many reasons.

The causes of civil wars are mostly political; civil wars signify failed political systems that could not perform essential governance functions, thereby generating political insurgencies. The need, therefore, is not to go back to precrisis conditions but to move in a different direction. Rehabilitating war-torn societies, then, involves redefining and reorienting relationships between political authority and the citizenry, revisiting relationships between different ethnic and social groups, creating a civil society in its broadest sense, promoting psychosocial healing and reconciliation, and reforming economic policies and institutions that foster entrepreneurship and individual initiative.

Further, in physical disasters, once hazards are over, people are able to resume their normal social and economic activities. But this is hardly possible in war-torn societies because of the widespread destruction of many critical economic, political, and even social institutions. Finally, rehabilitation is a long process; it takes several years, perhaps decades, before societies shattered by civil wars are able to effectively rebuild themselves and their governments to the point where they are able to perform the essential functions expected of them. In this chapter we have conceptualized rehabilitation broadly to encompass reform and reconstruction. As understood here, the rehabilitation process has three essential, interrelated elements:

1. *Restoration.* Depending on the nature of the devastation, physical infrastructure and facilities, basic social services, and essential government functions have to be restored.

2. *Structural reform.* Practically all war-torn societies require comprehensive reforms in their political, economic, social, and security sectors. This involves creating and/or dismantling organizations, institutions and administrative structures. For instance, a war-torn society that lacked adequate legislation to protect human rights needs new legislation for human rights and administrative mechanisms to enforce it. On the other hand, sometimes organizations created for internal security before and during the conflict need to be abolished to ensure political freedom.

3. *Institution building.* This type of rehabilitation involves improving the efficiency and effectiveness of existing institutions.

Therefore the terms *rehabilitation, reconstruction,* and *rebuilding* have been used interchangeably here: All refer to the efforts to rebuild political, economic, and social structures of war-torn societies.

The term *transition* also needs some clarification. The transition phase of a war-torn society begins when peace accords between warring parties are signed or when a party is soundly defeated and is not in a position to continue the war. This phase is over after some semblance of political order and stability has been restored, most if not all terms of the peace accords have been implemented (or are in the process of being implemented), and the government is in a position to resume its expected functions. Thus, transition is conceptualized here as a period between the cessation of hostilities and the establishment of political normalcy. In most instances, the transition phase lasts two to five years. However, a transition period is not always followed by an era of peace and stability. As the examples of Afghanistan, Angola, Rwanda, and Sudan have amply demonstrated, a country can well revert back to crisis.

Finally, the expression *the international community* is employed as a general category to refer to multilateral and bilateral agencies, intergovernmental organizations (IGOs), international nongovernmental organizations (NGOs), philanthropic organizations, relief agencies, and private sector firms that are involved in relief and reconstruction work in developing countries. The expression is somewhat of a misnomer but serves as a convenient means to refer to the many different actors working in this area.

Assistance for Political Rehabilitation

The most critical element in rebuilding war-torn societies is political rehabilitation. An intrastate conflict indicates that the state has failed to govern itself—that is, to meet the essential needs and aspirations of its people and to effectively accommodate and reconcile the demands of competing groups within the framework of economic growth and political stability. There is little doubt that in the absence of an effective and legitimate political authority, economic and social rehabilitation cannot occur, nor can further conflict and disintegration be prevented.

The political landscape of a postconflict era is hardly conducive to political reform and reconstruction. The signing of peace accords does not mean that the deep political cleavages between the warring factions have been bridged, nor does it signify that various factions have come to share a long-term commitment to peace and reconciliation. The truth is that during transitions, war-torn societies tend to remain extremely polarized. The extremist factions of warring parties constantly strive to undermine the peace accords. The case is even worse in countries where one party emerges victorious and sees little need for making significant political concessions. The presence of large groups of ex-combatants poses a continual threat to a fragile peace. The government also finds it difficult to make painful decisions, since both its political base and institutional capacity are limited. Moreover, the postcrisis climate is one of violence and suspicion, in which there is little respect for human rights and the rule of law—assuming that these existed prior to the onset of the conflict.

Although the need for political rebuilding is widely recognized, the international community lacks a well-defined framework for political reform and reconstruction that can inform its interventions. The primary focus of international assistance in the past has been on economic development; as a result, international actors do not have the necessary experience and expertise in the political sphere. But more important, bilateral and multilateral donors usually lack the will to expend their influence and resources to promote significant political change, except in geographical areas where they have vital, strategic interests. Consequently, the international community has most often initiated and implemented programs for political rehabilitation with neither firm commitment nor a strategic framework. Such programs have usually focused on institution building, promotion of elections, human rights monitoring, demobilization and reintegration of ex-combatants, and reforms in law enforcement agencies.

Institutional Capacity for Governance

In the aftermath of prolonged civil conflicts, governments are usually faced with three urgent problems. First, they are plagued with a critical shortage of trained personnel because of the systematic killing of the intelligentsia, emigration of the educated, and decay of existing educational and training institutions and facilities. Therefore, governments find it difficult to effectively operate in economic, social, and even internal security sectors. Second, and somewhat paradoxically, governments inherit a plethora of superfluous departments, agencies, and parastatal organizations—created or reinforced during the conflict to regulate production, trade, and civil supplies and to exercise political control over people. Such bloated bureaucracies are not only a severe drain on the precious resources of the government but also inhibit economic growth. The situation is most serious in countries that had command economies in the past. Finally, governments have to deal with the difficult problems of widespread inefficiency and a conspicuous lack of transparency, which are compounded during wars.

The international community has provided modest, though multifaceted, assistance to governments to address these problems. Donor agencies have funded salary support initiatives for public employees, supported training of government employees, and undertaken technical assistance projects to improve the performance of key government min-

---

Tapping the Cambodian Diaspora

In Cambodia, international agencies induced educated Cambodians living outside the country to return by providing modest financial incentives. The response has been quite encouraging. Many Cambodians living in France, the United States, and other democratic countries responded, often at considerable financial and personal sacrifice. Such returnees have been strong supporters of "pluralism, human rights, compromise politics, representative government, and other values and institutions that Cambodians formally adopted when they accepted the terms of the Paris Peace accord."   —*Robert Muscat, 1995*

istries and organizations. In Cambodia and Uganda, donor agencies have also devised and implemented projects to induce the educated overseas diaspora to return and help in the reconstruction process. In Rwanda, however, highly educated Tutsis returned spontaneously from neighboring countries without any support from the international community. Bilateral and multilateral donors have also given financial and technical support to dismantle or downsize public bureaucracies and to privatize public services and parastatals.

Many international agencies have preferred to build institutional capacities at the local rather than national level.[3] Such policies are justified on the twin grounds of efficiency and responsiveness. It is argued that local governments tend to be more efficient because they understand local problems better and can find innovative solutions. They are also more responsive because of their proximity to people. However, this sweeping generalization is not necessarily warranted by past experience.[4] The truth is that local officials can be as inefficient or corrupt as those at the national level. The experience of international donors with local governments has been a rather mixed one. For example, in Somalia, the international community had considerable success in galvanizing local governments into action, whereas in El Salvador, reliance on local governments often caused unnecessary delays and problems.

International donors have been slow to provide support for rebuilding the institutional capacity of interim governments. Such delays can erode public confidence in governmental institutions. A vicious circle can result: The international community does not channel substantial assistance through the interim government because the latter lacks institutional capacities; yet the government cannot rebuild its capacities without access to outside resources. For example, donors did not provide direct assistance to the government of Rwanda early during the transition. One consequence of this delay was the government's inability to perform even the rudimentary tasks expected of it. The line ministries did not have the staff or resources even to develop guidelines for NGOs and relief agencies, much less to coordinate their activities within an agreed framework (Kumar et al. 1996). Over time, the donor community realized its mistake and channeled resources to the Rwandan government.

Two problem areas have surfaced in international assistance programs for institutional capacity building. First is the limited relevance and high costs of training and technical assistance. There exists a widespread impression that highly paid expatriate experts lack an in-depth understanding of the local political and social landscape and often develop training activities that are not pertinent to the existing realities. This problem has not been unique to war-torn societies. Rather, it has been common to most of the international assistance programs.[5] But the problem is compounded in transition societies because of the intense pressure to solve urgent problems caused by personnel shortages. Second, international assistance programs have occasionally aggravated labor shortages in the public sector. In Cambodia and Rwanda, for instance, skilled and professional employees were lured away from the government to take up better-paying jobs in international agencies and organizations. Many professionals even preferred semiskilled jobs because of huge salary differentials (Brown and Muscat 1994).

Support for Elections

Peace accords invariably require holding free and fair elections with broad-based participation. Moreover, elections are supposed to settle the contentious issue of the political legitimacy of the government both inside and outside the country. More important, a responsive, representative political system is widely regarded as an effective mechanism for articulating the political aspirations of minority and other ethnic groups. Political competition based on ballots rather than bullets is also perceived to serve as an antidote to war and violence.

The international community has performed three distinct roles in support of elections. First, it has provided technical assistance to prepare electoral codes, manuals, voter lists, and personnel training.[6] Donor agencies have occasionally given financial assistance to political parties to enable them to effectively participate in elections, as was the case in Cambodia and Mozambique. International actors have also shared the costs of elections as an added inducement to resource-starved governments. Second, they have sent observers to monitor elections and to document irregularities and fraudulent practices. In a climate of mutual suspicion and distrust, the presence of international observers generates public confidence in the fairness of elections. Finally, bilateral and multilateral agencies have played a critical role as mediators between the warring parties before, during, and after elections. For example, when in October 1994 RENAMO threatened to withdraw from the election alleging widespread fraud on the part of the Mozambican government, only the timely intervention by the international community saved the situation.

Perhaps one of the most massive technical assistance programs provided for elections was in Cambodia, where the UN Transitional Authority in Cambodia (UNTAC) had to start from scratch. It had to draft the electoral law, regulations to govern electoral processes, and an electoral code of conduct. UNTAC also undertook to register voters, establish civil education programs, organize and conduct elections, count votes and, of course, persuade the parties to accept the outcome. Consequently, the per unit cost of each ballot cast was one of the highest for elections in recent times. Cambodia, however, has been an exceptional case; in other countries, the international community's level of involvement has been much more limited.

The holding of elections, even with the active involvement of international actors, has not always resolved the thorny issues of political legitimacy and minority representation in transition societies. The experiences of countries as diverse as Angola, Cambodia, Ethiopia, and Mozambique unmistakenly show that the ruling political parties seek to manipulate elections without compunction. Moreover, if they are defeated, as was the case in Cambodia and Nicaragua, it requires considerable outside persuasion and pressure to make them accept the election outcome. The record of the opposition parties is hardly better. They often charge fraudulent practices and also refuse to adhere to the results if they do not favor them.[7] Under these conditions, the claim of the victorious party to political legitimacy can remain dubious in the eyes of important segments of the population despite reasonably "free and fair" elections.

Further, the governments formed after elections have not always been strong or stable enough to promote reconciliation and development. Deep mutual distrust and antagonism exist between former adversaries. Moreover, leadership tends to derive its strength from ethnic, religious, or regional loyalties and therefore exploits these ascriptive affiliations to get votes. As a result, elections can aggravate those social and political cleavages that contributed to the violent conflict in the first instance. The case is different where ideological commitments were paramount in civil wars. For example, elections in El Salvador brought leftist forces within the framework of the democratic process and had a moderating influence on both the right and left. (Even then, there is a general perception in El Salvador that elections have been divisive—at least in the short run.)

There is growing recognition that a "free and fair" election in which all contesting parties accept the outcome is only a small step in the democratic rehabilitation of war-torn societies. It does not necessarily transform a society's deep-rooted political structures and culture. Holding an election does not guarantee that democratic political competition will be institutionalized in the country.[8] The majority of war-torn societies—Afghanistan, Angola, Cambodia, Ethiopia, Haiti, Mozambique, and Nicaragua—have been virtually one-party states. They did not have institutionalized democratic traditions and a strong middle class or a Westernized elite committed to democracy. Moreover, in most transition nations, as is the case in the developing world, political parties often revolve around a few charismatic personalities and are controlled by a small, urban-based elite who constantly change their loyalties.

Consequently, a long-term strategy of promoting political competition and participation through elections is necessary. To be meaningful, elections should be held regularly over time at different levels of political hierarchy and be followed by other initiatives—such as support for political decentralization, political parties, legislative strengthening, and civic education. Unfortunately, an integrated framework for elections has been absent in international assistance programs.

Human Rights Monitoring and Promotion

Human rights abuses persist, although with less severity and frequency, after the cessation of hostilities. Contributing to the persistence of violations are a climate of violence, the dominance of the military, and an internal security apparatus accustomed to unlimited license in the face of a powerless judicial system. A general improvement in the human rights situation is essential for political rehabilitation of war-torn societies. The fragile legitimacy of their governments can be further eroded if flagrant human rights violations continue to occur and guilty parties are not prosecuted and punished. Moreover, psychosocial healing and reconciliation at the community level cannot take place if human rights are not protected. But most important, respect for human rights is essential for building the foundations for a democratic political order.

With the active participation of NGOs, international agencies established human rights monitoring missions in Cambodia, El Salvador, Guatemala, Haiti, Rwanda, and Uganda. Such missions consisted of independent foreign observers who observed and documented human rights abuses in these countries. Although observers did not enjoy any judicial power, they could exert modest pressure on potential human rights violators by bringing them to public notice. For example, their presence has been a factor in the release of many detainees and prisoners in Cambodia, El Salvador, and Haiti. The United Nations Observers Mission in South Africa is also thought to have discouraged violence by security forces and political factions in demonstrations and marches. However, experience also shows that while the presence of foreign monitors may initially discourage violations, perpetuators again become emboldened if no action is taken against abusers. This appears to have been the case with human rights missions in Cambodia and Haiti (Golub 1995). In any case, the missions have been powerless in preventing large-scale human rights violations in the absence of strong political commitment at home and intense political pressure from outside.

In Cambodia, El Salvador, and Rwanda, missions also undertook public education programs in human rights. Such programs targeted a wide range of audiences—military officers, law enforcement authorities, political leaders, educators, and government officials. Seminars, symposia, public lectures, and training were held for this purpose.

In addition to missions, donor agencies have funded the establishment of special human rights commissions, like the Truth Commission in El Salvador, and international tribunals for the prosecution of war crimes and genocide, such as the one for Rwanda. By documenting human rights abuses in the past and the involvement of various individuals and groups in them, such commissions educate the public and improve the climate for the institutionalization of human rights norms in the society.[9] However, one of the limitations of truth and reconciliation commissions is that they do not have a way to enforce their recommendations.

The Commission on the Truth for El Salvador

The Commission on the Truth for El Salvador, comprising three foreign nationals, was formally established on July 15, 1992, as provided by the Salvadoran Peace Accords under the auspices of the United Nations. Its task was to investigate the violence that occurred in El Salvador between 1980 and 1991 and put an end to the perception—or reality—of impunity for officers of the armed forces. The commission focused only on the most egregious acts committed during the civil war.

The Commission had the authority to interview, freely and in private, any individuals, groups, or members of organizations; reveal the names of the perpetrators of the worst human rights violations; make recommendations concerning criminal trials and amnesties; and make binding recommendations to the government of El Salvador concerning legal, political, or administrative measures to prevent the repetition of such acts in the future. However, it was not a judicial body; thus, it did not hold public testimony nor subpoena financial or telephone records.

—*Thomas Buergenthal, 1994*

The international community has also provided both monetary and technical assistance to rebuild and reform judicial and law enforcement systems. For example, assistance has been given in Rwanda to train judges, prosecutors, and police; repair court buildings; and even construct new prisons. In view of the killing and migration of the judicial system's staff, such assistance has been necessary. Past experience suggests that "in general, the ambitious goals of legal reforms or transformations of the judicial systems have simply not been met" (Stolz 1995). In addition, bilateral and multilateral donors have helped universities, research institutions, and NGOs in many war-torn societies to build their capacities for human rights promotion, monitoring, and research. There are indications that such capacities frequently survive in the longer term; indigenous groups develop their own constituencies and are often able to draw external resources and support.

International efforts to promote human rights have been frequently criticized. Often host governments perceive human rights monitoring as an unwarranted intrusion in their internal affairs. In a few cases, government officials of war-torn societies have accused international actors of imposing Western standards that are inappropriate given their cultural traditions and political circumstances—a criticism that is usually a smoke screen to hide their authoritarian impulses and failure to prevent human rights abuses. A more valid criticism is that international interventions have focused more on strengthening formal legal mechanisms than on promoting respect for human rights through rehabilitation efforts. The latter approach includes such activities as instilling a culture of peace and tolerance through educational curricula and building a cross-ethnic component into rehabilitation projects.

Demobilization and Reintegration

The process of demobilization and reintegration of ex-combatants is essential for both political and economic reasons.[10] Successful demobilization and reintegration efforts can build mutual confidence among former adversaries, thereby reducing the risk of renewed hostilities. The experience of many war-torn societies indicates that when effective demobilization and reintegration programs were not or could not be implemented, fragile peace arrangements could be jeopardized and conflicts reignited (Refugee Policy Group 1994, 3). These programs also promote economic growth by reducing public expenditure and by making ex-combatants productive members of the society.

International donors have taken a leading role in supporting demobilization and rehabilitation programs in Angola, Cambodia, El Salvador, Ethiopia, Haiti, Mozambique, Namibia, and Uganda. Their support has been critical, because demobilization and reintegration initiatives involve a considerable financial burden, which transition governments can hardly afford in the face of many other volatile problems that require immediate and urgent attention. Further, in the absence of external pressure and assistance, former adversaries are reluctant to reduce the size of their armed forces and integrate them in a single entity.

Most demobilization and rehabilitation programs have encountered serious coordination problems that undermined their timeliness and effectiveness (Mahling-Clark 1995). The demobilization and reintegration process involves a wide range of sequential activities: identifying and discharging ex-combatants; assembling them in cantonment areas for limited duration; transporting them to the communities of their origin or the sites marked for their resettlement; providing benefit packages, usually in installments; providing training; and facilitating transition to civilian life. Obviously, many national, bilateral, and intergovernmental actors take responsibility for different activities, and they each have their own procedures, timetables, and mandates.

Many issues about the nature and delivery of reintegration assistance to ex-combatants remain unresolved. For example, should the assistance to ex-combatants be provided in cash or in kind? The advantages of cash payments are that they can be made in easy installments and they permit ex-combatants to expend the resources with reference to their distinct needs and circumstances. But the problem is that ex-combatants, especially those who have spent many years in the army, are not always prudent with their cash payments. They are more likely to utilize in-kind assistance for the intended purposes. However, in-kind assistance does not provide the flexibility the beneficiaries need.

Another issue concerns the targeting of rehabilitation assistance: Should it be targeted to ex-combatants themselves or to the communities where they reside? Because of their military training, unassimilated soldiers pose a serious threat to law and order and should be thus targeted directly. On the other hand, targeted assistance is very resource intensive. Moreover, there are many other vulnerable groups—refugees, internally displaced persons, women, orphans, and unaccompanied children—who are the direct victims of war and also deserve support.

The resettlement problems of demobilized female soldiers are often more complex than those of their male counterparts. Often they become accustomed to greater social and economic freedom than is the norm in their traditional societies. They usually lack marketable skills and find it difficult to engage in agriculture in the absence of previous experience. The international community has now realized this problem and recent demobilization programs tend to treat female ex-combatants as a separate group (Colletta et al. 1996).

International donors are also concerned that generous benefits to ex-combatants could generate what is called an "entitlement mentality." For example, prior to demobilization in Mozambique, many observers were apprehensive that the "more soldiers were given, or promised, the more they tried to obtain and the more aggressive they became." Subsequent events indicated that the earlier apprehensions were not without foundation; therefore, effective interventions should strike a balance between "ensuring the demobilized that they have not been abandoned and avoiding reinforcing their sense of themselves as a special group" (Ball 1995, 11).

Reforming the Security Sector

Closely related to the demobilization and rehabilitation of ex-combatants is the issue of restructuring and reforming the internal security regime. During civil wars, the distinction between internal security and defense against external threats, if such a separation existed in the country, is further blurred. The military is increasingly asked to maintain law and order and acquires unparalleled political power and authority. The police, too, amass additional power and are often able to indulge with impunity in acts of terror, illegal detention, and even murder. Reform of the internal security system, therefore, remains central to democratic political rehabilitation during transitions.

The international community has shown a marked reluctance to initiate and implement projects in this area for many obvious reasons. Support for internal security is outside the mandate of practically all NGOs, most IGOs, and most relief agencies. In fact, many bilateral agencies are prohibited by law from giving assistance to police. For example, in the aftermath of the Vietnam War, the U.S. Congress passed legislation prohibiting the involvement of the U.S. Agency for International Development (USAID) in police programs. In addition, host governments are also sensitive about foreign involvement in internal security matters. Consequently, the international community has provided significant assistance for comprehensive reforms in the internal security sector in only two countries: El Salvador and Haiti (Stanley 1995).

Three essential premises tend to inform international assistance in the internal security sector. First, a clear distinction should be made between the *internal* security function, which focuses on protecting human rights and maintaining law and order, and the *external* security function, which is concerned with defending the country against threats emanating from outside. In other words, the military should have no role in civilian affairs. Second, the military should be under the control of civilian authorities, who should determine its policies, budgets, and operations. Finally, the law and order function has to be performed by the civilian authorities within a framework of respect for essential human rights.

The international community has supported two sets of reform activities in El Salvador and Haiti. The first set concerns the armed forces' role in internal security: The entire armed force was demobilized in Haiti and was drastically reduced in El Salvador. Moreover, many organizational functions such as paramilitary patrols, which were earlier performed by the army in El Salvador, were discontinued and brought under the control of the civilian authorities. The second set of activities involved the creation of an almost entirely new national police force. In both countries, it necessitated disbanding existing institutional structures, recruiting and training police officials, and building a new organizational culture.

The assistance programs in Haiti and El Salvador faced many problems common to international interventions. There were unexpected delays, and the original timetables proved to be unrealistic. In El Salvador, delays in creating a new national police force partly contributed to a deterioration in law and order. Governments did not always share the framework for reform and failed to display the political will so necessary to introduce reforms. Donor nations too became lukewarm over time in their support for these activities. For example, in El Salvador, international donors did not always fulfill their financial commitments (Stanley 1995).

Assistance for Social Rehabilitation

Postcrisis societies face two major tasks. The first is to revive and restore shattered social services such as health, nutrition, and education, which decay during conflict because of widespread neglect and lack of resources. There is an additional strain on these services in the aftermath of war because of the many new problems the affected societies face. For example, anecdotal evidence from Rwanda indicates that HIV cases increased after the genocide as a result of the migration of vast populations, physical violence, and the high incidence of rape. Consequently, the country has no alternative but to expend more resources to combat that particular problem. In practically all war-torn societies, the fragile educational institutions have to cope with problems arising from the return of refugees and internally displaced persons (IDPs) and the widespread shortage of trained manpower in the public and private sectors.

The real challenge is not only to rehabilitate the vital social services in an environment of extreme scarcity and high expectations, but to revive them in such a way that they become sustainable—and possibly more efficient. Thus, there is a need to introduce innovative strategies and programs that can both reduce the overall costs of services and make them accessible to more people. Consequently, policy reforms in social sectors are undoubtedly as necessary as macroeconomic reforms.

The second task is to assist a variety of vulnerable groups created by war. Three groups deserve special consideration. The first consists of refugees and IDPs who return after the conflict and should be resettled. The second group includes unaccompanied and traumatized children; the former need to be reunited with their immediate or extended families, while the latter require assistance to overcome their emotional trauma. The last group includes war widows, sexually abused women, and women who are forced to become heads of households. The rehabilitation of these vulnerable groups is essential for both social stability and economic growth.

The international community has generously assisted war-torn societies in undertaking both these tasks by providing human and material resources. In fact, the international community seems to have been more effective in social rehabilitation than in political reconstruction partly because of its relatively long involvement in social sectors, such as health and education. Nongovernmental organizations, in particular, have played a critical role in rebuilding these sectors.

In the following sections, four areas in which the international community has been particularly active are briefly discussed. These pertain to the resettlement of refugees and internally displaced persons, the rehabilitation of social services, assistance to unaccompanied and traumatized children, and aid to women.

Repatriation and Resettlement of Refugees and Internally Displaced Persons

In many intrastate conflicts, a substantial portion of the population is forced to flee to more secure places within or outside the country. As much as one-third of the populations of Afghanistan, Lebanon, Rwanda, and Somalia migrated in search of physical security. The return and resettlement of the refugees and IDPs are necessary for social peace and economic growth.

An overwhelming majority of refugees usually return on their own without any direct involvement of international players. In fact, studies of Central America have shown that a substantial proportion tends to repatriate even before the conflict is over (Larkin, Cuny, and Stein

1991). Such spontaneous repatriation is individually planned or orchestrated by leaders of refugee groups. Massive return of nearly 1.5 million Afghan refugees from Iran and Pakistan, after the fall of the Soviet-supported Najibullah regime in April 1992, provides a most vivid illustration of a repatriation largely organized by refugee leaders. The return movement continued in 1993, though at a somewhat slower rate. The role of the international community is obviously very limited in such repatriation. The United Nations High Commissioner for Refugees (UNHCR), the lead international agency on refugees, does not endorse spontaneous repatriation but often provides assistance to returning refugees. For example, it gave returning Afghan refugees 300 kilograms of wheat and $150, monitored their return, and later supported their rehabilitation efforts inside Afghanistan (UNHCR 1993, 110).

International agencies and NGOs generally favor organized, orderly repatriation of refugees, which involves advance planning and careful preparation. The record of organized repatriation under the auspices of international organizations has not always been encouraging. While UNHCR succeeded in repatriating over 350,000 refugees to Cambodia, it had little success in Afghanistan, Mozambique, and Rwanda.

Two sets of factors shed light on the limited success of the international community with regard to the organized return of refugees.[11] One set relates to the underlying premise that all repatriation should be voluntary following a tripartite agreement between home and host countries and international agencies. International agencies are not expected to encourage, much less pressure, refugees to go back to the countries of their origin.[12] While this principle is laudable, the problem arises because

---

UNHCR's Repatriation Efforts in Cambodia

Between March 30, 1992, and April 30, 1993, more than 365,000 Cambodians returned home—a rate of 1,000 per day. Most of them had spent between ten and fourteen years in refugee camps in Thailand. About 2,000 of those who returned came from other countries in Southeast Asia. The repatriation, the largest logistical operation ever undertaken by UNHCR, was carried out under particularly difficult circumstances; the Cambodian infrastructure had been devastated by twenty-two years of war, and the situation in the country as a whole was far from secure. Yet, despite the uncertainty over Cambodia's future, many observers consider the repatriation program a success.   —*UNHCR, 1993*

refugees are a differentiated group and many of them are reluctant to repatriate. Some become accustomed to camp life, which provides them basic economic and physical security, while others are genuinely concerned about their safety upon return. Still others seek better economic prospects in host or other nations. Rwanda provides an extreme example of the refugees' refusal to repatriate. In March 1996, almost two years after the civil war and genocide, nearly 1.7 million refugees were still living in camps in Zaire, Burundi, and Tanzania. Although normalcy has been largely restored in Rwanda, these refugees are not willing to return, partly because of the influence of the camp leaders who had actively participated in genocide and who face punishment. The result is that the international community has to bear the extensive financial burden of maintaining the camps.

The second set of factors, which are perhaps more important, relate to the plans, timetables, and arrangements made by the international community. These are generally made without the direct involvement of the intended beneficiaries. Consequently, although they reflect the financial concerns of donors and the logistical concerns of the implementation organizations, the lengthy timetables and planning—which are typical of international bureaucracies—do not effectively respond to the needs of refugee populations for early return to their own communities.

International agencies involved in the repatriation of refugees have belatedly recognized that single female refugees returning home face two major problems, which should be taken into consideration while planning repatriation. First, women are highly vulnerable to sexual abuse by bandits, male refugees, and even the accompanying guards. Second, they do not receive their fair share of physical and material assistance (Martin 1992). Therefore, the concerned agencies have started taking steps to protect returning single women. NGOs particularly sensitive to women's needs have also begun to monitor the distribution of rations and other assistance to these returning refugees.

The resettlement of returnees, especially when substantial populations are involved, is a major challenge to the government and the international community. A prolonged stay in the protected environment of camps profoundly affects the attitudes, skills, perceptions, and values of refugees who become accustomed to the social services and economic security provided. While adults may idealize their past lives out of nostalgia, youngsters have no vivid recollection. Consequently, the process of the returnees' adjustment to their old environment is often painful and frustrating.

Three problems frequently hinder the resettlement of refugees and IDPs. The first is property rights, particularly land titles. Often the land, houses, and other property left behind by the returnees are appropriated by their relatives, friends, and others, who are naturally reluctant to hand them over to the original owners. For example, in Rwanda, some of the agricultural land belonging to the recent refugees and IDPs has been acquired by the old refugees who had fled the country in the 1970s and 1980s and returned following the installation of the RPF government. Although the government is firmly committed to the restoration of the land to its owners, it is questionable whether the government will be able to implement its stated policy (Kumar et al. 1996).

The second problem is the nonavailability of agricultural inputs. Often the returnees receive essential inputs such as seeds and tools, but these are usually not sufficient. Often too, the agricultural land is of poor quality and requires considerable preparation. At times the new sites differ ecologically from the returnees' original regions, which creates additional problems for the settlers. In all cases, refugees have difficulty obtaining credit. The third problem is finding gainful employment, particularly in rural areas. Often, refugees have been deskilled in their traditional occupations while in camps.

The experience of Cambodia, Guatemala, Mexico, and Nicaragua also demonstrates that the resettlement of refugees and IDPs in new communities generates a host of problems, which can be partly attributed to the poor planning, coordination, and implementation of resettlement programs. None of these problems is insurmountable, however. Quick impact projects, which are usually implemented through NGOs, often have been used to facilitate the rehabilitation of refugees. The experience of Mozambique indicates that these types of projects can help solve some urgent problems of returning refugees (Murungu 1995).

The programs that exclusively target returning refugees can generate tensions in local communities by arousing envy among those who did not migrate during the conflict. Cambodia and Mozambique attest to such tensions, which can be detrimental to initiating a process of reconciliation in the local communities (Murungu 1995). There is now a growing realization that assistance should be designed to foster the development of the entire community. Such programs should be need based and should target all vulnerable populations—refugees or nonrefugees.

A major problem the international community has yet to resolve is of the differential treatment of refugees and IDPs (Deng 1993). Because of internationally mandated conventions, refugees (or at least those who live in camps) are entitled to minimal economic and social facilities. Their essential needs are met and they enjoy basic civil rights. The case of IDPs is different, however. Few outside resources are available to them, and they are at the mercy of their governments. Their living conditions are invariably worse. A growing number of humanitarian organizations now agree that the artificial distinction between the two categories of migrant populations is untenable and unfair and should be abolished.

Reviving and Reforming Education and Health Services

Several factors contribute to widespread damage and disruption to health and education services during wars. Organizations lose their professional and technical staff. Doctors, nurses, paramedics, teachers, and administrative personnel die in conflicts, migrate to safer areas, or are simply unable to work because of the threat of violence. One of the worst examples in recent history is Rwanda, where over 80 percent of health care staff and educators were either killed or fled during the civil war, thus incapacitating primary health care centers and schools throughout the country.

Moreover, equipment, supplies, vehicles, and buildings are looted and/or destroyed during military operations. The facilities also deteriorate because of lack of maintenance. Thus, there is the common spectacle of health centers without medicines and schools without blackboards and chalk. Finally, damage to supporting physical and institutional infrastructures at the national and local levels further undermines the functioning of social services. Deterioration of roads, for example, makes it difficult to move medical supplies, and the absence of monitoring capacities in the departments of health and education prevents coordination and information sharing. The international community has played a vital role in rehabilitating essential social services in two ways.

First, international organizations have helped revive primary health and educational services in the areas devastated by warfare. For example, in Rwanda they successfully reactivated the country's 250 health centers and thirty of its thirty-four hospitals within six months after the cessation of hostilities. They provided supplies and medicines, brought in foreign health professionals, and trained local health staff. International agencies also helped launch nationwide vaccination and other public health awareness campaigns, which prevented the possible outbreak of epidemics (Kumar et al. 1996). In fact, in practically all recent civil wars, the international community has been instrumental in reviving or establishing primary health care systems throughout or in parts of the affected countries. Often the rehabilitation activities of the international agencies are a logical extension of their ongoing relief operations.

The international community has also provided assistance in rehabilitating educational institutions, particularly primary schools. UNICEF and UNESCO developed the "School-in-a-Box" kit for teaching children in refugee camps, which is now also used in many postconflict situations until regular schools can be reopened. This kit contains lesson plans, exercise books, slates and chalk, pencils and erasers, and other necessary teaching materials. It is designed to provide eighty pupils and a teacher with immediate psychological and material support to continue educational activities. Although such mobile schools cannot replace regular schools, they prevent the complete breakdown of the primary education system.

More important, international donors have funded teachers' salaries, designed training programs for teachers, and financed the repair of school buildings. Such assistance has proved to be extremely useful in Cambodia, Haiti, Mozambique, and Rwanda. Bilateral and multilateral donors have also given economic and technical support to reopen institutions of higher learning—although the amounts are modest and the delivery slow, partly because the functioning of institutions of higher education is not universally perceived as a priority by relief agencies.

Second, the international community has initiated and implemented programs to strengthen the physical and institutional infrastructure for social services. Such programs focus on promoting capacity building in line ministries and public institutions; restoring building and facilities such as cold storage for medicines, laboratories for medical testing, and even small plants to manufacture essential drugs; and importing essential commodities and technical expertise. International actors fund technical assistance, training, and the acquisition of computers, vehicles, and medical equipment. While questions have been raised about the cost effectiveness and timeliness of many of these interventions, there is little doubt about their relevance and impact. For example, modest economic and technical support provided by the donor community helped the ministry of health in Rwanda recruit and retain a small core administrative staff that formulated a nationwide plan for the rehabilitation of the health sector and coordinated the government's activities with over a hundred NGOs working in the country.

The involvement of numerous international nongovernmental organizations in rehabilitation efforts, particularly in the health sector, has not been without problems in many countries. The experience of Cambodia, Mozambique, Rwanda, and, to some extent, El Salvador indicates that international NGOs contributed to the duplication of efforts in many instances. Often NGOs, especially those lacking previous experience in the country or region, followed their own standards for providing health services, which are not always appropriate for local conditions. Moreover, they often competed for funding from the same sources and found it difficult to coordinate their activities with the government. It should be mentioned, however, that nongovernmental organizations are not a single homogenous group. The overall record of the established international organizations who have highly skilled professional staff has been much better than that of newly formed organizations without operational experience in developing nations.

There is often a tension between the provision of essential health services to needy populations and the sustainability of these services. During the emergency and immediately after the cessation of hostilities, health services are provided free or at nominal rates by health delivery organizations. Unfortunately, when international funding dries up, resource-starved governments cannot normally sustain them without generating huge budgetary deficits. But they cannot close clinics without encountering political resistance. It is clear, therefore, that "either donors need to make a long-term commitment to supporting recurrent costs, or make only limited investment in line with future national financing capacity" (Macrae and Zwi 1995).

Several bilateral and multilateral donor agencies have seen a window of opportunity in the initial postwar period for introducing much-needed policy reforms in social sectors. Consequently, they have been encouraging governments to review and reform their existing policies and have provided the necessary technical assistance. A number of reforms—such as providing an integrated framework for health and family planning, establishing a more rational division between public and private sector involvement in health care, and viewing of expenditures on health and education as investments—have been emphasized by these agencies. Donors have advocated charging users fees to beneficiaries and have supported increasing privatization of health care for improving its sustainability, quality, and access. They have also pressed for the increased access of educational and health services to women, ethnic minorities, and other vulnerable populations.

Assisting War-Stricken Children

Children are the voiceless victims of wars. Their health, nutrition, education, and psychosocial growth suffers tremendously during prolonged conflicts. While all children deserve attention, two categories of vulnerable children—unaccompanied and traumatized—require urgent assistance in postcrisis situations. The international community has taken a lead in highlighting their plight and has designed and funded programs to assist them.

The term *unaccompanied children* refers to children under the age of legal maturity without a guardian responsible for their well-being by custom or law. Many factors contribute to the swelling of the ranks of unaccompanied children during wars. Parents or guardians are killed or are unable to support children because of abject poverty caused by fighting. In other cases, children are separated from their families during migration to other countries or areas within the country, caused at times by evacuation rules, immigration procedures and refugee camp policies. The plight of unaccompanied children is aggravated in violent crises because traditional support systems are generally undermined. Extended families, local communities or even tribes, which traditionally look after such vulnerable children, find it difficult to assume their responsibilities in the face of declining economic resources, widespread social disorganization, and the large number of unaccompanied children.

The international community, particularly NGOs, have successfully implemented programs for reuniting unaccompanied children with their families in practically all recent conflicts. Most of these programs seek to reunite separated children with their immediate or extended families or place them in foster families. Typical programs trace children, prepare necessary documentation, provide interim care, locate immediate and/or extended families, and reunite them.

Most of the recent programs for unaccompanied children are based on three essential premises the international community has learned as a result of its active involvement.[13] First, even during hostilities, modest programs can be initiated to prevent the separation of children from their families. Programs that target single parents and other vulnerable families can provide in-kind assistance, loans, and skill training to enable them to meet their survival needs. However, such interventions should be designed after taking the community's own resources and capabilities into consideration; and should not disrupt existing social practices and support systems (Boothby 1994, 29). Second, institutional care should be considered the least desirable option. While orphanages and other child care institutions can provide food and shelter, they cannot fulfill the deep-rooted psychosocial needs of their wards for emotional warmth and social stimulation. In fact, institutional care can be "harmful for infants and young children, particularly in times of crisis when the quality of care is poor" (Boothby 1994, 29).[14] Third, the involvement of government agencies, affected families, and local communities is essential for the success of documentation, tracing, and unification efforts because they have their own informal networks for generating information.

The category of traumatized children is undoubtedly broader than that of unaccompanied children. It includes the children who have experienced severe physical and psychological abuse; witnessed acts of violence, particularly against their family members; participated in war as soldiers; or been deprived of the essential support of their family and the community. For instance, a UNICEF survey in Bosnia reveals that 57 percent of children interviewed reported that a massacre had occurred where they were living (UNICEF 1994). These children must live with the psychological results of these events, including a wide variety of classic trauma symptoms such as depression, insomnia, and obsessional memories. Many experts believe that unless these children receive professional attention, this trauma will continue to negatively impact their psychosocial development.

International relief organizations have organized a number of different therapeutic activities to help traumatized children. These include individual psychotherapy, family work, and art and creative group therapies. As expected, there are divergent views on the effectiveness of particular types of therapy. Mainstream psychologists and counselors advocate individual counseling, which they regard as the most effective therapy. On the other hand, many experts have questioned both the relevance and feasibility of individual psychotherapy in non-Western settings in which "experiences are verbalized and relived in a therapeutic setting" (Richman 1993, 1296). For example, it has been pointed out that the need is not to relive one's feeling but to contain them in many instances. Moreover, it may be after a relatively long period that children are able to talk freely about their experiences. Even if one ignores such criticisms, the high costs of individual counseling prevent its widespread use. Consequently, there is a trend toward employing group therapies. In Mozambican schools, an attempt has been made to help traumatized children through increased student-teacher communication, creative activities, and drama. It is reported that these methods helped to "re-integrate children who had participated in violent activities into families and communities" (Draisma and Richman 1992). In Cambodia and Rwanda, nongovernmental organizations have also initiated modest programs for traumatized children based on group therapies.

Assisting Women as War Victims

The plight of war widows, sexually abused women, and single female–headed households created by conflicts has been overlooked in the past by the international community, partly because such victims are not socially or politically visible. The conditions have begun to change in recent years. A growing number of international actors are now recognizing the need to assist vulnerable women during transitions.

A category of female victim who undoubtedly requires urgent assistance is the sexually abused. During wars, soldiers belonging to warring factions tend to violate women, particularly in conflict zones. As the examples of the Philippines, Mozambique, and Uganda show, it is not uncommon for soldiers to kidnap young women and force them into prostitution. In addition, stationed or advancing armies commit rape and other sexual abuses. In Bosnia and Rwanda, the raping of women belonging to the opposing ethnic group has been a deliberate policy for ethnic cleansing (El-Bushra and Piza-Lopez 1994, 184). In both these countries, the number of such victims runs into the tens of thousands. As many as 5,000 women were impregnated in Rwanda alone; most of them now carry children fathered by the killers of their spouses and family members (El-Bushra and Mukarubuga 1995).

The efforts by national and international relief organizations to help sexually abused women and girls are hindered, since most of the victims prefer to conceal such crimes out of shame or the threat of social ostracism. The few who are forthcoming confide only in their immediate families and friends. Moreover, the victims are widely dispersed and difficult to reach. Several international NGOs have taken the lead in Bosnia, Mozambique, and Rwanda by starting grassroots projects, but they have been able to reach only a small portion of the affected population.

The second and undoubtedly larger category comprises single female–headed households. In the aftermath of war, the number of such households swells because of the death of spouses in fighting, the migration of male family members, and general social disorganization. Relatively young and inexperienced women are forced to shoulder economic burdens for which they are often ill prepared. In predominantly agricultural economies, most of them fall back on agriculture as landless labor or farmers. Even women who are fortunate enough to have access to cultivatable land encounter numerous problems because of their subordinate social status and inexperience. For example, they face difficulties in procuring inputs such as seeds and fertilizers, especially when marketing networks are operated by men. If they do not have legal title to their land, they are denied credit by formal credit institutions and are forced to borrow from moneylenders who charge higher-than-market interest rates. Such women also experience obstacles in marketing their produce in distant areas because of transportation bottlenecks.

International donors have not targeted assistance to single female–headed households for many reasons. The process of identifying them is not only difficult but time consuming. It is undoubtedly easier to provide assistance to all female-headed households than to a particular subset; further, to single out a subset of the female population can generate tensions between these households and other female-headed households in the community. Consequently, the international community has designed projects and programs that seek to reach out broadly to all women. Such interventions have largely focused on providing agricultural inputs, particularly credit. For example, borrowing from the experience of Grameen Bank in Bangladesh, some NGOs have been supporting the formation of women's credit institutions in Cambodia and Mozambique.[15] Such initiatives help all women farmers and entrepreneurs.

Assistance for Economic Rehabilitation

After prolonged wars, the economies of conflict-ridden societies are invariably seriously weakened. Their institutional and physical infrastructures are damaged and in desperate need of repair. Postcrisis governments inherit huge budgetary deficits, overvalued exchange rates, and a low tax base. Military expenditure continues to remain high, at least during the first few years because of the continued influence of the military and fear of renewed hostilities. The alliance between government officials, traders, importers, and arms dealers that develops during conflict often survives, and it has a vested interest in perpetuating an environment of scarcity and maintaining the war machinery. The overall economic climate of transition societies is hardly favorable to investment or domestic savings. Business elites tend to invest overseas rather than within the country and are often responsible for capital flights. Overseas investors are naturally reluctant to invest in an uncertain environment. Under these conditions, the flow of substantial international aid is essential for economic rehabilitation.

The international community has a long history of involvement in economic rehabilitation, beginning with the Marshall Plan, which was instrumental in the recovery of European countries at the end of World War II. A large number of organizations have assisted in the physical and economic rehabilitation in the aftermath of major physical disasters. Moreover, multilateral and bilateral agencies have formulated and implemented programs for economic development all over Africa, Asia, and Latin America since the early 1950s. Consequently, there exists a vast body of codified knowledge, experience, and insights that are highly pertinent to the rehabilitation of war-torn societies.

The international community now recognizes that rebuilding institutional infrastructure shattered during conflict is as important as physical infrastructure—if not more important. Institutional infrastructure refers to the socially accepted norms of behavior without which economic activities cannot be performed. Its examples include legal or customary rights defining ownership of private property, contracts and their enforcement, and rules and regulations governing business transactions. The basis of institutional infrastructure is the expectation that the interacting parties will fulfill their respective obligations. Rebuilding shattered institutions is indeed a slow process. Unfortunately, this is an area that has been largely overlooked by the international community in the past.

The international community has provided assistance for a wide range of economic rehabilitation programs during the transition. Such programs focus on demining (which is undoubtedly both a social and economic problem), agriculture, physical infrastructure, and macroeconomic reforms. These are briefly discussed in the following sections.

Removing Landmines and Unexploded Ordnance

Landmines and unexploded ordnance (UXO), which continue to kill and maim innocent civilians, are undoubtedly among the most tragic human and economic legacies of wars. Over a quarter of a million people have been disabled by landmines. According to one estimate, one in every 230 persons in Cambodia is an amputee. The figures for Angola and northern Somalia are one in 470 and 1,000, respectively (Holtzman 1995, 20). Most of the victims tend to be small farmers, pastoralists, and village children. People in mine-affected areas live under constant fear and pay a heavy psychological price even when they are not physically harmed.

Consequently, landmines and UXO hamper agricultural growth and economic recovery. In countries such as Afghanistan, Cambodia, and Vietnam, some of the most productive agricultural lands were deliberately mined and remain unfit for cultivation. Moreover, in the absence of alternative sources of income and employment, subsistence farmers are forced to cultivate the mined agricultural land, thereby exposing themselves and their families to great risks. They are also often unable to procure agricultural inputs or market their produce because of the mining of secondary roads.

Although there are about 80 to 100 million unexploded mines planted in sixty-four countries of the world, nearly half of them are buried in developing countries that have witnessed violent conflicts in recent years, such as Afghanistan, Angola, Cambodia, Iraq, and Laos. Many factors have led to the widespread use of these landmines in civil wars. They can be easily procured in international arms markets, are relatively inexpensive, and can be quickly deployed. More important, they are highly effective in terrorizing innocent people. By deploying landmines on secondary roads and agricultural lands—and in wells, irrigation canals, schools, health centers, and other public places—civilian life can be disrupted and people forced to flee.

The international community has provided economic resources and technical expertise for demining. A number of NGOs have also started playing an important role not only in providing technical assistance but also in mobilizing public opinion against their widespread use.

During the past few years, the international community has learned many lessons that have significant programmatic implications. First, an integrated approach—involving systematic information gathering about minefields and setting up priorities—is required to deal with the problem. Second, public awareness campaigns are essential to educate vulnerable groups about protecting themselves against the dangers of mines and UXO. Last, and probably the most important, is the need to build up institutional capacities for demining in the country. Since local people could be easily trained by expatriate staff, it makes economic sense to build local training and support services in the heavily mined nations.

However, international resources pledged and allocated for demining in heavily mined countries are usually insufficient given the magnitude of the problem. Demining is an expensive and time-consuming operation; each mine must be identified and destroyed manually. The cost to clear one mine ranges from $300 to $1,000. Under these conditions, heavily mined countries cannot realistically shoulder the economic burden and massive international assistance is needed. For example, according to an estimate, "clearance of eight million landmines in Cambodia would cost the equivalent of more than five years of its gross national product and take as long as eight years" (Holtzman 1995, 20). Consequently, there is a growing recognition that the international community should consider demining as a social and economic investment and not merely a humanitarian endeavor.

Reviving Agriculture

In most war-torn societies, agriculture is the largest source of employment and is responsible for a major share of the gross national product and foreign exchange earnings. In addition, agricultural outputs are essential as inputs to industry. Although agriculture suffers because of nonavailability of inputs, transportation bottlenecks, and marketing problems during conflict, it usually performs better than manufacturing, construction, and other sectors. This is particularly true of subsistence agriculture which by its very nature is less vulnerable to external shocks. The situation is, however, different in geographical areas where extensive fighting has occurred. In such instances, subsistence agriculture, like other sectors, is devastated because of the threat to physical security and disruption to rural life.

At the end of hostilities, international agencies have often undertaken programs to provide essential seeds and tools to farmers for one or two seasons to revive agriculture. Originally, such assistance was limited to returning refugees, internally displaced persons, and demobilized soldiers; however, it was realized that whenever possible, it should be extended to all vulnerable small farmers in war-affected areas. Individually targeted assistance not only sows seeds of conflict in the local community, but it is also difficult to administer because of poor information about intended beneficiaries and the potential for corruption. In addition to seeds and tools, cereals for domestic consumption are also provided so that farmers do not eat seeds. Despite implementation problems and their possible adverse effects on seed markets, such programs have undoubtedly facilitated the recovery of agriculture in Afghanistan, Mozambique, and Rwanda.

In addition, the international community has supported interventions for reviving or establishing agricultural extension services and research, restoring village roads and irrigation systems, providing veterinary services and feed supplies, repairing or creating storage facilities, introducing agricultural sector reforms, and strengthening the institutional capacities of public and private sector institutions engaged in agriculture. International donor agencies and nongovernmental organizations have focused on short- and medium-term credit to small farmers to purchase seeds, fertilizers, and other inputs. However, the delivery of credit to small farmers from public sector institutions is not easy after war. For example, with international support, the Ugandan government tried to channel credit to small farmers through cooperatives in the late 1980s. Unfortunately, because of poor institutional infrastructure, bureaucratic delays, the government's cooptation of the cooperative movement, and the overall ineffectiveness of the movement, efforts were not particularly successful. Donors now promote and strengthen private sector institutions to provide agricultural credit.

In a few crisis-stricken societies, international agencies have supported the growth of nontraditional agricultural exports to generate income and employment in rural areas. These are essentially high-value cash crops that are exported to more affluent countries, particularly Western Europe and the United States. USAID, for example, has designed and implemented programs for nontraditional exports in El Salvador, Nicaragua, and Uganda. Because of the easy access to the large market of the United States, these programs have fared well in El Salvador and Nicaragua. The progress has been slow but encouraging in Uganda (Kumar 1995).

The recent experience of many war-torn societies has underscored the need for focusing on ownership issues surrounding agricultural land. In Mozambique, Rwanda, and Somalia, which faced massive transmigration of their populations during wars, returning refugees and internally displaced persons encountered serious problems in reclaiming their lands appropriated by others in their absence. In El Salvador, the land transfer program for ex-combatants has been stalled for various reasons. By the end of February 1995, only 17,000 beneficiaries out of 47,000 eligible recipients received land (Vilas 1995). Cambodia has a slightly different problem. The new government reestablished private ownership of agricultural land in 1989, which the Khmer Rouge regime had abolished. However, the laws were not consistent and the government failed to process claims quickly. Consequently, ownership issues were not settled and land disputes "generated more complaints to UNTAC than any other issue" (Kato 1995, 100). The disputes and delays concerning land ownership have undermined agricultural production and productivity in these countries. The affected farmers neither cultivated the disputed land nor made any investments in it because of uncertainty about ownership.

Another critical issue is the physical security in rural communities as a result of the deterioration in effectiveness of law enforcement agencies (which are invariably urban based), the presence of ex-soldiers, and widespread unemployment and poverty. Without reasonable security of life and property, agricultural production can hardly pick up. A major contributory factor to the revival of agriculture in Uganda has been improved law and order in the countryside. Unfortunately, the international community has played a limited role in this area.

Restoring Physical Infrastructure

One major casualty in all wars is the physical infrastructure—roads, bridges, railroads, airports, power generation and delivery, telecommunication, sewage and water supply, irrigation works, and so on. Physical infrastructure is deliberately incapacitated during fighting for military and political reasons, and it also deteriorates because of the nonavailability of resources for maintenance.

Restoration of physical infrastructure is undoubtedly a long-term process. Usually, the international community is reluctant to finance large-scale infrastructure investments immediately after war. Rather, it tends to focus primarily on small repairs and renovations that are essential for public safety (sewage and water supply) and for stimulating economic activity. Quick impact projects (QIPs) requiring very modest investments are designed and implemented to repair roads, minor irrigation systems, communication networks, and waterworks. In QIPs, the local community is asked to donate labor inputs to save resources and promote a sense of local ownership. The Food for Work Program, initiated and supported by the World Food Program, has also been effective in restoring roads and minor irrigation systems.

In many cases, infrastructure has been restored and even expanded for a different reason: to meet the needs of international peacekeeping operations. UN and other agencies have built roads, constructed bridges, restored power generation and repaired ports and airports for the effective functioning of the peace force. Nonetheless, such improvements have major positive consequences for the economy and polity.

Two issues have surfaced regarding the long-term rehabilitation of public utilities. The first issue is equity. Most of the public utilities—electricity, communication, piped water, and sewage systems—serve urban dwellers. Thus, the majority of the population, which is rural based, does not directly benefit from such investments. The second issue concerns cost recovery. In most of the developing world, public utilities are heavily subsidized by governments, which imposes a major economic burden on the public exchequer. Therefore, prudent reforms are necessary to ensure that users pay for the cost and maintenance of utilities. These issues should be critically examined by international donor agencies.

To promote investment, international financial institutions often push much-needed reforms in government policy toward physical infrastructure. Such reforms are based on the premise that infrastructure should be treated as a commercial service industry that responds to consumer demands (World Bank 1994, 2). This means that as far as possible, the private sector should participate in infrastructure management, financing, and ownership. Competition should be encouraged to improve economic efficiency and the quality of services provided. However, when a market orientation is insufficient to ensure accountability and cost effectiveness, users and other stakeholders should be involved in the planning and managing of physical infrastructure.

Instituting Macroeconomic Policy Reforms

Introducing macroeconomic stability remains perhaps the most important element of any economic rehabilitation endeavor. Almost all recent postconflict governments had followed flawed economic policies prior to wars; the situation worsened during the conflict, further compounding the problems of underdevelopment and widespread poverty. Macroeconomic stability is essential not only to facilitate economic recovery but also to lay the foundation for sustainable economic growth.

Although economists do not agree on the sequencing and timing of reforms, most agree on their nature and direction. The international community, particularly the World Bank, International Monetary Fund (IMF), and regional development banks, has emphasized a set of interrelated reforms based on their long experience in assisting developing countries.

The first set pertains to economic stabilization through prudent monetary and fiscal policies. In the aftermath of conflict, societies inherit huge budgetary deficits because of increased military expenditure and a stagnant, if not declining, revenue base. The international financial institutions, therefore, exert pressure on governments to restore the balance between revenue and expenditure, and often provide technical and economic assistance for this purpose. Generally, governments opt to severely cut their expenditures, because tax revenues may not be greatly enhanced in an environment of abject poverty and vast devastation caused by war.[16]

During wars, increased imports and declining exports create balance of payments problems, which governments attempt to stabilize with a regime of import and export controls. Overvalued currencies not only make exports less competitive in international markets, but also discourage domestic investment by making imports easily accessible. Currency devaluation is a major step in establishing an optimal exchange rate that reflects the market value. This, of course, imposes economic hardships on some segments of the population.

The second set of reforms involves liberalization. Broadly speaking, liberalization implies eliminating controls and regulations on the economy that block the functioning of market mechanisms. Many developing countries have instituted highly dysfunctional controls on investments, production, prices, wages, imports, and exports. Such controls rapidly expand during conflict. Consequently, international monetary institutions have universally supported a wide array of reforms, such as reducing tariffs, offering positive interest rates, relaxing or abolishing curbs on foreign investment, delicensing domestic investments, and dismantling price controls. Liberalization in countries like El Salvador and Uganda has spurred local entrepreneurship and initiative and contributed to a modest growth in foreign direct investment.

The third category, which can also be construed as a subcategory of liberalization, involves privatization of state-owned enterprises. Privatization prevents the constant drain on national resources by inefficient

---

Postwar Lending in Nicaragua

In Nicaragua, a state agricultural bank that served small farmers continued to function during the war. However, the structural adjustment measures forced the government to curtail the lending program by 75 percent in the three years following the war. This caused cutbacks in coffee exports and drove many farmers to subsistence production. Meanwhile, the new private banks established as a part of the structural adjustment program have refused to deal with the farmers.   —*Elizabeth Uphoff Kato, 1995*

and unproductive parastatals and creates space for the private sector. However, privatization usually encounters strong resistance from employees, managers, and government officials who control the public enterprises—and is also hampered by lack of liquidity.

Two general observations can be made about macroeconomic reforms pushed by the international community. First, while these reforms are necessary for sustainable economic growth, many might not be optimal solutions in the short run. A few simple examples can amplify this point. In Nicaragua, when imports were liberalized under a stabilization program, the balance of payments situation worsened, partly because it led to a large-scale import of luxury goods. The situation stabilized over time, however. Muscat (1995) has observed that in the absence of transparency and adequate supervision, the passage of a liberal foreign investment law in Cambodia has "introduced cronyism and natural resource stripping." He has also questioned the prudence of tax concessions granted to foreign investors, which will deprive the government of substantial tax revenues for several years to come. Collier and Gunning (1994) have argued that instead of devaluing their currencies, postwar governments may be advised to keep an initial overvalued exchange rate to prevent capital flight.

Second, macroeconomic reforms entail social costs that should not be underestimated. Cuts in government expenditures translate into cuts in social programs, which deprive vulnerable populations of their most essential support systems. Reductions in subsidies to agriculture and industry might result in a short-term decline in production and a rise in the prices of agricultural and industrial products. Market exchange rates increase the prices of imported goods and services. Privatization of state-owned enterprises and a downsizing in the government work force serve to aggravate the unemployment situation. Social safety net programs are often not adequate to alleviate the sufferings of vulnerable populations.

The social consequences of macroeconomic reforms can create severe problems for the fledgling political authority struggling to establish its control and legitimacy. The experiences of countries such as El Salvador, Nicaragua, Mozambique, Rwanda, and Uganda give credence to this observation. For example, in Nicaragua, stringent austerity measures imposed by the World Bank and IMF have partly contributed to a gradual erosion in the support of the ruling party, which might lose in the next election to a very conservative party, increasing the risk of further political polarization. In Rwanda, stabilization measures—in the face of falling international coffee prices and increasing defense expenditures—aggravated ethnic tensions in the aftermath of the Arusha accords. In Uganda, although the return of productive assets that were nationalized by an earlier government has stimulated industrial and business activity, it has also generated a growing apprehension that the economy might be dominated by a small ethnic group. In the present euphoria about reform, the undercurrents of discontent should not be overlooked. The obvious implication is that the noneconomic costs of macroeconomic reforms should be carefully examined at the outset.

A Few Policy and Programmatic Constraints

As mentioned earlier, problems of postconflict societies are invariably much more complex than those of developing countries during periods of stability. Civil wars not only destroy economic resources and physical infrastructures but also undermine social institutions, established roles and relationships, and political structures, which are essential for growth and stability. Therefore, along with the governments of war-torn societies, the international development community encounters major problems in designing and implementing effective projects and programs. These include overdesigned interventions that lack flexibility, untested intervention models, multiplicity of international actors, poor coordination among donors, bureaucratic red tape, delays in disbursing funds, inappropriate placement of projects, failure to create ownership of programs in implementing agencies, high costs of implementation and limited involvement of the beneficiaries in interventions. Such problems have been extensively discussed in the literature on relief and rehabilitation, and there is no need to dwell upon them here. However, three additional problem areas have surfaced in assistance programs for rebuilding war-torn societies.

Critical Gaps in Knowledge on Political Rehabilitation

The international community has accumulated a vast body of technical knowledge in designing and implementing economic and, to some extent, social assistance programs during the past three decades. Although the knowledge is not highly satisfactory, it is nonetheless adequate for all practical purposes. However, no such claims can be made for assistance in the political arena. The existing knowledge base is undoubtedly much more limited partly because the international community has only recently started providing significant assistance for political reconstruction. The interventions are essentially experimental in nature.

Consequently, those charged with designing and implementing political rehabilitation interventions lack appropriate conceptual frameworks, intervention models, concepts, policy instruments, and methodologies for assistance programs to rebuild civil society, establish and nurture democratic institutions, promote a culture favorable to the protection of human rights, reconstruct law enforcement systems, or facilitate ethnic reconciliation in a highly unstable political and social environment.

However, it should be recognized that as the international community gains more experience, the situation is bound to improve. In fact, technical knowledge has perceptibly advanced in the past few years, as the underlying frameworks, implementation, and effects of donor-supported political rehabilitation interventions are being analyzed and evaluated.

Lack of an Integrated Strategic Framework

Critical gaps in knowledge have partly contributed to the lack of an integrated strategic framework for political, social, and economic rehabilitation in postconflict societies. A strategic framework identifies priority areas, allocates appropriate resources for them, and relates interventions to the achievement of the twin objectives of peace and development.

Although, with the assistance of international organizations, transition governments have formulated comprehensive proposals for reform and rehabilitation of their societies, most of them can hardly be considered integrated strategic frameworks; rather, they are more a compilation of sectoral targets and plans without an overarching conceptual foundation. This has often created problems in prioritizing and sequencing major interventions. Individual programs are implemented in isolation of interventions in other sectors, which can undermine their effectiveness. For example, when a stable government did not exist, the implementation of economic stabilization programs aggravated social and political tensions, thereby hindering political reconciliation. In the same fashion, when programs for agricultural rehabilitation were not implemented, demobilization and resettlement initiatives for ex-combatants posed a threat to life and property in rural areas—which in turn adversely affected agricultural production and growth. An integrated strategic framework can help minimize such sequencing problems.

Inability to Make Long-Term Resource Commitments

In an environment of shrinking budgets and growing public disillusionment with international assistance, major donors are finding it increasingly difficult to commit substantial long-term resources to rebuild wartorn societies. Even when they make commitments, they are not always in a position to fulfill them. As a result, they follow what a perceptive observer has called "crisis management" rather than a balanced approach to fostering structural change in the body politic. For example, many of the highly visible interventions in human rights, elections, law enforcement and judicial systems, civil military relations, and even refugee settlement have the characteristics of quick fixes. They are neither conceived nor implemented as sustainable programs. Once the outside assistance comes to an end, the prospects for their long-term sustainability become remote at best. The international community cannot push a comprehensive agenda of reform and reconstruction that can reduce the probability of reoccurrence of the conflict and put these societies on the path of growth and stability without making long-term investments.

Many of the topics, issues, problems, and lessons discussed above are explored in depth in the following chapters, which are divided into three sections: political rehabilitation, social and cultural rehabilitation, and economic rehabilitation. Because substantive areas and issues pertaining to political rehabilitation are less understood, greater attention has been given to that subject.

Notes

1. For a comprehensive discussion of the subject, see Nicole Ball (1996).

2. Several articles have examined the concept of rehabilitation and explored the relationship between relief and development. See, for example, Buchanan-Smith and Maxwell (1994), Longhurst (1994), Seaman (1994), and von Meijenfeldt (1995).

3. For example, the U.S. Agency for International Development has followed this strategy in practically all transition societies.

4. For a good discussion on decentralization, see Rondinelli (1990), Smith (1985), and Smoke (1994).

5. For a good review of literature on technical assistance and capacity building, see Berg (1993).

6. Considerable literature on technical assistance for elections has been generated. The International Foundation for Electoral Systems (IFES) has prepared several manuals on a wide range of topics, ranging from pretechnical assessment to civic education programs. Also see Garber (1984).

7. This is, however, not unique to war-torn societies. Wozniak Schimpp and Petersen (1993, 9) mention a cross-country analysis by Michael Bratton in which the author found that in all African elections he studied, when the incumbent won the election, the opposition alleged fraud.

8. A review by Wozniak Schimpp and Petersen (1993) of fifteen case studies of USAID assistance for elections found that "free and fair elections have not always led to improvements in democracy, and in some cases have served to impede democratization."

9. The nature and functions of variations of such commissions has been documented in three volumes entitled *Transitional Justice*; see Kritz (1995).

10. Demobilization is the process of discharging combatants who are supposed to be demobilized when they have surrendered their weapons and uni-

forms, received discharge papers, and left the assembly area. Reintegration involves facilitating their integration to civilian life and has therefore physical as well as psychosocial dimensions. Sometimes an interim phase reinsertion, which lasts from six to twelve months, is also suggested (Colletta et al. 1996). However, reinsertion can also be conceptualized as an early phase of reintegration.

11. The experience of organized repatriation was discussed in a March 1994 international symposium entitled "Refugees and Development Assistance: Training for Voluntary Repatriation" at the University of Montana, where serious reservations were expressed about it.

12. It is generally suggested that the mandate, beliefs, and practices of the international agencies, particularly UNHCR, are not always conducive to the return of refugees. See Larkin, Cuny, and Stein (1991, 2).

13. Some of these lessons have been discussed in detail by Boothby (1994) and Ressler, Tortorici, and Marcelino (1993).

14. Boothby (1994) also notes that a review of institutional care facilities during World War II and recent wars in Korea, Vietnam, and Cambodia found that the quality of the care in all these settings was extremely poor, infant mortality rates high, and physical, emotional, social, and intellectual development of resident children jeopardized.

15. Little information is available about such projects except those reported in the press. Africa Information Afrique (AIA) sometimes covers such stories, which are filed electronically.

16. Even in an environment of abject poverty, there may be considerable scope for enhanced revenue collection. It may not solve the entire problem and may take some time to achieve, but the possibility exists.

References

Ball, Nicole. 1995. "Mid-Term Evaluation: Demobilization and Reintegration Support Project Mozambique." USAID/Mozambique. Internal document.

Ball, Nicole. 1996. "Making Peace Work: The Role of the International Development Community." Policy Essay no. 18. Washington, D.C.: Overseas Development Council.

Berg, Elliot J. 1993. *Rethinking Technical Cooperation: Reforms for Capacity Building in Africa.* New York: United Nations Development Programme.

Boothby, Neil. 1994. "Helping Unaccompanied Children Cope with the Consequences of War." In U.S. Agency for International Development (USAID), "Displaced Children and Orphans Fund," 19–32. Internal Report.

Boyce, James K. (ed.). 1996. *Economic Policy for Building Peace: The Lessons of El Salvador.* Boulder: Lynne Rienner Publishers.

Brown, Frederick Z., and Robert J. Muscat. 1994. "The Transition from War to Peace: The Case of Cambodia." Unpublished monograph.

Buchanan-Smith, Margaret, and Simon Maxwell. 1994. "Linking Relief and Development: An Introduction and Overview." *IDS Bulletin* 25(4):2–16.

Buergenthal, Thomas. 1994. "The United Nations Truth Commission for El Salvador." *Vanderbilt Journal of Transnational Law.* Vol. 27(3):497–544.

Colletta, Nat, Markus Kostner, and Ingo Weiderhofer. 1996. *The Transition from War to Peace in Sub-Saharan Africa.* Directions in Development. Washington, D.C.: World Bank.

Collier, Paul, and Jan Willem Gunning. 1994. "Policy Uncertainty, Repatriation and Investment." In "Some Economic Consequences of the Transition from Civil War to Peace," edited by Jean-Paul Azam et al. Policy Research Working Paper No. 1392, Public Economics Division, pp. 21–26. Washington: World Bank.

Deng, Francis M. 1993. *Protecting the Dispossessed*. Washington, D.C.: Brookings Institution.

Draisma, F., and N. Richman. 1992. "School Based Programs for Children in Difficult Circumstances: Final Report 1988–92." Maputo: Ministry of Education.

El-Bushra, Judy and Piza Lopez, E. 1994. *Development in Conflict: The Gender Dimension*. Oxford, UK: Oxfam Publications.

El-Bushra, Judy, and Cécile Mukarubuga. 1995. "Women, War and Transition." *Gender and Development* 3(3): 16–22.

Garber, Larry. 1984. "Guidelines for International Election Observing." Washington D.C.: International Human Rights Law Group.

Golub, Stephen. 1995. "Strengthening Human Rights Monitoring Missions." An option paper submitted to the U.S. Agency for International Development.

Holtzman, Steven. 1995. "Post-Country Reconstruction." Social Policy and Resettlement Division, Environment Department. Washington, D.C.: World Bank. Draft.

Kato, Elizabeth Uphoff. 1995. "When Shooting Stops: Helping Countries Rebuild After Civil War." Unpublished monograph.

Kritz, Neil J. (ed.). 1995. *Transitional Justice*. Washington, D.C.: United States Institute of Peace Press.

Kumar, Krishna. 1995. "Generating Broad-Based Growth Through Agribusiness Promotion: Assessment of USAID Experience." Washington, D.C.: U.S. Agency for International Development.

Kumar, Krishna, et al. 1996. "Rebuilding Post-War Rwanda: The Role of the International Community." Washington, D.C.: U.S. Agency for International Development.

Larkin, Mary Ann, Frederick C. Cuny, and Barry N. Stein. 1991. "Repatriation Under Conflict in Central America." Washington D.C.: Center for Immigration Policy and Refugee Assistance.

Longhurst, Richard. 1994. "Conceptual Frameworks for Linking Relief and Development." *IDS Bulletin* 25(4): 17–23.

Macrae, Joanna, and Anthony Zwi (eds.). 1995. *War and Hunger: Rethinking International Responses to Complex Emergencies*. London and Atlantic Highlands, N.J.: Zed Books.

Mahling-Clark, Kimberly. 1995. "Lessons Learned in the Implementation of Demobilization and Reintegration Programs." Washington D.C.: US Agency for International Development.

Martin, Susan Forbes. 1992. "Return and Reintegration: The Experiences of Refugees and Displaced Women." Unpublished paper.

Murungu, Diana Esther. 1995. "Gender Issues in Emergency Food AID: A Case Study of Two Districts in Sofala and Manica Provinces of Mozambique." Unpublished report.

Muscat, Robert J. 1995. "Conflict and Reconstruction: Roles for the World Bank." Unpublished paper.

Refugee Policy Group (RPG). 1994. "Challenges of Demobilization and Reintegration." Washington D.C.: RPG.

Ressler, Everett M., Joanne Marie Tortorici, and Alex Marcelino. 1993. *Children in War: A Guide to the Provision of Services.* New York: UNICEF.

Richman, Naomi. 1993. "Annotation: Children in Situations of Political Violence." *Journal of Child Psychology and Psychiatry* 34 (8): 1286–1302.

Rondinelli, Dennis A. 1990. "Decentralization, Territorial Power and the State: A Critical Response." *Development and Change* 20 (3):491–500.

Seaman, John. 1994. "Relief, Rehabilitation and Development: Are the Distinctions Useful?" *IDS Bulletin* 25(4): 33–36.

Smith, Brian. 1985. *Decentralization: The Territorial Dimension of the State.* London: George Allen and Unwin.

Smoke, Paul J. 1994. *Local Government Finance in Developing Countries: The Case of Kenya.* Nairobi: Oxford University Press.

Stanley, William. 1995. "International Tutelage and Domestic Political Will: Building a New Civilian Police Force in El Salvador." *Studies in Comparative International Development* 30(1):30–58.

Stolz, Walter. 1995. "Donor Experiences in Support for Human Rights: Some Lessons Learned." Report submitted to Netherlands Ministry of Foreign Affairs. Draft.

UNHCR (United Nations High Commissioner for Refugees). 1993. "The State of the World's Refugees." New York: Penguin Books.

UNICEF. 1994. "Women and Gender in Countries in Transition: A UNICEF Perspective." New York: UNICEF.

Vilas, Carlos M. 1995. "A Painful Peace: El Salvador After the Accords." *NACLA Report on the Americas* 28(6):6–11.

von Meijenfeldt, Roel. 1995. *At the Frontline for Human Rights: Final Report.* Evaluation of European Union Participation in the Human Rights Fields Operation in Rwanda. Photocopy.

World Bank. 1994. *World Development Report.* New York: Oxford University Press.

Wozniak Schimpp, Michele, and Lisa Peterson. 1993. "The US Agency for International Development and Elections Support: A Synthesis of Case Study Experiences." Washington, D.C.: U.S. Agency for International Development.

Part 1

Assistance for Political Rehabilitation

The six chapters in this section illuminate the different though interrelated dimensions of political rehabilitation of war-torn societies and the role that the international community can play.

Rafael López-Pintor, in Chapter 2, stresses the importance of elections as part of a broader process of reconciliation and political movement toward multiparty democracies. He focuses on recent electoral processes at the closure of protracted civil wars in Nicaragua, El Salvador, Cambodia, Angola, and Mozambique to highlight the unique nature of elections in postconflict transitions. López-Pintor contends that in "reconciliation elections" the political process is affected by an active presence of the international community, primarily the United Nations' organization and management; he also assesses the effectiveness of electoral procedures. Although elections are intended to settle the contentious issues of political legitimacy and peace building, López-Pintor concludes that an international presence cannot be a substitute for a genuine commitment to peace and to the cessation of hostilities by the armed opponents.

In Chapter 3, Peter Manikas and Krishna Kumar discuss international interventions designed to promote the observance of human rights in postconflict societies. They present a case study of the United Nations' Human Rights Fields Operation in Rwanda, examining its origin, mandate, and performance. The authors suggest that the operation was marred not only by conceptual confusion and inadequate administrative capability but also by the international donors' failure to adequately address the political obstacles to "restarting" Rwanda's justice system. Maintaining that each human rights emergency has its own peculiarities, Manikas and Kumar conclude that the response of the international community should be tailored to each crisis and that the intervention will likely have a greater chance of success if incorporated into a comprehensive strategy for promoting peace and respect for the rule of law in the society.

Nicole Ball, in Chapter 4, explores the subject of demobilization and reintegration of ex-combatants in a postconflict era. She identifies four phases of this process: assembly, discharge, reinsertion, and reintegration. Further, drawing from the international community's substantial experience in Africa, she outlines concrete and practical lessons learned about planning and implementing demobilization programs in each of these phases that minimize political and social risks and maximize benefits to the soldiers, their families, the most vulnerable populations, and communities. The author concludes that while our knowledge of the subject has grown in recent years, longer-term investigation of beneficiaries and detailed cost analyses of the intervention will help policymakers.

Bill Stanley and Charles Call, in Chapter 5, present a case study of the process of rebuilding a new civilian police force in El Salvador. The Chapultepec peace accords in 1992 greatly reduced the constitutional power of the armed forces, called for the complete elimination of the existing public security forces, and outlined a legal framework for the new police. There was a general consensus among national and international observers that the new system would substantially transform the relationship of citizen and state, improve both human rights and public safety, and eventually reduce political tensions. As outlined in the chapter, the new force after three years enjoys both a higher level of public confidence than the old police and an improved human rights record. However, implementation has proven difficult, particularly given rising crime levels following the war. The authors conclude that the El Salvador police project provides a cautionary tale about the need for political will in developing new police institutions, the difficulty civilian governments have in enforcing their independence from militaries, and the limited weight of international pressures relative to domestic political considerations.

In Chapter 6, John Cohen focuses on another dimension of political rehabilitation: "ethnic federalism" to reduce interethnic conflicts. In Ethiopia, the government that came into power in 1991 after prolonged civil war has followed a strategy of devolving public sector powers and tasks to regions dominated by the country's major ethnic groups. Cohen describes the context and nature of the devolution process. He also highlights the tension between political and economic objectives of "ethnic federalism." Even while promoting intraethnic peace, devolution of power to regions dominated by the country's major ethnic groups can undermine federal economic objectives. On the other hand, if the power of local governments to develop and finance their own objectives is limited, the political effectiveness of ethnic federalism as a strategy of peaceful reconstruction will be undermined. In concluding, Cohen discusses with cautious optimism Ethiopia's ability to succeed in implementing these reforms and the potential of aid agencies to assist in the process.

Barry Stein, in the last chapter of this part, discusses the vexing issues of repatriation and resettlement of refugees and internally displaced persons (IDPs), an essential prerequisite to political stability in many war-torn societies. In analyzing the return and resettlement of Central America's 18 million refugees and IDPs, Stein suggests that international assistance efforts focused on local needs, rather than on those of the returnees; attempted to link relief to long-term development; and tried, though not always successfully, to generate an integrated response to the problem. According to Stein, the two most significant outcomes of this repatriation and resettlement were the opening of humanitarian or political space and the expansion of civil society in the countries involved. Further, the implementation practices of the main international agencies also had a positive effect on the reconciliation process.

2

Reconciliation Elections: A Post–Cold War Experience

Rafael López-Pintor

In the early 1990s, competitive elections monitored by the international community were organized at the end of long-lasting civil conflicts that were fought for almost a decade in Nicaragua and El Salvador, and for longer than fifteen years in Cambodia, Angola, and Mozambique. Sometimes the conflict remained partially active while the elections were being organized, as was the case in Cambodia. Most frequently, as in the cases of Angola and Mozambique, a virtual ceasefire existed, but the political contenders participated in elections without being fully demobilized and disarmed. In all cases, the elections were mandated by internationally sponsored peace agreements, such as the Esquipulas II Agreements for the Pacification of Central America in August 1987, which were signed by all the presidents of the region and later ratified by Nicaragua in the Declaration of La Paz (El Salvador) in February 1989; the Paris peace agreements on Cambodia in October 1991; the Bicesse peace accords for Angola in May 1991; the peace accords for El Salvador, particularly the Mexico agreement in January 1992; and the Rome general peace agreement on Mozambique in December 1992.

These experiences shed new light on the importance of elections as part of a broader process of national reconciliation and political movement toward multiparty democracies. In these cases, the transition elections have traits distinctive from those of elections that have taken place elsewhere after peaceful reform by authoritarian governments. These elections can be denominated as "reconciliation elections." This chapter will provide a background on this type of election; analyze the results of the first multiparty elections after the cessation of hostilities in Nicaragua, El Salvador, Cambodia, Angola, and Mozambique; examine the electoral effectiveness of the processes facilitated by international organizations; and provide lessons learned from these countries.

Background on Reconciliation Elections

Three Different Conflictive Preelectoral Scenarios

Within the context of a concluding civil war, at least three different preelectoral scenarios can be identified. The least promising of them is illustrated by Liberia, where civil war ignited in December 1989. Repeated attempts to end the conflict through free and fair elections have failed. The process of national reconciliation and democratization has gotten started under international pressure, but minimum conditions have not coalesced to lay the groundwork for multiparty elections.

Following the highly publicized morbid execution of dictator Samuel Doe in September 1990, fierce tribal warfare exploded and continues throughout the country to this day. Fatal casualties are numbered at over 150,000, which would amount to 5 percent of a population of 3 million—half of whom have been displaced from up-country to the capital area of Monrovia. After a peace agreement was reached in May 1992, the Election National Commission was established in which the president and two of five commissioners were appointed by the new rebel leader, Charles Taylor. This commission was technically and/or financially supported by the UN, the Carter Center, and the International Foundation for Electoral Systems (IFES). An electoral budget was approved and a draft calendar for registration and elections prepared in June 1992, but hostilities resumed in July.

Early in 1994, contacts were reinitiated within the international community aiming to conclude the war and organize elections. In December of that year, the main contending groups signed a peace agreement in Accra, Ghana, which included a cease-fire, the establishment of institutions for a transition to democracy, and the holding of free elections. In January 1995, a power-sharing agreement was negotiated. However, in spite of the cease-fire agreement, hostilities among the half-dozen contending factions were still under way six months later. Thus, in the presence of the international community, the door to elections has intermittently been opened and closed.

A second scenario is one in which all conflicting parties engage in an electoral strategy under strong pressure from the international community but without full demobilization and disarmament of contenders. At some stage of this process, one of the parties may quit (e.g., the Khmer Rouge in Cambodia several months before the election) or threaten withdrawal (e.g., RENAMO in Mozambique). The election may even be denounced and warfare resumed after an unfavorable result, as was the case with Jonas Savimbi in Angola in October 1992. An armed conflict was still active in May 1995 when President Santos and rebel leader Jonas Savimbi met in Lusaka, Zambia—for the first time since 1992—to ratify the cease-fire and power-sharing agreement, which was signed in November 1994 after the successive failure of previous talks. In February 1995, the UN Security Council approved a new observer mission to Angola, including 7,000 blue helmets, to monitor the implementation of the Lusaka agreements. In all these cases, an election was held within technically acceptable standards. Nevertheless, with the election having been politically rejected by one of the contenders, the entire process thus falls back to the status quo prior to the peace agreements.

More frequently, however, postelectoral politics suffers from weaknesses due to incomplete demobilization and disarmament of contenders, as was the case in Cambodia and Mozambique. The former fighters may still have de facto control over certain areas of the territory. In Cambodia, the Khmer Rouge still has full control of the northwestern part of the country and keeps some threatening capacity in other areas. In Mozambique, the slow process of demobilization and disarmament, as well as the formation of a new army, was accelerated on the eve of the election of October 1994 in order to comply with the mandate of the peace agreements. There was a problem not only of political will among contenders, but also of uncontrolled disintegration of their respective armies—largely formed with soldiers who would desert without handing over their own weapons.

A third scenario exists in which more effective demobilization and disarmament are completed before the elections. Warfare is left far behind at the time of the electoral process. The former contenders are active in all the stages of the preparation of elections, which are held under the monitoring of the international community. The results are fully accepted by the loser—being either the governing party (e.g., Nicaragua) or an ex-combatant opposition (e.g., El Salvador). In this scenario, elections constitute the most effective step forward in the establishment of a multiparty democracy.

In all these scenarios, two main factors have been identified that condition the nature of the elections: a protracted civil war, and the formalized intervention of the international community. They both limit the degree of autonomy and efficacy of the election itself within the broader process of change; yet the holding of an election always implies some progress on the difficult path toward peace and democracy.

Elections with Civil War in the Background

Elections exist as part of the political process of concluding an armed conflict. The following causes seem apparent at the very least. The new international conditions of the post–Cold War era left the former contenders with neither the ideological justification for continuing the fighting nor the material support they were receiving from world powers. There have also been strong pressures, both political and economic, from the international community favoring the establishment of multiparty politics. Finally, exhaustion among contenders in a protracted war sets in when a clear prospect for victory by any of the parties is absent.

The existence of a civil conflict brings to the surface some basic problems of national integration and statebuilding. These have to do with the functioning of the state administration and the free movement of all contending parties throughout the country; safety conditions in areas where many people are still carrying arms; and the difficulty the government faces in getting the arms under control. For all these reasons, people may not feel confident enough to issue a free ballot, nor would they expect that the results of the election would be accepted by all conflicting parties.

Aside from the physical and psychological barriers to freedom of movement and expression, the persistence of armies of differing contenders, even under an effective cease-fire, can hamper the strengthening of civilian politics and diminish the political autonomy of the electoral process. The possibility of resuming fighting would always be there as an option, both psychologically and materially. In this context, the elections constitute a political alternative, but not the only alternative to the parties in conflict.

An Intervening International Community

Another major feature of elections in war-torn societies is intervention by the international community. The political process is formally affected by an active presence of the international community, represented primarily by the United Nations.[1] The presence of the international community both precedes and goes further than the organization of elections, having usually to do with mediation at the peace accords, the monitoring of demobilization and disarmament, and the support to state building and national development programs.

The degree of participation in the organization of elections by the international community in war-torn societies varies from country to country. Aside from missions limited to technical assistance, the UN practice has followed two other patterns. One is that of maximum intervention, where the UN organization assumes the functions of a national government in the organization and management of the elections, as was the case in Namibia in 1990 and Cambodia in 1993. In fact, in Cambodia, the elections were entirely organized and administered by the UN to the point where all the chief electoral officers at the polling stations were UN employees. The election was made possible with the logistical support of more than 20,000 blue helmets, though they might not have been able to guarantee the security of electoral officers and polling stations without the protective umbrella of the armed forces of the Hun Sen government.

A second, more frequent and less intensive, pattern is the one followed in Nicaragua in 1990, Haiti in 1991, Angola in 1992, and El Salvador and Mozambique in 1994. The UN gave technical assistance and logistical support for the organization of elections and monitored the extensive and intensive process throughout the territory. A strong intervention by the international community, most often with an observer military and police force, raises questions about the relative autonomy of the internal political process as well as the commitment to peace and democracy by former war contenders. Consequently, the electoral process by itself may not prove the most effective single element for the structuring of a new democratic order, though it could hardly be irrelevant.

Further, the presence of the international community has contradictory effects. On the one hand, it helps end the fighting and pushes the transition to democracy. On the other hand, by sharing the responsibility for organizing a new civil order and elections with local actors, the international presence can hinder the process by which contenders reach peace by themselves. Contrary to the situation after World War II, peace and democracy in post–Cold War times are a product of neither forceful international imposition nor the plain free will of local soldiers. The UN peacekeeping missions monitor and supervise but can never impose compliance to the terms of peace accords.

The effectiveness of the international community is a function of two main circumstances. First, there are the direct consequences the collapse of the USSR may have had in war-torn countries, as the armed parties used to be recipients of military and economic support from world powers. Second, there is the risk of losing economic aid from international donors. In this regard, international pressure seems to be effective, although the international community does not necessarily speak with a single voice. A variety of governments, international organizations and nongovernmental organizations (NGOs) are active in countries with conflict and may not share the same strategy. Nevertheless, the thrust of all pressures goes in the same direction—that of negotiated peace and multiparty politics.

The relationship between national actors and the international organization, usually the UN, is almost always problematic and ambivalent. Although the local parties have requested international assistance, they tend to be very sensitive to what they frequently define as interference in national sovereignty. The party promoting intervention by the international organization is usually the least critical of it (e.g., the Sandinista government in Nicaragua, the opposition FMLN in El Salvador, UNITA in Angola, or RENAMO in Mozambique). Nevertheless, it is to be expected that the "friends" of the international organization will become critical of it if the electoral prospects cease being favorable to their interests. Such was the case of the Hun Sen government in Cambodia, Savimbi in Angola, and Dhlakama in Mozambique. Accordingly, the party less sympathetic to the international organization may have a more friendly outlook after winning the elections and invoke international support as a guarantee of its electoral success. Such was the case of the opposition coalition UNO in Nicaragua, opposition FUNCINPEC in Cambodia, the MPLA government in Angola, and the FRELIMO government in Mozambique.

A question remains about what the reaction would have been by the parties less sympathetic to the UN had election results been contrary to their expectations—that is, had they won the election. The likelihood of accepting the eventuality of an electoral defeat might not have been the same by governing parties such as ARENA in El Salvador, MPLA in Angola, and FRELIMO in Mozambique; one reason is that they had different winning expectations—the least hopeful being the MPLA. As regards opposition contenders with little sympathies to UN intervention, one wonders about the likelihood of UNO in Nicaragua or FUNCINPEC in Cambodia accepting an unfavorable result. Most likely, the postelectoral scene still would have been problematic, particularly in Cambodia.

Sometimes, the seemingly weak electoral engagement of the national parties is frustrating for international actors. One of the contenders may threaten withdrawal in the middle of the campaign (UNO in Nicaragua and FUNCINPEC in Cambodia) or even after the polling has begun (RENAMO in Mozambique). To cite another example, a few days before the election in Angola, Savimbi announced that only fraud would impede his party (UNITA) from winning, and that an unfavorable result would lead them back to fighting—which is what actually happened. Thus, a situation arises in which the international organization seems to be the most interested single actor in supporting the election. In clear contrast to the less supportive attitude among certain elites, both the international organization and the national parties may feel pressure for elections coming from the general population. The people in war-torn societies tend to place great hope in elections as a way out of a conflict and onto a path to better living conditions in peaceful times.

A further paradox exists about the role of the international community: The armed conflict will not likely be stopped without external intervention, but at the same time, the external presence diminishes the autonomous strength of contenders—who somehow feel obliged to follow a path and an agenda that they themselves did not entirely set. Conversely, the experience of the unarmed transitions of the 1970s and 1980s in southern Europe, Latin America, and Asia took place under conditions of greater national political autonomy—precisely because civil conflicts were absent. This helps explain the higher political relevance of elections for the establishment of a stable democracy. Although the United Nations has been frequently criticized as ineffective in post–civil war peacekeeping operations, it is, moreover, the lack of national autonomy and of commitment to peace and democracy by former contenders that infuses the entire process with a pervasive weakness, not failure of the international organization.

The effectiveness of reconciliation elections should be judged by their contribution to the solution of the two main issues facing the political system: the ending of a civil conflict and the establishment of a state authority under democratic control all over the country. Reconciliation elections usually imply a problematic step forward in statebuilding and democracy, depending on the degree of demobilization and disarmament the national contenders and the international organization are able to attain. A variety of illustrations exist, from the more successful ones in Central America to the most dramatic failure in Angola. Nevertheless, there is always the possibility that the election would remain as a legitimate reference for future negotiations, as was the case in Haiti and may be the case yet in Angola. In Cambodia, a rare coalition cabinet with two prime ministers has been set up while a new constitution is being drafted. In Mozambique, the victorious Chissano government has to deal with pending problems of effective disarmament, the formation of a new army integrating ex-combatants from both sides, and state control over the entire territory.

Of course, elections where all existing forces compete for the first time should not be judged in isolation from previous electoral experiences. In Central America, reconciliation elections implied an advanced stage in the consolidation of political pluralism, which had been started long before. In Nicaragua, the main contending parties of 1990 had previously been partners in a coalition cabinet after they overthrew the Somoza dictatorship in 1979. Some of these parties participated in the 1984 parliamentary election, while some others withdrew not long before the election. Moreover, they all had accepted, with minor reservations, the 1987 constitution, which is still in effect. In El Salvador, there were both parliamentary and presidential elections during the 1980s with participation of opposition parties, including Christian Democrats and Socialists, although not the FMLN guerrillas. Those electoral processes were boycotted with varying intensity by the FMLN, which would participate in the 1994 elections only under the mandate of the peace accords.

The Electoral Results

Table 2.1 contains the returns of the first multiparty elections after the cessation of hostilities in Nicaragua, El Salvador, Cambodia, Angola, and Mozambique. In all five cases, the elections were held under a civilian government coming out of a single-party system with a Marxist orientation—except in El Salvador, where the government was sustained by a conservative party within a polity of limited pluralism. In all five cases as well, the UN participated both as a mediator of the peace agreements and as sponsor of an observer mission. Military and civilian personnel monitored of the implementation of agreements in all their terms: demobilization, disarmament and elections. At stake in all cases except Cambodia, where only a constituent assembly was being elected, were the president and a legislative assembly.[2]

There are several things to note from the data in Table 2.1. First, there was a high level of electoral turnout—almost always over 85 percent of registered voters. In all cases, registration included the largest part of the estimated population of voting age and required a major operation with technical support and monitoring from the UN. Although accurate demographic statistics were usually missing, local and UN electoral authorities have estimated registration rates of over 85 percent of the population eligible to vote: about 95 percent in Angola and Cambodia, 89 percent in Nicaragua, and 85 percent in El Salvador and Mozambique. With the partial exception of El Salvador, where it is all but impossible to produce accurate statistics, turnout rates for reconciliation elections are similar to those of the more participatory stable democracies, and higher than those of many opening elections in transition processes unrelated to civil war.[3]

In El Salvador, the official turnout figure was 57 percent, which is actually an unrefined figure given the imperfections of the electoral rolls. The list of voters for the 1994 elections was an updated registry from previous elections, where an undetermined number of deceased voters were still included. Furthermore, the proportion of registered voters living abroad, unable to vote under Salvadoran legislation, was also impossible to determine. An estimated million and a half Salvadorans out of a total population of over 6 million are living in the United States. With all these factors taken into consideration, a personal estimate of electoral turnout in El Salvador would amount to over 70 percent of those residents in the country *in possession* of an electoral card—since there were citizens registered to vote who did not pick up or were never issued an electoral card and who therefore were unable to vote.

Turnout statistics confirm the impression that the people have high expectations of what elections can bring them in terms of peace and a better life. In fact, in war-torn societies, electoral turnout is massive and orderly, regardless of the sacrifices entailed in going to the polls (e.g., long walks with elders and children, difficult climatic conditions, scarce food, etc.). International observers are usually amazed at the sight of orderly mass voting in the most remote and backward areas. The attitude of hope—sometimes devotion—with which the common people go to the polling stations clearly sends the message that the ballot is their power. In fact, the more recent the war, the higher the turnout—the highest being in Angola, Cambodia, and Mozambique.

Of the five cases included in the table, the party in government won the election in El Salvador, Angola, and Mozambique. The victory went to the opposition in Nicaragua and Cambodia. In the three cases where the government was the winner, only in Angola did an armed loser reject the results and go back to war. In the two cases with a winning opposition, that opposition was composed of conservative forces opposing a Marxist government. In only one case (Nicaragua) did the government hand over power to the opposition without any major obstacle, after negotiating certain military and economic matters. In the other case (Cambodia), the government reluctantly accepted the electoral results, retaining a portion of executive power within a coalition cabinet. Of the five cases, only Angola resulted in outright failure.

In reconciliation elections that represent the end to an armed conflict without heroes or victims, neither government nor opposition wins or loses by a landslide. The distribution of the vote between former armed contenders does not assign the winner much more than 50 percent, while the loser generally gets more than 30 percent of the vote.

Table 2.1 Reconciliation Elections in Nicaragua, Angola, Cambodia, El Salvador, and Mozambique

	Nicaragua Presidential election: 1st round 2/25/90	Angola Presidential election: 1st round[a] 10/29–30/92	Cambodia Constituent assembly election: 5/23–28/93	El Salvador Presidential election 1st round[b] 3/20/94	Mozambique Presidential election 1st round 10/27–29/94
Participation as a percentage of total registered voters	86.3	92.0	86.7	57.0	88.0
Vote to the party in government as a percentage of total valid vote	D. Ortega (FSLN)[c] 40.8	J. E. Santos (MPLA) 49.6	Ex-communist (CPP) 39.1	A. Calderón (ARENA) 49.0	J. Chissano (FRELIMO) 53.3
Vote to the opposition force that was a former war contender	V. Chamorro (UNO) 54.7	J. Savimbi (UNITA) 40.1	Royalist (FUNCINPEC) 46.5	R. Zamora (FMLN) 24.9	A. Dhlakama (RENAMO) 33.7
Vote to other parties	4.5	10.3	14.4	26.1	13.0
Total valid vote	100	100	100	100	100

continues

Table 2.1 (continued)

	Nicaragua Presidential election: 1st round 2/25/90	Angola Presidential election:[a] 1st round 10/29–30/92	Cambodia Constituent assembly election: 5/23–28/93	El Salvador Presidential election 1st round[b] 3/20/94	Mozambique Presidential election 1st round 10/27–29/94
Null votes as a percentage of all ballots issued	5.9	9.1	2.6	4.9	2.8

Source: Data from the election authority of the different countries as included in reports of the UN Secretary-General.
Notes: a. A mandatory runoff election was never held after the rejection by Savimbi of the results of the first round.
b. A second round was held April 24, 1994, with 50.6 percent turnout; 68.3 percent voted for ARENA and 31.7 percent for the second runner-up.
c. The following are the acronyms and the names of the political parties (by country and in the language): FSLN, Frente Sandinista de Liberación Nacional; UNO, Unión Nacional Opositora; MPLA, Movimento Popular de Liberaçao de Angola; UNITA, Uniao Nacional pela Independencia Total de Angola; CPP, Cambodian People's Party; FUNCINPEC, Front Uni Nacional pour une Cambodie Indépendente, Neutre, Pacifique et Coopérative; ARENA, Alianza Republicana Nacionalista; FMLN, Frente Farabundo Martí para la Liberación Nacional; FRELIMO, Frente de Liberaçao de Moçambique; RENAMO, Resistenza Nacional Moçambicana.

There is again the partial exception of El Salvador, where the armed opposition was but a fraction of all the opposition, which included the strong Christian Democratic Party; this party held the presidency in 1984–1989 as the result of the popular vote. The Christian Democrats obtained 18 percent of the vote in the first round in 1994; another old party, the promilitary PCN, obtained a sizable 8 percent.

The Appraisal of "Free and Fair" Elections by International Observers

One of the more visible components of reconciliation elections is the presence during the days before and after the polling of a large number of diverse international observers. Although this factor attracts a lot of media attention, the quality of elections within a process of national reconciliation depends only slightly on the work of international observers during the electoral season. However, the effectiveness of intensive and extensive observer missions as part of longer peacekeeping operations can be evaluated by certain basic standards of electoral effectiveness.

Electoral Effectiveness

Within a context of national reconciliation and transition to democracy, the international community is expected to appraise whether the elections were "free and fair," the most frequent evaluation criteria among international observers in well-established democracies. However, a contradiction in terms is inherent in this approach; because a nonroutine election is by nature full of uncertainty and irregularities, it cannot be judged by the standards of routine practice. Hence, it would be desirable for international observers to analyze elections in different political contexts in terms of "acceptability" rather than whether they were "free and fair." The free and fair concept implies a rather simplistic standard that was originally codified by the media in black-and-white terms—i.e., the election was either free and fair or it was not. This analytic tool has been very successful, precisely because of its simplicity. Nevertheless, it is of scant utility for evaluating the conduct of an election in both technical and political terms.

Another dubious standard is that of "historicity." International observers are sometimes unaware of the highly problematic political process to which the election belongs and do not hesitate to declare it a historic election; meanwhile, the election may turn out to be controversial and necessarily "imperfect." The long-term importance of the elections should be left for historians to evaluate. International observers should limit their appraisal to whether the elections were conducted according to those political and technical criteria which are deemed appropriate under given circumstances. In this context, my experience with peacekeeping electoral processes during the last few years suggests that the following criteria should be stressed.

First, acceptability of an election should depend not only on how the polling day or days unfolded, but also on the way in which the entire process was conducted: composition of the electoral authority, preparation of the voter rolls, conditions and development of the campaign, etc. It is particularly important that all contending parties be involved and participate at every stage of the process. Along the same lines, freedom of movement throughout the country, as well as access to the media, are to be carefully weighed. All these factors are proven too elusive to be assessed in terms of black and white.

Second, the acceptability of an election should be evaluated in global terms and be based on the distinction between irregularities and fraud. Irregularities constitute all those technical, administrative, and personal deficiencies that may abound throughout the electoral process but can be alleviated by consensus among contenders or action by electoral authorities. On the other hand, fraud has to do with ill-intended manipulation of sensitive electoral materials such as ballots and ballot boxes, voting and counting records, etc. Fraud may be limited or significant—i.e., that which would substantially affect the result of the election. In other words, had fraud not been present, the results would have been different. Only the existence of generalized significant fraud should make an election totally unacceptable and invalidate its results. In the case of limited fraud, the general validity of the election results should not be affected; the fraud can be addressed by the electoral authority and/or the judiciary by holding a by-election, by applying criminal law, or both.

Third, special attention should be paid to the fit between electoral procedures and the main purpose of the election, since procedures should support electoral political goals—and not the opposite. It seems apparent that the purposes of reconciliation and transition elections are not the same as the aims of elections in consolidated democracies. Routine elections in stable democracies are held to change the government according to a preestablished constitutional agenda. Reconciliation elections are aimed primarily at incorporating into a democratic political system political antagonists who related to each other by the use of sheer force prior to the election. Thus, acceptance of results by all contenders becomes a fundamental and necessary test for founding a democratic polity. In this context, substituting one government for another may turn out to be less important than contenders reaching a consensus on how to govern. It may be decided that the winning party should govern alone—as is the standard practice of stable democracies—or that there should be a coalition government, even if one contender has received a clear majority of the vote.

Although it is more an example of negotiated transition than of a post–civil war peace agreement, in South Africa the different political opponents preempted the possibility of any of them rejecting the results of the first fully democratic elections by negotiating that all of them would share in the government for a number of years. As a formula for reconciliation, it is illustrative of ex-combatants striving to achieve consensus to end war and establish a civil pluralist polity. This may also turn out to be the case if the 1994 Lusaka accords between Angolan adversaries are implemented—according to statements by the MPLA government and declarations by Savimbi after his meeting with President Mandela of South Africa in May 1995. In any case, the stability of the new regime will demand some sort of negotiation between government and opposition regarding fundamental matters, such as the drafting or reforming of a constitution, military affairs, basic economic policies, etc.

Some of the procedures established by electoral legislation may jeopardize the attainment of the main goals of national reconciliation and the founding of democracy. There are procedural practices that may contribute to a rarified political climate and hinder the acceptance of the elections as "free and fair." An example would be complex registration procedures, which may invite malpractice in voter registration in certain areas of the country or among less educated or socially deprived citizens. In El Salvador, for example, this was the most controversial issue both before and after the polling period. There may also be an emphasis on technicalities and/or political sensitiveness between local authorities and the international technical staff supporting or organizing the elections. For instance, personal energies and material resources are often concentrated on the "polling side" of the elections—that of bringing the people to vote—disregarding the counting of ballots and the announcement of results. With regard to these latter aspects, the form and time in which they are handled are politically crucial, as they have an extraordinary affect on the acceptance of the results and the postelection relationships between the parties. The ex-combatants, once transformed into civil adversaries, will in all likelihood have to engage in negotiations concerning the immediate future of the polity. Angola or Cambodia are poor models as regards the counting of votes and the announcement of results.

Electoral procedures should successfully satisfy two different needs: one individual, the other collective. On the one hand, the individual right to vote must be guaranteed; no citizen's participation is to be impeded or denied. On the other hand, collective representation has to be articulated in adequate manner and time. Thus, the safety of voters and control over the political process will suffer minimum risks. It is not only a problem of statistics and logistics but also a matter of political opportunity. It is critical that a maximum number of citizens turn out to vote, but it is at least as important that the ballots be counted and the results announced honestly and quickly. One questions the wisdom of collecting an additional number of votes by, for example, establishing more than one polling day, which increases political uncertainty and poses greater risks for the security of both the people and the electoral materials. At times, not enough attention is paid to producing ballot papers that can be easily handled by voters and electoral officials and to establishing organizational facilities for counting ballots. Consequently, the cost of a high proportion of null votes, or of a deficient and prolonged counting, may largely exceed the benefit that might stem from the great efforts that are normally devoted to registering voters and organizing polling days.

Within the context of civil conflict and regime change, an adequate conception and use of "political time" at elections may prove to be crucial for the unfolding of the entire process. Establishing several polling days in societies with enormous deficiencies in communications, security, and maintenance services may be particularly problematic. Two polling days are frequent; there were six in Cambodia. A prolonged counting of the vote, no matter the size of the voting population, is also common. In countries like Cambodia, Angola, and Mozambique, the counting took several weeks, creating a political atmosphere of uncertainty, mistrust, and confusion in political circles, the media, and the population at large. Results were announced in a partial and unsystematic manner as the counting proceeded, giving the impression of a partisan manipulation of the ballot.

Savimbi formally denouncing the Angolan election after the publication of early partial results that gave him a much smaller vote than the 40 percent that was finally his share after two weeks of counting illustrates well the sensitive issue of vote counting. In Cambodia, the different parties successively denounced the partial results, which UNTAC announced twice a day, according to whether they were favorable or damaging. Three days after the polling had finished, at the end of the second day of counting, only 800,000 out of more than 4 million ballots had been counted. On that day, the government was ahead of FUNCIN-PEC by a margin of 40 to 38, the reverse of the day before. The government declared its acceptance of the electoral results; thus, FUNCIN-PEC's position was that of waiting until the complete counting of the vote. In the meantime, the Khmer Rouge guerrilla called for the return to war because of election fraud. The following day, the government asked UNTAC to stop the publication of results after denouncing certain irregularities in the transport of ballot boxes from up-country to the counting facilities in Phnom Penh. One day later, the government declared it would reject the elections unless they were held again in the four provinces where the government party CPP was losing—Phnom Penh among them. At that time, FUNCINPEC was seven points ahead of the CPP.

Lessons for International Organizations and Donor Countries

Intervention by the international community plays an important role in peacekeeping operations and transition to democracy. However, the main lesson to be drawn from recent experiences is that international intervention does not substitute for the commitment to peace and democratic politics by the armed opponents. For well-equipped contenders in a civil conflict, continued hostilities can very rarely be stopped by international peacekeepers. The parties in conflict may keep on fighting as long as there is an even distribution of weaponry, soldiers, and strategic capacity.

Regarding the political value of elections coming out of a civil conflict vis-à-vis the value of other kinds of elections in transition to democracy, a main conclusion has to do with the effect of the election itself in strengthening the prospects for a stable pluralist polity. There is the historical evidence of consolidation of democracies that were established by force after the end of an international conflict, as was the case of Western Europe after World War II. There is also the evidence of consolidated democracies that emerged peacefully following the collapse of authoritarian regimes. Under both circumstances, though for different reasons, the electoral component seems to have infused much civil strength to the new polity, as the use of force as a political resource disappeared from the scene. Thus, historical experience from the second half of the twentieth century indicates that it was rather easy to exchange ballots for bullets when either the ballots were the result of an armed victory (e.g., World War II), or the weapons had lost their political ammunition (e.g., collapse of authoritarian regimes).

On the contrary, in recent peacekeeping operations and reconciliation elections, an option frequently remains open for political antagonists to resume fighting. Complete demobilization, encampment, and disarmament have not been an easy task under the rules of preventive international diplomacy in post–Cold War times. Therefore, the main weakness of the electoral process of reconciliation politics is that although the vote may be sincere and well organized, it may not have an explicit effect on the establishment of a lasting democracy. Clearly, there are instances where one of the contenders withdraws from the polls or refuses to accept the results, turning back to armed politics. Although it is too soon to evaluate the effect of peacekeeping elections upon the prospects for long-lasting democracy, it may at least be noted that immediate electoral success is directly related to effective demobilization and disarmament of former civil war contenders. In any case, the attempt to end a civil conflict by negotiation and peaceful leveling of historic differences is to be applauded, both ethically and politically.

Another main lesson to be drawn from the experience of active involvement by the international community in peacekeeping processes and the organization of competitive democratic elections has to do with the cost benefit of these types of operations, particularly in UN peacekeeping missions. It should be noted that the UN record of successful cases clearly outnumbers that of its failures. Nevertheless, as a working hypothesis for researchers and international strategists, the probability of political progress in the process undertaken by the international community is not directly related to the magnitude of the financial investment and the number of civilian and UN peacekeeping personnel. In fact, smaller, less costly UN missions like those in Nicaragua and El Salvador were most successful in solidifying the process of democratization, while the most costly mission in UN history (Cambodia) could only partially modify the status quo prior to the 1993 elections. In the case of the large and costly mission in Mozambique, involving some 7,000 blue berets and hundreds of civilian international personnel, it was not possible to reach election day under conditions of full effective disarmament of the ex-combatant electoral contenders.

Conclusion

The best explanations for such varied results are more likely to be found in the degree of civil autonomy and commitment to peace and democracy by contending parties than in the capabilities of international organizations. It has been demonstrated that effective demobilization and disarmament are fundamental for the success of the entire process and indeed of the elections. The attainment of such conditions is usually facilitated by international organizations, but it does not directly or basically depend on the number of civilian and military personnel deployed in the country. Consequently, it follows that the international presence could be limited to the minimum necessary for effective assistance—i.e. political, technical, and symbolic significance—without jeopardizing the success of the entire political operation. In this way, better use could be made of taxpayer resources from donor countries. A more supportive public opinion might develop with regard to a more limited international presence—as the public tends to make a simple linear association between the magnitude of a UN mission and the achievements of the political process. If the purpose is to achieve the electoral stage of a peace process after effective demobilization and disarmament of contenders, the political performance of local actors, as well as the quality performance of the international community and its organizations, is much more important than the sheer size and duration of the international interventions.

Notes

Rafael López-Pintor served in 1989–1995 as an electoral consultant to the United Nations in Albania, Angola, Azerbaijan, Cambodia, Guatemala, Lesotho, Liberia, and Nicaragua and also as Chief Electoral Officer of the UN observer missions in El Salvador and Mozambique. As he has been serving as a consultant to the UN in all of the countries addressed in the chapter, the positions stated reflect his own views and in no case are they necessarily those of the United Nations organization.

1. In the cases included in this chapter, the UN missions were denominated as follows: ONUVEN, Observadores de las Naciones Unidas para la Verificación Electoral en Nicaragua; ONUSAL, Observadores de las Naciones Unidas en El Salvador; UNTAC, United Nations Transitional Authority in Cambodia; UNAVEM, United Nations Angola Verification Mission; ONUMOZ, Oservadores das Naçoes Unidas em Moçambique. Other international organizations, worldwide or regional, are often involved to a lesser extent in these processes: Commonwealth; Interparliamentary Union; the Organization of American States (OAS), or the Organization of African Unity (OAU). There may also be present representatives of the European Union and a variety of NGOs involved in assistance programs of different kinds, including electoral technical assistance. Within this latter realm are the U.S. organizations International Foundation for Electoral Systems (IFES), International Republican Institute (IRI), National Democratic Institute (NDI), and the Carter Center. With a Latin American scope, there is the Centro de Asesoría y Promoción Electoral (CAPEL) with headquarters in Costa Rica.

2. A more detailed reference on these electoral processes can be found in the following publications: On Mozambique, see IFES (1994b). On El Salvador, see IFES (1994a). On Cambodia, see Roberts (1994). On Nicaragua, see López-Pintor and Nohlen (1991); Browning (1990); and Close (1991).

3. In fact, for the group of ten stable democracies with the highest turnout (Germany, Australia, Austria, Belgium, Holland, France, Italy, New Zealand, United Kingdom, and Sweden), I figured an average turnout of 88.8 percent for the period 1945–1979 and 86.2 percent for 1980–1990 (database in Crewe [1981,

236–238] and Justel [1994, 24]). As for transitional environments, electoral turnout at the first general elections of Spain in 1977 amounted to 80 percent; and it was 62 percent in Poland in 1989, 65 percent in Hungary that same year; and 72 percent in Lesotho in 1993.

References

Bogdanor, Vernon. 1990. "Founding Elections and Regime Change." *Electoral Studies* 9(4):288–294.

Browning, David. 1990. *Report on the Conduct and Context of the National Elections in Nicaragua on 25 February 1990.* London: HMSO.

Close, David. 1991. "Central American Elections 1989–1990: Costa Rica, El Salvador, Honduras, Nicaragua, Panama." *Electoral Studies* 10(1):60–77.

Crewe, Ivor. 1981. "Electoral Participation." In *Democracy at the Polls,* edited by David Butler et al., pp. 236–238. Washington, D.C.: American Enterprise Institute.

Diamond, Larry, Juan Linz, and Seymour Lipset (eds.). 1989. *Democracy in Developing Countries.* Boulder: Lynne Rienner Publishers. (Four volumes covering Southern Europe, Latin America, Asia, and Africa.)

IFES (International Foundation for Electoral Systems). "Election Results." 1994a. *Elections Today* 4(2–3):30.

IFES. "Election Results." 1994b. *Elections Today* 5(1):29.

Hermet, Guy, Richard Rose, and Alain Rouquie (eds.). 1978. *Elections Without Choice.* London: Macmillan.

Huntington, Samuel. 1994. *The Third Wave: Democratization in the Late Twentieth Century.* Norman: University of Oklahoma Press.

Justel, Manuel. 1994. "Composición y dinámica de la abstención electoral España." In *Comportamiento político y electoral,* edited by Pilar del Castillo, p. 24. Madrid: Centro de Investigaciones Sociológicas.

Lane, Robert E. 1965. *Political Life.* New York: Free Press.

Lijphart, Arendt. 1994. *Electoral Systems and Party Systems: A Study of Twenty-Seven Democracies, 1945–1990.* New York: Oxford University Press.

Linz, Juan J., and Alfred Stepan (eds.). 1994. *The Breakdown of Democratic Regimes.* Baltimore: Johns Hopkins University Press.

Lipset, Seymour M. 1959. *Political Man: The Social Bases of Politics.* New York: Doubleday.

López-Pintor, Rafael, and Dieter Nohlen. 1991. "Elecciones de apertura: El caso de Nicaragua 1990." In *Memorias del IV Curso Anual Interamericano de Elecciones,* Vol. 4, pp. 323–344. San José, Costa Rica: CAPEL.

O'Donnell, Guillermo, Philip Schmitter, and Laurence Whitehead (eds.). 1986. *Transitions from Authoritarian Rule.* Baltimore: Johns Hopkins University Press.

Roberts, David. 1994. "The Cambodian Elections of 1993." *Electoral Studies* 13(2):157–162.

Santamaria, Julián (ed.). 1982. *Transición a la democracia en el Sur de Europa y América Latina.* Madrid: Centro de Investigaciones Sociológicas.

Tocqueville, Alexis de. 1856 (quoted in the Spanish edition, 1969). *L'ancien régime et la révolution.* Madrid: Guadarrama.

3

Protecting Human Rights in Rwanda

Peter M. Manikas and Krishna Kumar

Human rights concerns are undergoing a transition in the post–Cold War era. In the aftermath of World War II, human rights issues generally focused on strong centralized states in which communist, authoritarian or military regimes repressed dissent, and there are several areas of the world in which these situations persist—such as Nigeria, Iraq, Iran, Burma and North Korea. During the past decade, however, human rights abuses have increasingly resulted from the collapse of regimes, as in the former Yugoslavia, Rwanda, and Somalia. In these nations, massive human rights problems have emerged in the context of armed conflict and regime breakdown. The human rights abuses that result from war, moreover, are likely to be compounded by refugee flows, disease, hunger, psychological trauma, and the destruction of homes and sources of economic support. The perpetrators of human rights abuses often include civilian militias and paramilitary groups, which lack the discipline and command and control structure of regular military forces; these groups are usually composed of ethnic, religious, or separatist extremists, who often act in support of an existing government.

Initial strategies for addressing human rights abuses concentrated on formulating treaties, adopting standards, and implementing procedures to remedy such human rights abuses as torture and arbitrary detention. Governments interested in promoting human rights used political pressure and economic sanctions in pursuit of their goals. These strategies, however, are of limited value where political order has broken down and a government, if it exists at all, can no longer conform its conduct to acceptable international standards.

In response to the problem of regime collapse, during the past decade new and more flexible international interventions have been developed. These include the deployment of UN human rights monitors in such countries as El Salvador, Cambodia, and Rwanda; the establishment of "truth commissions" in Nicaragua, El Salvador, and Haiti; the creation of a UN verification mission in Guatemala; the development of national human rights commissions in India and Mexico; and the establishment of international criminal tribunals for the former Yugoslavia and Rwanda.

Bilateral and multilateral assistance programs have also been initiated to strengthen institutions of accountability. These include efforts to reconstruct judicial and law enforcement systems, to ensure civilian control over the military, and to enhance civic institutions that can perform a mediative role between the state and the individual.

In the aftermath of the genocide in Rwanda, the international community, and donor nations acting bilaterally, launched efforts to address one of the greatest catastrophes of recent decades. The following discusses one such effort—establishing the UN's Human Rights Field Operation—Rwanda (HRFOR). The crisis in Rwanda, like crises everywhere, was shaped in part by circumstances that were peculiar to that country. Yet many of the issues related to the international community's response have appeared elsewhere and are likely to reemerge when future tragedies occur. These issues include the promptness of the international community's response, the ability of a human rights operation to coordinate its activities with humanitarian relief agencies, and the need to define clearly operational objectives, and to establish clear lines of authority for conducting a human rights field operation. The chapter ends with "Lessons to be Learned." It is hoped that many of the problems experienced in conducting the human rights field operations in Rwanda can be avoided in the future and that more effective policy and operational responses will be formulated and implemented in the complex emergency situations to come.

Background

In 1959, three years before Rwanda gained independence from Belgium, the majority Hutu population rebelled against the minority Tutsis, who had exercised power on behalf of Belgium's colonial administrators since the end of World War I.[1] By 1960, the Hutus' Parmehutu Party[2] had achieved political control over the country. Ethnic violence erupted again in 1963 when up to 20,000 Tutsi were killed and over 100,000 fled into exile. It has been estimated that between 40 and 70 percent of the Tutsi population left the country between 1959 and 1964, primarily for Uganda. The exiled Tutsi attempted to invade Rwanda on several occasions between the mid-1960s and 1990. After each unsuccessful attempt, Rwanda's minority Tutsi population faced severe reprisals.

In 1973, Juvenal Habyarimana, a Hutu, seized power and retained it for the following twenty-one years. Despite promised reforms in the 1970s and 1980s, government discrimination against the Tutsi population persisted. On October 1, 1990, the Rwandese Patriotic Army (RPA), the military arm of the Rwandese Patriotic Front (RPF),[3] invaded Rwanda from military bases in Uganda. The Rwandan government responded by arresting between 8,000 to 10,000 persons, primarily political opponents of the Habyarimana regime. The conflict, which lasted through 1992, resulted in thousands of deaths.

The Rwandan government and the RPF entered into negotiations in late 1991, and a cease-fire agreement was signed in July 1992.[4] Fighting erupted again, however, in February 1993, after the RPF alleged that the government had massacred 300 Tutsi in northwestern Rwanda. A new cease-fire agreement was signed on March 9, 1993, culminating in a peace accord signed in Arusha, Tanzania, in August 1993.[5] The agreement provided for the establishment of a transitional government, demobilization, the creation of an integrated military structure, and multiparty elections to be held at the end of the transitional period.[6] On June 22, 1993, the UN Security Council established the United Nations Observer Mission to Uganda—Rwanda (UNIMOUR) to help monitor the accord. An Organization of African Unity (OAU) team of fifty military observers from Nigeria, Senegal, and Zimbabwe had been deployed in August 1992 to help police the earlier peace agreement. The UN Security Council integrated UNIMOUR with the newly established United Nations Assistance Mission for Rwanda (UNAMIR) on October 5th, 1993. UNAMIR's mandate was to contribute to the establishment and maintenance of peace by securing the capital, Kigali, and monitoring the cease-fire agreement.

The incumbent head of state was sworn in as president of Rwanda on January 5, 1994, pursuant to the peace agreement. However, a transitional cabinet and National Assembly, which had been provided for in the accords, were not installed. After January 1994, the cease-fire agreement between the warring factions generally held, but violent demonstrations, assassinations of political figures, and politically motivated murders of civilians increased. On April 5, the Security Council expressed its concern over the escalating violence and extended UNAMIR's mandate until the end of July. The following day, April 6, a plane carrying the presidents of Rwanda and Burundi crashed as it approached Kigali. The systematic killing of Tutsi and Hutu political moderates began almost immediately. Several reports concluded that the killings were planned, well-organized, and fueled by radio broadcasts of hate propaganda. Many of the killings were carried out by militias known as *Interhamwe* ("those who attack together") and *Impuzamugambi* ("those who have the same goal"). These militias were established in 1992 by the ruling MNRD party and its allied party, the COR, and by the presidential guard.

On April 21, the Security Council decided to reduce UNAMIR forces to a minimal level because of the risk posed to the UN troops by the increasing violence. The withdrawn troops were evacuated to Nairobi. A supplement to the remaining UNAMIR contingent, however, was authorized on May 17, eventually increasing the UN forces to 5,500 troops. UNAMIR's mandate was expanded to include reporting on human rights violations. On April 7, RPA forces escaped from their barracks in Kigali, where they had been situated pursuant to the Arusha peace agreements. Almost simultaneously, RPA units that had been stationed in northern Rwanda opened several fronts. By May, RPF forces had captured the international airport and encircled Kigali.

On June 23, the French launched *Opération Turquoise* with the approval of the UN Security Council. The stated purpose of the intervention was to save civilian lives by establishing a "safe zone" in southwest Rwanda. The RPF opposed the French initiative because of France's role in arming the former government. The capital was taken by the RPA during the first week of July. On July 18, the RPF declared a victory and implemented a cease-fire. In the following days, the mass flight of Hutus, led by leaders of the former government, occurred.

Between April 6 and mid-July 1994, from 500,000 to 1 million persons were killed, and up to 2 million persons fled to neighboring countries such as Burundi, Tanzania, and Zaire. Another 1 million persons were displaced inside Rwanda. As a result of the massacres and the ensuing conflict between the Hutu-dominated former Rwandan government and the Tutsi-led RPA, millions of Rwandans have been traumatized by violence; many have suffered severe injuries, lost their homes, and seen family members and friends raped and murdered.

In addition, the country's governmental infrastructure collapsed, and along with it the framework of the nation's legal system. Court facilities were damaged and only forty of the 800 magistrates who were in office prior to April 1994 were working inside Rwanda one year later; the rest had been killed or had left the country. In October 1995, eighteen months after the massacre, there were few police officers to enforce the laws and almost no defense attorneys to protect the rights of the accused. By that time, already 50,000 prisoners accused of participating in the massacres were awaiting trial in Rwanda's prisons and in local detention facilities. Prisons were so overcrowded that some prisoners died from asphyxiation.[7] Three out of the eleven Courts of First Instance did not have a functioning prosecutor's office, and those that did were not processing cases of the detained if the alleged crime was associated with the genocide.

The violence in Rwanda that began on April 6, 1994, also led to the disruption of traditional law, called *gacaca*. *Gacaca* was often applied outside urban areas, but usually for non-serious crimes only. Nonetheless, *gacaca* had provided a mechanism to resolve disputes among those living in rural areas for crimes like stealing cattle or crops and small land disputes, thus providing access to an acceptable form of justice for many.[8] In sum, by August 1994, the entire civil judicial system, except for arrest and detention, had come to a grinding halt.

The international community's response to the genocide took place in a complex political environment. From April 1994 to August 1995, when Zaire expelled Rwandan refugees from its territory, the former government's army (Force Armée Rwandese, or FAR) remained largely intact in neighboring countries, situated in refugee camps on Rwanda's borders. The FAR, according to a Human Rights Watch report, was armed primarily by the governments of France and Zaire, and to a lesser extent by South Africa, the Seychelles, and China.[9] The refugee camps, then, posed a continuing threat to regional security.

Within Rwanda, civilian authority was not fully established. In August 1995, most arrests were performed by the RPA, and prosecutors complained of the army's interference in the judicial process. In any case, the role military authorities would play in a newly constructed Rwandan society was not yet clear. A nonelected, transitional National Assembly[10] exhibited some degree of independence in its deliberations over Supreme Court nominations. However, the legislature's legitimacy—as a body without an electoral base or an obvious constituency—was uncertain especially because the political reality had changed since the Arusha process. Many of Rwanda's new political leaders had only recently returned to the country after many years in exile. Few of them had any experience in governance. They were in the process of nation building and faced the practical tasks of constructing institutions, establishing their legitimacy, trying to jump-start the economy, and consolidating political power. At the same time, Rwanda's leaders confronted a more abstract, but overriding issue: What is justice for genocide? These and other factors shaped the political landscape in which the reconstruction of Rwanda's legal system was to take place.

The Protection of Human Rights and the United Nations Field Operation

The Special Rapporteur and the Commission of Experts

In May 1994, the UN Commission for Human Rights authorized the appointment of a special rapporteur to Rwanda to investigate the human rights situation and gather and compile information on possible violations of human rights, including acts of genocide. In June 1994, the special rapporteur submitted his first report to the commission, stating that gross violations of human rights had occurred in Rwanda. In July 1994 an impartial three-member commission of experts found that both the RPF and the former Rwandan government forces had perpetrated serious breaches of international humanitarian law and crimes against humanity. Forces of the former Hutu-dominated government were also found to have committed acts of genocide. The commission stated, however, that it had not uncovered any evidence that Tutsi elements had perpetrated acts committed with the intent to destroy the Hutu ethnic group.

Both the special rapporteur and the commission of experts called for establishment of a war crimes tribunal. On the basis of the reports submitted by the special rapporteur and the preliminary report issued by the commission of experts, as well as reports of the UN Secretary-General and the request of the government of Rwanda, the Security Council established the International Tribunal for Rwanda, pursuant to its powers under chapter VII of the UN Charter, on November 8, 1994.[11] Although the mandate for the commission of experts has lapsed, the special rapporteur for Rwanda continues to perform several functions, including following the progress of the Human Rights Field Operation in Rwanda, investigating genocide, and looking into such recent events as the tragedy at the internally displaced persons camp at Kibeho.[12]

International Tribunal for Rwanda

The International Tribunal for Rwanda, along with the International Criminal Tribunal for the former Yugoslavia, is the first attempt of the international community to prosecute violations of international humanitarian law since the close of World War II. The tribunal consists of eleven judges. Of these, five are shared with the tribunal for the former Yugoslavia, and six are specific to the Rwanda tribunal. Arusha, Tanzania, was chosen as the seat for the tribunal, and the Security Council appointed the prosecutor of the tribunal for Yugoslavia to serve also as prosecutor for the Rwanda tribunal. A deputy prosecutor has been appointed. A director of investigations was hired with the collateral duty of establishing a prosecutor's office in Kigali. The six trial judges of the Rwanda tribunal were elected by the UN General Assembly after governments submitted nominations to the Security Council. They were sworn in at The Hague in June 1995 and were beginning their work a year later.

High Rwandan officials have repeatedly voiced dissatisfaction with the tribunal. At its creation in November 1994, the Rwandan government strongly opposed the provision of the Security Council resolution that prohibited imposition of the death penalty. Rwandan government officials also urged that Kigali be named the seat of the tribunal, arguing that Rwandans were entitled to direct access to the proceedings. Finally, the government pressed for temporal jurisdiction of the tribunal to begin as early as 1992, instead of January 1994, so that planners, instigators, and organizers of massacres of Tutsis before commencement of the actual genocide, in April 1994, could be brought to justice. The officials were unable to convince the Security Council on any of these points. Additionally (and perhaps unrealistically) both survivors and government officials believed the tribunal would begin prosecutions before the end of 1994. They were disappointed when it did not.

In May 1995, the tribunal was facing problems of logistics, funding, and staffing, all of which caused long delays. Although such delays were not unexpected, the tribunal seemed unable to profit from relevant experience and resources of other UN agencies—for example, it suffered the same funding conundrums as those experienced by the tribunal for the former Yugoslavia. Long delays hindered staffing the prosecutor's office and all that task entails—recruitment, hiring, and deployment of personnel. One year from the beginning of the crisis, only five prosecutors and investigators were serving the tribunal, although thirty-one investigators, seconded from the United States, the Netherlands, and other governments, were expected to supplement the investigative staff. The registry was not yet operating, and judges of the trial chambers had just been nominated by the Security Council.

Hampered by an inadequate budget, the prosecutor was at first unable to establish a visible presence within Rwanda. The funds given to the tribunal were initially inadequate, and control over use of the funds was not at first fully vested in the tribunal. The tribunal received $2.9 million to cover the period January through March 1995. In May 1995, an additional $7 million was pledged by donor nations. Because of the tribunal's low budget, restrictions were initially imposed limiting personnel contracts to three months.

By year's end, the financial situation had improved; $9.5 million of the pledged amount of $9.9 had been disbursed, most of it ($7 million) by the Netherlands. Further delays and inconvenience were caused because the prosecutor lacked authority to hire staff or travel out of the country without approval of the UN's Office of Legal Counsel in New York. These problems were compounded when the UN Secretary-General froze all UN funds in September 1995. Until negotiations were completed exempting the tribunal from the generally imposed freeze, recruitment and travel at the tribunal ceased. After October 1995, when the tribunal installed a new director of investigations, the pace of investigations noticeably increased. On December 12, the tribunal issued its first eight indictments.

In establishing the tribunal, the Security Council stated that its aim was, in part, "to contribute to the process of national reconciliation and to the restoration and maintenance of peace." Delays in establishing the tribunal and making it operational have postponed reconciliation; there can be no reconciliation without justice. The prosecutor has taken steps to address the tribunal's deficiencies, but progress remains to be made in addressing the timeliness of investigations. There is need as well for progress in addressing the public perception, inside and outside Rwanda, of the prosecutor's lukewarm commitment to the success of this tribunal. Should the tribunal succeed in these endeavors, it is hoped that trust in its work will grow.

Human Rights Field Operation for Rwanda

The Human Rights Field Operation for Rwanda (HRFOR) was the first field operation to be undertaken under the auspices of the UN High Commission on Human Rights (UNHCHR) and to be administratively supported by the UN's Center for Human Rights in Geneva. In late August 1994, the UNHCHR reached an agreement with Rwandan officials to deploy 147 human rights field officers, one for each of the country's communes.

The objectives of the field operation were to: (a) carry out investigations into violations of human rights and humanitarian law; (b)monitor the human rights situation and, through its presence, prevent future human rights violations; (c) cooperate with other international agencies in establishing confidence and thus aid the return of refugees and displaced people and the rebuilding of civic society; (d) implement programs of technical cooperation in human rights, particularly in administration of justice.

To pursue these objectives, the field operation established three units: the Field Coordination Unit, the Technical Cooperation Unit (responsible for local training and education programs), and the Legal Analysis and Coordination Unit (responsible for special investigations). The UN Center for Human Rights recruited and hired most field officers and has provided overall management and logistical support for the operation. In October 1995, the original chief of mission for HRFOR was succeeded by a new one.

At its outset in September 1994, HRFOR faced a dilemma. Governments, the United Nations, and nongovernmental human rights organizations demanded that the high commissioner immediately deploy a human rights monitoring mission, but they failed to provide adequate funding for even the minimal prerequisites. The high commissioner complied with the request but had minimal support. More resources were available by December 1994, but recruitment and training of the personnel for HRFOR has been widely criticized.[13] The chief of mission was not involved in the original selection of staff, and many of the monitors initially did not have relevant background and experience. Moreover, no official announcements of the openings for HRFOR appeared in relevant newspapers and periodicals, limiting the pool of qualified applicants. The high commissioner's office, in cooperation with the European Commission, appears to have instituted more stringent recruitment standards, and the sophistication of field monitors has presumably increased.[14] There is, however, still substantial room for improvement.

Field monitors arriving in Kigali received no orientation or training until at least December 1994.[15] At that time, a small grant to the Center for Human Rights provided field officer training in Geneva and Kigali by the U.S. National Peace Corps Association. At first, the training program aimed at preparing field officers to work in a foreign environment, with little emphasis on operational aspects of their work. As HRFOR further developed its training program over the year, it grew to include additional topics such as the major human rights instruments. By April 1995, a total of 152 HRFOR personnel, including 114 field officers, had participated in at least some form of the training program, but it is unclear whether the content of the training program is adequate—in fact, several monitors surveyed indicate that important deficiencies remain.[16]

At the January 1995 Roundtable Conference and in subsequent revisions early in the year, donors committed approximately $9 million to human rights monitoring. By the end of the year, $14 million had been committed to the HRFOR, all of which had been disbursed, largely by the European Union and the United Kingdom.

Investigating genocide. An eight-member team of experts arrived in Rwanda in late October 1994 to support the special rapporteur and the commission of experts, as part of the HRFOR unit then called the "Special Investigations Unit." After about a month, they were succeeded by an American trial lawyer who, in turn, was replaced by a Swiss prosecutor and some forensic scientists from Spain. The investigations unit lacked a well-defined purpose and direction. It was expected to investigate violations of international humanitarian law, but, as one former member of the unit put it, "for whom or for what purpose was unclear."

In December 1994, the tribunal's prosecutor met with HRFOR in Kigali to request essentially that all investigations aimed at collecting evidence of those to be tried by the tribunal be henceforth conducted by tribunal staff only.[17] Further, he requested that evidence collected to date by HRFOR be organized and turned over to the tribunal. At that time, therefore, the Special Investigations Unit was left with a mandate to work for the special rapporteur and the Commission of Experts, to the extent their work did not touch on prosecutions within the mandate of the tribunal.

Before the December meeting between the prosecutor and HRFOR, the investigations unit had encountered several problems fulfilling its own understanding of its mandate. It was to work in support of the Commission of Experts and special rapporteur but report to the Center for Human Rights in Geneva and the HRFOR mission chief in Rwanda. Because neither the center nor the mission chief in Kigali was supervising investigations, no one could offer any significant direction; nor, apparently, did anyone assume responsibility for addressing the multifaceted problems encountered by the unit.

The unit lacked sufficient manpower and the necessary technical expertise and equipment to conduct a thorough and competent investigation of genocide, and the unit was hampered by uncertainty over whether it had the authority to request official records from government officials within and outside Rwanda. Without access to government officials and documents, collection of critical evidence for prosecutions was all but impossible.

Within this context, the members of the Special Investigations Unit directed their investigative work at collecting witnesses' statements and physical evidence at twenty-five massacre sites. Collection of this information was relevant, but insufficient for the investigative process envisioned by members of the unit. The leadership of HRFOR at the time seemed unable to resolve the resource–expertise–personnel problems or problems associated with access to official records, even those located in Rwanda.

Although the high commissioner for human rights communicated in one letter to the United States the need for more expert personnel and adequate resources, neither this effort nor any effort on the part of the HRFOR mission chief brought significantly more resources. The usefulness of the Special Investigations Unit was, by most accounts, very limited.[18] (Nonetheless, the high commissioner's office reports that when he handed over most of the HRFOR-collected evidence to the deputy prosecutor of the International Tribunal for Rwanda in March 1995, the deputy termed them "most valuable."[19])

In April 1995, after a visit of the special rapporteur, the Special Investigations Unit became the Legal Analysis and Coordination Unit (LACU), and its mandate was modified. HRFOR, primarily through its field officers, became involved in documenting the genocide through a variety of activities carried out by the Field Coordination Unit of

HRFOR coordinating with LACU and the newly appointed coordinator for the special rapporteur.

Monitoring human rights. After early 1995, the focus of field operations shifted from investigating violations of international humanitarian law to monitoring the ongoing human rights situation and cooperating with other international agencies in reestablishing confidence in Rwanda. Field officers hear complaints about human rights violations, investigate them, then file their reports, which are aggregated at the level of the prefecture and forwarded to the Field Coordination Unit. The unit writes a report based on a summary of the information contained in these reports. The mission chief periodically sends this summary to the high commissioner.

Until October 1995, HRFOR leadership had developed no discernible strategy for using these reports. According to the high commissioner's office, the reports were made available by him, "as appropriate," to the Secretary-General, governments, UN agencies, and intergovernmental and nongovernmental organizations.[20] Amnesty International has criticized this "as appropriate" distribution as ineffective for enhancing accountability for human rights violations in present-day Rwanda, but HRFOR failed either to adopt or articulate a policy concerning the reasons for its distribution policy. Consequently, it is not clear if these reports formed the basis for any actions or decisions.

In addition to the controversy over report distribution, the reliability of information contained in the reports was questioned—at first privately, later publicly.[21] HRFOR was unable to defend against such criticisms because it had not developed a comprehensive methodology for collecting information.[22] Additionally, HRFOR did not develop centralized policies, strategies, or guidelines for its field officers or unit leaders in Kigali for interaction with local or national officials during investigation and follow-up of alleged human rights violations. Because there was no agreement or missionwide understanding on these points within HRFOR, different officers in the field acted in different ways.

In October 1995, the new mission chief undertook to review and overhaul the structure and substantive work of HRFOR in the field and at its center. Establishing effective working relationships with ministerial-level officials appears to be a priority. Such relationships are essential to exchanging vital information and ensuring immediate action on allegations of current human rights violations.

A problem in monitoring current human rights violations is that the Rwandan government considers reporting partisan and unfair. Leaders feel the government is being subjected to critical scrutiny, whereas the perpetrators of genocide are being fed by the international community.

One explanation for this criticism is that HRFOR has failed to adequately publicize its assistance to the judicial system and information it has collected about the genocide.[23] Another explanation is that the Human Rights Field Operation may have directed its attention toward current violations with little regard for the desperate need to take a leading role on justice issues as they relate to perpetrators of genocide[24] though a welcome change recently began with HRFOR's efforts to work systematically with Rwandan officials on arrest and detention procedures.

Monitoring the return of refugees *to* Rwanda and monitoring detention centers *in* that country are two tasks that deserve special consideration. Until April 1995, HRFOR's monitoring of returnees from neighboring countries was characterized by the same local variability as its other monitoring activities; effectiveness depended on the persistence and talent of individual field officers. When Zaire expelled 15,000 Rwandans in August 1995, HRFOR tried to implement a coherent monitoring strategy. Field officers initially played a supporting role to UNHCR teams with regard to the logistics of moving and tracking returnees to all relevant locations, especially prisons. Later, field officers traveled to communes and worked with local authorities to assist in the reentry process. They monitored alleged killings, property disputes, numbers of individuals detained, and living conditions in the communes. At the national level, the Field Coordination Units contacted the relevant ministries to coordinate activities.

HRFOR has also been monitoring conditions for inmates in central, communal, and military prisons. Field monitors have reported serious maltreatment in both communal and central prisons and have sometimes been able to persuade local authorities of their duty to investigate and discipline. They have also raised with local authorities the issue of illegal detention of people accused of crimes not related to genocide. Coordination between HRFOR and the International Committee of the Red Cross in prison monitoring has been problematic since the inception of the mission, for several reasons, one of which is the special, independent mandate that the Red Cross must follow. Nonetheless, recently HRFOR did create written reporting procedures to be used by HRFOR and provided to the Red Cross for better coordination.

Technical cooperation program. The Technical Cooperation Unit of HRFOR has become increasingly important. It has attempted to coordinate foreign assistance for rebuilding Rwanda's judicial system. The Technical Cooperation Unit completed in March 1995 a nationwide survey (conducted in cooperation with UNDP and the Ministry of Justice) of short- and long-term material and personnel needs for rehabilitating the judicial system. Then field officers distributed to the prefectures the material assistance needed for the short term. More elaborate material assistance so desperately needed has failed to materialize, in large part for reasons beyond the control of HRFOR. In this context, HRFOR and UNDP may have jointly miscalculated the desire of the Rwandan government for a proposed plan to deploy fifty foreign legal experts who would have provided assistance to the judicial system as legal advisers. The program has been suspended until it can be reexamined by the new minister of justice.[25]

The unit has organized training and seminars on human rights for the local population, women, and government officials. In June 1995, the unit sponsored a seminar on human rights and press freedoms. More recently it implemented a series of prefecture-level workshops on arrest and detention procedures. Increasingly, HRFOR has taken responsibility for training gendarmes at the National Gendarmerie School. The success of these efforts appears to be determined more on the training and background of the individual field officer than on a specific strategy or program developed by the unit, although Rwandan judicial personnel seem to appreciate the assistance.

Conclusion

From its inception, the UN's field operation in Rwanda was marred by conceptual confusion and an inadequate administrative capability. Perhaps most important, the international donors supporting the operation, as well as those who were in charge of managing it, failed to address the political obstacles to "restarting" Rwanda's justice system. The Rwandan government's delay in bringing the accused perpetrators of the genocide to trial was as much the result of the internal political dynamics of a newly reconstituted government as it was a matter of a lack of resources.

In addition, the field operation was saddled with a multifaceted mandate that was difficult to operationalize and that failed to establish priorities among its objectives of carrying out investigations of human rights and international humanitarian law violations; monitoring the ongoing human rights situation; facilitating the return of refugees and displaced persons; and implementing technical cooperation programs in the administration of justice. The field operation, therefore, had to act as a critic and adversary of government in preventing ongoing abuses and as their partner in implementing technical cooperation programs. Moreover, the refugees who would be encouraged to return included many who might well be accused of participating in the genocide. They would be encouraged to return, then, by the same organization that was helping prepare for their prosecution.

Further, since no priorities were established among the mandate's diverse goals, how would the field operation's performance be measured? In August 1995, HRFOR reported that "the principal responsibility of the human rights field offices continues to be close cooperation with local authorities at the commune and sector levels to improve the process of reintegration of returnees to their home communes."[26] Eventual return of the refugees, however, was affected by many factors, such as intimidation by the leadership of the refugee camps; leadership consisted largely of officials of the former Hutu government. More realistic benchmarks were needed to determine if the field operation was successful.

The prosecution of those who were awaiting trial for participating in the massacres was at a standstill as late as October 1995, eighteen months after the genocide occurred. Over 50,000 persons were detained; many had not been formally charged with a crime and no trials had taken place. Nor had the government made an attempt to classify the prisoners according to their alleged culpability so that prosecutorial priorities might be established.

The prosecution of members of a former regime by a newly established government has taken place with increased frequency since the mid 1970s.[27] In Greece, Argentina, Colombia, Venezuela, the Phillipines, and Romania such prosecutions have occurred. In many of these countries, however, prosecution and punishment was largely confined to the former dictator, his family and selected high-ranking officials.[28] As Huntington noted, these nations' decisions to prosecute or not prosecute "was little affected by moral and legal considerations. It was shaped almost exclusively by politics, by the nature of the democratization process, and by the distribution of political power during the transition."[29]

Delays in the prosecution of former officials, then, can be expected. The rulers of the new regime need time to make political calculations and answer such questions as, How will the military respond to the prosecutions or allow a pretrial amnesty? Who should be prosecuted? What is the appropriate punishment for those found guilty of human rights violations?

In December 1994, for instance, the trial of the Derg—the military group that governed Ethiopia from 1974 until 1991—was just getting under way after three years of preparation. The trial of the forty-four former military leaders is expected to take years to complete.[30] The trial, however, is only part of a larger undertaking. In October 1995, 1,500 other officials of the former Derg regime were in custody awaiting trial.[31] The delay in bringing the former officials of the Derg to trial is due at least in part to the concern that the prosecutions will impede efforts to unify the nation. Ethiopia incorporates several language groups and has experienced ethnic rivalry between the Amhara and the Tigrayans. In Ethiopia, as in Rwanda, impunity and national unity (or reconciliation) are the terms that inform political debate.

The situation in Rwanda, however, was different than the other cases in two important respects: There were 50,000 persons awaiting trial under appalling conditions; and border incursions by the hostile exiled army of the former government threatened Rwanda's, and the region's, stability. The political obstacles to bringing officials of a former regime to trial that emerged in other nations might have put the international community on notice that new approaches would be needed if prosecutions were to begin expeditiously. No new initiatives, however, were forthcoming.[32] In October 1995, eighteen months after the genocide, the impasse continued.

Lessons to Be Learned

Each human rights emergency situation has its own peculiarities, and the response of the international community should be tailored to the specific circumstances of particular crises. The situation in Rwanda is unique in that the perpetrators of massive human rights abuses fled the country. They were replaced by a ruling coalition that was dominated by the ethnic group that had been the victim of a genocide. That ruling coalition, in turn, was heavily influenced by the military forces of the formerly exiled Tutsi. While the situation in Rwanda is unique, it nevertheless suggests lessons for future crises. Many of the problems that have emerged are the result of operational procedures and organizational structures that must be addressed if the performance of international human rights agencies is to improve. The following observations are designed to be a guide in responding to future emergencies:

1. Human rights field operations appear to have a greater chance of success when they are incorporated into a comprehensive strategy for bringing peace to the region. In the context of Rwanda, this means that a human rights field operation should be incorporated into an overall regional approach that would focus on (a) disarming the FAR who are in refugee camps located on Rwanda's borders; (b) separating those who are suspected of having committed violations of international humanitarian law from those who are not suspected; (c) providing an environment conducive to repatriation for refugees who want to return (who may be relatively few in number); and (d) policing Rwanda's borders to deter violent incursions on the part of the

current government and the FAR. When seen as part of an overall settlement, human rights activities are most likely to be viewed as being
impartial and fair.

2. Mandates for human rights field operations should be drafted
carefully by persons who are familiar with the details of the crisis. In
Rwanda, for example, several problems might have been avoided if the
mandate had been drafted after a study team went to the country, became familiar with the internal political dynamics of the current regime,
and consulted with leaders of the current government regarding their
views on what an appropriate mandate should contain. While a mandate
may be broad so as to provide flexibility to those responsible for carrying it out, it must not include potentially conflicting responsibilities.
Monitoring and protecting the human rights of persons who may be accused of crimes should not be conducted by the same agency that is assisting in the prosecution of those crimes.

3. In establishing a field operation, there should be a clear chain of
command, and overlapping reporting requirements should be avoided.
Persons conducting a criminal investigation, for instance, should report
only to the prosecutor or another person directly responsible for the
investigation. Furthermore, persons should be required to report to
only one authority; for example, investigators should not be required
to report to a Special Rapporteur, a Commission of Experts, and the
Centre for Human Rights in Geneva. Reporting requirements should
be clearly established. Periodic reports should be filed and circulated
to national, and international officials. Reports, or parts of them that
do not contain confidential information, should be available to the
public. The purpose of such reports should be made clear; that is, the
reports should form the basis for the decisions of the High Commissioner or the special rapporteur.

4. The leadership of human rights field operations is critical to
their success. It is not sufficient for leaders to be selected on the basis
of general experience in emergency relief work or because they possess the requisite foreign language skills. They must have substantive
knowledge of and experience in the areas involved in their work. This
substantive knowledge is needed for three reasons: (a) the leaders of
the field operation must be able to think strategically about implementing human rights, thus they must be familiar with the institutions
and procedures involved in protecting and promoting human rights;
(b) leaders must be familiar with the content of major human rights instruments and with international humanitarian law so that they are
knowledgeable about the applicable international obligations of the
parties involved in a conflict; (c) the knowledge and experience of
leaders affects the credibility of the field operation with the parties in-

volved in a conflict, and also affects their ability to recruit and retain highly skilled and knowledgeable assistants.

5. A training program for field officers should be established that focuses on their operational responsibilities. It should include instructions concerning the applicable international human rights instruments as well as information concerning the particular crises.

6. The leadership of a human rights field operation must be able to assess and deal with political as well as administrative obstacles that arise. Political problems do not readily yield to technocratic solutions. A major obstacle to the commencement of trials in Rwanda was political in nature (i.e., the delay of the National Assembly in appointing members of the Supreme Court and Council of Magistrates). High-level political negotiations were needed to break the impasse. The international donors, for example, could have appointed an emissary to meet with Rwandan officials to determine what was needed to get prosecutions and trials under way.

7. An early-warning system is needed to trigger the deployment of peacekeeping troops and UN human rights monitors. Some studies suggest that three factors are present in most states in which genocides or mass killings have occurred.[33] These factors are the existence of sharp internal cleavages, a history of intergroup conflict, and the lack of foreign powers' interest in or constraints on the ruling elites. All of these factors were present in Rwanda.[34] In Rwanda, moreover, the withdrawal of UN forces when violence broke out probably signaled to the leaders of Rwanda's former government that few or no constraints would be imposed on how the civil conflict could be waged.

Communal conflict, such as interethnic conflict, may follow a dynamic that differs from revolutionary violence. Some studies suggest, for instance, that several factors make intense communal conflict more likely. These are: (a) the presence of two or more ethnic groups with deep historically based hostilities; (b) ethnic identifications that have not been diluted by other identifications, such as those based on class or other group associations; (c) economic inequalities that reinforce discriminatory patterns of behavior, especially where disadvantaged groups are relatively large compared to advantaged groups.[35] Such indicators, when coupled with an event that threatens to exacerbate inequalities or disrupt the status quo, such as the 1990 RPA invasion, appear to be strong predictive factors.

Models for predicting genocides or mass killings are clearly in need of refinement. There appears, however, to be sufficient information on which to structure an early-warning system on which the deployment of large numbers of peacekeepers or human rights monitors could be based.

Notes

This chapter is largely based on "Rebuilding Post-War Rwanda," a 1996 evaluation written by Kumar et al., part of a larger 5-volume set entitled *The International Response to Conflict and Genocide: Lessons from the Rwanda Experience* (Copenhagen: Steering Committee of the Joint Evaluation of Emergency Assistance to Rwanda).

1. Rwanda, a German colony from 1890 to 1916, was mandated (along with Burundi) to Belgium by the League of Nations after World War I. See African Rights (1994, 5–14). Under Belgian rule, the Tutsi held all of the nation's forty-three chiefdoms, 549 out of 559 subchiefdoms, and over 80 percent of government positions in fields such as the judiciary, agriculture, and veterinary sciences. See U.S. Committee for Refugees (1991, 4). It has been estimated that during this period Tutsi constituted approximately 15 percent and Hutu 85 percent of Rwanda's population. The Tutsi and Hutu are subgroups of the Banyarwanda, a Bantu people who are East Africa's largest ethnic group. U.S. Committee for Refugees (1991, 2).

The relationship between the Tutsi and Hutu during the period of Belgian rule has been termed "ranked ethnic subordination," characterized by clientage relationships and an ideology of inferiority for the subordinate group. See Horowitz (1985, 29–30). Also see Lemarchand (1968).

2. Party for the Emancipation of the Hutu People (partie de l'Emancipation du Peuple Hutu).

3. The RPF was founded in 1979 by Tutsi exiles in Nairobi, Kenya. It was first known as the Rwandese Alliance for National Unity. Lorch (1994, A10).

4. See "The N'sele Ceasefire Agreement Between the Government of the Rwandese Patriotic Front, as Amended at Gbadolite, 16 September 1991, and at Arusha, 12 July 1992."

5. See U.S. Institute of Peace. See also "Peace Agreement Between the Government of the Republic of Rwanda and the Rwandese Patriotic Front," Arusha, 4 August 1993 (English translation obtained from the Embassy of Rwanda, Washington, D.C., USA).

6. The accords were seen by many within the ruling MNRD party (Mouvement National pour la Révolution et le Développement) as making too many concessions to the RPF. According to Lemarchand (1994), "The decisions made by the parties represented were never fully endorsed by the MNRD rank-and-file, and only reluctantly by the leadership."

7. Twenty-four prisoners died from asphyxiation in a detention facility near Kigali in April 1994. There are currently over 9,000 prisoners in Kigali's prison, which has the capacity to hold only 2,000 persons. In April 1994, it was estimated that 1,500 additional persons were being arrested each week. See UN Office of the Humanitarian Coordinator, Rwanda: Humanitarian Situation Report, April 15, 1995, p. 6. Nationwide, approximately 30,500 persons are being held in eleven major facilities with the collective capacity of 12,550. United Nations High Commissioner on Human Rights, Report No. 1, "Sur l'état de la justice au Rwanda, 2 Mai 1995."

8. By May 1995, there were sporadic reports that *gacaca* had begun to function in a nonofficial capacity in various regions of Rwanda.

9. As reported in the *Chicago Tribune,* May 30, 1995, p. 7. The newspaper article also quotes the Human Rights Watch report as stating that "additional money and assets in foreign countries (including at least Kenya, Tanzania, Zaire,

and the Netherlands) controlled by the ousted Rwandan government continue to be available to its leadership in exile."

10. When the RPA ousted the former government in July 1994, the new government pledged to establish a government according to the relevant agreements in which the Arusha process had resulted. Articles 60 through 79 of the Arusha accords provide for a transitional National Assembly. The deputies are appointed by their political parties. The parties and the numerical distribution of seats in the National Assembly are identified in Article 62 as follows: MRND: eleven; RPF: eleven; MDR: eleven; PSD: eleven; PL: eleven, and PDC: four.

11. See UN document S/res/955/1994. The vote was 13 in favor of the resolution, one against (Rwanda), and one abstention (China). It is generally believed Rwanda voted against the resolution because it precluded application of the death penalty.

12. See UN document E/CN.4/1996/7 (28 June 1995), p. 1.

13. For example, Amnesty International "Rwanda and Burundi: A Call For Action By the International Community" (September 1995, 11); African Rights "A Waste of Hope: The United Nations Human Rights Field Operation" (1995, 48–49).

14. Seven of twelve monitors surveyed were "satisfied" with the selection process, at least with regard to the EU contingent. See Roel von Meijenfeldt, "At the Frontline for Human Rights: Final Report," Appendix H (1995, 4). No survey has been conducted for non–EU monitors.

15. From "Response of the High Commissioner on Human Rights to Recommendations Contained in 'Rebuilding Post-War Rwanda: Evaluating the Impact of International Assistance with Regard to Human Rights'," p. 12.

16. See Roel von Meijenfeldt, "At the Frontline for Human Rights: Final Report" Appendix H (1995, 5–6).

17. Additionally, there was discussion between the prosecutor and HRFOR concerning preservation for the tribunal of the massacre sites for its own expert staff.

18. See, for example, Human Rights Watch, "Human Rights in Rwanda—1995" (1995, 8); Adam Stapleton, "Amateurs Posing As Professionals," in *Human Rights Tribune* (June–July 1995, 13–15); African Rights, "A Waste of Hope: The United Nations Human Rights Field Operation" (1995, 7–10).

19. From "Response of the High Commissioner on Human Rights to Recommendations Contained in 'Rebuilding Post-War Rwanda: Evaluating the Impact of International Assistance with Regard to Human Rights'," p. 4.

20. From "Response of the High Commissioner on Human Rights to Recommendations Contained in 'Rebuilding Post-War Rwanda: Evaluating the Impact of International Assistance with Regard to Human Rights'," p. 7. However, the high commissioner's office fails to note whether these reports were regularly provided to the government of Rwanda for comment, and if so, whether and when its response was distributed.

21. See African Rights. "A Waste of Hope: The United Nations Human Rights Field Operation" (1995, 14–28).

22. In April 1995, HRFOR hired a senior officer to head the Field Coordination Unit and address that weakness.

23. Amnesty International. "Rwanda and Burundi: A Call For Action by the International Community." AI Index: AFR 02/24/95, 12.

24. African Rights. 1995. "A Waste of Hope: The United Nations Human Rights Field Operation."

25. From "Response of the High Commissioner on Human Rights to Recommendations Contained in 'Rebuilding Post-War Rwanda: Evaluating the Impact of International Assistance with Regard to Human Rights'," p. 11.

26. High Commissioner for Human Rights, Update on the Activities of HRFOP: August 1, 1995; August 25, 1995.

27. For a discussion of such prosecutions see Samuel P. Huntington, *The Third Wave: Democratization in the Late Twentieth Century* (Norman: University of Oklahoma Press, 1991, 211–231).

28. The situation in Rwanda differs from that which has prevailed elsewhere in the magnitude of the crimes committed by the former regime. Nevertheless, the political considerations made by Rwanda's leaders appear to be much the same as others who faced the issue of whether former governmental leaders should be punished. If trials were to commence in the near future, the international donors needed to develop a political strategy to break the impasse; no such strategy was forthcoming.

29. Huntington, *The Third Wave* (1991, 215).

30. For a discussion of the trial, see John Ryle, "An African Nuremberg," *The New Yorker,* October 2, 1995.

31. Ibid., p. 52.

32. The steps that the Rwandan government intends to take subsequent to the November 1995 conference are still unclear.

33. See, e.g., Barbara Harff, "The Etiology of Genocides" in Isidor Wallimann and Michael N. Dobkowski (eds.), *Genocide and the Modern Age: Etiology and Case Studies of Mass Death* (1986, 41–59). Also see Leo Kuper, *Genocide: Its Political Use in the Twentieth Century* (1981). These works are discussed in relation to Africa in Ted Robert Gurr, "Theories of Political Violence and Revolution in the Third World," in Frances M. Deng and I. William Zartman, *Conflict Resolution in Africa* (1991, 153–189), especially 174. For other discussions of genocide, see Frank Chalk and Kijrt Jonassohn, *The History and Sociology of Genocide: Analyses and Case Studies* (1990); Robert Jay Lifton and Erik Markusen, *The Genocidal Mentality: Nazi Holocaust and Nuclear Threat* (1990); and Ervin Staub, *The Roots of Evil: The Origins of Genocide and Other Group Violence* (1989).

34. A test of this theory, however, would also require a showing that these factors were absent in nations where genocides did not occur.

35. Ted Robert Gurr, "Theories of Political Violence," 184. Also see Donald L. Horowitz, *Ethnic Groups in Conflict* (1985, 597–599).

References

African Rights. 1995. "Rwanda—A Waste of Hope: The United Nations Human Rights Field Operation." London: African Rights.

African Rights. 1994. *Rwanda: Death Despair and Defiance.* London: African Rights.

Amnesty International. 1995. "Rwanda and Burundi: A Call For Action By the International Community." New York: Amnesty International.

Bassiouni, M. Cherif (ed.). 1994. *The Protection of Human Rights in Administration of Justice: A Compendium of United Nations Norms and Standards.* Irvington-on-Hudson, N.Y.: Transnational Publishers.

Chalk, Frank, and Kurt Jonassohn. 1990. *The History and Sociology of Genocide: Analyses and Case Studies.* New Haven: Yale University Press.

Gurr, Ted Robert. 1991. "Theories of Political Violence and Revolution in the Third World." In *Conflict Resolution in Africa,* edited by Frances M. Deng and I. William Zartman, pp. 153–189. Washington, D.C.: Brookings Institution.

Harff, Barbara. 1987. "The Etiology of Genocides." In *Genocide and the Modern Age: Etiology and Case Studies of Mass Death,* edited by Isidor Wallimann and Michael N. Dobkowski, pp. 41–59. Westport, Conn.: Greenwood Press.

Horowitz, Donald L. 1985. *Ethnic Groups in Conflict.* Berkeley: University of California Press.

Huntington, Samuel P. 1991. *The Third Wave: Democratization in the Late Twentieth Century.* Norman: University of Oklahoma Press.

Kuper, Leo. 1982. *Genocide: Its Political Use in the Twentieth Century.* New Haven: Yale University Press.

Lemarchand, René. 1968. "Revolutionary Phenomena in Stratified Societies: Rwanda and Zanzibar." *Civilizations* 18 (March).

Lemarchand, René. 1994. "Managing Transition Anarchies: Rwanda, Burundi, and South Africa in Comparative Perspective." *Journal of Modern African Studies* 32 (4).

Lifton, Robert Jay, and Eric Markusen. 1990. *The Genocidal Mentality: Nazi Holocaust and Nuclear Threat.* New York: Basic Books.

Lorch, Donnatella. "Rwanda Rebels: Army of Exiles Fights for a Home." *New York Times,* June 9, 1994, p. A10.

Ryle, John. "An African Nuremberg." *New Yorker,* October 2, 1995, pp. 50–61.

Staub, Ervin. 1989. *The Roots of Evil: The Origins of Genocide and Other Group Violence.* Cambridge: Cambridge University Press.

U.S. Committee for Refugees. 1991. "Exile From Rwanda: Background to an Invasion." Washington, D.C.: U.S. Committee for Refugees.

von Meijenfeldt, Roel. 1995. *At the Frontline for Human Rights: Final Report.* Evaluation of European Union participation in the Human Rights Field Operation in Rwanda. Photocopy.

4

Demobilizing and Reintegrating Soldiers: Lessons from Africa

Nicole Ball

The last thirty years have offered enormous opportunities and challenges to the countries in sub-Saharan Africa. Although important progress has been recorded in both economic and social sectors, the gains have often come more slowly and unevenly than anticipated, especially during the 1980s. Consequently, economic stagnation has combined with deteriorating terms of trade, rapid population growth, exceptionally high levels of indebtedness, and the effects of prolonged conflict to produce a significant economic crisis.

In the political arena, one-party rule, military juntas, and authoritarian regimes have far outnumbered multiparty systems, offering citizens little opportunity to provide input into the decisions that shape their lives. The crisis in governance has intensified the economic crisis as resources have been put to unproductive uses, retarding efforts to achieve sustained development. The crisis in governance has also contributed greatly to the conflicts that have afflicted the region. Some of these have resulted from protracted decolonization struggles and from foreign military intervention. Prior to 1990, African conflicts were often exacerbated by the Cold War. But in many cases, domestic political and economic inequalities have played a central role.

Fundamental to both improved governance and sustained economic and social development is a reexamination of the role of the security sector. While the armed forces can play an important role in nation building, they can also severely constrain national well-being by absorbing too many resources, preventing the growth of responsible, accountable government, and encouraging conflict over compromise. In these respects, the military has imposed a heavy burden on sub-Saharan Africa. Reducing the size and political power of the security sector can substantially increase economic and political stability and thereby significantly enhance a country's long-term development prospects.

Restructuring the security sector involves demobilizing troops; separating internal and external security functions; enhancing transparency, accountability, and civilian control; reassessing missions; and, in some cases, creating entirely new security forces. This chapter focuses solely on the demobilization of troops, their initial reinsertion into civilian life, and their long-term reintegration as productive members of society. Seven African countries have significantly reduced the size of their security forces since the early 1980s—Chad, Eritrea, Ethiopia, Mozambique, Namibia, Uganda, and Zimbabwe. The coming years could witness troop reductions in perhaps another half-dozen or so African states. Development cooperation agencies have increasingly been asked to provide technical and financial support. A review of recent demobilization and reintegration efforts suggests that while some unresolved questions remain, considerable valuable experience has been accumulated.

This chapter begins by describing the four phases of the demobilization-reintegration process and identifying the roles played by the various actors involved. Three categories of lessons are then discussed: general lessons, lessons pertaining to assembly, and discharge, and lessons applicable to reinsertion and reintegration.

The Demobilization-Reintegration Process

While military life sometimes provides soldiers with technical and administrative skills that will stand them in good stead in civilian life, most African ex-combatants constitute a specially disadvantaged group. The typical veteran is semiliterate at best, is unskilled, has few personal possessions, often has no housing or land, and frequently has many dependents. Some veterans are also physically and psychologically handicapped by wartime experiences. Many find it difficult to take independent initiatives and to cope with the ordinary demands of civilian life. Even when they possess a marketable skill, such as mechanic or driver, ex-combatants tend to have little or no experience in the labor market, having taken up arms at an early age. They also tend to have an imperfect understanding of the state of the economy. Consequently, ex-combatants often have unrealistic assumptions about civilian life and require a period of adjustment to assess their personal situation and options. These characteristics are particularly relevant for former foot soldiers, whose opportunities for education and personal advancement were more limited than those of the officer corps, and for members of the armed opposition.

Donors and nongovernmental organizations (NGOs) have sometimes been reluctant to assist veterans following conflicts because of their role in uprooting noncombatants from their homes and causing considerable loss of life, destruction of physical infrastructure, and suffering. Still, peace agreements often specify such assistance, and it may be very difficult from a political standpoint to avoid aid to demobilized soldiers—even if it is not mandated by peace accords—in view of their capacity to disrupt the peace process. Demobilization-reintegration programs for ex-combatants and in some cases their families have been and will continue to be part of the transition landscape in Africa (World Bank 1993; Colletta, Kostner, and Wiederhofer 1996).

The demobilization-reintegration process consists of four major phases through which soldiers progressively pass: assembly, discharge, short-term reinsertion, and longer-term reintegration. The first two constitute the demobilization stage; the latter two the reintegration stage. The duration of these four phases varies from country to country, but experience from Africa and elsewhere suggests that donors should anticipate remaining involved for three to four years.

Assembly

Soldiers are typically assembled, or cantoned, as the first step in the demobilization-reintegration process. Following conflicts, assembly has primarily political and security objectives: to account for all combatants and their weapons and, where wars end without a clear winner, to build confidence between the former warring parties that each side will maintain the commitments expressed in the peace accords. Some soldiers are exempt from cantonment in order to maintain the functioning of the armed forces. Senior officers may also not be required to enter assembly areas.

The precise needs of cantoned troops vary considerably. When confined to barracks as most government troops are, the requirement for supplementary shelter, food, clothing, sanitation facilities, and medical care may be minimal. However, governments, which often owe their troops substantial back pay, may not have the resources to provide for soldiers' basic needs during cantonment. Opposition forces typically require that everything be provided for them, and they often need this assistance urgently. Finally, cantoned soldiers may have special health needs, particularly members of the armed opposition who have frequently had access to only very basic medical care for many years. Prior to discharge, soldiers often receive orientation to help them adjust to civilian life.

Because of the political context in which they occur, postconflict demobilization processes governed by negotiated settlements rarely, if ever, adhere to the timetables established by peace agreements. As the

Table 4.1   Potential Support to Ex-Combatants During Assembly and Discharge

Assembly	Discharge
Food	Short-term food supplements
Shelter	Transport
Clothing	Orientation on conditions in district of
Sanitation	residence
Medical exams	First tranche of reinsertion benefits
Medical care	
Basic education	
Leisure activities	
Orientation on adjusting to civilian life, including financial counseling, health counseling, civic duties, income generation (for soldiers and spouses)	
Assistance to child soldiers	
Census	
Discharge documentation	

cantonment period is extended, provisioning the encamped soldiers becomes more costly, and new needs are created. For example, it can be difficult to avoid providing some services, such as basic medical care, to the soldiers' families—who progressively join them in assembly areas—and to nearby civilians.

Discharge

When large numbers of soldiers are demobilized, they are generally discharged over a period of time. From a social and economic perspective, it may be preferable to discharge troops over a several-year period. For political-military reasons, however, postconflict demobilizations, particularly those governed by negotiated settlements, are often required to be completed within the space of one year, and the discharge of troops may be closely linked to compliance with other provisions of the peace accords.

Upon discharge, soldiers are generally transported to their home districts, which tends to be less expensive and safer than independent travel and facilitates the initial geographic dispersal of ex-combatants.

They are usually provided with food for the journey or given funds to purchase food. In some cases, veterans are required to attend postdischarge orientation meetings upon their arrival in their home districts. In addition, soldiers often receive some portion of their reinsertion benefits at the point of discharge. Table 4.1 illustrates the types of support provided by the international community during the assembly and discharge phases.

Reinsertion

Reinsertion assistance is a form of transitory safety net that provides veterans with the basic necessities of life—such as shelter, medical care, food, clothing, and household goods—for a period of between several months and two years. Delivery methods include cash payments, vouchers (for medical care and children's school fees), and in-kind transfers (housing material, food, clothing, transportation). Some reinsertion programs have offered special support to physically handicapped veterans. Psychological problems have received less attention. Some assistance has been provided to help veterans regenerate their traditional coping

Table 4.2   Potential Support to Ex-Combatants During Reinsertion and Reintegration

Reinsertion	*Reintegration*
Food supplements	Job generation, including public works, community development, micro-enterprises, salary supplements to employers, cooperatives
Clothing and personal items	
Housing material	
Short-term medical care	
Basic household goods	Job placement services
Land	Training, including apprenticeships, formal vocational training, managerial/administrative training
Basic agricultural supplies (seeds/ tools)	
Severance pay/other cash allowances	Credit schemes
Veteran/spouse information/counseling	Education
Assistance to child soldiers	Agricultural extension services
Rehabilitation for physically/mentally disabled soldiers	Veteran/spouse information/counseling
	Rehabilitation for physically/mentally disabled soldiers

skills through the creation of organizations to which soldiers can turn for advice and information.

Reintegration

The objective of reintegration is to incorporate the veteran and his family into civilian society and the attainment of financial independence through involvement in productive activities. Refugees, internally displaced persons, and veterans have many needs in common, and donors increasingly agree that programs to reintegrate ex-combatants into civilian life in postconflict environments are most appropriately linked with economic revitalization activities at the community level. To date, however, most assistance has targeted ex-combatants. The most frequently employed mechanisms are cash payments, counseling (employment and psychological), vocational training, apprenticeships, formal education, job generation, support for job search, access to land, credits, technical assistance, and support in identifying market needs. Table 4.2 illustrates the types of support provided by the international community during the reinsertion and reintegration phases.

Major Actors

The demobilization-reintegration process is both highly politically charged and administratively complex. Governments frequently request economic and technical assistance to devise a framework for demobilization-reintegration efforts, and to develop and implement specific programs for demobilized soldiers. They may also require external political support to overcome obstacles to the timely completion of the demobilization process. In addition, for a variety of reasons, programs are frequently implemented by nongovernmental organizations, both domestic and international, and by public international organizations. Table 4.3 summarizes the major actors in the demobilization-reintegration process and the roles each commonly plays during its four phases.

General Lessons

1. *Flexibility in planning and implementation is crucial. Postconflict demobilizations are particularly vulnerable to delays and other program changes. All involved should anticipate and plan for the unexpected.* Demobilization is inherently a political process and as such is subject to a variety of political pressures: to slow implementation, to speed implementation, to change the beneficiary pool, to alter the benefits package.

Table 4.3 Roles of the Major Participants in Demobilization and Reintegration

Government	In principle, governments are involved in assembly, discharge, reinsertion, and reintegration. In practice, peace agreements governing the transition in countries with no clear winner may require government to cede some of their responsibilities to other actors. Government tasks include: identifying assembly areas; provisioning assembly areas; selecting soldiers for discharge; developing benefits packages for assembly, reinsertion, and reintegration; identifying implementing agencies; ensuring that programs for ex-combatants harmonize with government priorities; delivering benefits; and monitoring reinsertion and reintegration programs.
Armed opposition	The armed opposition typically participates in selecting assembly areas and developing benefits packages for assembly, reinsertion, and reintegration. It may also participate in delivering benefits.
Demobilized soldiers	Demobilized soldiers frequently have little input into the demobilization-reintegration process. They have, however, sometimes been involved in developing and implementing benefits packages and counseling other ex-combatants.
UN peacekeeping operation	UN PKOs have provided military, technical, and political support for the demobilization process. UN troops have helped select, establish, monitor, and provision assembly areas and disarm combatants. UN staff have helped design and implement programs for assembly, reinsertion, and reintegration programs. Special Representatives of the Secretary-General have played an important role in helping to overcome political obstacles to demobilization.
UN development and humanitarian assistance bodies	UN development and humanitarian assistance bodies have participated in the development, implementation, and monitoring of reinsertion and reintegration programs. They have also provided funding for such programs.
Bilateral governments	Bilateral governments have supported the Special Representative of the UN Secretary-General in creating conditions conducive to demobilization.
Bilateral aid agencies	Bilateral aid agencies have participated in the development, implementation, and monitoring of reinsertion and reintegration programs. They have also provided funding for such programs.
NGOs/PIOs	Nongovernmental organizations and public international organizations have participated in the development, implementation, and monitoring of reinsertion and reintegration programs.
World Bank	The World Bank has participated in the development, implementation, and monitoring of reinsertion and reintegration programs. It has also provided funding for such programs.

Following conflicts that produce no clear winner, these pressures are particularly strong. Personnel have to be able to adapt rapidly to new circumstances. Enhanced flexibility does not, in and of itself, solve all problems. However, without the ability to respond to changing circumstances, programs face an even greater chance of failure.

> A plan is an agreed-upon basis for change.
> —*United Nations peacekeeping official, Mozambique, January 1995*

2. *Flexible, quick-disbursing funds are essential to the success of demobilization and reintegration programs.* The importance of financial flexibility has been stressed time and again by development practitioners involved in demobilization-reintegration efforts, but this lesson has not yet been fully internalized by development assistance bureaucracies. Although both relief aid and development assistance are routinely employed in demobilization-reintegration efforts, neither are well suited to this purpose. Development assistance is slow disbursing, and the more accessible relief aid is often limited to activities that save lives. Mechanisms urgently need to be developed to speed disbursement, including means of overriding any restrictions on assistance to military organizations where necessary.

One possible mechanism would be a "transition/postconflict waiver authority" to support demobilization-reintegration activities. Alternatively, donors could cofinance structural adjustment loans with the multilateral development banks to increase the volume of quick-disbursing funds available to governments. Redirecting funds already appropriated for other programs offers a third option that donors frequently use, but significant funds are not always available for this purpose.

Equally important, special attention needs to be given to UN procurement practices in view of the central role accorded UN peacekeeping operations (PKOs) when conflicts end in negotiated settlements. One means of increasing the flexibility of UN funding would be to provide PKOs with reasonable local expenditure authority so that only major expenditures would have to be referred to New York.

3. *For demobilization-reintegration to proceed smoothly and with maximum possible effectiveness, planning should begin well before troops enter assembly areas. This means that donors should be prepared to act early on, ideally before wars actually end.* Governments invariably require financial and technical assistance to plan as well as implement

their demobilization-reintegration programs. Thus, if planning is to begin early, donor support must begin early. Adequate lead time will facilitate the timely delivery of assistance and enable donors to determine if ongoing programs—health care, vocational training, credit, and so on—could be expanded to meet the needs of ex-combatants.

There are three additional reasons in favor of early donor involvement. First, it is possible that the process of reaching peace agreements could be expedited if the parties to the conflict knew that specific programs would be available to their soldiers to ease the difficult transition to civilian life. Second, when wars end in negotiated settlements, demobilization tends to begin before a legitimated government is established, this generally through internationally supervised elections. Indeed, demobilization may be a precondition for holding the elections. Under these conditions, mistrust of transitional governments among the armed opposition may necessitate some degree of international supervision of the demobilization-reintegration process. Third, postconflict countries typically suffer from extreme institutional weakness. Their governments are overextended and unable to fulfill key functions and deliver critical services. It would be helpful in these situations for the donors to work with appropriate government officials (at the national, regional, and local levels), relevant international NGOs and multilateral institutions, representatives of the opposition, local communities and nongovernmental bodies, and the soldiers themselves to plan demobilization-reintegration activities.

4. *As with any development program, a key element in the success of the demobilization-reintegration process is adequate institutional support. Three functions that must be fulfilled are: (a) strategic planning, (b) coordination within the government and with the donor community, and (c) oversight of implementing bodies.* The governments of war-torn countries invariably have substantial institution-strengthening needs. If they are to develop the capacity to fulfill key functions and deliver essential services, some level of material and technical assistance will be necessary. The planners of demobilization-reintegration efforts should, therefore, incorporate institutional-strengthening and human resource capacity building into their programs where appropriate and feasible.

Strategic planning. To assess institutional needs, donors might encourage the establishment of an informal forum in which donors, the government, and the armed opposition could engage in dialogue on the overall policy and institutional framework within which demobilization-reintegration activities will occur; the key tasks for government and the appropriate level of government to assume responsibility for each task; methods of incorporating the views of the soldiers to be demobilized; and the specific roles that individual donor agencies and NGOs will play to help implement demobilization-reintegration programs.

Coordination. Recent experience suggests that a civilian, quasi-governmental commission is the best mechanism for guiding the overall demobilization-reintegration process and effecting coordination between the country undergoing demobilization and the donor community (Colletta, Kostner, and Wiederhofer 1996, 25). The primary objective must, however, be to assist veterans, not to create an elaborate administrative structure. In addition, donors must make every effort to encourage such commissions to operate in a problem-solving mode and to avoid falling prey to the postconflict power struggles that afflict countries when conflicts end with no clear winner.

To facilitate donor-government coordination, the resident donor community should appoint a lead donor—a bilateral aid agency, the World Bank, or the UN Development Programme (UNDP). Where demobilization occurs as part of a peace process supervised by the United Nations, a PKO may be responsible for coordination. In these cases, an effort must be made to draw as much as possible on existing donor coordination mechanisms—both formal and informal. Whatever the donor coordination mechanism is employed, it is critical that the individual responsible for overall coordination possess a collaborative, inclusive, personal style. It is also important that the donors give priority to veterans' needs rather than to their own interests, something that has not always occurred in recent demobilization-reintegration efforts.

Implementation oversight. Local oversight mechanisms are typically discredited or severely weakened in countries that have experienced lengthy civil wars. One means of strengthening local capacity would be to constitute community-based committees composed of government representatives, community leaders, local NGOs, businesspeople, and other local citizens, including ex-combatants. Such committees could initially provide input on project/program design and implementation and ultimately assume oversight responsibility. Involving local representatives in this way should increase the community's stake in the successful incorporation of veterans.

Although time consuming to establish, the return on investment from such committees is likely in most cases to outweigh the costs in terms of more appropriate programs, enhanced local capacity, and more rapid social integration of ex-combatants. If this approach is to succeed, however, local participation must be genuine. Community members must be consulted, not informed; authority must be progressively transferred from central and regional governments to local entities (Colletta, Kostner, and Wiederhofer, with Mondo, Sitani, and Woldu 1996, 170–171, 179–180).

5. *Program planners should take into account the needs of special vulnerable groups.* The disabled, the chronically ill, child soldiers, and women are among those most frequently cited as requiring special attention. In some African countries, a significant number of the soldiers discharged from military service are infected with HIV. Other veterans carry the physical and psychological scars of lengthy wars. Female combatants and the wives of male veterans face a variety of social and economic constraints and burdens that derive to a large extent from the traditional role of women in African societies. If not overcome, these can cause considerable hardship for the women and their children. Child soldiers are a particularly unfortunate legacy of war.[1] Even soldiers who are in their twenties at the time of demobilization may need special assistance because they have had no experience of civilian life as an adult. Although there have been some efforts to address the problems of these especially vulnerable groups, they have generally received less attention than warranted (Colletta, Kostner, and Wiederhofer 1996, 21).

6. *A crucial component of any demobilization/reintegration scheme is an effective monitoring and evaluation capacity.* To conserve increasingly scarce resources, it is vital that assistance reaches its intended beneficiaries, that programs are cost-effective, and that leakage is minimized. In addition, monitoring and evaluation in the course of project execution enable midcourse corrections, which can be extremely valuable in maximizing beneficiary satisfaction. This is accomplished by making adjustments in program content and the way in which benefits are delivered. A unified database is critical to these functions and should be created at the beginning of the demobilization-reintegration process.

Lessons from the Assembly and Discharge Phases

1. *Lengthy periods in assembly areas prior to demobilization can create significant political and social problems and increase costs substantially. They should therefore be avoided whenever possible.* It is widely understood that there are significant economic, political, and social benefits to be gained from minimizing the amount of time troops spend in assembly areas (RPG and DHA 1994, 10). Nonetheless, demobilizations following wars that end without a clear winner invariably encounter political obstacles to rapid discharge. It is therefore critical that planners of postconflict demobilizations under these conditions develop

contingency plans on the assumption that significant delays will occur in implementing the peace process and that soldiers will remain in assembly areas considerably longer than anticipated in the peace accords timetable.

2. *One method of mitigating problems associated with lengthy periods in assembly areas is to update cantoned troops regularly on the status of the demobilization process and, whenever possible, avoid communicating "dates certain" to them.* Although it is probably impossible to eliminate the frustration of long encampment periods, explaining the complexity of the process to the soldiers and keeping them constantly updated on progress (or the lack thereof) may help to mitigate some of the tensions that develop. In order to facilitate this communication, it is important to ensure that as many of the personnel supervising assembly as possible speak local languages.

3. *It is desirable to begin preparing soldiers for civilian life prior to discharge.* Soldiers can usefully receive information on a broad range of subjects that will help them reintegrate into civilian life. It is desirable to include soldiers' wives (or husbands) in these orientations whenever possible. Where soldiers are encamped for lengthy periods of time, the predischarge orientation can be more detailed than in situations where they are assembled for a shorter time, and basic skills enhancement can be provided as well. However, assembly periods should never be lengthened solely to provide soldiers with training.

When veterans arrive in their home districts, it may be helpful to provide a post-discharge orientation before they and their families disperse. The purpose of this exercise would be to familiarize the new arrivals with the local economic situation, customary rights of women, and other relevant information, and to acquaint them with representatives of local government and relevant NGOs (Colletta, Kostner, and Wiederhofer 1996, 13–14).

4. *Child soldiers should not undergo assembly.* Every effort should be made to identify child soldiers, to remove them from assembly areas or encampments around assembly areas, provide them with psychological counseling if at all possible, and reunite them with their families. Armed forces, reluctant to admit that they have child soldiers in their ranks, often refuse to give relief workers early access to the children. Donors need to make every effort to overcome these obstacles and should be supported in their efforts by the key members of the diplomatic community, including the Secretary-General's Special Representative.

5. *If time permits, it is desirable to conduct a trial run of assembly-discharge activities in order to fine tune the process.* By discharging some 400 soldiers several weeks before the formal start of the demobi-

**Uganda Veterans Assistance Board Predischarge
Orientation for Soldiers and Their Wives**

Soldiers were demobilized in three phases in Uganda between 1992 and 1995. During this period, the content of the predischarge orientation was progressively refined. As a result, the length of the orientation sessions was extended from a short briefing period prior to mustering out in phase I to at least 20 hours spread over five days in phase III. During phase I, soldiers' wives were not included; during phase III, the sessions were conducted jointly with wives to the extent possible.

The eight phase III predischarge orientation modules were:

- Entitlements (banking and installments, education and health, roofing materials)
- Veterans' associations and veterans' experience to date (projects undertaken, economic opportunities, personal finances)
- Women's legal rights and civil responsibilities
- Services and cost-sharing at local health facilities
- Household health issues (preventive care, first aid)
- AIDS/HIV (basic information, access to counseling and support resources)
- PTA fees and importance of basic education for veterans' children
- Women's legal rights issues (basic education for both veterans and veterans' wives)

—*Nat Colletta, Markus Kostner, and Ingo Wiederhofer with Emilio Mondo, Taimi Sitani, and Tadesse Woldu.* Case Studies in War-to-Peace Transitions: De-Mobilization and Reintegration of Ex-Combatants in Ethiopia, Namibia, and Uganda, *Working Paper (Washington, D.C.: Africa Technical Department, The World Bank, 1996), p. 23.*

lization process, the Uganda Veterans Assistance Board was able to identify program design and implementation weaknesses and make a number of adjustments to their procedures. Some of the lessons learned were that it is desirable to have military escorts accompany veterans and their families during transportation to the district reception centers; it is desirable to take out group insurance to protect against the loss or theft of benefits distributed at the time of discharge during transport to the districts; and it is important to fully prepare re-

ception and temporary sleeping arrangements at the district reception
point to accommodate veterans and their families while they await
transport to their home villages.

Lessons from the Reinsertion and Reintegration Phases

1. *Demobilization-reintegration programs should include a combination
of benefits (which are available to all demobilized soldiers), and opportunities (which are available to ex-combatants who meet certain criteria). To
minimize the potential for discontent among veterans, the distinction between benefits and opportunities needs to be communicated clearly and
consistently.* Providing all veterans with relatively short-term reinsertion
benefits that function as a transitory safety net addresses both their real
physical needs and their psychological need for formal recognition of
the personal sacrifices they made during their years of military service.
Where different benefit packages are provided—based on personal
characteristics (female, child soldier, disabled), destination (rural or urban), or intended occupation—every effort should be made to develop
packages of roughly equivalent value. In addition, it is probably preferable to distribute benefits to soldiers only as long as they remain in large
groups, that is, during the assembly and transport phases.

Longer-term reintegration assistance should be presented as a series
of opportunities, since it is highly unlikely that employment, training,
and education opportunities can be provided to all veterans, particularly
in postconflict societies where the lives of large numbers of people have
been disrupted by war and resources are exceptionally constrained.

2. *The benefits package should consist of short-term reinsertion subsidies, in cash or in kind, to tide soldiers over the initial period of return
home. Opportunities should include medium- and long-term assistance
aimed at identifying immediate employment openings, supporting economic revitalization, promoting community development, and increasing
longer-term employment possibilities.* To minimize the increase in polarization among social groups that demobilization-reintegration programs
might cause, it is important to limit the number of targeted programs
and shift as early as possible to community-based programs and/or programs benefiting all the most severely war-affected populations.

Short-term reinsertion assistance. Short-term reinsertion assistance
can provide ex-combatants with a vital breathing space while they establish themselves in the civilian economy. It also reduces the burden that
veterans and their dependents place on the communities to which they
return and enhances veterans' self-esteem by ensuring that they will be
able to finance their basic needs. Reinsertion assistance in the form of

cash can help remonetize the economy and stimulate local production of basic goods and services. The duration of reinsertion programs depends on local circumstances but should probably be six to twelve months. The value of the reinsertion package should take account of regional variations in purchasing power, as well as the local cultural environment and mode of subsistence. It is important, of course, that this assistance not come to be considered an entitlement. Therefore, a termination date should be established at the start of the demobilization process and communicated clearly and consistently to veterans.

Although financial payments arguably provide the demobilized and their families with greatest flexibility and are the least costly method of providing benefits, the most appropriate method of delivering reinsertion assistance—cash payments, in-kind assistance, vouchers—depends on local conditions. Each of these methods should be considered during the planning phase. When cash payments are the chosen form of assistance, payments spread over several installments with an option of advances for investment purposes are preferable to lump-sum payments. Cash payments can also be used to strengthen the capacity of local financial institutions.

Donors should be aware of the ways in which the type of assistance they offer influences program design, costs, and outcomes. Whatever form their assistance takes, donors should make every effort to provide it in a timely fashion to avoid the negative impact that disbursement delays can have on program beneficiaries.

Medium- and long-term reintegration support. Demobilized soldiers and their spouses require three types of assistance to facilitate their productive reintegration into the civilian economy: information about economic and social programs from which they could benefit; information about specific job opportunities; and means of acquiring or upgrading skills essential for employment.

Past experience has demonstrated the value of both information (benefits and opportunities) and referral (employment and training) services for ex-combatants, even in countries where the local economy is extremely weak and job opportunities outside the family agriculture sector are limited. In the future, however, it would be worthwhile to determine if the focus could be on the community as a whole. Since a growing economy provides the best hope for long-term reintegration, it makes good sense to focus as many resources as possible on strengthening the local economy.

A community information and referral capacity could be established to provide community members with referrals to employment and training opportunities. This capacity could be attached to existing local government offices or be lodged in a community center. In the

Donor Influence on the Housing Component of Reinsertion Assistance in Uganda

"The following assistance was rendered to a veteran for erecting a simple house: twenty galvanized corrugated iron (GCI) sheets and five GCI ridges in kind as well as in-cash contributions for the purchase of poles, doors, windows, nails, vents, and skilled labor.

It was initially contemplated to provide veterans with a total cash package to reduce logistical and transaction costs of procuring, storing, transporting, and distributing such large numbers of iron sheets and ridges; however, one donor willing to entirely support this component could only contribute to the program through commodity provisions ...

Pledged in the autumn of 1992 [for phase I demobilization, December 1992–July 1993], actual delivery took place between September and December 1993....

Phase II procurement experienced similar delays, this time due to the late arrival of funds and due to the procurement procedures.... The iron sheets for phase II veterans were finally delivered in the summer of 1995...

Ideally, veterans would receive the in-kind housing benefits immediately after returning to the community. Only then would they be able to make full use of this component. Until the house was built, a period of maybe one to three months, they were expected to stay with relatives or friends. As a result of these delays, however, many veterans did not have adequate shelter for a prolonged period of time after arrival, though few veterans were actually homeless two to three months after discharge....

Because in-kind and cash benefits were not provided at the same time, in fact more than one year apart, many veterans were not able to save the cash components until the sheets arrived...."

As a result of this experience, it was decided the cash payments equivalent to the value of the iron sheets would be substituted for the sheets themselves during the third round of demobilization.

—*Nat Colletta, Markus Kostner, and Ingo Wiederhofer with Emilio Mondo, Taimi Sitani, and Tadesse Woldu. 1996.* Case Studies in War-to-Peace Transitions: Demobilization and Reintegration of Ex-Combatants in Ethiopia, Namibia, and Uganda. *Working Paper. Africa Technical Department. Washington, D.C.: The World Bank: 258–259.*

latter case, it could possibly house NGOs and other agencies providing a variety of information and services and even become the locus of community-based conflict management and reconciliation efforts where necessary and appropriate. In either case, the objective would be to designate specific staff members to work solely with veterans and their families. It is important, particularly in the first months following demobilization, that there is a place where veterans can obtain advice and support.

Rather than establish job and credit schemes specifically for veterans, additional funding could be made available to existing community development, microenterprise, public works and other relevant programs to enable them to absorb a certain number of ex-combatants or their spouses into ongoing activities. Resources could be allocated on a priority basis to districts with particularly high concentrations of veterans and few employment opportunities.

A number of recent African ex-combatant reintegration efforts have included training programs intended to raise skill levels and enable some ex-combatants to become self-employed. These experiences suggest that such programs are not an efficient use of limited resources, particularly in countries with limited employment opportunities and weak training infrastructure. Rather, future reintegration schemes for demobilized soldiers should concentrate first on developing apprenticeship opportunities that help overcome the training-employment disconnect and various problems associated with training centers, such as quality, capacity, and geographic distribution. According to the World Bank, apprenticeships are "a feasible and cost-effective option for the most urban ex-combatants" (Colletta, Kostner, and Wiederhofer 1996, 21). An additional priority would be to provide vouchers for formal education and vocational training to qualified veterans. Incentives can also be offered to private sector firms to hire veterans.

3. *Surveys of the socioeconomic characteristics and employment aspirations of soldiers and the local opportunity structure and institutional capacity will result in more appropriate programs and help manage expectations.* In the absence of detailed information, donors often make unwarranted assumptions about demobilized soldiers, the capacity of the economy to absorb labor in specific sectors, and the ability of institutions, such as training facilities and local governments, to contribute to reintegration efforts.

In Africa, reintegration planners commonly anticipate that the agricultural sector will absorb most veterans and that by virtue of their peasant background, most veterans know how to farm. Reality is often quite different. Government troops in particular are frequently urbanized. In many countries, many farmers find that off-farm employment is necessary to supplement the family income. Equally important, in no country does a peasant background guarantee that an individual has the necessary skills to become a successful farmer. Indeed, many African soldiers have entered military service at an early age and spent long periods under arms.

One reason demobilization-reintegration programs are based on untested assumptions in postconflict environments is the difficulty that almost always exists in obtaining information about the intended beneficiaries and particular localities prior to the end of hostilities. In countries where wars end without a clear victor, this situation often extends into the early days of the peace process when levels of mistrust are still very high. The speed with which programs have to be developed can also limit local input.

It is possible that access to beneficiaries could be increased and implementation facilitated if donors engaged the parties to the conflict in discussions of reintegration-reinsertion issues during the course of peace negotiations. It may also be possible to overcome

---

The Importance of Assessing
the Local Opportunity Structure

In 1994, the German Technical Cooperation Agency (GTZ) agreed to finance an on-the-job-training program for thirty demobilized soldiers in Manica province in Mozambique through its Open Reintegration Fund. One-third of the trainees were to become shoemakers while the remainder were to become shoe repairmen. All were to receive kits and start-up material to help them establish themselves in the informal sector. While GTZ believed that there would be a demand for shoemakers and shoe repairmen, no market survey was conducted to verify this. In addition, once training got under way, it was realized that the self-employed shoemakers would experience difficulty in obtaining raw materials on a sustained basis. A second project was established to provide the newly employed shoemakers with raw materials at reasonable prices. It can be predicted, however, that most of the trainees who attempt to become self-employed will end up concentrated in a small area and that only a few of them will survive in the medium to long term. Indeed, GTZ has recognized that some trainees may not succeed in establishing viable businesses.

—Interviews by author

some of the constraints on obtaining timely information on the local situation by adapting strategies that have worked in similar circumstances. For example, vocational training programs for ex-combatants could usefully be viewed as a special form of adult basic education program (UNDP 1993, 72).

4. *It is important to promise no more than can be delivered.* Governments emerging from long periods of civil strife that are eager to consolidate their power, reward loyal followers, or enhance their legitimacy frequently promise benefits they cannot deliver. In view of the economic constraints facing most countries undergoing demobilization, it is difficult for governments to finance extensive benefits packages. In addition, the highly contentious political environment that characterizes many postconflict countries can complicate government efforts to redistribute assets such as land.

Unfulfilled promises to ex-combatants only exacerbate the political problems facing these governments. It is important for donors to assist governments in shaping programs that are as realistic as possible, thereby avoiding frustrations and resentments that can all too easily generate social discontent.

5. *Reinsertion-reintegration is a family affair.* One clear lesson from recent African experience is that reinsertion-reintegration programs should be aimed at the soldiers and their dependents, not just the soldiers themselves. Programs that do not take into account the fact that many veterans must provide for dependents (and frequently a sizable number) will not provide the degree of support these former soldiers need and may delay their productive reintegration into society.

6. *Reinsertion-reintegration is also a community affair.* The more community support veterans receive, the greater their chance of rapid reintegration. Since extended families can be an important source of support to newly demobilized soldiers, veterans should be encouraged to take up residence in communities where family members reside. For a variety of reasons, however, including past personal experience with the security forces, communities may have negative attitudes toward demobilized soldiers. It would therefore be desirable to survey communities during the planning phase to ascertain their attitudes and their capacity to assist veterans. Where necessary, community sensitization efforts can be undertaken to enhance local understanding of challenges facing veterans and their families and the role the community can play in helping them make the transition to civilian life. One method of strengthening community acceptance of veterans and their families would be to offer communities that absorb a substantial number of veterans some tangible benefit, such as the resources to finance a rehabilitation project to be chosen by the community.

Conclusion

The lessons outlined in this chapter constitute a first step toward charting a course for demobilization-reintegration efforts during the first three to four years following the cessation of hostilities. They are based on a growing body of very recent evaluations of demobilization and reintegration activities.[2] These evaluations suggest that additional longer-term investigations of beneficiaries and detailed cost analyses would be fruitful.

In addition, it would be helpful for donor agencies to meet at a senior policymaker level—perhaps under the auspices of the World Bank or the OECD Development Assistance Committee—to discuss a broad framework for demobilization and, especially, reintegration assistance, and to develop a preliminary division of labor. Conclusions reached as the result of such a meeting should be communicated clearly and consistently to field staff. In particular, it would be helpful if field staff could receive guidance on the issues pertaining to country-level donor coordination.

Notes

1. According to "The Convention on the Rights of the Child," adopted by the United Nations General Assembly on November 20, 1989, and entered into force on September 2, 1990, "A child means every human being below the age of eighteen years unless, under the law applicable to the child, majority is attained earlier" (Article 1).
2. In addition to the items cited in the text, this chapter has made use of the following reports: Ball (1995), Clark (1996), Colletta and Ball (1993), International Labour Office (1995a, 1995b), Klingebiel et al. (1995), and Organization of African Unity and Global Coalition for Africa (1995).

References

Ball, Nicole. 1995. "Mid-Term Evaluation: Demobilization and Reintegration Support Project (656-0235) Mozambique." USAID/Mozambique. Internal document.

Clark, Kimberly Mahling. 1996. *Mozambique's Transition from War to Peace: US-AID's Lessons Learned.* Washington, D.C.: The U.S. Agency for International Development.

Colletta, Nat, and Nicole Ball. 1993. "War-to-Peace Transition in Uganda." *Finance and Development* (June):36–39.

Colletta, Nat, Markus Kostner, and Ingo Wiederhofer with Emilio Mondo, Taimi Sitani, and Tadesse Woldu. 1996. *Case Studies in War-to-Peace Transitions: Demobilization and Reintegration of Ex-Combatants in Ethiopia, Namibia and Uganda.* Working Paper. Africa Technical Department. Washington, D.C.: World Bank.

Colletta, Nat, Markus Kostner, and Ingo Wiederhofer. 1996. *The Transition From War to Peace in Sub-Saharan Africa.* Directions in Development. Washington, D.C.: The World Bank.

International Labour Office. 1995a. *Reintegration of Demobilized Combatants Through (Self) Employment and Training: An Issues Paper.* Geneva: International Labour Office.

International Labour Office, Vocational Training Systems Management Branch. 1995b. *Reintegrating Demobilized Combatants: Experiences from Four African Countries.* Geneva: International Labour Office.

Klingebiel, Stephan, Inge Gärke, Corinna Kreidler, Sabine Lobner, and Haje Schütte. 1995. *Promoting the Reintegration of Former Female and Male Combatants in Eritrea. Possible Contributions of Development Co-operation to the Reintegration Programme.* Berlin: German Development Institute.

Organization of African Unity and Global Coalition for Africa. 1995. *Post-Conflict Demobilization in Africa: Report of the Workshop, November 9–10, 1994, Kampala, Uganda.* Addis Ababa and Washington, D.C.

RPG (Refugee Policy Group) and DHA (United Nations Department of Humanitarian Affairs). 1994. *Challenges of Demobilization and Reintegration: Background Paper and Conference Summary.* New York: United Nations Department of Humanitarian Affairs.

UNDP (United Nations Development Programme). 1993. *Launching New Protagonists in Salvadoran Agriculture.* San Salvador: UNDP.

World Bank. 1993. *Demobilization and Reintegration of Military Personnel in Africa: The Evidence from Seven Country Case Studies.* Working Paper. Africa Technical Department. Washington, D.C.: World Bank.

5

Building a New Civilian
Police Force in El Salvador

William Stanley and Charles T. Call

The Political Significance of Civilian Policing

Internal Security Versus National Defense

As unprecedented numbers of Latin American countries have undergone transitions from military to civilian rule, scholars have begun to focus on how countries can move beyond mere elected civilian rule to establish more broadly participatory, genuinely competitive electoral systems, impartial judiciaries, and accountability for those in office to the publics they represent and serve. One of the potential barriers to deepening democracy in Latin America is the entrenched presence of militaries in internal security and domestic intelligence roles (Bayley 1993).

José Manuel Ugarte (1990) argues that these militarized internal security institutions, and the practices and philosophy they embody, represent a fundamental impediment to more profound democratization. According to Ugarte, the defining characteristic of national security institutions and doctrine is that they do not distinguish between the realm of *national defense*, which involves the organization and maintenance of force and intelligence to defeat potential enemies, and *internal security*, which is the task of protecting the rights of citizens as defined under the norms of liberal democracy. National security doctrine places a priority on protecting the nation as an organic whole: Applied to internal security, this approach negates the importance of individual rights and defines entire classes of people and currents of political opinion as threats to the security of the nation (Lopez 1986). The tendency to define citizens as enemies leads to the practice of waging war against them, usually through the illegal detention, torture, and murder of citizens. The forces that "fight" such "dirty wars" expect, and usually enjoy, impunity for their actions, even after transitions to civilian rule.

Unless civilian governments carry out a fundamental transformation of internal security institutions—separating them completely from national defense institutions—policing remains in the hands of untouchable forces who view much of the free political expression and organization that underlie democratic politics as a threat to the state. In such a context, repression is likely and the capacity of a new democracy to channel discontent into the political system is jeopardized.

A growing current of scholarly opinion argues that civil-military relations can improve if militaries refocus their efforts on less politically contentious national defense issues (Norden 1990; Stepan 1988; Zagorski 1992; NDI 1990a). Separating internal security and national defense functions is thus arguably a prerequisite for civil-military cooperation. Once militaries get out of the role of political police, civilian legislators and executives are likely to find them less threatening and are likely to be more receptive to their professional concerns and needs; and militaries are less likely to perceive and treat civilians as subversive enemies. This can lead, at least in theory, toward mutually respectful dialogue and increased civilian participation in the management of national defense, leading eventually toward effective civilian supremacy along the lines of Western democracies.

In practice, civilian regimes have found it relatively difficult to wrest control of internal security from the military. In a handful of cases—Argentina, Panama, Bolivia, and Haiti—the demilitarization of internal security occurred where the military was especially weak politically at the time civilians took office. In other cases—Chile, Guatemala, Honduras, and Nicaragua—the military was in a position to manage its own withdrawal from power, and the transition to civilian rule has not entailed full civilianization of internal security.

In this context, the police civilianization project in El Salvador, part of the January 1992 Chapultepec peace accords that ended the civil war between the government of El Salvador and the Farabundo Martí National Liberation Front (FMLN), constituted one of the most radical attempts to date to put internal security firmly under civilian control.[1] The Salvadoran project provided for a completely new National Civilian Police (PNC) force, which incorporated relatively few personnel from the military-controlled security forces it replaced. The peace agreements greatly reduced the constitutional powers of the armed forces, called for the complete elimination of the existing public security forces, and provided a very specific institutional and legal framework for the new police force and a timetable for its development and deployment. The international community provided unprecedented levels of technical assistance, training, on-the-job supervision, and material assistance to the new police force. The development of the PNC in El Salvador therefore represented a critical test of how rapidly and effectively civilian policing could be established, and of how the international community could contribute to such a process of institutional development. From promising beginnings, the El Salvador police project developed into a cautionary tale about the crucial importance of political will for developing new police institutions, the difficulty civilian governments have in enforcing their independence from militaries, and the limited weight of international pressures relative to domestic political considerations. This chapter will explore the achievements and failures of the PNC project in El Salvador and consider what lessons it may carry for civilianization of internal security in other contexts.

Internal Security in El Salvador

Internal security in El Salvador was historically based on vigilance by militarized security forces and paramilitary organizations under the direct control of the military. For most of the twentieth century, in fact, the military's primary mission was internal security and control of the population.[2] The Chapultepec peace accords changed all of this. Under the accords, the government agreed to eliminate the old public security forces—the National Guard, Treasury Police, and National Police (PN)—and disarm and abolish the paramilitary patrol structure in the countryside.[3] Constitutional reforms included in the peace accords prohibited the armed forces from participating in internal security, except under emergency conditions and with approval of the Legislative Assembly. In place of the military and its auxiliary forces, the accords provided for creation of the PNC, a completely new, civilian-controlled institution with a new training academy, a new doctrine emphasizing the protection of individual rights and minimal use of force, and a majority of personnel who took no part in the armed conflict from either side.

PNC agents, inspectors, and commissioners were to be better educated than personnel of the previous security forces, with higher levels of professional police training. After an initial transition period, PNC personnel would live in their own homes as part of the civilian community, rather than in barracks as a society apart. The law and doctrine regulating the new police, and the curriculum of the new academy, conform to modern standards for police conduct, accountability, and democratic civilian control and were specifically designed to uphold the spirit and letter of the peace accords. These were developed with extensive participation of an international technical advisory team made up of civilian police officials and academy administrators.[4] The implementation of the accords was monitored by a Salvadoran agency, the Commission for the Consolidation of Peace (COPAZ), created by the accords and made up of representatives of political parties, and by an observer mission of the United Nations called ONUSAL.

The replacement of the old security forces is a vital part of El Salvador's transition to a more fully democratic society. The old forces were explicitly political and ideological institutions; they were an integral part of the armed forces, and until the mid-1980s their officers were trained in the military academy with an emphasis on anticommunism and counterinsurgency. Even after distinct training programs were developed for the security forces, officers continued to move freely between security forces and regular army assignments. Because the military as an institution governed the country between 1932 and 1979 in alliance with civilian social elites, an important role of the military's security forces was political repression and exclusion. This politicized role continued, under the rubric of counterinsurgency, despite the transition to civilian rule in 1982.

Security forces at the local level were very closely associated with powerful landowners, functioning virtually as private security forces, with barracks sometimes actually located on large private farms. As political opposition and labor unrest grew in the 1960s and 1970s, the security forces became the primary instruments of political surveillance and repression. From the late 1970s through the early 1980s, units of the security forces tortured, killed, and "disappeared" thousands of regime opponents and activists of popular organizations in what can only be characterized as a campaign of state terrorism.

Besides being politicized, the old security forces were not very good at policing, and their approach to their work was fundamentally hostile to the rights of individuals in a democratic society. The essence of the old system was to maintain order through vigilance and intimidation. The security forces had poor investigative skills and lacked the most basic skills for protecting, recording, and using evidence. Activities focused on counterinsurgency; suspects of political infractions were arrested, detained without trial, and subject to torture and abuse, largely to obtain information. The old security forces seldom obtained convictions and gave little attention to crime.[5]

Negotiating Police Reforms

The idea of creating a wholly new civilian police force had its origins in the concerns of the FMLN for the safety of its members as they reentered the political and social life of the country. Given the ideological and repressive background of the existing internal security regime, broadening the democratic political spectrum clearly required some sort of profound reform. Initial proposals by the FMLN sought to abolish the military, but the unacceptability to the government of this proposal led to a scheme under which the armed forces would be retained but confined to national defense duties, with a new civilian police force taking over internal security functions.

The basic framework for this solution was put in place by the Mexico accords of April 1991, which included constitutional reforms excluding the military from internal security functions, subjecting the armed forces more clearly to civilian control, and reforming the judiciary to reduce partisan political control of the courts. The FMLN continued for several more months to insist on either abolition of the armed forces or integration of FMLN units into the armed forces; but in the September 1991 round of negotiations in New York, the FMLN accepted that the safety of its members would be adequately protected by having presence in the new police force so long as additional measures were taken to ensure that the military would function within the bounds of its new, more restrictive constitutional mandate. This concession by the FMLN, combined with pressure on the government from the United States, which was unwilling to continue financing the war, and from United Nations Secretary-General Javier Pérez de Cuéllar, who had taken a personal interest in the negotiations, pushed the Cristiani government (and the Salvadoran military) into agreeing.

The New York accords provided for a purge of the armed forces, a new armed forces doctrine, reforms in military education, major reductions in the armed forces, the formation of COPAZ to verify compliance with the peace accords, and an agreement that former FMLN members could participate in the PNC without discrimination so long as they met the admissions standards.[6] A secret agreement accompanying the New York accords provided that a majority of PNC members would be civilians with no role in the armed conflict, but permitted the participation of former FMLN combatants and, implicitly, former members of the National Policemen.[7]

The final accords signed in Mexico City on January 16, 1992, filled in the details of the general framework approved in New York in September, providing specifications for reforms to the armed forces that would help ensure that they remain excluded from internal security activities: The accords required that the paramilitary patrol system be disarmed and legally abolished and that the intelligence system of the armed forces be abolished and a new civilian-controlled intelligence entity be created under the direct control of the president. The army was required to cut its forces by approximately one-half, including the demobilization of the special counterinsurgency battalions that had conducted the majority of offensive operations against the FMLN during the war. Other institutional reforms provided by the accords include the creation of a human rights ombudsman's office with broad powers to investigate rights violations, to inspect police and military facilities without advance notice, and to refer cases to the courts. The judicial system was also to be reformed, with an increased budget, measures to require broader political consensus for the appointment of judges, and new minimum standards of professional qualification.

The final accords provided a detailed discussion of the doctrine, structure, functions, personnel, and training of the PNC, including drafts of secondary legislation (*leyes orgánicas*) for the PNC and the new National Public Security Academy (ANSP), which were annexed to the final accords. Former FMLN combatants and former National Police members were limited to 20 percent membership each. These laws, which had been developed with extensive technical assistance from the UN, were subsequently approved by the Legislative Assembly with minor changes. The doctrine of the PNC gives highest priority to the protection of individual rights, to minimum use of force by the police, and to absolute adherence to apolitical conduct by the police. The PNC is composed of nine divisions: public safety, criminal investigations, immigration and border control, finance, arms and explosives, protection of important persons, environmental protection, anti-narcotics, and regulation of ground transportation. It is the only armed police institution with national jurisdiction, replacing all existing organizations with responsibilities in the above areas. The PNC is commanded at the departmental level by commissioners who are required to have university degrees (though some exceptions have been made to educational requirements, see below). Subdelegations are commanded by inspectors who are supposed to have at least three years of university education (again, exceptions have been made), and sergeants with at least a high school education command smaller posts. All commissioners and inspectors were to receive at least ten months of training at the ANSP or abroad, though in practice some former antinarcotics officers without such training held command positions in 1993 and 1994.

The PNC was to be deployed over a two-year period, dating from the opening of the National Public Security Academy. During that transition period, the public safety division gradually deployed throughout the national territory, then other divisions were formed and took over functions previously carried out by the PN and other entities. During the transition, the old PN would continue to function, but under the supervision of the 277-member police division of ONUSAL. The PN was to be demobilized progressively as the PNC took over its functions, though in practice its demobilization was considerably delayed. The PNC was to be considered fully deployed when it reached 5,700 agents and 240 inspectors and commissioners, though it had over 9,000 members as of early 1996 and will continue to increase personnel.

Developing the New Force

Selection and Training

The importance of the police reform to the overall peace process, and the urgency of completing the transition from the old force to the new during the brief tenure of the UN observer mission, led to an extremely ambitious timetable—three and a half months—for development of the new ANSP. Delays set in almost from the outset. Devising a curriculum took longer than anticipated, and the government initially failed to provide funds for recruitment, testing, students' uniforms, food, stipends, and other operating costs. International donors, nonplussed by the government's own lack of commitment, held back, and a kind of stalemate ensued.[8] The military contributed to delays and resource shortfalls by refusing to hand over the existing public security academy, which the military instead appropriated as a new facility for its own academy.[9] The military even went so far as to strip one smaller facility that it did turn over, removing doors, lockers, window frames, and even the lightbulbs (GAO 1992a). The ANSP set up in a sweltering, ill-equipped temporary facility at Comalapa on the coastal plain, which the government spent a million dollars during 1992, and an additional $3.5 million during 1993, to refurbish.

The recruitment and testing processes were predictably fraught with organizational problems. Some of the initial tests were not well adapted to Salvadoran conditions, and early testing placed priority on physical fitness rather than intellectual skills, leading to entering classes of cadets whose aptitudes were not optimized for the new institution's emphasis on knowledge of the law, intelligence, and interpersonal skills rather than force. Following criticism from ONUSAL and COPAZ, the exams were changed.[10] Throughout the first two years of recruiting, the number of applicants was lower than anticipated. At the outset this resulted from a lack of publicity; thereafter, low police salaries and public perceptions of other, more attractive economic opportunities (especially in the eastern part of the country) seemed to be the main obstacles.[11]

Admissions to the ANSP are governed by the Academic Council, which included representatives of a broad political cross-section. In contrast to COPAZ and its subcommissions, where the political balance built into the commission's makeup led to fairly consistent adherence to the peace accords, the Academic Council was essentially controlled by the government.

The quality of training at the ANSP has been somewhat mixed. While enormous credit is due to all involved for training a completely new national force in little over two years, some aspects of training have been shortchanged. The first PNC delegations to deploy quickly showed that they did not know how to deal with common policing situations. Moreover, there were numerous vehicle and firearm accidents, including some involving fatalities. This was partly a start-up problem; the early classes had been trained without access to such basics as handcuffs, batons, fingerprinting sets, basic crime lab equipment, a photography lab, vehicles, a driving instruction track, adequate firearms, and a shooting range. The U.S. Justice Department's International Criminal Investigative Training Assistance Program responded to some of these problems, but firearms handling and knowledge regarding the use of force remained serious problems as of October 1994.[12] Legal training proved overly theoretical and lacking in practical guidance on how police agents may conduct themselves, and ANSP graduates remained ill-trained in specifics of criminal procedure and legal norms. ONUSAL officials believe these deficiencies contributed to a number of lapses in due process protections as well as to the more serious human rights violations that began to emerge in late 1993.[13]

Some of the best training the new PNC has received has actually been outside the country, particularly at an academy in Puerto Rico, where sixty officers received an accelerated training course to serve as transitional commanders during the initial deployment of the first PNC contingents. Officers who attended this program were uniformly positive about the experience.[14] Some of the future commissioners also received additional training in Spain.

With the pressures to quickly prepare a basic public security force, the ANSP had little time or resources to develop the capacity to provide specialized training for regulation of ground transportation, immigration and border control, customs, drug enforcement, control of arms and explosives, criminal investigations, fiscal investigations, environmental protection, and protection of VIPs, all of which are legally mandated divisions of the PNC (United Nations 1994b, 7). These gaps were gradually overcome by bringing in foreign instructors and sending some PNC personnel abroad for specialized training, enabling them to return as ANSP instructors.

Deployment and Development of the PNC

As with the ANSP, the PNC was initially plagued by serious resource shortfalls. When the PNC first deployed to the rural department of Chalatenango, the provisional commanders in charge felt they had been sent there to fail. Virtually no organizational work had been done prior to their return from Puerto Rico, so they found that they had to take it upon themselves to design the force they would command. Working night and day, they accomplished more in the few days before the actual deployment than the PNC administration had accomplished in months.[15] The PNC began its work with severe shortages in uniforms, radios, sidearms, vehicles, and fuel. Living conditions at many of the posts were extremely austere. There were also some instances of PNC agents receiving their pay months late, causing particular hardships for those with dependents.

The most severe problems were gradually resolved as funds began to flow, but by late 1993, ONUSAL still characterized the government's support for the PNC as "blatantly insufficient" (United Nations 1993c, 9). U.S. embassy officials correctly pointed out that PNC posts are already better equipped than those of the old PN; however, the PNC has taken on the duties of three former public security forces bolstered by the army and various paramilitary structures.[16] For a force of almost 10,000 police to maintain security in a country of almost 6 million, it needs mobility, communications, and the ability to conduct investigations rather than depending on catching criminals in the act. From this point of view, the PNC was still severely short of equipment as of early 1996.[17]

In its first year, the PNC lacked the most basic investigatory tools, such as fingerprinting equipment, making it very difficult for them to gather sufficient evidence to obtain arrest warrants. Many posts lacked handcuffs, which forced them to restrain individuals they arrested by tying their thumbs together with the prisoners' shoelaces, a practice historically associated with the security forces and death squads. Moreover, since many PNC posts lacked jails, prisoners had to be watched constantly, increasing the strain on personnel.

The overall effect of these material shortages was to strain the morale of the new force. Although members of the PNC began their work with great enthusiasm and voluntarism, the poor working and living conditions and lack of sufficient material support compromised the new force's ability to perform its job effectively and establish a positive reputation for itself (United Nations 1993c, 9). The resource problems for the PNC stemmed in part from the fact that El Salvador had in the past had little equipment that was appropriate for the needs of ordinary policing (GAO 1992b). Nevertheless, ex-PN, ex-FMLN, and civilian personnel in the PNC showed remarkable capacity to work effectively and cooperatively as professionals alongside one another, giving the PNC in its first six months the reputation of being one of the most important and effective venues of national reconciliation.

One of the PNC's most urgent tasks was to secure the trust of the population in order to build political support for the institution and to enable the PNC to operate effectively on the basis of information provided by the public. One of the greatest weaknesses of the military's security forces was that they were more feared than trusted, and therefore received little information and assistance from the population. The PNC initially made signficant strides toward earning popular confidence, aided part by the fact that the first communities to which it was deployed were ones that had received little or no service from the police in the past. This led to helpful cooperation from citizens, such as lending horses to enable PNC agents to reach remote communities. In Cabañas, the PNC acted on tips from citizens to capture members of two notorious gangs who had been operating in the department with impunity since the mid-1980s.[18]

As it deployed to new areas, the PNC found it needed to orient the population to its different way of operating. PNC personnel held meetings with organized sectors of the population to inform them of the new community service approach of the PNC. At the same time, people were warned that customary practices of the past, such as operating vehicles without proper licenses and documents, dealing with infractions by bribing police agents, and paying the police to mediate and resolve minor legal disputes, would be discontinued. Citizens were given a one-month grace period to get their legal affairs in order, after which laws would be enforced to the letter.

The PNC's novel insistence on actually enforcing the nation's laws generated friction between the police and the not-yet-reformed judicial system. The PNC's higher activity level, and its greater propensity to investigate crimes and seek arrest warrants, increased the workload on local justices of the peace, many of whom had held office for years despite not being lawyers. In some cases, local judges failed to respond to PNC requests for arrest or search warrants, despite carefully prepared documentation. In other situations, the shortage of public defenders forced judges to release suspects without trial. PNC officials interviewed for this study expressed the hope that by doing their own work efficiently, they might eventually pressure the judiciary into greater activity and professionalism, but saw a growing risk that the influence would flow the other way.

The Threat of Expediency

Despite positive early developments of the new force, the reform effort suffered setbacks that can largely be traced to expediency. Faced with urgent public security needs, Salvadoran decisionmakers (often with U.S. and other international backing) repeatedly chose to retain existing human resources and organizational structures rather than take the time to develop new ones. The decision in mid-1993 to appoint an ex-military officer (Captain Oscar Peña Durán) as sub-director for operations of the PNC is illustrative: as a former military officer who led an anti-narcotics unit, Peña offered experience not possessed by any of the available civilians. His appointment, in addition to being a violation of the stipulation of the peace accords that the PNC be commanded by civilians, proved to be disastrous for the development of the PNC. Sub-Director Peña brought with him a combination of political bias, militarism, and disregard for human rights that quickly and seriously eroded the efforts of the international community to inculcate democratic values in the PNC (Call 1994). He eventually resigned under pressure from the United Nations and the United States.

One of the costs of Peña's appointment was his severing relations with ONUSAL, perhaps in retaliation for ONUSAL's opposition to his appointment. During the first six months of PNC deployment, the ONUSAL police division played a crucial role in helping compensate for the new force's lack of equipment by providing between 70 percent and 80 percent of the vehicular transportation and lending ONUSAL's radio communications network for messages. ONUSAL police observers also accompanied PNC agents in their duties, tutoring them in both practical and legal aspects of policing, helping to fill gaps in their training and compensate for their lack of experience. Though ONUSAL's training role was not well coordinated, the sheer number of people at ONUSAL's disposal (277 officers in the police division, plus dozens of human rights officials) meant that ONUSAL's technical assistance role was the most substantial contribution by the international community to the PNC project. Peña's break with ONUSAL suspended this advising role until after his resignation and led the international community to question why it should provide further material assistance to the PNC while the PNC itself was rejecting free advice and on-the-job training from UN police observers.

Another expedient but harmful decision was the incorporation of hundreds of detectives and technical support personnel from two old security units (the Special Investigative Unit, or SIU, and the Anti-Narcotics Unit, or UEA) into the PNC, where the majority of them performed badly, refused additional training to adapt them to the new civilian institution, and ultimately resigned en masse. Critical time was wasted trying to preserve a group of agents who lacked commitment to civilian, rights-oriented policing. This decision forced public security authorities to start over to create an investigative division for the PNC.

While the old SIU and UEA were negotiating for severance pay, a small group of civilian recruits in the PNC was transformed, with international assistance, into an increasingly effective task force to tackle organized crime. At the behest of a joint United Nations/Salvadoran government commission, the Salvadoran government in February 1995 created the Organized Crime Investigations unit (DICO) to look into politically motivated crimes. Despite their inexperience, the unit quickly broke some key cases, including cases implicating active-duty PNC officers and members of the former SIU.[19] The success of this unit was achieved despite continuing efforts by members of the old SIU and security forces to sabotage its development. This experience demonstrates that the PNC could have obtained better—and possibly even faster—results by training new investigators rather than transplanting a cancerous organizational culture from the old institutions into the PNC.

Human Rights and Accountability

Human rights groups, international observers, and Salvadoran analysts all agree that the human rights performance of the PNC remains superior to that of the old security forces. Cases of homicide and torture by PNC agents have been exceptional and political motivations rarer still. Former National Police officers now in the PNC reported in interviews that under the new police, abuses are often reported by fellow PNC officers, something unheard of under the old regime.[20]

However, the Salvadoran experience shows that a transition to civilian policing does not necessarily mean a transition to an accountable police force. In 1995, a widespread perception emerged that the PNC's human rights record had notably worsened. It became increasingly common to hear comments from citizens comparing the PNC to the old PN. Complaints against the PNC filed with the government's Human Rights Ombudsman's Office rose from 326 in the first three months of 1995 to 519 in the trimester May-July 1995, although the majority of these charges were for violation of due process rather than more serious abuses such as murder and torture.[21] Of respondents in a March 1995 survey, only 39 percent believed that the PNC consistently respects human rights. Twenty-two percent said it did not respect rights, and 33 percent said it did so "sometimes."[22]

Perhaps the most visible abuses of the PNC have involved repeated incidents—too many be to considered exceptional cases—of excessive force during 1995 in responding to public demonstrations, labor strikes, and protests.[23] Two people have been killed in such protests, and police officials agree that in some cases excessive force has been employed. Poor organization and preparation contributed to these abuses, but the Public Security Ministry and the PNC leadership have been criticized for sending in baton-wielding riot police rather than allowing time for negotiators to reach pacific solutions. These incidents have marred the public image of the PNC in terms of human rights.

Slow development of institutions of accountability have facilitated the rise in PNC abuses. An inspector general was not appointed until after the Calderón Sol government took office in June 1994—eighteen months after the PNC was first deployed. The lack of a working Office for Internal Affairs and Discipline for the first year of the PNC's existence probably contributed to very lax standards of conduct evident during the formative months of the new force. The delay in developing these institutions was due partly to government reticence, partly to the urgency of deploying operational units quickly, and possibly to an over-reliance in early stages on the UN police and human rights personnel present in the countryside.

Hazards of the Transition

Crime and Government Policy

There are few valid crime statistics on El Salvador, for the simple reason that most crimes go unreported because most citizens see nothing to be gained by reporting them (IUDOP 1993). Even official figures showed a marked increase during the transition. ONUSAL statistics based on complaints filed with the National Police showed a 300 percent increase in violent crime from January to September 1993 (United Nations 1994a, 24). The transitional regime dramatically reduced the felt presence of government authority and vigilance throughout the country. The suppression of the National Guard and Treasury Police abruptly cut the available personnel for public security from 14,000 to roughly 6,000. Combined with the demobilization of half the government's army and all the rebel army (which had informally policed zones under its de facto control), the end of the war reduced the overall forces of vigilance from roughly 75,000 to around 6,000.[24]

Popular perceptions of crime centered on armed robbery and murders, both astonishingly frequent and often carried out with weapons of war, including fully automatic assault rifles, submachine guns, and grenades. In a February 1993 survey by the University of Central America, 34 percent of respondents from urban areas said either they or an immediate family member had been robbed in the past four months, clearly an extraordinarily high rate.[25] While the poor are the most heavily affected, social elites are also extremely concerned about crime, including armed robberies, organized thefts of the coffee crop during the harvest season, and, in mid-1994, frequent kidnappings.

In 1995, evidence emerged that criminal elements, some from the old security forces, had infiltrated the PNC. A PNC investigative agent has been directly implicated in the assassination of an FMLN leader in 1993, and when the agent's involvement became known, he was able to escape arrest and flee to the United States, apparently with the help of others in the PNC. And a gang of citizens and PNC officers and agents were arrested in mid-1995 for planning and carrying out private executions of known criminals in the department of San Miguel.

Demobilizing the Old Police

Not surprisingly, the problem of crime created considerable political pressures on the government to take strong measures to protect citizens. While full deployment of the PNC represented the best strategy in the long run, the government had no choice in the early months of the transition but to depend on the PN. However, rather than dealing with the PN's lack of material resources, which would have required a confrontation with the military over the vehicles and other equipment appropriated by the Defense Ministry, the government responded by increasing the PN's personnel, initially by transferring over 1,000 Treasury Police and 111 National Guard effectives into the National Police, in clear violation of the peace accords. The United Nations challenged this practice, and the government agreed in May 1992 to stop it (United Nations 1993b). Despite the government's promises, however, ONUSAL subsequently discovered that several self-contained army units from a demobilized counterinsurgency battalion, complete with officers, had been transferred into the National Police in what the United Nations characterized as "a redeployment of army personnel" (United Nations 1993a, 9–10).[26]

The United Nations also questioned the intent of the Salvadoran government to comply with the peace accords' requirement to demobilize the National Police by September 1994 (United Nations 1993b). The National Police training school continued to operate until December 1993, graduating between sixty and a hundred new police agents every month. The Cristiani administration, which delayed over a year in preparing a demobilization plan, finally began demobilization under UN pressure, only to suspend the process in early 1994. In May 1994, days before the inauguration of president-elect Armando Calderón Sol, the target date for demobilization was extended to March 1995. The political tide finally turned against the PN, however, when a gang of former PN and National Guard personnel, including someone bearing close resemblance to the second-in-command of the PN Criminal Investigations Division, Lt. José Rafael Coreas Orellana, was videotaped carrying out an armed car robbery. The ensuing scandal uncovered a web of complicity of PN and ex-military personnel involved in organized crime.[27] Newly inaugurated President Armando Calderón Sol summarily dismissed the entire 700-member Criminal Investigations Division of the PN and advanced the date for final PN demobilization by three months. Calderón, as a relative hardliner within the ARENA party, could afford politically to act against the interests of the old military security forces. Unlike Cristiani, Calderón had not been responsible for signing the peace accords that stripped so much power from the military, purged its officer corps, and exposed it to highly public human rights criticisms. At the same time, Calderón lacked Cristiani's cachet with the international community and therefore had incentives to yield to UN and U.S. concerns about the PNC in order to build greater credibility.[28]

The Military and the Internal Security Reforms

Concerns about the remilitarization of internal security were compounded when the government began proposing in late 1992 to deploy the military in a "dissuasive," quasi-internal security role. De facto policing activities contradict both the peace accords and the constitution, which mandate that the armed forces be used in internal security only when the Legislative Assembly has been informed that "ordinary means of maintaining internal peace have been exhausted." The United Nations consistently questioned the necessity of such deployments, proposing various measures such as accelerated deployment of the PNC as highway patrol and the temporary transfer of vehicles and radio communications equipment from the military to the National Police.

In July 1993, without formally informing the legislature, the government deployed military troops as a "dissuasive presence," mainly along highways. Although no serious incidents were reported as a result of these deployments, they did pave the way to further involvement of the armed forces in internal security. In one case, when military personnel were ordered to assist in policing a bus strike in San Miguel, two civilians and one army sergeant were killed. In March 1995, the government initiated Plan Guardián, creating joint commands of military and police personnel to conduct patrols and to deal with particularly violent public order situations in the rural areas of El Salvador.[29] With Plan Guardián, a team of military personnel was introduced into each regional police headquarters. Although police officers were given nominal operational control, some senior army officers stated in interviews their belief that PNC control over operations applies only until a patrol encounters a suspect found in the act of committing a crime (as would be the case if soldiers encountered rock-throwing demonstrators).[30] While public criticism of the military's role in policing functions ebbed, the important demarcation between external defense and internal security responsibilities was eroded.

The main decisions regarding the deployment of the military in internal security roles during the transition appear to have been made by the Cristiani and Calderón governments. There is little if any evidence that the military actively sought to wrest public security functions from the PNC, and the Defense Ministry even resisted some policing duties.[31] Nevertheless, its position cannot be characterized as supportive. The armed forces wholly failed to collaborate in providing resources to the PNC. And its occasional public positions on public security have not been positive. In 1993, the official journal of the military high command published a scathing critique of the new public security regime,[32] and in January 1996, newly appointed defense minister General Jaime Guzmán cited the inability of the PNC to provide security as his main defense against cutting the military's personnel and budget.[33] In interviews some military officers speculated that the military might in future regain a role in public security.[34]

Political Support for the New Police

Ultimately, the completion of the transition from the old regime of armed vigilance to a modern system of professional law enforcement depended on the ability of the PNC to prove its capacity and develop a political constituency, a constituency stronger than that of the armed forces and the PN. Initially, the PNC was viewed with considerable hope and anticipation by almost all sectors of society except the military. Leaders of business associations interviewed indicated they felt that their personal safety and that of their businesses had been ill served by the PN and the armed forces. The PNC leadership began cultivating private sector support through seminars during which PNC officers explained the nature and goals of the new institution. The main concern of business leaders was that the PNC not be politicized, but most were optimistic that it would become a professional, apolitical force.[35] Popular confidence in the old PN was extremely low, and 56 percent of respondents in a survey of the urban population expected the crime situation to improve once the new PNC was deployed (IU-DOP 1992, 1993).

It is significant that the opposition parties, including the FMLN, the Democratic Convergence, and the PDC, were extremely cautious in criticizing the preservation of the PN and the deployment of the military, perhaps because of the intensity and political saliency of public concerns about crime made it politically dangerous to oppose *any* measure that appeared to offer some promise of relief from crime. Representatives of the opposition Christian Democrats went so far as to call for expansion of the deployment of the military, asking only that the president act through proper constitutional channels (CENITEC 1993).

Despite a general recognition of the improvements represented by the PNC, public confidence in the new police declined in 1994 and 1995. When the PNC first deployed to the departments of Chalatenango and Cabañas, 71 percent of people polled by the University of Central America evaluated it as good or very good, and less than 2 percent considered it bad or very bad (the bulk of the remainder said "regular"). In February 1995, with the PNC deployed throughout the country, a nationwide poll showed those figures had changed significantly—to 33 percent good and 15 percent bad.[36] By December 1995, the respective figures were 35 percent and 30 percent bad, with negative responses doubling. Other polls showed that, in the face of the questionable ability of the PNC and judicial system to catch and punish criminals, almost half the Salvadoran population supported reliance on other sources of protection, including the army and illegal vigilante groups such as the *Sombra Negra,* or Black Shadow. Persistent negative press in late 1995 led prominent leaders of all political parties, including ARENA party legislators and the president of the Supreme Court, to seek a cleansing of the police in late 1995.

One of the more difficult aspects of the police reform effort in El Salvador was the relatively slow movement by groups in civil society—human rights NGOs, community organizations, unions, think tanks, the business community, journalists, etc.—to determine their role in the process. Human rights NGOs, for example, were unable to make recommendations for institutional development in a timely fashion and became vocal only when human rights problems became manifest. The scarcity of national experts on crime, policing, and public security planning within civil society probably contributed to what emerged as an extremely ad hoc public security policy by the Ministry of Public Security in 1995. In this sense, the transition showed that while the influence of the international community can be positive and important, it is also limited. The idea that coercive forces and security policies are the exclusive domain of police and military institutions has deep historical roots in

Latin America. If civil society is unable to monitor, investigate, and make positive proposals regarding public security issues, this idea is unlikely to change.

The difficulties in the transition process demonstrate a central dilemma in the consolidation of a civilian-controlled law enforcement regime: To build public support for its deployment and budget, for the definitive exclusion of the military from internal security roles, and for the timely demobilization of the old militarized police, a new civilian police force must demonstrate its effectiveness, thereby establishing a political counterweight to the claims of the military and old police forces that they are necessary to maintain public order. But to be effective, a small, inexperienced new force needs more equipment and better salaries, as well as ongoing access to international training and advising. In the Salvadoran case, neither the government nor the international community (see below) had the needed resources. The members of the PNC themselves compensated through exceptional dedication and voluntarism during the first months of deployment, but it remained in doubt whether this would prove to be sufficient, and durable enough, to realize a full transition to civilian policing.

International Cooperation

The Salvadoran government has consistently claimed that UN and U.S. officials gave assurances during the peace negotiations that the international community would pick up the tab for the predictably expensive process of creating a new police force from scratch. In practice, such support was not forthcoming, in part because donors were leery of contributing to a project that the government itself seemed reluctant to support. As noted, the government's early commitments to both the ANSP and PNC were lackluster at best.

The meager support from the international community is especially noteworthy in view of the fact that support for the public safety components of the peace process was markedly lower than support for other aspects, such as land transfers. Using the government's estimates of needs and international commitments for 1993 as an example, international donors committed 26 percent of the $491.7 million needed for reconstruction activities in 1993. For reconstruction activities related to public security, however, international donors promised to provide only 12 percent of the costs. Overall, the international community promised to support only about 9 percent of the costs of public security reforms for 1993 and 1994.[37] Repeated appeals by the UN Secretary-General, the United Nations Development Programme (UNDP), and the United States went largely unanswered. The ability of the United

States to provide additional funds in 1995 and 1996 was further hampered by its heavy commitment to the new civilian police development project in Haiti.

The lack of international support for these programs was extremely unfortunate in light of the importance of the transformation of public security institutions to the overall democratization goals of the peace accords. Unlike many elements of the reconstruction program that benefited only particular groups such as ex-combatants or residents of formerly conflicted areas, the reform of internal security institutions affected all Salvadorans and clearly had a major impact on the political environment of the country, despite flawed and underfunded implementation.

One possible explanation for the inaction of the international donor community is that relatively few countries have legal mechanisms in place to provide assistance to foreign police forces. Negative past experiences with police aid that merely fed into corrupt and politicized police forces have made many countries leery of establishing such programs (Anderson 1993). As United Nations officials Alvaro de Soto and Graciana del Castillo (1993) have written, financing for the ANSP and the PNC

> not only suffers from being outside the mainstream of the international donor community's pet projects; it falls into the category of projects which this community normally does not *want* to assist; indeed, taxpayers oppose them almost as a reflex action. This is precisely because the police tends to be bunched together in the mind with the military, and is associated not with what is commonly understood as "development" but rather with the idea of "violent repression."

Ironically, the high cost of the Salvadoran police development project stemmed precisely from the fact that it was designed to overcome problems of earlier police development projects by creating a completely new force. Material and technical assistance to the ANSP and PNC had the potential to reinforce the formation of a new institutional culture, rather than being co-opted and misused by an old one.

One international aid observer commented that "in the end, it's their police force, and they have to find a way to fund it." A sober analysis of the Salvadoran national budget, however, reveals that there was very little room for savings in any spending categories other than the military, given the urgent postwar need to maintain spending in health, education, and poverty alleviation.

Indeed, the only two obvious sources for budget resources transferable to the PNC were the PN and the military. The PN's budget for 1994 amounted to over $20 million, for a force with declining responsibilities.

Defense spending fell by only 6.4 percent between 1992 and 1993, despite the military's reports of an approximate 45 percent cut in military personnel, and remained constant in nominal terms between 1993 and 1994 at $100 million, or roughly 9 percent of the 1994 national budget, compared with the 3 percent allocated for the PNC.

Nonetheless, it may not have been realistic for international donors to hope for cuts in defense to finance the PNC. The civilianization of internal security, and all the reforms embodied in the peace accords, were *coerced* by the armed forces of the FMLN.[38] The creation of the PNC represented a radical reduction in the prerogatives and political powers of the armed forces. There continued to be extreme distrust both within the military and in many sectors of political society regarding the intentions of the FMLN, and the military retained considerable capacity to manipulate this distrust for its own political—and budgetary—advantage.

Conclusion

There is a growing consensus in the international community that prospects for both development and political democracy can be enhanced by reducing the resources and prerogatives of militaries. In countries where militaries have played a prominent role in internal security based on broad, heavily ideological national security doctrines, police civilianization has the potential to substantially change the relationship between citizen and state. El Salvador's police project is a test of whether one of the more visible elements of the authority of the state, the police force, can be converted from oppressor to public servant.

Many of the features of the Salvadoran experiment seemed especially conducive to success. The plan to create a wholly new institution made it more likely that old patterns of abuse and impunity would be broken, and that the PNC would remain genuinely independent of the military. The accords created an environment in which significant international attention and resources were devoted to carrying out, advising, and observing the project; in which the international community had an important stake in the outcome; and in which the government was at least somewhat accountable to the United Nations for carrying out the project as designed. Even in this unique situation, international support was less than needed. The failure of international donors to more actively support the Salvadoran reform process, despite its visible successes, points to the need to establish new international mechanisms for assisting genuine civilian police development programs. The need for international assistance is made all the more urgent by the fact that any police civilianization project worth its salt is, by definition, taking away from the military one of its established roles and, in many cases, one of its main bases of political power. It is unrealistic for the international community to expect governments with tenuous authority over military institutions to civilianize policing without encountering some effective resistance by the military, whether in the form of impeding the transfer of facilities or resisting budget cuts. International assistance can play a crucial role in temporarily easing zero-sum budget conflicts, at least until new civilian forces can prove themselves and gain domestic political support sufficient to offset the more established constituency of the military. Such assistance may be a necessary cost of demilitarization.

That said, it is important to note that for police civilianization to be successful, a government must have the will to actually implement the project, even if its initial ability to provide material support to the project is limited by overall budgetary constraints and/or military resistance. Some of the greatest failings of the Salvadoran process resulted from initial government sabotage of the substance of civilianization, including efforts to smuggle military personnel into the new force, to preserve the old PN, to suppress contacts between the civilian police and international police observers and advisers, and to retain a substantial de facto role for the armed forces in internal security. The government's posture on these issues was to some extent predictable in view of the historical ties of the ruling party to the military and the still extreme polarization of Salvadoran politics; nonetheless, the remarkable capacity of the government to undercut the civilian nature of the PNC within months of its creation, despite intense international involvement and scrutiny, is a very sobering lesson. The El Salvador police project clearly shows that international donors should not contemplate assisting police projects in other countries unless the government demonstrates unequivocal political will to carry out the project in good faith, especially since almost nowhere (with the possible exception of Haiti) will a police development project enjoy the degree of international supervision seen in El Salvador.

Another lesson from the Salvadoran experience is that considerable attention must be given to how the state will deal with the problem of crime during the transition from one internal security regime to another. While El Salvador's situation was particularly difficult in this regard, given the massive demobilization of security forces combined with postwar unemployment and superarmament, any police civilianization process likely involves the risk that crime will increase, undercutting political support for the new force and reinforcing elements who favor a return to the old ways of maintaining order.

The Salvadoran experience points to the delicacy of the transition period in setting up a new police force. The benefits of excluding members of previous militarized and abusive forces are clear. Even a small number, viewed as the "old hands" by newcomers, can undermine police reforms aimed at enhancing transparency, accountability, and civilianization. Yet these personnel are often the only ones with policing experience—and the temptations of expediency are great. And putting hundreds or thousands of such persons, trained in the use of arms, out of work is likely to contribute to the crime waves that accompany postconflict scenarios. Balancing these factors in the transition period is one of the most difficult aspects of demilitarizing police forces. International financing for retraining such personnel for other tasks may be one of the better investments in public security reforms.

The Salvadoran case shows the benefits of immediately setting up mechanisms of accountability and control, right alongside operational units. Political attention was given to these mechanisms only late in the process, after well-publicized police abuses. The delays and problems in establishing the inspector general's office and the Internal Discipline unit undermined the establishment of an institutional culture of strict standards of conduct and an expectation of constant monitoring. Furthermore, the negotiators and international experts who designed the PNC gave no consideration to setting up mechanisms of accountability, such as citizen review boards.

Finally, one of the central lessons of the 1980s for the United States in assisting the Salvadoran military was that it was easier to teach techniques than to change attitudes and institutional norms. The same problem applies to civilianization of police. There is an inherent tension between preserving and taking advantage of the existing knowledge and experience of available personnel from the old force, and creating an institution that breaks from past practices. The negative impact of the subdirector, Peña, and the Executive Anti-Narcotics Unit on the PNC project in El Salvador suggests that such conflicts are best resolved in favor of newness and good will, at the expense of experience and technique, even if this results in initial errors. The likelihood of creating a new and distinct organizational ethos is greater without representatives of the old order in charge.

Notes

Field work for this chapter was financed by grants from the United States Institute of Peace and from the Latin American Institute of the University of New Mexico. Earlier drafts of the chapter benefited from comments and criticism from George Vickers, Jack Spence, officials of the United States Embassy in San Salvador, and officials of the United Nations. Portions were previously published in the journal *Studies in Comparative International Development (SCID)*, and this chapter reflects improvements suggested by *SCID* editor John Martz and anonymous reviewers. The authors bear sole responsibility for the contents of the chapter, including all errors.

1. Only Panama and Haiti might be considered more radical, in the sense that their militaries were eliminated rather than merely downsized as in El Salvador. Nonetheless, the comprehensiveness of Salvadoran police reforms themselves is unmatched.

2. One illustration of this is that most military barracks are located in densely populated areas near the center of towns.

3. The National Guard and the Treasury Police were absorbed into the army as the Special Brigade for Military Security, which combines military police functions and readiness to perform border security functions in the event of a cross-border military conflict. The security forces had an extensive network of informants regarding political activities, and these connections no doubt occasionally served to call police attention to crimes, but general community relations were poor.

4. The initial plan for the police, embodied in an annex to the peace accords, was largely the work of Jesús Rodés, as Spanish Police Academy director on assignment to the UN. Subsequent work was elaborated by the Spanish and U.S. technical teams, which included five members each. The U.S. technical team belongs to the Justice Department's International Criminal Investigative Training Assistance Program. Two Salvadoran military officers represented the government. As a result of an oversight by the UNDP, which coordinated the police project, the FMLN was not included in the process at the outset. Following FMLN protests, it was included in regular meetings from April 1992 onward.

5. National Police, Treasury Police, and National Guard intelligence units were highly effective at counterinsurgency work during the war but functioned more as death squads, particularly early in the war, than as legal investigatory agencies. For an illustrative case of the use of extrajudicial confessions, see Popkin (1993, 90).

6. COPAZ was made up of two representatives each from the government and the FMLN, and one each from the political parties represented in the Legislative Assembly at the time, including the National Republican Alliance, the National Conciliation Party, the Authentic Christian Movement, the Christian Democrats, the Democratic Convergence, and the National Democratic Union. This makeup usually created a deadlock, since the first three parties generally sided with the government and the last three generally did not. The composition of the COPAZ sub-commission on the National Civilian Police was similar.

7. The parties subsequently agreed that 60 percent would be noncombatants, while 20 percent each could be ex-FMLN and ex–National Police. In practice, the FMLN had difficulty fully utilizing these quotas, as too few of their personnel met the educational standards and physical stature required for the PNC. This difficulty reflected the class makeup of the FMLN's army.

8. The initial budget estimate developed by the joint technical team for the first two years of operation of the ANSP came to $42 million. Of this, the Salvadoran government committed $13 million, the United States pledged $10 million, Spain pledged almost $3 million, and Norway offered $300,000. This left an anticipated budget shortfall of over $15 million. In practice, the govern-

ment was very slow to actually disburse the amounts it had committed. Moreover, the first year of operation of the ANSP revealed the initial estimates to have been conservative, leading the government to increase its estimates for the cost of the ANSP for 1993 and 1994 to $69 million. The government committed $28 million for this period and received pledges for an additional $12 million committed by the United States, Spain, and Norway. This left a balance of $29 million for which support was not yet available. See Presidencia de la Republica de El Salvador (1993a, 2).

9. The military school had little need for the old 114-acre public security academy, since entering classes had fallen to their prewar level of around 110, attrition would reduce graduating classes to about 35, and the total student population was unlikely to exceed 300, in contrast to the peak enrollment of over 2,200 at the ANSP (United Nations 1994b, 6).

10. Interviews with ONUSAL officials and members of the COPAZ subcommission on the ANSP/PNC, September-October 1992. It was recognized from the beginning that many ex-combatants would not meet the formal educational requirements for the "basic" level, so special remedial courses were set up with the cooperation of the Ministry of Education to bring former combatants up to the ninth-grade level. The government did not finance the program, however, which mainly benefited members of the FMLN. After some delay, a European donor provided the necessary funds for the first several months of operation. Funding for these minicourses was soon exhausted, complicating the task for the FMLN of preparing enough qualified candidates to fill their 20 percent quota. Interviews with Miguel Eduardo Mira (September-October 1992) and Claudio Armíjo (August 1993). Both were members of the FMLN committee that monitored development of the PNC.

11. Interviews with UN officials, October 1994.

12. Ibid.

13. Personal communication with ONUSAL officials, January 1994.

14. Significantly, both ex–National Police and ex–FMLN members of the PNC command made extremely favorable comments about the Puerto Rico program. Interviews with PNC commissioners and inspectors in Chalatenango and Cabañas, March and July, 1993.

15. Interviews by David Holiday and Tommie Sue Montgomery with PNC officials in Chalatenango, March 1993 and August 1993, respectively.

16. Interviews with U.S. Justice Department officials, San Salvador, August and September 1993.

17. Interviews with UN officials, September 1993, October 1994, October 1995.

18. A special operation by the PNC in Usulután arrested two gang leaders, one ex-FMLN and one ex-military, using tips from the population (Fundación Flor de Izote 1993).

19. These cases include the implication of former SIU agent Carlos Alfaro Romero in the murder of FMLN commandant Francisco Velis and the implication of a handful of PNC officers and agents in a death squad operating against alleged criminals in the San Miguel area.

20. Anonymous interview by Charles Call with PNC agent, January 1996.

21. Some of this increase was to be expected as the PNC deployed steadily greater numbers throughout the country and began working in more complex urban communities. Part of the increase is probably also attributable to growing popular confidence in the Human Rights Ombudsman's Of-

fice, which finally established offices in all fourteen provinces of the country by January 1995.

22. *Estudios Centroamericanos*, April 1995, 360.

23. See ONUSAL XIII Report of the Division of Human Rights, and "La frontera entre el cumplimiento de la función policial y los excesos de la represión in *Defensor del Pueblo* 1(1), publication of the Human Rights Ombudsman's Office of El Salvador.

24. Subsequent transfers of military and security personnel into the PN raised its numbers to around 8,000, though only about 6,800 of these were regular patrol personnel, the balance performing administrative and investigative functions.

25. The Ministry of Justice's (1993) figures show that crime increased by 83 percent between 1990 and 1991, prior to the signing of the final accords. In the IUDOP poll on crime, only 22.4 percent of those who claimed to have been victims of crime reported the incident to authorities. Of those who did not report crimes, over 60 percent reported that they were either afraid to do so or felt it would accomplish nothing. See IUDOP (1993).

26. As noted above, it proved difficult for ONUSAL to track the transfers of military personnel into the National Police because of lack of access to records. One UN official interviewed estimated that half the new recruits of the National Police were from the army.

27. Interviews with diplomatic sources. In the end, Coreas was not convicted for the robbery because the poor quality of the videotape left some doubt as to the identity of the lead assailant, while fellow National Police officers provided Coreas with an alibi. The failure to convict was mocked in political cartoons in the Salvadoran press that depicted caricatures of the distinctive-looking Coreas and that asked who else it could be on the videotape. The Salvadoran justice system remains notoriously weak in recognizing physical evidence.

28. This analysis from David Holiday, personal communication, July 1994.

29. The armed forces continue to deploy annually in the "Plan Grano de Oro"—joint PNC/military patrols to protect the coffee harvest at the end of the year. In October 1995, the current year's plan, which according to Defense Minister Corado will involve 2,000 soldiers, was put into operation. See "En marcha plan 'Grano de Oro,'" *Diario de Hoy*, October 21, 1995.

30. Interviews with army colonel, July 1995; diplomatic official, May 1995.

31. For example, General Humberto Corado, then defense minister, resisted calls to undertake joint military-police patrols in crime-ridden areas of the capital in 1995.

32. See "Ausencia de la Fuerza Armada y auge de la criminalidad," *Revista Militar: De la Fuerza Armada de El Salvador*, published by the Estado Mayor Conjunto (Joint High Command), undated, released in 1993.

33. Cited in "PNC incapaz de brindar seguridad," *La Noticia*, January 4, 1996.

34. Interviews with army brigade commanders, July 1993 and June 1995; interview by David Holiday with army brigade commander, October 1995.

35. Interviews with representatives of the National Association of Private Enterprise, the Salvadoran Foundation for Economic and Social Development, the Chamber of Commerce, the Center for Democratic Studies, and the Cotton Growers' Cooperative, July and August, 1993.

36. *Estudios Centroamericanos*, November-December 1993, 1154; and January-February 1995.

37. The ANSP received commitments of $13.3 million from the United States, Spain, and Norway for its first years of operation. The PNC initially received little support: During 1993, only $650,000 from the Swedish government and ten vehicles from the United States were delivered to the PNC. The United States subsequently obligated $11.75 million for the PNC, part of which was delivered during 1994 (Call 1994, 9). Besides the United States, donors to the ANSP and PNC include Spain ($3 million), Sweden ($1.3 million), Germany (<$1million), and Norway (<$1million). See Call (1994) and Presidencia (1993a, 1993b).

38. The international community, including the United Nations and the "four plus one" countries—the United States, Mexico, Venezuela, Spain, and Colombia—played an important role in pushing for these reforms as well, but in the final analysis there is no reason to think that the Salvadoran government would have undertaken such profound changes had it not been coerced by the FMLN.

References

Anderson, M. A. 1993. "International Administration of Justice: The New American Security Frontier." *SAIS Review* 13 (1):89–104.

Bayley, D. H. 1993. "What's in a Uniform? A Comparative View of Police-Military Relations in Latin America." Paper presented for the conference "Between Public Security and National Security: The Police and Civil-Military Relations in Latin America," Woodrow Wilson Center, Washington, D.C., October 21–22.

Call, C. 1994. "Recent Setbacks in the Police Transition: El Salvador Peace Plan Update #3." Washington D.C.: Washington Office on Latin America.

CENITEC (Centro de Investigaciones Tecnológicas y Científicas). 1993. "Los patrullajes de la Fuerza Armada." Paid advertisement published in *La Prensa Grafica*, August 3, p. 27.

de Soto, A., and del Castillo, G. 1993. "Post-Conflict Peace-Building in El Salvador: Strains on the United Nations System." Typescript.

Estado Mayor Conjunto. 1992. "Ausencia de la Fuerza Armada y auge de la criminalidad." *Revista Militar, Fuerza Armada de El Salvador*, July , pp. i–ii.

Fundación Flor de Izote. 1993. *Cronología de El Salvador.* No. 84, September 6. Electronic publication.

Fundación Flor de Izote. 1994. *Weekly Report.* No. 25, June 27. Electronic publication.

GAO (General Accounting Office). 1992a. "Aid to El Salvador: Slow Progress in Developing a National Civilian Police." Washington D.C.: Congressional Record, S14801 (September 23).

GAO (General Accounting Office). 1992b. "El Salvador: Efforts to Satisfy National Civilian Police Equipment Needs." Washington, D.C.: GAO/NSIAD-93-100BR (December).

IUDOP (Instituto Universitario de Opinión Pública). 1992. Los Salvadoreños ante los acuerdos finales de paz." San Salvador: Universidad Centroamericana José Simeón Cañas.

IUDOP (Instituto Universitario de Opinión Pública). 1993. "La delincuencia urbana." *Estudios Centroamericanos* 534–535 (April/May):471–479.

Lopez, G. A. 1986. National Security Ideology as an Impetus to State Violence and Terror. In *Government Violence and Repression,* edited by M. Stohl and G. A. López. Westport, Conn.: Greenwood Press.

Ministerio de Justicia. 1993. *El sector justicia de El Salvador en números.* San Salvador: Ministerio de Justicia.

NDI (National Democratic Institute). 1990a. *Hacía una nueva relación: El papel de las fuerzas armadas en un gobierno democrático.* Washington, D.C. and Buenos Aires: National Democratic Institute and Fundación Arturo Illia.

NDI (National Democratic Institute). 1990b. *Panamá: Hacía un modelo policial: El informe de un misión international.* Washington, D.C.: National Democratic Institute.

Norden, D. 1990. "Democratic Consolidation and Military Professionalism: Argentina in the 1980s." *Journal of Interamerican Studies and World Affairs* 32 (3).

Partido Demócrata Cristiano (PDC). 1992. "PNC: 10,000 ¡Ya!" San Salvador: PDC.

Popkin, M. 1993. "El Salvador's Negotiated Revolution: Prospects for Legal Reform." New York: Lawyers Committee for Human Rights.

Presidencia de la República de El Salvador. 1993a. "Requerimientos de cooperación internacional para el funcionamiento de la Académica Nacional de Seguridad Pública." San Salvador, June.

Presidencia de la República de El Salvador. 1993b. "Requerimientos de cooperación internacional para el funcionamiento de la Policía Nacional Civil." San Salvador, June.

Stepan, A. 1988. *Rethinking Military Politics.* Princeton: Princeton University Press.

Ugarte, J. 1990. *Seguridad Interior.* Buenos Aires: Fundación Arturo Illia.

United Nations. 1992. "Acuerdos de El Salvador: En El Camino de la Paz." UN Document DPI/208-92615. New York: United Nations.

United Nations. 1993a. "Report of the Director of the Human Rights Division of the United Nations Observer Mission in El Salvador up to 31 January 1993." Documents A/47/912 and S/25521. New York: United Nations.

United Nations. 1993b. "Report of the Secretary-General on the United Nations Observer Mission in El Salvador." Documents S/25812 and S/23999. New York: United Nations.

United Nations. 1993c. "Further Report to the Secretary-General on the United Nations Observer Mission in El Salvador." Document S/26790. New York: United Nations.

United Nations. 1994a. "Ninth Report of the Director of the Human Rights Division of the United Nations Observer Mission in El Salvador (ONUSAL), 1 August–31 October 1993." UN Document A/49/59 S/1994/47. New York: United Nations.

United Nations. 1994b. "Report of the Secretary-General on the United Nations Observer Mission in El Salvador." Document S/1994/561. New York: United Nations.

United Nations. 1994c. "Calendario para la ejecución de los acuerdos pendientes más importantes." Document S/1994/612. New York: United Nations.

United Nations. 1994d. "Report of the Secretary-General on the United Nations Observer Mission in El Salvador." Document S/1994/1000. New York: United Nations.

Zagorski, P. 1992. *Democracy vs. National Security: Civil Military Relations in Latin America.* Boulder: Lynne Rienner Publishers.

6

Decentralization and "Ethnic Federalism" in Post–Civil War Ethiopia

John M. Cohen

Since the end of World War II, governments of advanced industrial countries have sought to help three successive Ethiopian governments address critical policy issues related to reconstruction and development. For Haile Selassie's government, which was attempting to consolidate a state forged by nineteenth-century Abyssinian military expansion and disrupted by the Italian occupation and civil resistance, the critical issues were to establish a modern public sector and promote development. The failure of the government and its Western supporters to address problems relating to institution building and agrarian reform substantially contributed to the 1974 revolution (Ottaway and Ottaway 1978; Markakis and Ayele 1978; Cohen 1984). The major issues the military government faced in attempting to consolidate power during the instability of the 1974–1990 period were formation of a civilian vanguard party, establishment of a command economy, and promotion of agrarian socialism. Assistance focused on these issues was provided by the Eastern bloc. Again, the government and its communist supporters failed to effectively achieve these politically difficult objectives (Clapham 1988). Moreover, the military government and its Eastern bloc supporters exacerbated long-simmering resistance movements, leading to civil war; the overthrow of the government by insurgent rebels; and the current need for Western assistance to a transitional government with a new set of state reconstruction objectives (Woodward and Forsyth 1994; Henze 1991a, 1991b). The complexities and risks of these transitional objectives and the new wave of foreign assistance in support of them are the focus of this chapter.

Assistance for an Emerging Transitional Government

In May 1991, forces led by the Tigrayan People's Liberation Front (TPLF) overthrew the ruling military government, promising political and ethnic reconciliation, economic liberalism, human rights, and democratic governance (Henze 1992). A July 1991 national conference, brokered by Western embassies and attended by most political groups, formed a transitional government (TGE). For many observers, the TGE was from 1991 to 1995 essentially a de facto military regime that operated de jure as a civilian government (Brietzke 1995, 20–27). Since the approval of the constitution in late 1994, parliamentary elections in mid-1995, and the selection of a president and prime minister subsequent to those elections, Ethiopia has become the Federal Democratic Republic of Ethiopia (FDRE).

From the beginning, the TGE was dominated by the Ethiopian People's Revolutionary Democratic Front (EPRDF), a coalition controlled by the TPLF. Its leader, Meles Zenawi, was named president in 1991 and was charged with leading the country through the transition period. Shortly thereafter, despite the persistence of fundamental problems related to the politics of ethnicity and administrative and fiscal capacity, the TGE began to take steps toward effectively reconstructing the state (Henze 1991b, 1992). Foremost among the TGE's transitional objectives were to draft a constitution, hold regional elections, rebuild physical infrastructure, implement macroeconomic reforms aimed at stimulating the economy, rehabilitate public service infrastructures, reform the judiciary, promote human rights, support the emergence of an independent media, decentralize power to regions and districts, and encourage the emergence of a free press and democratically oriented civic organizations.

From the beginning, Western governments and aid agencies were prepared to support TGE efforts to achieve these objectives. But reaching them requires more than foreign aid coupled with committed leadership. The deep structure of state reconstruction requires the design and implementation of complex interlocking policy reforms, all of which involve difficult political decisions that are politically risky. It also requires rebuilding a number of established (and launching new) public sector tasks that demand scarce financial and personnel resources. Given the complexities of the TGE's set of transitional objectives, this chapter focuses only on decentralization reforms. This is justified on the grounds that (1) a chapter-length review of all the reforms required to rebuild Ethiopia's war-torn state would be too general to have any utility (cf. Keller 1994); (2) a number of political leaders, aid agency professionals, and academics are examining the utility of administrative decentralization reforms as a strategy for responding to ethnic, religious, and regional separatists; (3) it illustrates the extent to which ethnicity can pose a serious threat to the success of state reconstruction; and (4) a review of the complexities of this single objective requires all the space available, and it demonstrates how essential it is for analysts to get below the surface details of reconstruction. The complexities of and current progress on the other transitional objectives are described in detail in other studies I have done, from which materials in the chapter are drawn.[1]

Decentralization Assumptions and Realities

Before reviewing the legal, administrative, and fiscal complexities of Ethiopia's decentralization reforms, it is useful to review briefly the task environment uncertainties existing at the beginning of the transition period. In mid-1991, aid agency professionals, who had limited field experience in the country, wrote program documents based on optimistic assumptions about the TGE's capacity to design and introduce devolution in a historically deconcentrated system of administrative decentralization. The most important assumptions they held relative to this transition objective were: (1) a constitution would be drafted that would clarify the structure and functions of the regional government system, most likely along federal lines, and effectively address issues related to policy and implementation powers, judicial authority, taxation, budgeting, and expenditure; (2) during the transition period political and administrative reforms would be adopted that would move government closer to the people and lower ethnic-based pressures toward secession; (3) Ethiopians from all ethnic groups and classes, particularly those in leadership positions, would embrace the National Charter's principles and support decentralization policies; (4) electoral processes and procedures that allow parties to form and openly contest national and local-level elections would be put in place; (5) the government would fairly manage democratic elections for offices in the emerging devolved governmental units and would invite the participation of the opposition parties; (6) central government administrators and professionals would support decentralization reforms and be effectively redeployed to devolved governmental units; and (7) revenues from central and local-level governmental jurisdictions would be allocated in support of both equity and development.

Aid agency optimism about this limited set of assumptions rapidly declined as the complexities of decentralization were revealed. Among the major events and problems that have hampered administrative decentralization components of larger state reconstruction efforts are: (1) proclamations on administrative and fiscal aspects issued during the transition period neglected or left unclear a number of important issues; (2) during the transition period, conflicting statements about the structure, functions, and legal responsibilities of the proposed system of administrative decentralization created substantial misunderstandings among TGE leaders, central government ministries, political parties, Ethiopian citizens, and aid agencies over the legal, administrative, technical, fiscal, and budgetary powers to be granted to all local-level governmental units; (3) delays in the constitutional drafting processes led to the extension of the transition period for an additional year, thereby perpetuating uncertainties about decentralization reforms; (4) low political tolerance from various ethnic groups led major opposition parties to withdraw from participation in democratic processes, seriously hampering the government's efforts to move toward multiparty democracy; (5) decisionmaking processes within the TGE, never particularly open to public view, were becoming less transparent with regard to decentralization; (6) information on the administrative status and financial requirements of decentralized governmental levels was inadequate; and (7) decentralization reforms were not clearly linked to other major policy reforms being implemented by the government (Cohen 1994, 1995; National Democratic Institute 1992; International Human Rights Law Group 1994).

Decentralization and "Ethnic Federalism"

From the beginning, the leaders of the TGE have been committed to pursuing an administrative strategy that transforms Ethiopia from a highly centralized unitary state, which for decades administered its rural and urban areas through tightly controlled deconcentration (Cohen and Koehn 1980), into a federal government based on what is generally labeled "ethnic federalism": a strategy of devolving public sector powers and tasks to regions dominated by the country's major ethnic groups. It is estimated that Ethiopia contains approximately ninety distinct cultural-linguistic groups. Based on the 1980 and 1984 censuses, which are subject to bitter dispute by opposition parties, the principal ethnic groups are Amhara (38 percent), Oromo (35 percent), Tigrinya (9 percent), Gurage (3 percent), and Sidamo, Afar, and Somali with 2 percent each (Brietzke 1995, 30).

Four terminological issues complicate this review of ethnic federalism. First, the Western term *ethnic* is used throughout this chapter even though in Amharic, Ethiopian officials use the term *nation* or *nationality*. Second, the term *federal* is used even though knowledgeable observers argue that even if the new constitution labels the new country as a federal state, it is, in fact, based on a constitutional system more akin to "confederation," an innovative form that looks like federalism but appears closer to an international treaty among ethnic groups with the power to secede (Brietzke 1995, 30). Third, the term *state* is used by some observers to describe the component parts of the new federation, because this is the term used in the English translation of the new constitution. But the Amharic version of the Constitution and both Amharic and English translations of proclamations on decentralization issued since 1991 use the term *national regional administrations*. Fourth, the conceptual definitions of *administrative decentralization*, as well as its subtypes *deconcentration* and *devolution*, are those used by the majority of comparative public administration specialists.[2]

Initial Policy Decisions

Beginning in 1991, the Constitutional Committee (CC), charged with preparing a draft constitution, was considering the advantages and disadvantages of confederal, federal, and unitary systems of governance. Despite their deliberations, assisted by conferences funded by the U.S. Agency for International Development (USAID), involving international constitutional law experts and technical assistance, it was clear to the drafters that some form of federalism was the only option they had. This is because the TGE leadership had declared its decentralization objectives to be (1) reducing the interethnic conflict that has divided Ethiopian society for centuries; (2) addressing the effects of military dictatorship, civil war, failed agrarian socialism, and famine; (3) building a polity based on democratic principles; (4) promoting equitable material conditions for all of the country's 55 million people, the majority of whom are subsistence farmers and peri-urban unemployed; and (5) improving the efficiency and effectiveness of project and program implementation. Somewhat naively, the TGE's leaders argued that they could use devolution to promote these objectives without threatening other important objectives, such as economic growth and political stability.

Before the deliberations of the CC were complete, the TGE decided not to pursue confederation. Hence, in 1993 it allowed Eritrea to hold a referendum on secession. The outcome of this exercise led to the peaceful transition of that region into an independent state (Kendie 1994). TGE leaders assumed they could promote regional autonomy without further secession because, unlike Eritrea, the remaining regions of Ethiopia did not have a history of separate existence or the potential to be economically viable on their own.

By 1992 it was clear that the TGE was committed to some form of ethnic-based federalism. This was made clear through a series of proclamations that defined an interim system of decentralization that would prove to be remarkably similar to the one eventually established by the 1994 constitution.

Interim Transitional Proclamations

The march toward this devolved federalism began in early 1992, when the TGE issued Proclamation No. 7, which was based on Chapters II and XIII of the National Charter. It aimed at establishing a provisional "federal" system of twelve regions based on ethnic identities and two urban regions that were too diverse to be subdivided by cultural-linguistic identities. The regions *(kilil)* were divided into zones and districts *(wereda)*. The demarcation of ethnic boundaries was not without difficulty, particularly with regard to *weredas* located along the borders of regions. As of mid-1995, some boundaries were still contested and not all zonal boundaries specified. But ethnic-based boundary disputes were anticipated by the 1992 proclamation, which provided that the TGE continue to revise boundaries as the "details of geographical borders of each nation, nationality and people are specifically laid down." The constitution contains similar provisions for dealing with boundary disputes and revisions.

Proclamation No. 41 of 1992 elaborated the interim system through which administrative bureaus responsible to regional, zonal, and *wereda* councils carry out the responsibilities devolved to them. Proclamation No. 33 of 1992 outlined the revenue and budgeting relationships between the central government and lower-level governmental units. In support of the provision of public goods and services, the TGE seconded some central personnel to the bureaus of local-level governmental units. These provisions were difficult to communicate to field agents of formerly highly deconcentrated ministerial systems, much less to local grassroots political leaders elected to organize regional councils and to supervise the activities of the new governmental bureaus.

This is not surprising, for it has taken more than 200 years of legislative debate and judicial deliberation to clarify center-local relations in the United States, under conditions far more advanced than those found in Ethiopia. Throughout the 1991–1994 period, many observers believed the language of these proclamations strongly suggested that regions and their subunits would be technically subordinate to the federal government. Government efforts to clarify what the administrative decentralization proclamations were seeking to promote only muddied the water further (Regional Affairs Sector 1994). Field agents did not help matters by continuing to act as if they were responsible to their home ministries and agencies. The fact that the center continued to set policies and standards, collected 85 percent of revenue, and controlled budget allocation processes further complicated efforts by central and local civil servants to understand exactly what the relationship was to be between the center and the periphery (Mirsha 1993, 1995).

Risks Inherent in Transitional Strategy

The TGE's attempt to promote devolution is full of risks. Foremost among these is that devolution to large regions reinforces the demands of some ethnic groups for regional secession or partition (Engedayehu 1994). This risk is compounded by the fact that the TGE's federal strategy can generate internal violence when ethnic majorities are intolerant toward minority groups in their jurisdictions, as has been the case in the Southern Peoples' Administrative and Somalia Regions (Abbink 1993). A further risk is that the promotion of devolved ethnic governments hampers central government efforts to build a democratic system, for the emerging regionally based ethnic parties have frequently disagreed with the administrative systems and electoral rules being formulated at the center. Finally, regionally based ethnicity is a development risk because it can limit the mobility of capital and labor required to take advantage of economic opportunities, create entitlements based on ethnicity that can undermine rational allocation of scarce capital budget resources, and lead to irrational use of energy and resources. In this regard, it threatens to disenfranchise a number of Ethiopians who, over the past few decades, have moved into regions dominated by other ethnic groups, most notably northern farmers who were resettled in the south in the 1980s.

Initial Resistance to Devolution

Initial bureaucratic resistance to devolution and confusion over emerging intergovernmental relations delayed and complicated the implementation of TGE's decentralization reforms. To a large extent, this was because senior TGE decision makers failed to anticipate and did not have the luxury to consider the complex policy, regulatory, personnel, communications, service provision, revenue, and budgetary issues that had to be resolved in order to translate the promised devolutionary strategy into a functioning reality. In addition, despite their political statements in support of devolution, many senior public servants in the deconcentrated and long-established line ministries generally favor maintaining established patterns that determine and implement policies, regulations, programs, and projects. Given the tendencies of bureaucracies to resist change, it should not be surprising that some headquarters staff in the line ministries wish to continue the pattern of unintegrated prefectoral deconcentration that has existed since the mid-1940s.

Continuing the former deconcentrated administrative system is also favored by some longtime field personnel, such as administrators, finance and budget officials, tax collectors, auditors and accountants, and clerks. This view is difficult to challenge because many field-level personnel are unfamiliar with the new administrative strategy, the center currently dominates revenue and budget allocations, and the EPRDF's coalition of regionally based parties continues to look toward central party leadership. While these conditions are not likely to last indefinitely, it is clear that getting headquarters and field personnel of line ministries to buy into devolution reforms is a major challenge.

Constitutional Provisions

The 1994 constitution did not clarify matters. It established the FDRE, comprising eight rural, ethnically based regions: Tigray, Amhara, Benshangul-Gumaz, Afar, Somali, Oromia, Southern Ethiopia People's, and Gambela. In addition, there are three ethnically mixed urban areas: Harar, Dire Dawa, and Addis Ababa. Harar is a region, and there is a strong probability that Dire Dawa will eventually be declared a region. The capital city, Addis Ababa, is defined as a federal district and region. In effect, there are currently ten regions (see map in Cohen 1995, 24). Most of these, including Tigray, Amhara, Oromia, and Somali, are dominated by one ethnic group. Others are more diverse, such as Southern Ethiopia People's, which is composed of at least forty-five ethnic groups.

Ethnicity was the major criteria used in drawing boundaries. Indeed, Ethiopians are to be registered according to their ethnic group. Identification of ethnicity is not precisely spelled out in Ethiopian law, but the major factor for defining groups appears to be linguistic. So, while under the new constitution the official language of the state is Amharic, all Ethiopian languages are to enjoy equal recognition, with each region having the right to determine its respective official language. This important provision poses many questions, such as the effects a multiplicity of languages will have on the operation of regional bureaus or the ability of bureau staff to communicate with counterparts working in the bureaus of other regions.

There is great variation among regions. In drawing their boundaries, little attention was given to their respective geographical size, population densities, agriculture and resource bases, levels of infrastructure, existing administrative capacity, or ability to generate tax revenues. For example, Oromia has a population of 17 million, while Gambela has a population of 110,000; Oromia surrounds the three largest cities in the country (Addis Ababa, Harar, and Dire Dawa), while Benshangul is isolated by distance and infrastructure from any urban center; and Somali is largely a poverty-stricken, arid, and semiarid region characterized by livestock production and limited infrastructure, while Oromia contains some of the country's most productive farmland and supporting agrarian infrastructure. The number of zones and *weredas* in each region also varies greatly. Throughout the 1991–1995 period these units were being both collapsed and expanded. It is estimated that as of mid-1995 there were approximately 50 zones and 670 *weredas*.

Briefly, under the new constitution: (1) the federal government is headed by a prime minister and a nominal head of state; (2) the legislative function is performed by two parliamentary chambers based on a division of labor rather than different bicameral powers, namely: (a) an upper house, or Council of Federation (CF), appointed by ethnic groups or the councils of the regions and charged with interpreting the constitution and, most important, deciding revenue-sharing questions; and (b) a lower house, or Council of People's Representatives (CPR), composed of representatives elected by secret ballot every five years and charged with passing federal laws for the president's signature; (3) the prime minister and the Council of Ministers are accountable to the lower house; (4) regions have, subject to specified conditions, the right to secede; (5) regions may prepare their own constitutions, decide their own official language, establish their own governmental institutions and organizations, exercise authorized tax powers to generate the revenue required to carry out their devolved public sector tasks and establish separate police forces; and (6) the federal government sets federal policies, guidelines, and regulations.

The constitution is the supreme law of the land, taking precedence even over customary law. It combines presidential and parliamentary forms of government in ways that minimize the separation of powers and the checks and balances seen in the U.S. Constitution, devices thought by legal scholars to be critical to the promotion of economic growth, facilitation of federalism, and protection of human rights (Brietzke 1995). Further, the constitution provides only limited guidance on how federal-regional relationships will be managed. In most federal systems this is done by the courts. However, legal experts on Ethiopia do not believe the judiciary, as currently empowered, organized, and staffed can carry out this role. Further, unlike successful federal systems where the constitution is the product of a contract entered into by subunits to form a federal government, Ethiopia's federal system was created by the center, posing the ever present threat that at some future date the center could declare a return to a unitary state.[3] Finally, most legal scholars hold that federal systems should not allow a right to secession. But the constitution recognizes this right, though it is politically and procedurally difficult to exercise it (Cohen 1995, 13). Clearly, this right entered the constitution because politicians and the drafters believed it might help control the kind of armed conflict that led to the independence of Eritrea. It should also be noted that the constitution allows regions to either join together to form a new and larger region or divide into a smaller set of regions.

Over the next few years, considerable attention must be focused on how much power will be devolved to and exercised by regions, particularly with regard to policy formulation, planning, tax revenue and budgeting, and personnel administration. Under the constitution, both the federal and regional governments have legislative, executive, and judicial powers. Aside from the expected fiscal, monetary, trade, foreign policy, immigration, defense, and public safety powers, which, as in most countries, are held by the central government, the constitution grants the federal government such major powers as: (1) preparing and implementing general economic plans and policies for the country; (2) preparing and implementing federal standards and policy measures with respect to basic human needs, science, and technology; (3) enacting laws relating to the protection of land, natural resources, and historical heritage; and (4) enacting laws relating to political organizations and elections. Regional governmental units are given such powers as: (1) establishing their own administrative systems, police force, and democratic order; (2) borrowing from domestic lending sources and levying authorized dues and taxes; (3) preparing, approving, and implementing their own budgets; (4) directing and supervising social and economic activities in accordance with the relevant policy of the federal government; (5) establishing and managing social and economic development institutions and enterprises; and (6) administering land and natural resources.

Administrative and Financial Capacity of States

The most obvious point this outline of responsibilities suggests is that substantial capacity and institution building are required to provide the personnel and structures to allow civil servants to administer, finance, and provide public goods and services. This effort begins with secondary and university training and extends to in-service training for government decisionmakers, professionals, administrators, and technicians. Foreign aid could play a major role in promoting this task, a task made all the more difficult by the death or emigration of many of Ethiopia's "best and brightest" and the dramatic decline in the quality of education that marked the years of military rule (Cohen 1995).

There are at the moment few specific details on how relationships between the federal government and the regions will be managed on a sector-by-sector basis. This is to be expected, for it has taken a century or more for Western federal governments to settle these relationships through legislation, regulations, litigation, and customary practice. But recent studies of the education sector shed some light on the complexities involved and remaining to be resolved (DeStefano et al. 1992; Ethio Education Consultants 1994; Sachs, et al. 1995). These aid agency–funded studies demonstrate how technical assistance can assist both the government and aid agencies to understand the complexities inherent in a given state reconstruction reform.

With regard to tax revenue, Articles 95–100 of the constitution attempt to distinguish federal from regional sources. These are complex and have been analyzed elsewhere (Chole 1994; Mirsha 1993, 1995; World Bank 1995). Suffice it to note that current constitutional provisions and supporting legislation fail to effectively address such fiscal decentralization questions as: (1) Which budgeting and allocation responsibilities are to be transferred to devolved governmental levels? (2) What rules will govern revenue sharing between the center and the regions? (3) What systems of grants-in-aid (general, specific, or matching) will be established and what formula will govern them? (4) How will these formulas deal with the conflicting goals of promoting equity in all regions and investing in growth in promising regions; (5) What conflicts are likely to arise between what the people or officials in individual regions want and what the central government decides? and (6) What arrangements will govern revenue sharing and tax-base sharing? (Chole 1994, 8–9, 13, 20). Beyond this, the federal government has yet to begin to design a monitoring mechanism that can track the capacity of devolved local governmental units to collect revenue, budget effectively, accountably expend allocations, or effectively administer the implementation of public sector programs and projects.

The only studies that have been done on revenue and budgeting suggest that under the constitution and current supporting proclamations, the federal government will dominate the regions through its control of major revenue sources and budgetary allocations (Mirsha 1993, 1995; World Bank 1995). Data in these studies demonstrate that approximately 15 percent of domestic revenue is collected by the devolved government units and 85 percent by the federal government. The center's domination of revenue is due to the fact that the most significant sources of revenue come either from import and export taxes, which are constitutionally outside the jurisdiction of the regions, or from excise taxes levied on manufactured goods, which are largely collected in Addis Ababa. If external assistance is considered, the federal government controls approximately 90 percent of total revenue.

To date, regions have not collected the revenues projected for them, but some, particularly Oromia and Harar, have been more successful in generating revenues than had been expected. Currently, about 45 percent of the federal budgetary allocations go to regions as budget deficit support, subsidies, and block grants. In terms of current regional budgets, the evidence suggests that 10 percent comes from locally collected revenue and 90 percent is provided by federal grants.

While there is some hope that regions will be able to increase their revenue collection, it is very unlikely that these revenue and budgetary relationships will change over the midterm. In this regard, regions with better land resources and infrastructures may eventually be able to cover their recurrent costs. But it is unlikely that any region can meet its capital budget needs. Under the constitution, regions can borrow from domestic financial markets, though none appears to have done this yet. But they cannot deal with foreign banks or accept external aid agency project loans.

Further, budget and allocation decisions are dominated by the federal government. The political strategies regions are likely to follow to gain more influence are described elsewhere (Cohen 1995, 19–21). What is important here is that simply addressing the systems and procedures of revenue collection, budgeting, grant supervision, and accounting will create great burdens on the public sector—burdens aid agencies can address only through advisory support, training programs, and the provision of microcomputer-based management information systems.

At the heart of the coming struggle between the federal government and the regions for definition of structure, organization, and powers will be the revenue and budget system. Substantial debate and accommodation has to take place over how revenue will be shared and grants-in-aid will be formulated. Revenue sharing will depend on the economic policies pursued, their impact on growth in the regions, and the capacity of regions to collect the increased revenues meaningful growth should generate. Block grants are linked to decisions on where to target economic growth and efforts to stimulate economic and social development in less developed areas. In this regard, much attention must be given to: (1) levels and formulas for fiscal resource transfers to regions; (2) equity and efficiency weights to be attached to such formulas; (3) what mechanisms will be used—general (preferred by regions), specific (preferred by the center), or matching grant (perhaps required by law) (Chole 1994, 14–15, 21); (4) how priorities will be set for selecting among specific grant awards; and (5) how conflicts over transfers and formulas will be resolved. Until these issues are settled, it will not be known how tax revenues will be administrated relative to federal versus regional priorities, how revenue sharing relative to common tax sources will be handled, how budgetary equity will be ensured (between the federal and regional governments, as well as among zones and *weredas* within regions), and how interregional conflict over budgetary allocations will be resolved.

Clearly, developing a growth-oriented and equitable revenue and budgetary allocation system for a country as ecologically diverse and economically imbalanced as Ethiopia will be much more difficult than current statements by the government suggest. Moreover, if the center intends to maintain technical supervision over the implementation of regional projects and programs it funds, then it is also likely that the federal ministries will assert extensive control over revenues, budgets, and expenditures.

As noted earlier, there are marked interregional disparities that affect the capacity of various regions to raise revenues, staff governmental units with capable personnel, and administer or implement federal and regional policies, regulations, programs, and projects. Given the range of interregional disparities, serious attention must be given to reallocating resources from wealthier to poorer areas. To date, little thought has been given to such disparities or their implications for broad economic growth and political stability. This poses a problem, because these disparities are sure to affect the coming debate over how to shape and implement the constitution's directives for administrative decentralization.

It can be argued that the new constitution and the TGE's previous proclamations create a hybrid pattern of administrative decentralization, one that is still part deconcentrated and part devolved. The dominant line ministries appear to have control over policy and technical standards. This, coupled with federal control over revenue and budgetary allocations, suggests more deconcentration than devolution. On the other hand, the central government's statements suggest a real commitment to devolution of substantial regional control over the production and provision of public goods and services.

If Ethiopia is following a hybrid strategy of administrative decentralization, two questions arise. First, how long will it take for it to deliver meaningful devolution? Public administration specialists closest to the situation have concluded that it will take considerable time. Second, can meaningful devolution be delivered in time to offset the potential instability embedded in an ethnic-based federal system with a weak center and limited potential for economic development? Many observers conclude it probably cannot. Others see grounds for hope. As yet, there is little debate between proponents of these two views and little empirical evidence in support of their positions.

Recognizing these questions, and aware that the government's federal and devolutionary reforms are more problematic than initially thought, most aid agencies have worked with the government to get a better picture of personnel and financial resources and emerging administrative, legal, and jurisdictional issues. But other aid agencies have sought to assist this devolution without a detailed understanding of the constraints and problems discussed in this chapter (Picard 1993; UNDP 1994). Aid in support of Ethiopia's development needs will flow, however, when and if the government clears up ambiguities surrounding the administrative decentralization reforms. It is likely that most aid agencies will provide, through the federal budget, support to regional governments on a sector-by-sector basis, since this simplifies the design and implementation of the projects they typically fund. It can be expected that these projects will follow a similar model: supporting planning efforts at the center and in the regions; supplying local-level governmental units with computers, vehicles, office equipment, furniture, communications gear, and other commodities; funding long-term training workshops and short-term overseas training; and providing technical experts to assist sectoral ministries and regional bureaus to design systems and draft regulations that help them carry out the functions that appear to have been devolved by the central government, particularly in the areas of agriculture, conservation, health, and education.

In sum, it is likely to take years before the overall structure, organization, and allocation of powers to the federal and devolved regional governments is clarified. This is because the bureaucracies, political parties, opposition groups, and civic associations involved in debating how to implement ethnic federalism have different (1) expectations about the possibilities and difficulties of empowering local populations; (2) experience in managing large-scale institutions other than military units; (3) understanding of the difficulties of formulating policies essential to development and implementing such policies through the preparation of regulations, the provision of basic goods and services to urban and rural populations, and the identification, design, and implementation of sustainable development–oriented projects and programs; and (4) appreciation of the complexities of public sector planning processes, revenue generation, budgeting, expenditure, and accounting procedures in line ministries and agencies. Debates and power struggles among these parties and associations will play a major role in determining the final structure, functions, and scope of Ethiopia's administrative decentralization reforms.

Conclusion

Just before the May 1995 elections, a Western diplomat summed up the uncertainty of Ethiopia's new system of decentralization: "In recognizing ethnicity for what it is—a very powerful issue … they are sitting on an ethnic time bomb. They have come up with a possible solution, which is to tackle it pre-emptively. It is a frightening experiment. Will it work? I don't think anybody knows" (Lorch 1995, 3). A recent aid agency study of the devolution process in Ethiopia optimistically argues that while the reform is still at an early stage, it has been less troublesome than expected, a good start has been made in building personnel capacity and strengthening local-level public institutions, local revenue collection is likely to increase, and friction between the federal government and devolved units has been minimal (World Bank 1995). Still, the new Constitution and its supporting 1991–1994 legislation represent an aspiration unlikely to be realized in the near future.[4]

Clearly, this is a case of a government and an administrative decentralization reform still in flux with important steps yet to be taken. It is a case that illustrates the ways in which political and economic objectives of devolution can be in conflict. If regions are granted extensive power to determine development priorities, establish economic and social policies, and control revenue and budgetary allocations, then devolution can undermine the federal economic objectives and reforms while serving as an effective tool of conflict resolution through regional self-governance. On the other hand, if the federal government retains substantial policy, revenue, and budgetary control while limiting the capacity of devolved government levels to determine and finance their own priorities, then the political effectiveness of ethnic federalism as a strategy of peaceful reconstruction will be undermined. Finding the balance between these two objectives will take a good deal of the attention of political leaders and senior decisionmakers over the next few years.

Further, Ethiopia's post-1991 experience with administrative decentralization demonstrates how difficult it is to implement devolution— much less all the other actions required to effectively rebuild a war-torn state—when personnel and financial resources are limited, ethnicity pervades all action, the center is weak, and the country has well-established patterns of centrally controlled administrative deconcentration. In Ethiopia's case, the elaboration of federal-regional relations is probably going to take place on a sector-by-sector basis. It is also going to be implemented unevenly, for there is great variability among the regions in terms of economic potential, administrative and financial capacity, and political stability. Given the perseverance of the government in promoting devolutionary reforms over the past four years, there is some hope that a viable federal system will emerge within the next decade. It appears to most observers that central to this prediction are the requirements that the country experience substantial economic growth and that useful aid agency funding be available to support the devolution reforms. But whatever the outcome, the Ethiopian experience is going to generate insights into the complexity and potential for fragmented states to use the administrative decentralization strategy of devolution as an effective approach for dealing with demands for greater autonomy from regionally based ethnic, religious, and nationalist groups.

It is also difficult to be optimistic about the potential of aid agencies to assist the FDRE in addressing major state reconstruction tasks such as decentralization reforms. First, the forty-year history of foreign assistance, as shown at the start of this chapter, is marked by more ineffectiveness than success. Second, the subtleties of ethnicity, language, political culture, and historical administrative structures that began this review illustrate the complexities that, with the possible exception of USAID (Cohen, Hammick, and Simmons 1994), few aid agency professionals working in Ethiopia understand. These subtleties limit the capacity of such personnel to work effectively in Ethiopia's complex task environments. Thus, they lower the probability that aid agencies will provide useful technical assistance. Third, the same degree of complexity that marks the formulation and implementation of the government's administrative decentralization initiative also marks all the other reforms the government is simultaneously carrying out. Again, these range from establishing an electoral system and rebuilding the judiciary to forming a modern army and police force, restructuring central ministries and agencies, and formulating new fiscal, monetary, and economic policies. Given the FDRE's limited administrative and financial resources, it is doubtful that Ethiopia's political leaders and public servants, even with the additional provision of aid resources and technical assistance, can effectively implement the complex and wide-ranging reforms and initiatives required. Fourth, the political and administrative intricacies briefly revealed here relative to center-periphery relationships, demonstrate how difficult it is for aid agencies to understand both policy and implementation issues and administrative structures and capacities. The ambitious, ill-informed, and potentially wasteful UNDP plans to assist regionalization attest to the saliency of these points (Picard 1993; UNDP n.d.; UNDP 1994). On the other hand, the useful work by USAID and World Bank professionals on current patterns and potential problems embedded in the area of decentralized revenue and budgeting gives grounds for hope that careful work by knowledgeable specialists can assist the government (Mirsha 1993, 1995; World Bank 1995). If aid agency professionals can overcome their hubris and patiently formulate their technical assistance packages on the basis of Ethiopia-specific knowledge and close counterpart relationships, there is some reason to expect that foreign aid can be useful to political leaders and senior public sector decisionmakers seeking to rebuild war-torn Ethiopia.

Notes

1. Extensive documentation supporting the discussion in this chapter of decentralization, and reviewing progress relative to other objectives of the TGE is found in three lengthy studies: Cohen, Hammick, and Simmons (1994); Cohen (1994); and Cohen (1995). These documents should be consulted by those seeking sources and materials related to the assertions and analyses presented in this chapter. Additional documents reviewing the 1991–1995 progress toward aid-assisted state reconstruction in Ethiopia are: National Democratic Institute (1992); Picard (1993); Harbeson (1994); International Human Rights Law Group (1994); and Fox (1994).

2. Definitions of the types and forms of "decentralization" are important. Failure to understand and use these definitions with legal precision has made it difficult for aid agency professionals and government officials to communicate within their organizations and with their outside counterparts. This chapter adopts the dominant view (Rondinelli, Nellis, and Cheema 1984, 9–15; Silverman 1992). Briefly, "deconcentration" is the transfer of authority over specified decisionmaking, financial, and management functions by administrative means to different levels under the jurisdictional authority of the central government. This is the least extensive type of administrative decentralization and the most common found in late-developing countries. "Devolution" occurs when authority is transferred by central governments to autonomous local-level governmental units holding corporate status granted under state legislation. Federal and confederal states are by definition devolved, though the extent of legally defined and shared powers devolved by the federal government to lower-level government units can be quite limited. Devolution is not common in unitary states, largely because many late-developing countries are characterized by weak central governments weary of losing political or administrative control to local-level governmental units. "Delegation" refers to the transfer of government decisionmaking and administrative authority for carefully spelled out tasks to institutions and organizations that are either under its indirect control or independent. Most typically, delegation is by the central government to semi-autonomous organizations not wholly controlled by the government but legally accountable to it, such as state-owned enterprises and urban or regional development corporations.

3. Most federal states result from a centralization process: a search for unity by the voluntary alliance of previously autonomous or self-autonomous units. Ethiopia is a case where the center is devolving to regions under a form resembling a federal system. In terms of ethnicity, the only other country where the center has devolved to local-level units based on cultural-linguistic lines is Belgium. That country is somewhat more extreme than Ethiopia in that there is no hierarchy between the Union and the federated entities, which are seen as

completely juxtaposed autonomous authorities. For example, the twenty-seven communes are entitled to conclude treaties whose subject falls within their jurisdiction. On the other hand, the Belgian constitution does not mention self-determination, much less secession. The Belgian experience, therefore, deserves close attention by the Ethiopian government, as do the cases of Canada and Switzerland.

4. Brietzke (1995, 37) describes the constitution and its supportive laws as more like the Magna Carta, the Declaration of Independence, and the Rights of Man, which can be "made to come true in the future by people of good will. Without such behavior from such people, all is doomed under even the best of constitutional documents." He uses Spain's constitution of 1978 as an example, generating hope that Ethiopia can succeed with its stated constitutional goals.

References

Abbink, Jon. 1993. "Ethnic Conflict in the 'Tribal Zone': The Dizi and Suri in Southern Ethiopia." *Journal of Modern African Studies* 31 (4):672–682.

Brietzke, Paul H. 1995. "Ethiopia's 'Leap in the Dark': Federalism and Self-Determination in the New Constitution." *Journal of African Law* 20 (1):19–38.

Chole, Eshetu. 1994. "Opening Pandora's Box: Preliminary Notes on Fiscal Decentralization in Contemporary Ethiopia." *Northeast African Studies* (New Series) 1 (1):7–30.

Clapham, Christopher. 1988. *Transformation and Continuity in Revolutionary Ethiopia.* New York: Cambridge University Press.

Cohen, John M. 1984. "Foreign Involvement in Land Tenure Reform: The Case of Ethiopia." In *International Dimensions of Land Reform,* edited by John D. Montgomery, pp. 169–219. Boulder: Westview Press.

Cohen, John M. 1994. "Transition Toward Democracy and Governance in Post Mengistu Ethiopia." Development Discussion Paper No. 493. Cambridge: Harvard Institute for International Development.

Cohen, John M. 1995. "'Ethnic Federalism' in Ethiopia." Development Discussion Paper No. 519. Cambridge: Harvard Institute for International Development.

Cohen, John M., William Hammick, and Emmy Simmons. 1994. "Evaluation Report: Ethiopia Democracy/Governance Support Project." Addis Ababa: USAID.

Cohen, John M., and Peter H. Koehn. 1980. *Ethiopian Provincial and Municipal Government: Imperial Patterns and Post Revolutionary Changes.* East Lansing: African Studies Center, Michigan State University Press.

DeStefano, Joseph, et al. 1992. "Ethiopia: Education Sector Review." Addis Ababa: USAID.

Engedayehu, Walle. 1994. "Ethiopia: The Pitfalls of Ethnic Federalism." *Africa Quarterly* 34 (2):149–192.

Ethio Education Consultants. 1994. "Organization and Management of Regional Education Bureaus Under the Policies of Regionalization and Educational Decentralization." Addis Ababa: USAID.

Fox, Leslie M., et al. 1994. "An Assessment of USAID's Capacity for Rapid Response in Support of African Civil Society." Washington, D.C.: Associates in Rural Development.

Harbeson, John W. 1994. "Ethiopia's Democratic Transition: A Preliminary Assessment." Nairobi: USAID/REDSO.

Henze, Paul B. 1991a. "Ethiopia in 1990: The Revolution Unraveling." Report No. P-7707. Santa Monica, Calif.: Rand.

Henze, Paul B. 1991b. "Ethiopia in 1991—Peace Through Struggle." Report No. P-7743. Santa Monica, Calif.: Rand.

Henze, Paul. 1992. "The Defeat of the Derg and the Establishment of New Governments in Ethiopia and Eritrea." Santa Monaco: Rand Report No. P-7766.

International Human Rights Law Group (IHRLG). 1994. "Ethiopia in Transition: A Report on the Judiciary and the Legal Profession." Washington, D.C.: IHRLG.

Keller, Edmond. 1994. "Remaking the Ethiopian State." In *Collapsed States: The Disintegration and Restoration of Legitimate Authority,* edited by I. William Zartman, pp. 129–139. Boulder: Lynne Rienner Publishers.

Kendie, Daniel. 1994. "Which Way the Horn of Africa: Disintegration or Confederation?" *North East African Studies* (New Series) 1 (1):137–167.

Lorch, Donatella. 1995. "Ethiopia Holding Elections in Federal System," *New York Times,* May 7.

Markakis, John, and Nega Ayele. 1978. *Class and Revolution in Ethiopia.* Nottingham, England: Russell Press.

Mirsha, Satish Chandra. 1993. "Public Expenditure Implications of Regional Economic Devolution." Nairobi: USAID/REDSO.

Mirsha, Satish Chandra. 1995. "The Economic Dimensions of Regionalization in Ethiopia." Nairobi: USAID/REDSO.

National Democratic Institute for International Affairs (NDI). 1992. "An Evaluation of the June 21, Ethiopian Elections in Ethiopia." Washington, D.C.: NDI.

Ottaway, Marina, and David Ottaway. 1978. *Ethiopia: Empire in Revolution.* New York: Africana Publishing Company.

Picard, Louis A. 1993. "Regionalization in Ethiopia: Preparation of a Strategic Action Plan." Management Development Programme. New York: United Nations Development Programme.

Regional Affairs Sector. 1994. "The System of Regional Administration in Ethiopia." Addis Ababa: Prime Minister's Office.

Rondinelli, Dennis A., John R. Nellis, and Shabbir G. Cheema. 1984. *Decentralization in Developing Countries: A Review of Recent Experience.* Washington, D.C.: World Bank, Staff Working Paper No. 581.

Sachs, R. et al. 1995. "Operationalizing Decentralization in Education." Addis Ababa: UNESCO.

Silverman, Jerry M. 1992. "Public Sector Decentralization: Economic Policy and Sector Investment Programs." African Technical Department, Technical Paper Number 188. Washington, D.C.: World Bank.

UNDP (United Nations Development Programme). n.d. "Programme Document: Support to Economic and Financial Management: Supplementary Funds Requirements for the Ethiopian Regionalization Process." Addis Ababa: UNDP.

UNDP (United Nations Development Programme). 1994. "Capacity Building for Regional Administration in Ethiopia." Addis Ababa: UNDP.

Woodward, Peter, and Murray Forsyth (eds.). 1994. *Conflict and Peace in the Horn of Africa.* Aldershot, England: Dartmouth Publishing.

World Bank. 1995. "Ethiopia: Public Expenditure Review: Issues in Public Expenditure." 2 vols. Washington, D.C.: World Bank.

7

Reintegrating Returning Refugees in Central America

Barry N. Stein

By the early 1980s, more than 10 percent of Central America's 18 million people were displaced—internally or externally—by internal social revolutionary conflicts in Nicaragua, El Salvador, and Guatemala, which directly affected the neighboring states of Costa Rica, Honduras, Belize, and Mexico, as well as the more distant United States.

International assistance to reintegrate uprooted populations in Central America—primarily through the Development Program for Refugees, Displaced and Repatriated Persons in Central America and the process begun by International Conference on Central American Refugees—took place in advantageous circumstances created by a regional peace process, buttressed by the political will of the concerned governments, and generously supported by international donors. The political impact of the international assistance proved to be its most important outcome by increasing humanitarian or political space and expanding civil society. Though the implementation practices of the main international agencies—the United Nations High Commissioner for Refugees (UNHCR) and the United Nations Development Programme (UNDP)—had a positive effect on the reconciliation process in the war-torn countries, these agencies were less successful in promoting effective collaboration and cooperation between themselves, and the international assistance effort was unable to tie reintegration assistance into sustainable national development processes.

Affected Regions and the Peace Process

Refugees in general, and those of Central America in particular, flee their homelands because of a fear of violence and persecution. Sometimes they flee the impersonal danger of a war zone, but more often they flee the violence and persecution aimed at them by their own government. Such governmental violence strains and can break the normal bond of trust and loyalty between the citizen and the state.

In 1988, UNHCR was assisting approximately 120,000 Central Americans who were officially recognized as refugees.[1] At the same time, the United States General Accounting Office (GAO 1989), using Department of State reports and information from governments, estimated there were almost 2 million Central American refugees, with as many as 650,000 Nicaraguans in Honduras, Costa Rica, and the United States; 1 million Salvadorans in the United States and Mexico; and 300,000 Guatemalans in Mexico and the United States. In addition to approximately 2 million refugees, more than 1 million Salvadorans, Nicaraguans, and Guatemalans were internally displaced within their countries and large numbers of people—stayees—were in their homes but severely affected by the conflicts. The refugees, returnees, and displaced persons, along with former combatants, are often referred to as "uprooted populations."

The Central American refugee problem encompasses four refugee flows from three of the region's six republics:

1. Nicaraguan refugees from the Miskito and Sumu indigenous ethnic groups, on the Atlantic side of the country, fled to the Miskito region of Honduras because of attempts by the revolutionary Sandinista government to "take control of their communal way of life" (Zinser 1991, 192). In 1987, the Sandinista government of Nicaragua reversed its policies toward the Miskito and Sumu communities and agreed to give them greater autonomy. Approximately 12,000 Indians returned in the next two years, and the remaining 12,000 returned after the 1990 elections.

2. Nicaraguan *campesinos* fled to Honduras or Costa Rica because of the revolutionary policies of the Sandinistas or because of the counterrevolutionary conflict, either as its victims or to support the contras. In 1990, the nine-year civil war in Nicaragua ended when the Sandinista government was defeated in national elections. By the end of 1991, approximately 117,000 refugees, members of the resistance, and their supporters and dependents had returned to Nicaragua with the assistance of UNHCR and the Organization of American States (OAS) (GAO 1992).

3. Guatemalan refugees, overwhelmingly *campesinos* from the Maya-Quiche indigenous groups, fled to the bordering, southern Mexican state of Chiapas, to escape brutal, indiscriminate, counterinsurgency campaigns of the Guatemalan army. Negotiations to end a thirty-year civil conflict between the government of Guatemala and

the Unidad Revolucionaria Nacional Guatemalteca (URNG) have continued under the mediation of the United Nations—the Secretary-General has appointed a Special Envoy for the Guatemala Peace Process. A number of agreements were signed in 1994 and 1995 dealing with such topics as the rights of indigenous peoples, resettlement of the population groups uprooted by the armed conflict, and establishment of a commission to clarify past human rights violations and acts of violence. A 1994 agreement led to the establishment of the United Nations Mission for the Verification of Human Rights and of Compliance with the Commitments of the Comprehensive Agreement on Human Rights in Guatemala (MINUGUA).

4. Salvadoran *campesinos* from rural war zones in the northern regions of El Salvador, and many others from other regions of the country, fled to Honduras and Costa Rica to escape the cross fire of a civil war or direct attacks by the Salvadoran military. In January 1992, El Salvador's twelve-year civil war ended with the signing of a cease-fire between the government and the Farabundo Martí National Liberation Front (FMLN). The United Nations, which assisted the peace process with the United Nations Observer Mission in El Salvador (ONUSAL), declared the war officially over in December 1992.

The United States was deeply involved in the conflicts: supporting a counter-revolutionary force against the Sandinista Government of Nicaragua; and, assigning a high priority to defeating the insurgency in El Salvador. Furthermore, while not directly supporting the murderous, military government of Guatemala, in earlier decades the U.S. had aided its landed oligarchy in suppressing peasant action for social change.

For the most part, three of the four refugee problems were resolved by 1992. By mid-1996, all the formal refugee camps had been closed and the Guatemalan refugees were the main group still being assisted. Repatriation and reintegration programs for Central American refugees have been focused on those refugees who remained in the immediate region and were receiving international assistance. Most of the more than 1 million exiles who went to North America, however, have not returned to the region.

Regional governments were reluctant to recognize victims of violence as refugees, out of a concern that recognition would entitle them to legal rights and assistance and make them into a permanent problem. Further, some governments were guided by foreign policy concerns; the refugees' claims of persecution were not accepted if they came from friendly countries. The United States was hostile to refugee claims from El Salvador, whose government it supported, and much more generous to asylum seekers from Nicaragua, whose government it was trying to overthrow.

Fortunately, the Central American peace process and the international assistance to returnees were not restricted by formal legal categories. Rather, they "recognize[d] that solutions to the problems of refugees, returnees and displaced persons form an integral part of the efforts for peace, democracy and development taking place in the region" (CIREFCA 1989).

Because refugee problems were part of Central America's security problems, a balance between national security and humanitarian interests was necessary. Mexico and Costa Rica saw the conflicts in Central America as a regional issue requiring a regional solution, and both had condemned U.S. actions against Nicaragua.

The Central America Peace Process

In 1987, "the Central American Presidents took matters into their own hands" (Crosby 1990) with the signing of the Arias Peace Plan, also known as the Esquipulas II Declaration. The plan took an integrated, regional approach to peace rather than seeking partial or national solutions. It called for cease-fires, coexistence between Nicaragua and its neighbors, and guarantees of U.S. security concerns; and it undertook to prevent interventions in the internal affairs of other nations. Moreover, the agreement recognized that "there can be no lasting peace without initiatives to resolve the problem of refugees, returnees and displaced persons" in the region and appealed for international aid for these efforts.

The Esquipulas II Declaration led to two related, but politically different, courses of action. One was a UN-centered effort to support the peace process, focused on the General Assembly and UNDP, which produced the Development Program for Refugees, Displaced and Repatriated Persons in Central America (PRODERE). The other effort, the International Conference on Central American Refugees (CIREFCA), was a collaboration of European donor governments, some of whom were trying to counterbalance U.S. policy in the region, and UNHCR, whose goal was to increase protection for the uprooted.

PRODERE was established in 1989 to aid the social and economic reintegration of uprooted peoples. It was financed by an initial $115 million contribution from Italy. PRODERE planners assumed that reintegration "required creating conditions conducive to sustainable development" (Sollis and Schultz 1995).

In 1988, as a further follow-on to the Esquipulas II Declaration, the presidents of Costa Rica, El Salvador, Guatemala, Honduras, and

Nicaragua called on the UN Secretary-General, UNHCR, and UNDP to convene an international conference to address the problems of refugees, as well as displaced persons and repatriates. The 1989 conference, CIREFCA, adopted a Concerted Plan of Action (CPA) which considered the problems of refugees, returnees, and displaced persons to be an indispensable component of the regional efforts for peace and development. The "CIREFCA process," as it came to be known,[2] headed by UNHCR, implemented the CPA from 1989 until June 1994 and was an important support and adjunct to the Central American peace process.[3]

The states of the region not only engaged in a peace process that reduced their involvement in the Cold War; as a region they explicitly sought international resources to support their peace, reconstruction, and development efforts. PRODERE and CIREFCA are just pieces of this larger regional process and program, which includes peace treaties, elections, and UN peacekeeping and peace building efforts. Their part in this process is to provide strictly humanitarian and impartial international economic assistance to address the problems of refugees, displaced persons, and returnees throughout the region. The international community's response was to commit itself to provide political and financial support, while UNHCR and UNDP agreed to lend their support to ensure the successful implementation of both programs. PRODERE, which had been designed, funded, and operational before the CIREFCA meeting, was later integrated into the CIREFCA framework.

The Challenge

The first Salvadoran refugee *masiva* from Honduras, 4,000 refugees from the Mesa Grande camp returning to five Salvadoran communities in areas contested between the military and the FMLN, took place only two months after the Esquipulas II summit meeting. Widely covered by the press, the Mesa Grande *masiva* raised awareness that thousands of rural refugees could soon return to marginal areas inhabited by the local poor and the internally displaced. Castillo and Fahlen (1995) describe the challenge for international assistance:

> Personalized humanitarian returnee relief assistance would under such circumstances be both difficult and inappropriate. The only solution was to integrate these people into a social and economic development process in an atmosphere of reconciliation and justice. But there was nothing like an economic development process taking place in the war-torn areas of return and, least of all, in the municipalities and rural communities to which people actually came back.

The challenge, however, was much more than economic development. The civil wars had sprung from conditions of deep social, economic, and political inequality; and now these rifts had been exacerbated by death, destruction, and armed conflict. In the rural areas, all parties felt a profound mutual distrust. The first returns were occurring without peace, into areas dominated by rebel and government military forces.

A central advantage of the international assistance programs for Central America's returning refugees was the strong expression of political will by the concerned governments at Esquipulas II and the CIREFCA meeting, which committed those governments to attaining peace and resolving the crisis of displacement. This level of political will and commitment in a small and homogeneous region with a relatively manageable refugee problem had a positive impact on international funding support and assistance.

This tremendous increase in international resources, as well as the direct link to the regional peace process, gave the international community substantial leverage in dealing with governments, regional and local officials, and polarized local interests. International projects and involvement with the uprooted and needy populations shifted the terms of debate within the societies receiving international assistance and transformed the condition of these uprooted groups from an internal matter subject to the sole discretion of the government into a "benchmark for the international community to monitor" progress on a host of domestic issues and problems (Sollis and Schultz 1995).

Repatriation and Reintegration

Although the regional peace process and the CIREFCA and PRODERE assistance processes are important unifying elements in the reintegration of the Central American returnees, it is important to note that only the Nicaraguan *campesinos* affected by the contra war returned home in the presence of both peace and international assistance programs. In two of the four refugee movements—the *masivas* to El Salvador and the Miskito return to Nicaragua—almost all the refugees returned home before the assistance programs were established and while war was still raging in their countries. In Guatemala, there have been significant repatriations while waiting for a peace accord, but the majority of the refugees are still in Mexico.

Repatriation of refugees to their homeland is a sign that safety and control over one's own life has the possibility of being restored, but it does not necessarily mean that the bond of trust and loyalty has been restored. This is especially so in cases such as El Salvador, Guatemala, and the Miskito of Nicaragua, where the returns were challenges to the government. Indeed, in the *masivas* to El Salvador, the refugee communities had the "intention to turn the repatriation process ... into a political confrontation." "The refugees wished to demonstrate to the Salvadoran government, through their collective repatriations to the zones of conflict and guerrilla control, the extent of their political will and organizational strength" (Fagen and Eldridge 1991). And, learning from the example and experiences of the *masivas*, the Guatemala refugees in Mexico have not waited for peace and have taken matters into their own hands to organize collective returns home.

Repatriation as a Beginning

Most voluntary repatriations occur during conflict, without a decisive political event such as elections or a peace agreement and without major change in the regime or the conditions that originally caused flight. Countless individual refugees and sizable groups of well-organized refugees return home in the face of continued risk—frequently without amnesty, without a repatriation agreement or program, without the permission of the authorities in either the country of asylum or of origin, without international knowledge or assistance, and without an end to the conflict that caused the exodus. International assistance and protection play a minor role in refugees' decision to repatriate. Many refugees leave behind international assistance programs in their country of exile to return unassisted and unprotected to their homeland.

The refugees are the main actors in the contemporary practice of voluntary repatriation. They are the main decisionmakers and participate in determining the modalities of movement and the conditions of reception. In the absence of coercion, refugee-induced repatriation is a self-regulating process on the refugees' own terms. The refugees apply their own criteria to their situation in exile and to conditions in their homeland and return home if it is safe and better by their standards. Although refugees are commonly thought of as powerless, they are making a choice when they decide to flee or to repatriate. In comparing alternatives, refugees attempt to conserve and strengthen their control over their own lives, to reduce stress, and to seek security.

People who are physically home but are not participating in the economic and political life of their country are still uprooted persons. In many cases, they may be back in their homeland but far from their own communities. The danger exists that repatriation alone is a relocation that converts refugees into internally displaced persons.

Nonetheless, all four Central American refugee groups have returned to highly stratified and polarized homelands rent by bitter struggles over social, political, and economic justice. Although the immediate struggle was somewhat moderated at the time of return, the refugees returned to lands seething with danger and militarism and the potential for resumed violence.

A decade or more of internal conflict can leave the homeland devastated: resources are depleted, indebtedness burdens the economy,[4] infrastructure is destroyed, institutions are weakened, and the peace may be fragile. However, the return of refugees to poverty and frustration does not necessarily overturn a durable solution. While social and economic improvements are desirable conditions for repatriation and reintegration, they are neither necessary nor essential. There is little evidence of renewed refugee flight due to economic conditions. Renewed flight, which is relatively rare, is usually in the context of resumed fighting or persecution. Nonetheless, experience shows that poor, stagnant economic conditions can contribute to political fragility and danger, while growth and progress improve political conditions.

The Central American refugees were primarily from rural areas near their country's international border. These rural, border areas are peripheral and marginal in many ways; they are typically neglected in national development plans and provision of basic infrastructure and state institutions, other than the military. Often, due to insurgency, they are highly militarized, with military authorities controlling all significant activities to serve national security goals. Refugee repatriation alone, in the absence of substantial international assistance, was unlikely to reduce military activity or to increase development priorities in these areas. In a sense, once refugees cross a border in relative safety, repatriation is fairly complete and a durable solution is achieved. However, mere return home is not enough. Returnees must be reintegrated into their countries of origin.

Reintegration of returning refugees is a complex political, economic, social, and cultural process that goes beyond a simple physical reinsertion of refugees in their home communities.[5] Violence and conflict and the passage of time have an effect on individuals and societies. Exile changes the refugees, and their children may know nothing of "dear old home." Refugees may undergo a major cultural and social transformation; they may be urbanized, politicized, educated, and develop new skills and attitudes. Although the refugees' memory and image of home may be idealized and frozen at the moment of flight, conflict and politics may have transformed the homeland, the hometown, and the home folks. Some of those who stayed behind may have been on the other side of the conflict. Others who stayed may have endured sufferings and experiences not shared by the repatriates.

Departure from Traditional Reintegration Assistance

International organizations and agencies, such as UNHCR and UNDP, are limited in their programs and operations by their respective governing mandates and available resources. UNHCR is mandated to assist and protect refugees and is not a development agency, thus the fact of repatriation serves to limit UNHCR's responsibility for those who have voluntarily returned to their homelands. While UNDP, as a development agency, might be seen as well placed to assume this responsibility for returnees, its programs are in fact primarily aimed at long-term development of geographic regions, and UNDP works primarily through governmental channels. Further, UNDP's monies cannot be easily shifted to deal with returnee problems.

Through the end of the 1980s, traditional or typical UNHCR postreturn assistance was short-term aid mostly directed toward individual refugees. It provided them with transport, food assistance for less than one year, shelter materials, seeds, tools, cash grants, and other agricultural inputs. In addition, some UNHCR repatriation programs provided for some community-based assistance for returnees in the form of repair of infrastructure. UNHCR has long accepted the idea that reintegration assistance should include the local population in the affected area and that it should be for a longer period, tying return assistance into long-term development processes. However, such assistance was beyond UNHCR's mandate and resources.

Integral reintegration assistance tries to restore the institutions of civil society and the bond between citizen and state. Rather than limiting itself to the emergency relief needs of returned refugees, reintegration assistance makes an integrated response to the rehabilitation and development needs of local communities and the larger society. Rather than treating "the returnees as one undifferentiated mass" (Allen and Morsink 1994), appropriate reintegration assistance attempts to develop programs for localities, vulnerable populations, individual refugees, and organized groups, and to connect these programs to national development and political efforts.

Although such integral reintegration goals are sometimes given rhetorical voice in repatriation planning, it is extremely rare to find a solid attempt to achieve them. Central America is a special case, where the momentum of the Esquipulas II regional peace process produced not only the CIREFCA and PRODERE international assistance programs, but a significantly higher level of national political will and international commitment and funding to the tasks of reintegrating uprooted populations and rebuilding societies.

PRODERE and CIREFCA

The CIREFCA process and PRODERE were related programs; PRODERE was eventually integrated into the CIREFCA framework, but their institutions, missions, and operations were quite different, reflecting the differing mandates and operational cultures of UNDP and UNHCR. Although UNHCR participated in PRODERE and UNDP had a role in CIREFCA, in practice "UNHCR was reluctant to assume anything beyond a symbolic presence in PRODERE" (Sollis and Schultz 1995), and for UNDP, "CIREFCA was perceived as first and foremost a UNHCR venture" (Castillo and Fahlen 1995).

Refugees and uprooted populations are central to UNHCR's mandate and are normally its only reason for being involved in a situation. For UNDP, the problem of the uprooted is only one of many issues regarding peace, democracy, economic recovery, and sustainable development that are central to its mission and involvement in the region.[6]

UNHCR, a crisis-oriented agency, is concerned with speed in a crisis, and with urgent coordination to avoid omission or duplication. UNHCR's focus is to protect refugees and to deal with their related problems. In particular, although UNHCR is rhetorically committed to sustainable development, development is a goal and process outside UNHCR's mandate and experience. UNHCR is more concerned with short- and medium-term activities. UNHCR tends to work with ad hoc, emergency systems or counterparts set up by governments rather than through permanent linkages with the principal planning and development ministries.

UNDP is a long-term and strategic development agency concerned with principles, methods, standards and plans. UNDP places great importance on securing technical assistance, carrying out feasibility studies, establishing planning processes and documentation, building and consolidating local program and project execution capacities, and strengthening mechanisms of community participation—before it begins project implementation. A two- or three-year delay working on these matters before beginning the major flow of funds for project implementation may be considered time well spent. Reintegration programs are not part of UNDP's normal mode of operation.

PRODERE

PRODERE was a development program aimed at assisting the social and economic reintegration of uprooted populations in war-affected areas of Central America. It had a $115 million budget[7] and was executed by UNDP's Office of Project Services from 1989 to 1995. Assistance was provided in fourteen territorial areas of intervention, twelve rural and two urban, in six countries: $23 million for each of the refugee source countries—El Salvador, Guatemala, and Nicaragua; $7 million for Costa Rica; $5 million for Honduras; and $3 million for Belize. There was a National Coordinator in each country who worked with the UNDP Resident Representative and a designated government counterpart. Area Coordinators did field implementation at the local level. A Regional Technical Support subprogram provided PRODERE with specialist support regarding the complementary activities of other UN agencies, including UNHCR. The PRODERE "approach" emphasized building participatory local mechanisms, decentralized management, and "joint decision making between local governments, State institutions and civil society" (Castillo and Fahlen 1995). PRODERE's strategy focused on local communities greatly affected by the conflict and treated all who were needy—returnees, displaced persons, and local population—equally as beneficiaries.

CIREFCA

The CIREFCA process,[8] which implemented the CPA of the 1989 CIREFCA conference, was a forum for consensus and dialogue between Central Americans and for dialogue and negotiations between Central Americans and the international community. The process was also a fund-raising mechanism—which raised some $438 million, including PRODERE, through 1994—and an attempt to reduce displacement in Central America. The main actors were UNHCR, donor governments and the Central American governments; UNDP, NGOs, and beneficiary organizations played lesser roles.

"CIREFCA projects were those that underwent consultation in the various national fora of CIREFCA and were then presented for funding at international pledging conferences" (UNHCR 1994a). Many projects that were presented directly to the donors or at CIREFCA forums, without going through the CIREFCA consultation mechanisms, were considered to be "in the framework of CIREFCA." Donors preferred to channel resources through UNHCR, UNDP, or nongovernmental organizations (NGOs) rather than directly funding some Central American governments.

The institutional center of the CIREFCA process was the Joint Support Unit, which worked on coordination of activities and on project planning, promotion, presentation, and reporting. With a four-person staff in Costa Rica and consultations throughout the region, this unit served as technical support, troubleshooter, liaison, and fund-raiser for the process. UNHCR and UNDP provided the staff for the unit, with

UNHCR serving as the lead agency until 1993, when the role was taken over by UNDP.

Humanitarian or Political Space

Even though CIREFCA and PRODERE operated separately for the most part, they did have a significant, complementary impact on the expansion of humanitarian or political space in the countries of return. Although the concept of political or humanitarian "space" is quite ambiguous, it can be a vital achievement of international assistance to politicized societies:

> This protection is defined as the perceived "space" or opening in society that provides the refugees not only some measure of physical protection, but also material and moral support. Space can be seen so narrowly as to give a single refugee the freedom to choose to return to the community of origin, or it can be understood so broadly as to permit a collective return of a community. (Larkin 1991)

> ...

> Humanitarian space expands and contracts depending on circumstances. It may be circumscribed, or expanded, by the actions of political and military authorities; it may also be enlarged, or contracted, by humanitarian actors themselves. In short, humanitarian space is neither durable nor transferable but elastic. Rather than filling existing space, external organizations and personnel may, through their own presence, enlarge and extend it. (Sollis and Schultz 1995)

Prior to the CIREFCA and PRODERE programs, the needs of the uprooted populations were dealt with as a national security problem primarily within a counterinsurgency framework rather than as a humanitarian problem. In the peripheral, conflicted areas of return, military authorities controlled all activities and tried to manipulate humanitarian programs to serve national security goals. In both Guatemala and El Salvador, the confrontational demands of the refugees, to return to conflicted areas that were to be demilitarized, were supported by UNHCR and UNDP—not on the political terms favored by the refugees or the military, but in terms of supporting international law and commitments, the humanitarian rights of civilians, and the peace process.

Most of the money for refugee reintegration from international donors was used to improve the economic status of the returnees and their communities. This focus was understandable given the devastation caused by the civil conflicts and the significant groups of needy and vulnerable people. The long-term obstacles to reintegration are only partially rooted in economics. The roots of the original refugee flows are deep and are entwined around resentments of power and privilege, mutual suspicions, and fundamental economic and social injustices. However, the implementation practices of the CIREFCA and PRODERE economic projects had a substantial impact on the process of reconciliation in Central America.

At the local level, CIREFCA and PRODERE projects were discussed and negotiated with all concerned: "Talking and talking and negotiating every single humanitarian project eventually created a new culture of dialogue between the sides, instead of violence" (Redmond 1995). UNHCR and UNDP had a mediating role between the various sides and eventually helped establish a climate of cooperation between former foes. Both agencies were able to use their economic and political leverage to bring civilian government ministries back into marginalized areas where previously all projects had to be cleared with the military.

When additional resources are introduced into peripheral regions, they become the subject of intense competition. The UN agencies' policy of neutrality and evenhandedness and their willingness to deal impartially with all civilian actors helped create humanitarian space and strengthen civil society. And, at times, the simple presence of international institutions and personnel moderated the behavior of polarized forces.

The UNDP-implemented PRODERE program, drawing on established UNDP practices, attempted to deal with the political and social obstacles to cooperation by emphasizing the role of civil society in the reintegration of uprooted populations. UNDP helped to create local institutions for consensus building among those on opposite sides in the conflict, to build less antagonistic relationships between the community and the state, and to create local institutions in previously marginalized areas that would continue in place after international assistance efforts had ended. Similarly, UNHCR embraced neutrality by choosing "to work with historically opposing forces in the same" project (Ortega et al. 1993), thus helping to depolarize recipient municipalities.

The international effort to create greater political space went beyond UNHCR and UNDP to also involve the United Nations Secretariat and the donor governments. The UN and the donors, together and separately, worked to secure the political commitment of all parties involved to the return of uprooted groups, to assistance projects, to institution building and political participation, and to inclusion of previously marginalized groups in the political process. The UN role, through the

Secretary-General and his special envoys—as well as peacekeeping, monitoring and observer missions—was as an impartial, neutral participant in negotiating, tracking, monitoring, and evaluating the follow-up and compliance with formal agreements.

The donor governments, primarily European[9] and North American, had an interest that was far broader than the CIREFCA/PRODERE programs and projects. The donors made their continued involvement and financial support for reconstruction and development conditional on progress in democratic reforms, human rights, demobilization, reform of the security services and judiciary, and other matters directly related to opening up the political process. Further, by funding a large part of CIREFCA assistance through NGOs, "the donors effectively pressured governments to widen the civil consultation process to include NGOs" (UNHCR 1994a).

Civil Society

The establishment, restoration, and strengthening of civil society is part and parcel of the effort to expand political space for returnees. Civil society is all those autonomous associations, groups, networks, and organizations that give form and substance to community life. Rather than government being the only social and political force in a community, civil society is the NGOs, churches, private enterprise, workers' organizations, political parties, trade unions, community groups and countless other associations by which people articulate their needs and preferences, organize to achieve their goals, and popularly participate in the social, economic, and cultural development of their locale. Civil society can be diverse and powerful enough to organize daily life with little outside involvement, or so weak, cowed, and damaged as to be almost nonexistent.

Internal conflict, in particular, can polarize and politicize even the most friendly and benign activities, thus contributing to social disintegration and the violent resolution of disputes. When civil institutions are weakened and attacked and security interests are paramount and pervasive, participation in civil society can be dangerous. Populations are uprooted, either internally displaced or as refugees, when violence replaces consensus building, when normal, legitimate concerns and needs are labeled subversive.[10] Returnee reintegration will be precarious without the re-creation of a functioning civil society at the local, regional, and national levels. Castillo and Fahlen (1995) comment:

> Both UNHCR and UNDP, through PRODERE, were instrumental in establishing entities of civil society. For UNHCR, this was a means,

rather than an end, to ensure effective delivery and implementation of humanitarian assistance. For UNDP/PRODERE, on the other hand, it was a deliberate objective of building local capacities for socio-economic development, i.e. an end in itself.

UNHCR, through CIREFCA, made two important contributions to strengthening civil society: the use of NGOs as project implementers, and development of its community-based quick impact projects.

Nongovernmental organizations. "The inclusion of the non-governmental sector in the CIREFCA process brought about a relationship between governments in the region and civil society that was previously unknown in Central America" (Castillo and Fahlen 1995). Prior to CIREFCA, the relationship between NGOs and governments was based on mutual suspicion: Governments were seen as the source of persecution and oppression allowing human rights violators to act with impunity; governments saw NGOs as subversive supporters of revolution.

UNHCR and the CIREFCA process allowed local and national NGOs to have unprecedented and increasing access to official channels, giving the NGOs legitimacy and resources. In customary UNHCR fashion, the CIREFCA conference and follow-up meetings included NGOs in their deliberations, and almost "40% of CIREFCA funds" for project implementation were channeled through NGOs (Castillo and Fahlen 1995). Contact with regional and international NGOs provided local NGOs with allies and additional resources. Working relationships and even partnerships were established between NGOs and government or military programs.

UNHCR normally implements programs in an operational partnership with NGOs. "NGOs provide a significant proportion of the global resources dedicated to refugees and returnees, and an increasingly large percentage of UNHCR's budget is also channelled through NGO partners" (UNHCR 1993). In Central America this mutually supportive relationship included UNHCR efforts to encourage and improve the links between NGOs and UNDP and the UN system. A 1993 meeting of the International Council of Voluntary Agencies, representing international NGOs, and the Regional Association for Forced Migration, representing ninety Central American NGOs, "agreed that CIREFCA had facilitated their participation in discussions with the governments of the region regarding the uprooted and permitted new possibilities for concerted action on their behalf" (CIREFCA 1993). Donors insisted, through the CIREFCA process, that NGOs be involved not only in the implementation of projects but in the earliest design and negotiation processes.

Quick impact projects (QIPs).   QIPs were developed by UNHCR in 1991 in the course of assisting the reintegration of returnees in Nicaragua. Since then, QIPs have become a major component in UNHCR reintegration programs globally. In the 1990s, there are increased opportunities for repatriation, but these are returns to devastated countries in a context of fragile peace. In Nicaragua, to consolidate reintegration, UNHCR assistance "focused on returnee impacted communities rather than on specific categories of people to avoid discrimination between returning refugees, internally displaced persons and other locally war-affected populations in addressing the collective needs of these people to rebuild their communities in confidence and reconciliation" (UNHCR 1994a).

QIPs are small-scale interventions made up of simple inputs and activities intended to be an immediate injection of support to meet community-based needs. QIPs build on the active involvement of communities "from identification of priorities, design of interventions to implementation of projects" (UNHCR 1994b). QIPs are implemented—primarily by NGOs, with a preference for indigenous NGOs—over the course of a few weeks to several months, and specific projects generally cost less than $70,000. (From 1991 to 1993 there were over 350 QIPs in Nicaragua, costing more than $12 million.) The QIPs are simple, speedily implemented microprojects requiring relatively modest investments and addressing basic and urgent needs in the sectors of infrastructure, health, social services, income generation, and crop and livestock production.

The aim of community benefit and participation is to enable previously displaced people to become members of "a social and economic community, which through outward interaction with broader segments of the civil society is linked to a national development framework" (UNHCR 1994b). More important, the QIPs enlarged the political space and reconciliation of civil society in Nicaragua and elsewhere by adopting a clear political perspective in favor of reintegration and neutrality. An evaluation of the Nicaragua QIPs found that

> the neutrality was expressed in the decision to not work exclusively with one sector of the uprooted population. The QIPs were not influenced by the desires of some sectors to exclude others from the projects. ... It is also a political decision to choose to work with historically opposing forces in the same QIP. ... From this political perspective, the QIPs play a determinant role in depolarization in those municipalities where they have influence. (Ortega et al. 1993)

UNDP/PRODERE.   Regarding strengthening civil society, UNDP's customary approach was similar to UNHCR's approach in its emphasis on neutrality and reconciliation and in its focus on communities in ex-conflict areas. Local and regional development-related institutions were created in which historically polarized groups would negotiate and cooperate, discuss issues of common interest, and establish the practice of toleration and reconciliation. However, beyond these similarities with UNHCR, there were fundamental differences in the UNDP/PRODERE approach to reintegration assistance. Although UNHCR promoted a greater role and funding for community participation and for NGOs, this increased role was "not accompanied by a proportionate amount of training and institution building" (UNHCR 1994a). On the other hand, the entire basis of UNDP's traditional program is to strengthen the institutional base of community participation, to build local capacities for development, and to deliberately enlarge civil society.

PRODERE operated as a pilot program, focusing on two or three territorial sites in each country, areas that were greatly affected by conflict or displacement and had concentrations of uprooted groups; it did not focus directly on the groups themselves. The strategy focused on local communities and households with a concern for the social integration of uprooted populations with their communities. An evaluation of PRODERE found that

> the origins of the Central American conflicts can be found in the lack of participation and weak democratic institutions. PRODERE proved sensitive to this issue, and was especially responsive to civil society's quest for a protagonist's role. Among its achievements, the organization of civil society and its involvement in decision-making processes, through, for instance, the legalization of organizations previously lacking legal status, is worth mentioning. Moreover, in the areas where PRODERE operates, many preexisting organizations and initiatives were given legitimacy thanks to its activity and presence. (Arias et al. 1995)

UNDP's global strategy emphasizes sustainable human development, grassroots participation, and human rights. UNDP "assumed that effectively reinserting uprooted populations into national economic and social life required creating conditions conducive to sustainable development" (Sollis and Schultz 1995). Sustainability requires the revitalization or even the creation of local institutions to build capacity for community-based project implementation and participation. PRODERE served as a facilitator for the creation of local development mechanisms, training, technical assistance, and credit. This concern with capacity and institution building ensures an impact even after the economic program ends.

Regarding civil society, PRODERE was the first development program to include the issue of human rights as one of its components. This was in societies where "the expression 'human rights' had for decades had a subversive connotation, especially where the armed forces' repressive action was guided by the national security doctrine" (Arias et al. 1995). The UNDP projects and presence "broke the warring forces' institutional monopoly" (Arias et al. 1995) and trained human rights promoters, financed monitors, conducted workshops and distributed literature on international human rights, and worked to strengthen independent judiciary and to repair the social fabric of society. The aid was to provide a functional framework for mediation and democratic participation.

In the territorial areas, PRODERE sought to decentralize government programs and to develop working relations between the government, communities, and NGOs. PRODERE operated a flexible, demand-sensitive program through decentralized operations in the intervention area. "With 800 local committees in place, PRODERE's project interventions were later able to address priorities identified by participatory decision-making approaches involving beneficiary communities" (Sollis and Schultz 1995).

In the end, returnees reintegrate at the local level and local authorities play a major role in the success of a repatriation program. Through their control of local institutions, taxes, and spending, local authorities are influential in the allocation of resources, funding of recurrent costs, and a myriad of other important decisions. The community-based reintegration assistance approach of both UNHCR and UNDP brings resources and rewards to local authorities to encourage their interest and participation in reintegration. Greater use of local structures to formulate and deliver assistance can also help lessen the returnees' dependence on international aid.

In countries where international assistance is attempting to "rebuild civic institutions," the need to focus and rely on the local level and local authorities has important consequences for the design of reintegration assistance. Even in the best of times, local authorities have few resources and relatively little power. Reintegration projects that are integrated, coordinated, multiphased, staged, multidimensional, long-term, multisectoral, technically sophisticated, multicomponent, linked, etc., are likely to be beyond the ability, will, and resources of local authorities to support and implement. Reintegration assistance projects should be kept simple.

The CIREFCA process and PRODERE supported the Central American peace process by working and improving conditions in the outlying rural areas where conflict was centered. Although both programs had strong economic components, in the end the political component was more successful than the economic. This is not disturbing, however, because from the beginning of PRODERE and CIREFCA, the political impact of their economic activities has been a major concern. "It is clear that the political environment of the uprooted populations has improved dramatically and their situation and importance is better understood and appreciated by all" (Castillo and Fahlen 1995).

Lessons Learned

The continuing problems of Guatemala caution that even a regional peace process with political will and massive international assistance has limits in its impact on certain politicized societies. Further, the continuing economic problems and the nonreturn of millions of refugees indicate that the Central American peace process, which has accomplished a great deal, is a long way from completion. However, there are also some important lessons in Central America about the ability of international aid to improve political conditions for returnees. And I believe these lessons can apply even in cases that lack a regional peace process with significant international assistance.

Increasing Political Space and Expanding Civil Society

There are two main lessons and two additional cautions that emerge from this examination of reintegration in Central America. The lessons are that international assistance, which was primarily sought and defined in economic terms, had mostly a positive political impact by increasing political space and expanding civil society. Further, these beneficial impacts were not the primary goal of international assistance, but instead resulted from implementation practices of consensus building and impartiality that encouraged reconciliation. The cautions relate to the continued inability of international agencies to collaborate and to coordinate their efforts, and the difficulties of making a transition from integration assistance to sustainable development.

Even more problematic than physical and socioeconomic reintegration is the political and civic reintegration of returning refugees. Many refugees fled their homelands because they were viewed and targeted as a subversive force by the security authorities. Reintegration of returnees into political life and civic participation has to deal with the root causes of flight and a fundamental change in the political and security orientation of the society. Economic assistance and repatriation packages can restore household and community functioning, but political improvements are needed to restore the bond of trust and loyalty between citizen and state.

In Central America, UNHCR and UNDP separately used their resources and economic assistance programs to open up greater political and humanitarian space in the recipient countries and to create, restore, and support the institutions of civil society. Refugee problems are rooted in politics and violence, and those programs that support talk and negotiation, that bring historically opposed forces together for common goals, that fairly and impartially deal with all segments of society, and that foster consensus rather than conflict will promote lasting reintegration by restoring the bond of trust and loyalty between citizen and state.

The reintegration programs had much greater success in assisting and protecting the clearly defined population of returned refugees—who had legal status and international protection in exile—than in dealing with the needs of the internally displaced. Although aiding the internally displaced was a central CIREFCA objective, the displaced populations remained an enigma that confounded the international and NGO assistance community, which had scant information on their whereabouts or needs and no institutions specifically mandated to assist them. And the far larger numbers of refugees who were not officially recognized and protected were largely ignored by the programs.

"CIREFCA excelled as a forum for dialogue in a war-torn region, and will be remembered most for its political contribution in bringing opposing parties together" (UNHCR 1994a, 3). International involvement led to depolarization of issues and groups. National authorities had viewed many uprooted peoples as subversive, and this suspicion extended to groups and agencies that worked with them. PRODERE and CIREFCA worked with officials from the local to the national level and with military leaders to greatly increase their awareness of their responsibilities toward their citizens who were uprooted and to fortify their legal rights and status. The programs greatly widened the internal political processes by committing governments to consultation and consensus building with a wider range of actors than normal, particularly at the local level.

Some of the most important reintegration assistance had only the most tenuous connection with refugees, repatriation, and reintegration. Programs that reform the political and security landscape of a homeland in transition from war to peace and that promote reconciliation, human rights, sustainable development, peace processes, and democratic change will ultimately have a greater impact on reintegration than economic assistance. However, well-designed refugee reintegration programs and traditional reintegration packages can provide supplementary support to these broader political processes.

International Cooperation and Collaboration

Interagency collaboration within the UN system tends to be weak. The CIREFCA process and the PRODERE program were viewed as significant opportunities for UN agencies to cooperate and develop integrated approaches to human problems, stretching from humanitarian relief to development. Prior to the CIREFCA conference in 1989, the General Assembly requested close cooperation between UNHCR and UNDP. For the most part effective collaboration on assistance activities did not occur, especially in the early years of the programs. PRODERE was UNDP's program and CIREFCA was UNHCR's program.

Recent reviews of CIREFCA (Castillo and Fahlen 1995; UNHCR 1994a) and PRODERE (Sollis and Schultz 1995) indicate that UNHCR and UNDP started out with sour relations, personality clashes, institutional turf battles, serious misgivings, wrong assumptions, and a lack of experience and familiarity between the two agencies. PRODERE formulated its country projects in barely over a month, allowing little opportunity for other agencies to participate in the process. UNHCR perceived that UNDP was interfering in its mandatory field of competence (the sensitive and conflictive area of UNHCR-government relations regarding refugee protection), while UNDP perceived this as a matter of economic reintegration into national economies. However, Castillo and Fahlen indicate some hope for future collaboration:

> One of the problems of inter-agency cooperation during CIREFCA was that both agencies had preconceived ideas of what the other should do without making the effort to fully understand the scope and limitations of each other's mandates and resources. ... It was only when UNHCR and UNDP eventually appreciated that their different operational and institutional cultures did not necessarily go against cooperation that the two agencies started to identify and develop mutually supportive activities.

Nonetheless, the overall experience of interagency collaboration in Central America is disturbing. Despite a convergence of goals and interests concerning refugees, displaced persons, returnees and uprooted groups, human rights, and other issues, cooperation, collaboration and coordination were not achieved. The reviews of the five-year joint efforts of the CIREFCA process and PRODERE emphasize lessons of what to avoid in the future rather than examples on which future cooperation can be built.

The lost opportunities of coordination and complementarity are not trivial. UNHCR and UNDP were part of a larger UN system involvement, and therefore a larger coordination problem, in Central America. There was "little coordination of activities among all the national and international actors working in protection and assistance activities" (UNHCR 1994a). Operating separately, these institutions can create only limited and transitory humanitarian spaces and support for human rights. "When agencies fail to collaborate, human rights space can only be circumscribed. Institutional actors, working jointly to confront formidable obstacles, can mount multifaceted action supporting peace process and the protection and promotion of human rights" (Sollis and Schultz 1995, 15). Instead, by sticking to their mandates and operational cultures, the agencies lost many opportunities to learn from one another, to identify and bridge gaps in assistance, to consolidate one another's gains, to build on the other's respective networks and relationships, and to utilize the comparative advantages of each institution.

Ties to Sustainable Development

The homelands to which the refugees are returning often have disrupted development processes. The same forces, conflicts, and political disputes that produced refugees have chased away investors, destroyed infrastructure, led to the imposition of foreign sanctions, and otherwise retarded the country's development.

Refugee return often occurs during conflict, very early in the process of reconciliation and peacemaking and before any resumption of development is possible. Attempting to tie returnee aid to national development is a laudable goal but is most likely to be an unrealistic goal, at least at first. At the time of refugee return the most pressing needs are for rehabilitation and reconstruction. Development is a very distant goal.

Although the CIREFCA process and PRODERE explicitly linked the solutions for uprooted populations to economic and social development in the region, it must be emphasized that this linkage was additional and peripheral to the national development plans in each country. The fact that returnees or uprooted populations are present in an area does not change it from a marginal region into a development dynamo, especially if the national government views the population as sympathetic to its opposition, or even worse, as guerrilla supporters. Additional external funding can reduce the neglect of these peripheral regions for the duration of the international assistance program; it is unlikely to change the fundamental political realities of political and economic marginality for these zones and people.

Linking reintegration assistance to development is not a trouble-free, win-win proposition. The creative use of reintegration assistance to support development objectives—for example, QIPS—is not without financial and administrative costs and problems. Development-oriented programs and projects need to be planned, designed, and managed; investments in one activity necessarily involve trade-offs and opportunity costs regarding other possible investments; implementation of development connections may overload systems and delay other programs; and adding a reintegration component to a development activity can greatly increase its cost and lower its productivity.

UNHCR hoped through the CIREFCA process and the QIPs to provide a connection between short-term reintegration assistance and longer-term development programs. "CIREFCA's greatest challenge…is to…ensure the sustainability of actions carried out to date and their incorporation into broad-based development programmes" (CIREFCA, 1993). However, because the QIPs tended to be discrete with no linkage or follow-up to a larger program, progress was limited to the specific activity with little long-term impact. In particular, the anticipated linkage to UNDP did not take place, as differences in mandate, working methods and relationship to government made it difficult for UNHCR and UNDP to collaborate in operational activities. The overall program lacked a comprehensive strategy and the many small projects had limited sustainability. Nonetheless, even without a development connection, the economic programs eased the initial difficulties of reintegration and had a longer-term beneficial impact by increasing political space and the reconciliation of civil society.

UNHCR's view of the transition from relief to development is focused on the idea of a "handover" of responsibilities from a relief agency to a development agency at some midpoint in the process. In this view, UNHCR's relief activities are carried through to a point where they can be "phased out" and responsibility "turned over" to another agency, such as UNDP, which is assumed to be willing and able to carry out development assistance. The QIPs developed by UNHCR in Nicaragua are emblematic of this approach; they are small and quick community-based reintegration and rehabilitation projects with limited sustainability but an assumed linkage to development.

Conclusion

Despite being a special case, Central America also has some potential to be a model for reintegration programs elsewhere. The international assistance efforts centered on CIREFCA and PRODERE have been concerned with local needs that go beyond those of the returnees; have attempted to connect relief and rehabilitation assistance with broader, sustainable development processes; and have tried to produce an integrated response by the major international agencies such as UNHCR and UNDP.

Most important, reintegration in Central America indicates the importance of implementing assistance programs in ways that consciously and deliberately enlarge political and humanitarian space and foster civil society.

Notes

1. In examining these refugee exoduses, it is important to note the distinction between officially registered refugees and unofficial refugees—often considered illegal aliens or undocumented migrants—because the distinction has a major impact on one's perception of the scale of the problem and the degree of its resolution. The countries of asylum determine whom to officially recognize as a refugee: 47,917 refugees were from Nicaragua; 28,059 were from El Salvador; and, 43,585 were from Guatemala.

2. CIREFCA refers to both an international conference held in Guatemala City in 1989 and to the five-year follow-up process to implement the Concerted Plan of Action adopted at the meeting. In the remainder of this chapter, CIREFCA will refer to the process or program of assistance.

3. The CIREFCA process, including PRODERE, raised $438 million from 1989 through 1994. The relative scale of these programs can be seen by the fact that UNDP's indicative planning figure for 1987 to 1991 for the six countries was only $47.4 million, and the $150 million PRODERE project was "the largest and most complex single operation" ever undertaken by UNDP (UNDP 1993).

4. Nicaragua's external debt is more than six times its gross domestic product "and higher per capita than anywhere else in the world" (United Nations 1995).

5. Harrell-Bond (1986, 7) offers a "very simple definition of integration," as being a situation in which "host and refugee communities are able to co-exist, sharing the same resources—both economic and social—with no greater mutual conflict than that which exists within the host community." Although this definition "will not stand up to detailed analysis" (Harrell-Bond 1986), it does remind us that reintegration involves several communities—which may be hostile to or suspicious of one another. And they will be sharing and competing for the same resources, which are likely to be very scarce.

6. Other differences in mandate and approach between UNHCR and UNDP can be summarized as follows:

• UNHCR deals directly with the target population, and with protection, political, and humanitarian problems. UNDP focuses on macrolevel development, looking at the needs of a given geographic area.

• UNDP tends to operate through governments by supporting their development aspirations. UNHCR cooperates with governments where possible, but it sometimes finds itself at odds with governments. UNDP has long-standing development assistance relations with the concerned governments, while UNHCR's relationships begin because of the conflicts.

• UNHCR often designates nongovernmental organizations (NGOs) as its implementing partners rather than serve, itself, as an executing agency. UNDP can act as an executing agency and/or work through government agencies, but it does not have an extensive history of working with NGOs.

7. The initial grant of $115 million came from Italy. Additional financing from the United Nations and the Central American governments increased the total budget to over $150 million by the end of 1994.

8. As a dynamic and multifaceted *process,* CIREFCA is particularly difficult to define. A questionnaire sent to "selected persons who had had a direct working relationship with CIREFCA" (Castillo and Fahlen 1995) elicited diverse responses to the query "What was CIREFCA?" including: fund-raiser; forum for dialogue; forum for negotiation; durable solutions program; peripheral program; and promoter of change in the region.

9. "European donor countries provided almost 90% of the total funds for CIREFCA" (Castillo and Fahlen 1995).

10. Zolberg, Suhrke, and Aguayo (1989) define refugees as having a "well-founded fear of violence." They indicate "flight-inducing violence may also be an incidental consequence of external or internal conflict…and affect groups that are not even parties to that conflict. Violence may also be inflicted indirectly, through imposed conditions that make normal life impossible."

References

Allen, Tim, and Hubert Morsink, 1994. "Introduction: When Refugees Go Home." In *When Refugees Go Home: African Experiences,* edited by Allen and Morsink, pp. 1–13. Geneva: UNRISD.

Arias Foundation for Peace and Human Development; Refugee Policy Group; Friedrich Ebert Foundation; and International Centre for Economic Development. 1995. "External Evaluation Report: Development Programme for Displaced Persons, Refugees and Returnees in Central America (PRODERE)." United Nations Development Programme, United Nations Office for Project Services.

Castillo, Gonzalo Pérez del, and Marika Fahlen. 1995. "CIREFCA: An Opportunity and Challenge for Inter-Agency Cooperation." Joint UNDP/UNHCR Review. Geneva: Internal document.

CIREFCA (International Conference on Central American Refugees). 1989. "Declaration and Concerted Plan of Action in Favour of Central American Refugees, Returnees and Displaced Persons." Guatemala City: CIREFCA/89/14.

CIREFCA. 1993. "Third Status Report on Implementation of the Concerted Plan of Action of the International Conference on Central American

Refugees (CIREFCA)." CIREFCA Joint Support Unit. San José, Costa Rica: CIREFCA.

Crosby, Benjamin L. 1990. "Central America." In *After the Wars: Reconstruction in Afghanistan, Indochina, Central America, Southern Africa, and the Horn of Africa,* edited by Anthony Lake. New Brunswick, N. J.: Transaction Publications.

Fagen, Patricia Weiss, and Joseph T. Eldridge. 1991. "Salvadoran Repatriation from Honduras." In *Repatriation Under Conflict in Central America,* edited by Mary Ann Larkin, Frederick C. Cuny, and Barry Stein, pp. 117–186. Washington, D.C.: Georgetown University.

GAO (General Accounting Office). 1989. "Central America: Conditions of Refugees and Displaced Persons." National Security and International Affairs Division. Washington, D.C.: GAO/NSIAD-89-54.

GAO (General Accounting Office). 1992. "Aid to Nicaragua: U.S. Assistance Supports Economic and Social Development." National Security and International Affairs Division. Washington, D.C.: GAO/NSIAD-92-203.

Harrell-Bond, B. E. 1986. *Imposing Aid: Emergency Assistance to Refugees.* Oxford: Oxford University Press.

Larkin, Mary Ann. 1991. "Conference Report: Repatriation Under Conflict: The Central American Case," Washington, D.C.: Center for Immigration Policy and Refugee Assistance, Georgetown University.

Ortega, Marvin, Ricardo E. Chavarria, Sergio Santamaria, and Celia Aguilar. 1993. *Evaluation of Quick Impact Projects (QIPs).* Final Report to UNHCR Mission Office. Managua: Center of Socio-Economic Research and Consulting (CINASE), Institute of Human Promotion (INPRHU), Itztani Research Institute.

Redmond, Ron. 1995. "The Human Side of CIREFCA," *Refugees* 99(1).

Sollis, Peter, and Christina M. Schultz. 1995. "Lessons of the PRODERE Experience in Central America." Washington, D.C.: Refugee Policy Group.

UNDP (United Nations Development Program). 1993. "1992 UNDP Annual Report: Human Development at Work," UNDP Division of Public Affairs.

UNHCR (UN High Commissioner for Refugees). 1993. "Information Note on PARINAC (UNHCR/NGO Partnership in Action)." Executive Committee of the High Commissioner's Programme, 44th Session. A/AC.96/INF.177, September 23.

UNHCR. 1994a. "Review of the CIREFCA Process." EVAL/CIREF/14.

UNHCR. 1994b. "Policy and Methodological Framework for Quick Impact Projects (QIPs) as a Means of Facilitating Durable Solutions Through Integration." Working draft.

United Nations. 1995. "International Assistance for the Rehabilitation and Reconstruction of Nicaragua: Aftermath of the War and Natural Disasters." Report of the Secretary-General. General Assembly, 50th Session. A/50/535, October 10.

Zinser, Adolfo Aguilar. 1991. "Refugee Repatriation in Central America: Lessons from Three Case Studies." In *Repatriation Under Conflict in Central America,* edited by Mary Ann Larkin, Frederick C. Cuny, and Barry Stein, pp. 187–212. Washington, D.C.: Georgetown University.

Zolberg, Aristide R., Astri Suhrke, and Sergio Aguayo. 1989. *Escape from Violence: Conflict and the Refugee Crisis in the Developing World.* New York: Oxford University Press.

Part 2

Assistance for Social and Cultural Rehabilitation

The three chapters in this section focus on rebuilding the health sector, promoting psychosocial healing at the community level, and assisting traumatized children.

Joanna Macrae, in Chapter 8, raises three critical questions about the rehabilitation of the health sector. First, she questions who should be responsible for determining the allocation of large sums of international assistance and through which types of organizations these funds should be channeled, in the absence of a legitimate government or national mechanism for decisionmaking. Second, Macrae raises the question of how to move beyond the focus on delivery of critical services and building institutional infrastructure to the underlying crisis of long-term financing and management. Third, she examines the dilemma of ensuring the coherence of the international community's efforts in rehabilitation policy and planning during the transitional period from relief to longer-term development. By focusing on Cambodia, Ethiopia, and Uganda, the author provides health planners with guidelines for future strategies.

Kimberly Maynard, in Chapter 9, discusses the psychosocial injury to individuals and communities in intrastate conflicts and the need for international interventions, beyond the largely economic and physical, to promote healing and reconciliation at the community level. She notes that while the traditional coping mechanisms for dealing with trauma are undermined, the local communities are overwhelmed by fear and distrust between groups. Maynard proposes a five-phase approach to psychosocial recovery at the community level: establishing safety; instituting a process of communalization and bereavement; rebuilding trust and the capacity to trust; reestablishing personal and social morality; and reintegrating and restoring democratic discourse. She examines current international efforts with respect to these five phases and suggests specific steps to enhance prospects for comprehensive rehabilitation of postwar communities.

Sara Gibbs, in Chapter 10, cautions against the conventional Western paradigms for dealing with traumatized children. Drawing from her ethnographic research in Mozambique, she argues that childhood and trauma are perceived differently in different cultures. For instance, in Mozambique, children do not perceive themselves, nor are they perceived, as passive, vulnerable, or unable to work. Further, people consider many reconstruction activities—such as building homes and planting fields—as integral to the healing process for individuals and communities. Gibbs also discusses the role of churches and traditional healers in promoting reconciliation and forgiveness through acknowledging and celebrating people's return and through confessions. Thus, Gibbs suggests that an understanding of the wider cultural milieu is needed to design and implement programs for traumatized children and adults in non-Western societies.

8

Dilemmas of Legitimacy, Sustainability, and Coherence: Rehabilitating the Health Sector

Joanna Macrae

This chapter raises three dilemmas related to international assistance for rehabilitating the health sector in postconflict situations. (The achievement of peace is typically a relative and incremental process; the main focus of a particular conflict may be over but violence may persist intermittently or continuously, nationally or within particular geographical areas. I use the term *postconflict* to indicate this.) The first dilemma is of legitimacy: Who should set priorities for determining the allocation of international resources during the transitional period when the legitimacy of the government is questionable? The second dilemma concerns the framework for and direction of rehabilitation. Should rehabilitation efforts seek to recreate or reform preconflict institutions and systems, including health services? The third dilemma pertains to the mandates and agendas of international aid agencies. The chapter explores the impact of conflict on health care systems and examines the subsequent dilemmas related to rehabilitation, focusing in particular on experiences in Cambodia, Ethiopia, and Uganda. It concludes that resolving the dilemmas of rehabilitation implies a fundamental change in the objectives and strategies of aid in postconflict situations.

Impact of Conflict on Health Systems

Violence exerts direct and indirect effects on health status and health systems (Zwi and Ugalde 1989). Direct effects are those related to military action and include death and injury and destruction of the health infrastructure and equipment. However, more significant in terms of aggregate mortality and morbidity are the indirect effects of the social, political and economic changes that both underlie conflict and are pre-

cipitated by it. At the same time, the capacity of health systems to respond to increased health needs is critically reduced by the erosion of
national capacity for health financing and provision. There is therefore a
need to expand capacity for health service delivery. This expansion often
takes two forms in postconflict situations. First is the need to rehabilitate
damaged infrastructure and/or to incorporate health units that have
been out of government control in rebel-held areas. Second, there is
likely to be a need to expand health systems to include previously underserved populations as part of the process of peace building.

The following examples highlight a few of the main challenges confronting health systems.

Impact on the Human Resource Base

Informants in Soroti, a northern district of Uganda affected by conflict
between 1986 and 1992, described the impact of conflict on the human
resource base as follows:

> "[There were] different factors which affected the human resource base
> for health: some health workers who were not from Soroti, particularly
> Bantu health workers [from the south] fled because they were targeted
> by the rebels. Most of these fled the district. ... They were often the most
> highly trained staff and prior to the war had made up 50% of the estab-
> lished staff. Others feared that they would be forced to treat rebels if
> they remained in the rural areas. If they had been caught they would
> have been punished by the NRA (the government army). In Soroti hos-
> pital, we currently have one doctor for a 250 bed hospital and even he is
> disabled by a war injury." (Quoted in Macrae, Zwi, and Birungi 1993)

This extract demonstrates how a combination of ethnic division, fear
of reprisals, and injury affect the distribution and availability of human
resources in conflict-affected communities. Particularly important are
the transfer of resources from rural to urban areas and the fact that it is
the most senior and skilled health professionals who are likely to leave
first. Many interviewed in Soroti in 1993, when the conflict was substantially over, thought that the problem was likely to intensify rather than
diminish in the future; the disruption to the education system, combined
with high levels of poverty in the immediate postconflict period has
meant that relatively fewer people are leaving secondary school in the
area and entering university.

Impact on Policy and Management

The effects of the brain drain, fear, and a breakdown in the financing of
health systems have a major effect on national capacity for policymak-

ing, planning, and management in conflict-affected countries. In Uganda, in addition to the loss of key human resources, the environment of oppression and political chaos also meant that "for years [health] policy was established by decree. ... No one knew what the health policy really was. ... Over the years it had become an ad hoc collection of declarations rather than an integrated legal framework for government action" (interview with a senior health professional, reported in Macrae, Zwi, and Birungi 1993). Being isolated during the 1970s and early 1980s, Uganda was denied opportunities to participate in international health debates, particularly those relating to primary health care. The combination of these effects of conflict on policy and management meant that when relative peace returned to most parts of the country in 1986, national capacity for policy development to guide the rehabilitation process was extremely limited.

Impact on Health Financing

Measuring the economic impact of conflict is complex, not least because it is often difficult to distinguish between economic stress as a factor promoting vulnerability to violence and economic stress caused by violence; they are clearly mutually reinforcing. The most important features to note regarding the economics and financing of health care in conflict-affected societies are the reduction in the public budgets available for health, the privatization of finance and provision, and the changing modalities of international support for health financing.

The availability of public finance for health care typically declines substantially in conflict-affected societies. Stewart (1994) notes that there are substantial variations in the economic policies and performance of war-affected countries and in their capacity to raise public revenue and so sustain public services. Once again, these variations appear to be linked with the type of conflict and in particular the capacity of governments to regulate the economy. Interestingly, Stewart suggests that tax capacity and government choices of expenditure are more important in determining the availability of finance for the public sector than the effects of militarization (Stewart 1993, 369). In both Uganda and Cambodia, the capacity of the central government to raise taxes was significantly interrupted by conflict. In Uganda, for example, revenue from taxation in 1986 accounted for only 6 percent of GDP in contrast with the regional average of over 20 percent (Lateef 1990).

As public capacity for health financing diminished in Uganda, private provision increased. Whyte (1990) points out that self-management—the most extreme form of privatization—was often the only option available to people. At the same time, the role of traditional healers increased. In both Uganda and Cambodia, health workers previously working in the public health system resorted to private practice to maintain their incomes as government salaries deteriorated below subsistence levels.[1] In Ethiopia, however, despite incremental declines in the overall health budget during the 1980s, health worker salaries were fixed above subsistence rates and were paid regularly, enabling health workers to remain in place and within the public health system.[2]

A final aspect of privatization is the changing role of international nongovernmental organizations (NGOs) in providing health services in conflict-affected countries. Where international donors are not prepared to engage with national authorities, NGOs become a primary means of channeling resources, particularly for health. Hanlon (1992) has documented this phenomenon in Mozambique, arguing that it has resulted in considerable distortions in the health system. The proliferation of NGOs, each working within its own micropolicy domains, bounded by project areas rather than national guidelines, can threaten the development of a coherent and efficient health system. Duffield (1991) has similarly commented on the emergence of the NGO-driven welfare safety net put in place to maintain basic services in conflict zones. The key issue that emerges in the transitional period is whether and how NGO services can be integrated within a national health system.

Rehabilitating Health Systems in Postconflict Situations

The challenges confronting the international community in rehabilitating health systems in 'post'-conflict situations are enormous. Developing health systems that simultaneously respond to the health needs of conflict-affected populations and are also financially viable implies confronting three major dilemmas. These can be summarized as the dilemmas of legitimacy, sustainability, and coherence.

The Dilemma of the Legitimacy of Transitional Government

Historically, the principal partner for development assistance from multilateral and bilateral sources has been the government of the recipient country. While the 1980s saw considerable shifts in debates concerning the role of the state in financing and delivering social services, access to international development finance continues to rely largely on the presence of an internationally recognized government. By contrast, access to emergency relief is not subject to the same conditions. Humanitarian aid is increasingly delivered outside formal government structures and may be delivered without a government's formal approval (Borton 1994).

The transformation from relief to development assistance implies therefore international recognition of a new regime and its being accorded legitimacy. If rehabilitation is seen primarily as a developmental activity, rather than as a relief intervention, the presence and recognition of a legitimate national government will be a necessary condition for international finance. Alternatively, rehabilitation may be conceived as an activity that lies between relief and development and that does not confer legitimacy on either the government or other recipient partners.

The legitimacy dilemma has two distinct, but related, implications for health planning: First, what type of decisionmaking body should be responsible for determining the allocation of national and international health resources in the transitional period? Second, through which institutions should resources, particularly aid resources, be channeled? These questions are particularly urgent in transitional situations, because large sums of assistance relative to the scale of government finance are released quite suddenly into resource-poor environments where a national policy framework to guide resource allocation for health is absent.

In Ethiopia, for example, where the new political regime was recognized very quickly by the international community and where bureaucratic structures remained relatively intact throughout the war, the donor community was willing to channel the majority of its resources for rehabilitation interventions through government channels. Through the mechanism of the World Bank–led Emergency Recovery and Rehabilitation Program, essential drugs valued at approximately $40 million were channeled through the Ministry of Health to facilities throughout the country. This program, rapidly designed and implemented, came at a time when the country's supply of drugs had been reduced to a critical level because of a shortage of foreign currency and interruption of local production. By providing drugs, health facilities could return quickly to providing basic services, encouraging health staff to stay, and restoring levels of utilization. Critical to the success of the program were the availability of relatively large levels of finance at short notice, the umbrella for donor coordination provided by the World Bank, and adequate capacity within the public administration at central and local levels for the design and implementation of the program.

188

The Legitimacy Dilemma: Issues for Future Strategy

Defining objectives of rehabilitation: There is a paradox in that in many transitional situations there is a perceived need to promote the development of strong state institutions in order to promote stability; at the same time, because many rehabilitation interventions are implemented outside state structures, the rehabilitation process often does not serve to strengthen these institutions in the longer term. While the desirability of strong states may be debatable, they are needed to reestablish long-term development activities and implement economic and sectoral reform programs.

To increase capacity for planning and management in the health sector in the transitional period and the long term, it will be important to work with national civil servants, health professionals, and community representatives to increase the skills base in the country and community to develop consensus on directions for health policy for the future. International aid agencies, including NGOs, can serve an important function in facilitating such a dialogue, which can contribute to wider aims of political reconciliation.

Finding a constitution for decisionmaking: Ensuring effective coordination of health sector rehabilitation implies establishing basic principles for different actors to follow and designing a mechanism to enforce these principles. Where a recognized government is in place, providing support to the responsible central and local government ministries to define and monitor adherence to such guidelines is crucial. Where no central government is in place, donor and major multilateral agencies can exert considerable leverage in defining basic health planning rules (some of which are identified in more detail below). Identifying a neutral party, which can act as a mediator between governmental, multilateral, and nongovernmental agencies, such as the World Health Organization, can be effective. Both these strategies imply expanding investment in management and coordination functions; this should not be seen as diverting funds from operational activities, but as a precondition for increasing their effectiveness.

Conditionalities and leverage: In both Uganda and Ethiopia, very few conditions for rehabilitation assistance were made. There is considerable scope to explore the potential use of conditionali-

—continues

ties in transitional situations to promote accountability and define basic reform measures—for example, reallocating military budgets to match international contributions to the health care sector and developing strategies for decentralization and health financing. Such tools could be used to promote accountability of transitional regimes and to set the framework for future partnership with the international aid community.

The Ethiopian experience of rehabilitation provides an increasingly rare example of a transitional regime that had both the authority and competence to steer the process of recovery. It stands in sharp contrast to the experience of a number of other countries where national mechanisms for decisionmaking have been either absent or regarded as illegitimate or incompetent. In these contexts, a number of strategies have been developed to accommodate the conditions of transition.

Absent national mechanisms for decisionmaking. In Cambodia, for example, the Paris Accords, which laid the legal framework for the transition, provided for the creation of the Supreme National Council, comprising representatives of all the major factions in the country. Under the peace agreement, it was determined that the authority for ensuring implementation of the accords and for initiating rehabilitation would be delegated to the United Nations Transitional Authority in Cambodia (UNTAC) This responsibility would cease when a constituent assembly had been elected.

Echoing the principles of the Paris Accords, the World Bank stressed the importance of starting from the premise that public services are delivered by public administrations, not by NGOs or international agencies. It also cautioned against the creation of parallel but similar programs for different population groups such as returnees, internally displaced populations, and demobilized soldiers (World Bank 1994a; CCC 1992). At a ministerial conference in Tokyo in June 1992, pledges of more than $800 million were made by donor countries and international aid agencies, an amount far in excess of the appeal made by the UN Secretary-General (Curtis 1994).

Despite the warnings of the World Bank, aid flows to the health sector during the transitional period largely bypassed central government. Bilateral and multilateral donors both sought to support public health facilities at the local level, often by disbursing funds through NGOs (World Bank 1994a). The transitional period saw a rapid expansion of the role of NGOs in health provision. In 1988, it was estimated that twenty-seven NGOs provided approximately $10 million per year in relief and development assistance, a high proportion of which went to the health sector. A recent survey indicated that in 1992 US$28 million was channeled to the health sector through NGOs (CCC 1992).

This expansion in NGO assistance reflects the increased availability of international finance for Cambodia and the reluctance of bilateral donors—and to a lesser extent multilateral organizations—to engage directly with the government until or after the elections in mid-1993 (CCC 1992). This pattern of donor assistance mirrors the experience of Uganda and Somaliland, where rehabilitation interventions largely consist of NGO-led interventions at the microlevel. While enabling an expansion of service provision, these NGO interventions were not implemented within a coherent national policy framework, increasing the risk of fragmented organization and financing of health services (Macrae, Zwi, and Birungi 1993)[3]; Forsythe, personal communication).

In Cambodia, an attempt was made to develop such a framework. In 1991, the Coordinating Committee for Health (CoCom) was established, which drew on high-level representation from the Ministry of Health and from international and nongovernmental agencies (CCC 1992). The World Health Organization provided support for the CoCom secretariat (WHO 1994). The development of this mechanism for coordinating health policy in Cambodia in the transitional period could be of significant international interest. CoCom represents one of the few attempts to work with existing health authorities to provide a coherent management framework for health services rehabilitation to guide international aid interventions.

Its capacity to influence internationally financed health programs, however, was constrained by a number of factors. Biberson and Goemare (1993) argue that because CoCom was chaired by the vice-minister for health, a member of the Vietnamese-backed government, UNTAC was reluctant to work with it. UNTAC strictly interpreted its mandate to work equally with the different factions, causing it to avoid being seen to legitimize the capacity of one authority, in this case the Ministry of Health, to develop policy (Utting 1994). It might also be argued that international agencies, particularly NGOs empowered with relatively substantial resources and encouraged by the example of UNTAC, could safely ignore policy prescriptions and guidelines developed by CoCom (World Bank 1994a; Macrae and Zwi 1994).

The experience of Cambodia is echoed in Palestine, where a different strategy has emerged. The Palestinian Economic Council for Economic Reconstruction (PECDAR) was established in October 1993 by the Palestinian National Authority, with support from the World Bank, as a semiautonomous organization with central responsibility for managing international aid for reconstruction and development. A major motivating factor behind the creation of PECDAR was the desire to separate the technical elements of policy development and political decisionmaking (Forsythe and Zwi 1994). Such a division has not been sustainable in practice and the increasing politicization of PECDAR has undermined donor confidence, slowing the pace of funds disbursement. Under these conditions, NGOs—seen as politically neutral and bureaucratically efficient—become an attractive mechanism to increase implementation rates. However, in the politically complex environment of Palestine, where different groups aim to maximize their political credibility, NGOs can become an instrument for political groups to raise resources and generate popular support. In this environment, assumptions about the neutrality of NGOs require careful scrutiny.

Sustainability of Rehabilitation: Which Way Forward?

Perhaps unsurprisingly, in most countries the major focus on rehabilitation initiatives in the immediate postconflict period has been on rebuilding the physical infrastructure. In addition to providing the material base for the future development of the health system, restoration of buildings is also often seen to have important symbolic and psychological value, providing a sense of a return to normality.

However, the experience of a number of countries suggests that heavy investment in rebuilding health facilities has two major drawbacks: First, it presumes that the infrastructure in place prior to the conflict is appropriate in the postconflict era. This was clearly not the case in Uganda, where before the war there were major inequalities in the distribution and type of health services in different areas of the country. In 1986, 41 percent of the health sector rehabilitation budget was allocated to the rehabilitation of the central teaching hospital in Kampala, despite the fact that this served only a fraction of the country's population. Overall, most rehabilitation funds were spent on rehabilitating district hospitals, with comparatively little attention placed at health center level. In this case, rehabilitation was identified with restoring the preconflict health system almost in its entirety, with little emphasis on adjusting health service provision toward primary health care and increased equality of provision.

Second, there has also been a tendency for health sector rehabilitation to be characterized by highly vertical programming (Macrae, Zwi, and Burungi 1993). While vertical programs are common in many developing countries, particularly for the Expanded Program of Immunization (EPI) and the Control of Diarrheal Diseases (CDD), these of-

The Sustainability Dilemma: Issues for Future Strategy

Rehabilitation: relief or development? Conflict exacerbates underlying weaknesses in health systems. If rehabilitation is to provide the basis for long-term health services development, it must include a holistic analysis of the problems confronting the health system—one that identifies both infrastructural and structural constraints to health service delivery. Moving beyond a relief-oriented, supply-driven approach to rehabilitation implies investing in policy, planning and management systems, and human resource development. Such a strategy implies a time frame beyond the usual eighteen to twenty-four months that defines rehabilitation. In Somalia and Afghanistan, where state structures have collapsed and traditional institutions have reemerged as an important force, there is a need to think beyond state-defined models of health care. Even within this more fragmented framework for policy action, basic guidelines for resource allocation should be developed, particularly in relation to capital finance.

Planning for health financing: Rethinking rehabilitation also suggests reexamining conventional expectations of national health care systems in resource-poor environments. Assuming that impoverished and weak national governments will be able to sustain complex, resource-intensive health systems without very considerable international subsidy is likely to be unrealistic in most countries. Donors financing rehabilitation activities need to ensure a careful balance between capital and recurrent support for rehabilitation. Existing preferences for capital spending serve to promote investment in physical infrastructure often at the cost of maintaining salaries and drug supplies, which are more important in determining the functioning of the health system. If donors wish to support rapid expansion of health systems in transitional situations, such investment needs to be planned with respect to a long-term framework for health planning that forecasts the availability of both national and international resources.

Experimentation and innovation: The policy vacuum that characterizes situations of postconflict transition represents an opportunity as well as a threat. There is considerable scope during the transitional period for innovation and experimentation: for example, establishing pilot projects looking at different mechanisms for

—*continues*

health financing. The scope for operational research in these environments is considerable; the poverty of the information base is such that there is a considerable need for experimentation with different models of financing and provision. The results of these experiments can be used to inform the process of policy development once a recognized government is in place.

Salaries of public health workers: The Ethiopian experience suggests that where health staff remain in place, the capacity of health services to survive conflict and postconflict transition is enhanced. A key factor enabling staff to remain at their jobs was that they continued to be paid. While this is explained in part by the fact that key bureaucratic institutions, including payroll departments, continued to function in large parts of the country, also important is that resources were made available to pay them. As salaries were fixed above subsistence levels, the incentives to staff to work privately were reduced. In the immediate postconflict period, considerable attention should be placed on strategies to maintain salaries for public health workers.

ten dominate the health sector in countries recovering from conflict. This is in part because vertical programs form an integral part of many relief activities and are therefore easier to sustain and expand during the transitional period prior to the reestablishment of public health services. For incoming governments, vertical services, particularly EPI, are also popular because they are a visible demonstration of commitment and of the capacity to reach populations in areas they have not previously controlled. The potential problem in these contexts, as in non-conflict-affected areas, is that the promised integration of these vertical programs into horizontal service delivery is often elusive. The focus on infrastructure and the delivery of key services through vertical programs reflects a wider tendency of rehabilitation programs to focus on the material crisis affecting health systems in conflict-affected countries, rather than the deeper, underlying crises of financing and management (Duffield 1994b). It can be argued that in this sense, rehabilitation programs are nearer in concept and design to the strategies of emergency relief than to those of long-term development.

What is at issue is not whether physical rehabilitation and immunization should take place, but how they will be financed in the longer term given the impact of conflict on national and household income. There is a risk that rapid expansion of the physical infrastructure (either by rehabilitating previously nonfunctioning facilities or by building new facilities in previously underserved areas) and the establishment of vertical programs during the transitional period cannot be sustained in the longer term.

In Cambodia, for example, total health care spending by the public sector in 1993 amounted to about $7 million, less than $1 per capita (World Bank 1994a). It is estimated that in the same period, donor expenditure on health services was about $35 million. Even if it is assumed that 40 percent of this amount is allocated to expatriate salaries, external resources still represent health expenditures of $4.4 per capita, a figure that exceeds government budgets fourfold (World Bank 1994a).

Similarly, in Uganda in 1985, it was estimated that to restore health service functioning to its 1970s levels would have required an expansion in the national health budget between five and twelve times (Scheyer and Dunlop 1985). In Ethiopia, a similarly dramatic (and unlikely) increase in health budgets of 30 percent will be required to meet the recurrent costs of new and rehabilitated health facilities in the country (World Bank 1994b).

In both Cambodia and Uganda, donors are pressing national governments to enact a process of health sector reform to reduce high levels of aid dependency and the inappropriate patterns of provision that have reemerged, in part because of the process of rehabilitation (World Bank 1994a; Okounzi and Macrae 1995). Because rehabilitation programs have tended to reinforce the urban, curative bias of the preconflict era, in the longer term there is a need to reorganize the health system in order to increase the efficiency and effectiveness of health care expenditure. The scope for such a redefinition remains to be seen in countries where absolute levels of public health financing are well below the $12 per capita recommended by the World Bank (1993) to deliver a minimum package of health services. In the majority of postconflict situations, while it is clearly desirable for national public health systems to be re-created or created, it is unclear whether it is feasible. Indeed, with respect to donor policy, there are frequently contradictory tendencies in this respect, with considerable international resources devoted to restoring the public health infrastructure; at the same time, public expenditure comes under intense pressure in the context of stabilization and adjustment programs.

Improving the Coherence of Rehabilitation Policy and Planning

Ensuring the coherence of rehabilitation interventions during the transitional period is important in order to address the fragmentation of financing and provision characteristic of health systems during conflict.[4] This fragmentation is typically institutional, in the sense that many different actors—government, rebels, NGOs and multilateral organizations—are all doing different things in different places. It is also geographical in that different populations have differential access to health resources for historical, security, and political reasons. Ensuring coherent health planning is also important because the pattern of investment during the transitional period will influence the long-term prospects for health systems development.

A constraint to developing coherence and long-term vision of international rehabilitation assistance is that "when it comes to rehabilitation, no one has been sure who is responsible. Everyone is doing little bits" (interview with UN official, reported in Macrae and Zwi 1994). For example, "emergency rehabilitation" is defined as the responsibility of the Department of Humanitarian Affairs within the UN, and of the Emergency Aid Department of the British Overseas Development Administration. "Nonemergency" rehabilitation in the former falls within the remit of the UN Development Programme (UNDP), and in the latter to the geographical desks. The distinctions employed are not very clear in principle, and in practice they are reflected in the wide range of agencies engaged in "rehabilitation."

Achieving coherent planning implies the existence of a competent and legitimate coordinating body. G. Meier, writing about macroeconomic reform, has highlighted the need to identify what he calls "constitutive mechanisms" of decisionmaking in order to define and implement policy change. In other words "decisions have to be made about how decisions can be made" (Meier 1993, 387). Such a constitution needs to identify mechanisms that define both how different actors relate to a national authority, and how agencies relate to each other.

The absence of a clear mandate for rehabilitation between the specialist agencies of the UN and the different desks of donor agencies and some NGOs has meant that agencies and personnel experienced in relief are increasingly engaged in rehabilitation initiatives. For example, the involvement of the UN High Commissioner for Refugees (UNHCR) in reintegrating refugees in a number of countries has effectively extended its domain of activity beyond its traditional role of providing protection and relief for refugees and into one of community development. The rationale for this expanded involvement is grounded in an awareness that maintaining the durability of the repatriation solution is contingent on meeting the basic needs of returnees and those of receiving communities. The potential difficulty, however, is that by their very nature these interventions are designed quickly and for a short duration (twelve to eighteen months). In the case of UNHCR, the interventions are designed by an agency that

The Coherence Dilemma: Issues for Future Strategy

Special budget lines: The lack of clear budget lines reflects the awkward place rehabilitation occupies within the international aid system. The chronicity of complex political emergencies and the increasing number of transitional situations suggest that the institutional abyss currently separating relief and development assistance cannot be sustained. The creation of special budget lines for rehabilitation may form part of the solution but will not be sufficient, particularly if these special funds continue to replicate the strategies of relief (heavy reliance on NGOs and on material supply responses). Such budget lines will meet their objectives only if the speed of response is matched by simple mechanisms to assess criteria of appropriateness and sustainability at both project and country level.

Information sharing: Developing such a strategy would be facilitated by interdonor and interagency assessment of needs to share information and analyses, promote a common vision, and maximize leverage. Management of such a process could be delegated to the UN Department of Human Affairs (DHA) or the World Bank, and should be conducted over an extended period of several months rather than weeks. Sectoral needs assessment and coordination should be delegated to a specialist agency. Such an assessment procedure would require close collaboration with national political and professional actors; in the absence of consensus about resource allocation and use, successful implementation is likely to remain elusive. An overall review setting guidelines—for example, in relation to capital and recurrent financing, coordination, and cooperation with national professional and government institutions—could then be used as a basis to guide the development of sectoral strategies.

Developing expertise: Agencies and personnel who have developed expertise in relief, but who find themselves increasingly engaged in rehabilitation planning, should expand their expertise in long-term health systems development through training and cooperation with specialist agencies. Encouraging long-term development agencies to establish programs during the transition period could be encouraged by extending the time frame for rehabilitation programs.

may have experience of the returning refugee population but not of the community to which they return. In the case of the health sector, a typical quick impact project (QIP) comprises the rehabilitation of a health facility and recurrent cost support for salaries and drugs for a one-year period (UNHCR 1994). Implicit in this strategy is that another authority will take over responsibility for these activities after the first year; experience suggests that this is often problematic (van Brabant 1994).

The absence of a clear mandate for rehabilitation is mirrored in many agencies by the lack of procedures to accommodate rehabilitation funding and activities. While the objectives of rehabilitation clearly envisage a movement away from the short-term, resource-intensive programming of relief, providing assistance relatively quickly to support the transition to peace does not conform with the usually stringent and time-consuming process of development programming.

The limitations of existing procedures have resulted in a number of adjustments within donor agencies. For example, in 1992, the European Commission established 100MECU Special Rehabilitation Program for Africa, drawing on preexisting relief and development budget lines (European Commission 1993). Similarly, the new budget of $20 million (1993/94) for the Office of Transition Initiatives within the U.S. Agency for International Development (USAID) is drawn equally from relief and development lines. However, usual appraisal and administrative procedures to which development programs are subject are largely bypassed to ensure rapid project identification and implementation; both USAID and European Commission initiatives rely almost exclusively on NGOs to propose and implement projects. The strengths of these innovations is also their weakness: In the search for instruments that enable fast-disbursing support, the very procedures used to assess sustainability and efficiency are often bypassed.

In emergency situations, many bilateral and multilateral agencies cannot or do not carry out a country programming exercise to guide their strategy. The absence of mechanisms to link donors with a national policy framework, combined with the high degree of donor dependence on NGOs for project design and implementation, tends to reinforce the inclination of rehabilitation programs to adopt the highly decentralized, unintegrated approaches of relief rather than those of development. The difficulties posed by the absence of a strong national government policy framework make it all the more essential that donors and international agencies develop their own clear strategies and work to develop interagency consensus on priorities and guidelines for implementation.

Conclusion

The weaknesses of rehabilitation interventions in countries as far apart as Uganda, Cambodia, and Ethiopia can be traced back to a misunderstanding of the nature of war and to the difficulties facing the international aid system in an environment of globalization and weakening state structures.

Responding to the complex emergencies and their aftermath implies defining humanitarian crises not primarily as material supply crises, but rather as crises of economic, political, and social systems. It also requires acknowledging that neither relief nor rehabilitation nor development assistance is politically neutral; introduction of resources into these complex and resource-poor environments necessarily implies strengthening one group, potentially at the cost of others (Keen and Wilson 1994). The concern is therefore to ensure that the rehabilitation process strengthens the vulnerable rather than rewards the violent, that it enables reconciliation rather than exacerbates inequalities and increasing political tension.

It appears that the international aid system is still unable to respond to the rehabilitation challenge. The dilemmas are profound and not amenable to a quick, technical fix. Rather, even responding to the apparently simple challenge of health services rehabilitation strains developmentalist models of aid, if all developmental models remain premised on the presence of strong states with strong formal economies (Duffield 1994b). In the twilight zone of transition and rehabilitation, there is a kind of institutional paralysis. At the same time, there is often a feeling of wanting to do something, anything to make things better.

Confronting the dilemmas of rehabilitation will imply a combination of pragmatism and modesty of purpose and pace. Initiatives need to be planned in line with local resources and capacity. There is also a need for flexibility and sensitivity to the complex politics of peace building—in other words, an approach that integrates political and sectoral perspectives. This suggests a need to improve the quality of analysis of the nature of the rehabilitation task and to find ways of enabling recipient populations to define *their* priorities for a healthier peace. Cash and wishful thinking alone will not be sufficient.

Notes

Many thanks go to colleagues at the London School of Hygiene and Tropical Medicine, particularly Anthony Zwi, who supported successive studies on health sector rehabilitation. John Borton, Martin Griffiths, Kelley Lee, and

Catherine Spencer cast their critical gaze over earlier reports and papers resulting from the studies reported here, and with their usual insight enriched the chapter. Finally, thanks to Vivienne Forsythe who has proved a trusted mentor. Any weaknesses that remain are my own.

1. Whyte 1990, and personal communication of de Sweemer, human resources consultant with the World Health Organization.

2. Based on personal interviews in East Hararghe; personal communication of Christian Gunnenberg, Save the Children Fund project manager in Eastern Ethiopia.

3. Also personal communication of Forsythe, an independent research/ consultant with considerable experience with NGOs in Somalia and Uganda.

4. Biberson and Goemare (1993) refer to the "lost agenda" of health care reconstruction.

References

Biberson, P., and E. Goemare. 1993. "Health Care Reconstruction: The Lost Agenda." In *Life, Death and Aid: the Médecins Sans Frontières Report on World Crisis Intervention,* edited by F. Jean. London and New York: Routledge.

Bond, G., and J. Vincent. 1990. "Living on the Edge: Changing Social Structures in the Context of AIDS." In *Changing Uganda: The Dilemmas of Structural Adjustment and Revolutionary Change,* edited by H. Hansen and M. Twaddle. London: James Currey.

Borton, J. 1994. "NGOs and Relief Operations: Trends and Policy Implications." ESCOR Research Study R47774. London: Overseas Development Institute.

Cassels, A. 1992. "Implementing Health Sector Reform." Report prepared for the Health and Population Division. London: Overseas Development Administration.

CCC (Cooperation Committee for Cambodia). 1992. "NGOs and the Rehabilitation of Cambodia." Phnom Penh, Cambodia. Photocopy.

Curtis, G. 1994. "Transition to What: Cambodia, UNTAC and the Peace Process." In *Between Hope and Insecurity: The Social Consequences of the Cambodian Peace Process,* edited by P. Utting, pp. 41–70. Geneva: United Nations Research Institute for Social Development.

Davies, S. 1994. "Public Institutions, People and Famine Mitigation." *IDS Bulletin* 25(4):46–54.

Duffield, M. 1991. "War and Famine in Africa." Oxfam Research Paper No 5. Oxford: Oxfam Publications.

Duffield, M. 1994a, "Complex Political Emergencies: An Exploratory Report for UNICEF." Birmingham, England: University of Birmingham.

Duffield, M. 1994b. "Complex of Emergencies and the Crisis of Developmentalism." *IDS Bulletin* 25(3):37–45.

Duffield, M. 1994c. "The Political Economy of Internal War: Asset Transfer, Complex Emergencies and International Aid." In *War and Hunger: Rethinking International Responses in Complex Emergencies,* edited by J. Macrae and A. Zwi. London and Atlantic Highlands, N. J.: Zed Books.

European Commission. 1993. "Special Rehabilitation Support Program in Developing Countries." Communication from the Commission to the Council and the European Parliament, COM(93)204, final, May 12.

Forsythe, V., and A. Zwi. 1994. "Health Care in Situations of 'Post'-Conflict Transition: A Preliminary Review of the Palestinian Situation." London School of Hygiene and Tropical Medicine. Photocopy.

Hanlon, J. 1992. *Mozambique: Who Calls the Shots?* London: James Currey.

Kaplan, R. 1994. "The Coming Anarchy." *Atlantic Monthly,* February, pp. 44–76.

Keen, D. 1991. "A Disaster for Whom? Local Interests and International Donors During Famine Among the Dinka of Sudan." *Disasters* 15(2):150–165.

Keen, D., and K. Wilson. 1994. "Engaging with Violence: A Reassessment of the Role of Relief in Wartime." In *War and Hunger: Rethinking International Responses in Complex Emergencies,* edited by J. Macrae and A. Zwi, pp. 209–221. London and Atlantic Highlands, N. J.: Zed Books.

Lateef, K. 1990. "Structural Adjustment in Uganda: The Initial Experience." In *Changing Uganda: The Dilemmas of Structural Adjustment and Revolutionary Change,* edited by H. Hansen and M. Twaddle. London: James Currey.

Macrae, J., and A. Zwi. 1994. "'Post'-Conflict Rehabilitation of the Health Sector: A Preliminary Assessment of Issues and Implications for International Aid Policy." Report prepared for the Health and Population Division. Overseas Development Administration and London School of Hygiene and Tropical Medicine.

Macrae, J., A. Zwi, and H. Birungi. 1993. "A Healthy Peace? Post-Conflict Rehabilitation of the Health Sector in Uganda 1986–1992." Final report. London School of Hygiene and Tropical Medicine and Makerere University.

Macrae, J., A. Zwi, and V. Forsythe. 1995. "Aid Policy in Transition: A Preliminary Analysis of 'Post'-Conflict Rehabilitation of the Health Sector." *Journal of International Development* 7 (4):669–684.

Meier, G. 1993. "The New Political Economy and Policy Reform." *Journal of International Development* 5(4):381–389.

Okounzi, S., and J. Macrae. 1995. "Whose Policy Is It Anyway? International and National Influences on Health Policy Development in Uganda." *Health Policy and Planning* 10(2):122–132.

Scheyer, S., and D. Dunlop. 1985. "Health Services Development in Uganda." In *Crisis in Uganda: The Breakdown in Health Services,* edited by C. Dodge and P. Wiebe. Oxford: Pergamon Press.

Seaman, J. 1994. "Relief, Rehabilitation and Development: Are the Distinctions Useful?" *IDS Bulletin* 25(4):33–36.

Sen, A. 1986. *Famines and Poverty.* Oxford: Clarendon Press.

Sivard, R. 1993. *World Military and Social Expenditures 1992–3.* Washington, D.C.: World Priorities.

Smallman-Raynor, M., and A. Cliff. 1991. "Civil War and the Spread of AIDS in Central Africa." *Epidemiology of Infectious Diseases* 107(1):69–80.

Stewart, F. 1993. "War and Underdevelopment: Can Economic Analysis Help Reduce the Costs?" *Journal of International Development* 5(6): 357–380.

Stockton, N. 1989. "Understanding Conflict in Africa." Oxford: Oxfam. Photocopy.

UNHCR. 1994. Restricted document.

UNICEF. 1989. "Children and Women in Uganda: A Situation Analysis." Kampala: UNICEF.

USAID. 1994. "Strategic Plan." Office of Transition Initiatives, Office of Disaster Assistance, May 11.

Utting, P. 1994. *Between Hope and Insecurity: The Social Consequences of the Cambodian Peace Process.* Geneva: United Nations Research Institute for Social Development.

van Brabant, K. 1994. "Bad Borders Make Bad Neighbours: The Political Economy of Relief and Rehabilitation in Region 5." *Relief and Rehabilitation Network*, Network Paper No. 4. London: Overseas Development Institute.

WHO (World Health Organization). 1994. "The World Health Organisation in Cambodia 1980–1994." Strengthening Health Systems Project. Phnom Penh: WHO.

Whyte, S. 1990. "Medicines and Self-Help: The Privatisation of Health Care in Eastern Uganda" In *Changing Uganda: The Dilemmas of Structural Adjustment and Revolutionary Change*, edited by H. Hansen and M. Twaddle. London: James Currey.

World Bank. 1993. *World Development Report: Investing in Health*. New York and Oxford: Oxford University Press.

World Bank. 1994a. *Cambodia: From Rehabilitation to Reconstruction*. Washington, D.C.: World Bank.

World Bank. 1994b. *Ethiopia: Public Expenditure Review*. Washington, D.C.: World Bank.

Zwi, A., and A. Cabral. 1991. "Identifying 'High Risk Situations' for Preventing AIDS." *British Medical Journal* 303:1527–1529.

Zwi, A., and A. Ugalde. 1989. "Towards an Epidemiology of Political Violence in the Third World." *Social Science and Medicine* 28(7):633–642.

9

Rebuilding Community: Psychosocial Healing, Reintegration, and Reconciliation at the Grassroots Level

Kimberly A. Maynard

The dramatic changes brought about by the end of the Cold War have not been limited to world politics. The global balance shift has unleashed hidden animosities and new power struggles, giving birth to a different kind of warfare, unprecedented in measure. Many past, ideologically rooted, interstate conflicts have been replaced by internal strife of a communal, inter-group nature. These more numerous and pernicious wars are fought on a local level between neighbors and community members across identity lines. Bosnia, Somalia, Tajikistan, Rwanda, and Chechnya are all recent examples.

As a result, the number of civilians subjected to violence has risen considerably in the past five years, presenting a different victim profile from that of past wars. Today, 80 to 90 percent of all war-related deaths are civilian casualties from massacres, ethnic cleansing, indiscriminate attacks, and collateral killings in cross fires. Earlier, most casualties occurred among established fighting units such as government military troops and armed opposition groups. Although often such wars also vitiated economies, infrastructure, and political stability, even affecting large populations, the damage was nevertheless usually geographically isolated. In contrast, contemporary wars coincide with large-scale human migration; failed economic, political, and social structures; and food insecurity, creating complex humanitarian emergencies. Consequently, they negatively impact all levels of society through death, dislocation, famine, and disease.

Communal violence has a far-reaching effect on individual and community life. Intimate exposure to brutality and subsequent displacement and civil disorder leave individuals psychologically scarred and the intricate network of social interaction deeply torn. Traditional support systems have disintegrated along with communal cohesion in intergroup violence. Conventional international relief such as food, health care, and shelter does not directly address these less tangible war wounds. The substantial methodological improvements in humanitarian assistance in the past decade have remained largely in the physical and economic spheres and have not yet reached psychological or social issues. However, with the rise in both occurrence and banefulness of intergroup violence and subsequent complex emergencies, international relief and development professionals are gradually recognizing the implications of these issues on recovery efforts. This new component in the rehabilitation equation deserves significant attention on the operational end, as well as in headquarters and in academic and policy circles.

To begin with, the parameters of these new violent struggles have yet to be defined. While the magnitude of warfare has been determined quantitatively by defining "major conflict" as those accumulating over 1,000 deaths, distinctions between various types of, and motivations behind, violent disputes are a bit more nebulous. The West's tendency to codify most of today's wars as ethnic oversimplifies the root causes. Although ethnicity plays a primary role in much of contemporary warfare, other factors, such as religion, political power, language, and regionalism, may also figure prominently. The study of conflict has provided a plethora of causal theories and variations—for example, territoriality, ethnonationalism, economic interest, group worth, and elite manipulation. Notwithstanding the continued debate, most agree that the common bond in contemporary warfare is its identity-based, internal nature. In this chapter, the term *intergroup* loosely denotes interaction between collective identities based on shared cultural characteristics.[1] The words *war* and *conflict* are used interchangeably within the context of intergroup violence.

This chapter examines the growing phenomenon of psychological and social injury resulting from community violence and the need for successful programs in grassroots psychosocial recovery. It outlines a five-phase approach and examines current efforts against it. Finally, it proposes future directions in international assistance for promoting psychosocial rehabilitation.

The Psychosocial Damage of War

Although the ruinous effect of war has been documented since Greek civilization, the widespread exposure to personal attack in today's conflicts brings forth some new repercussions. Since warfare is no longer primarily the domain of trained fighters on the battlefield, but is within the realm of ordinary citizens in house-to-house combat, the effects are plebeian and widespread.[2] The typical war survivor today is a civilian—often a female who has lost close family members, possibly her home, and many of her possessions in the war. Her experience of violence has been extremely personal; she has conceivably been assaulted herself, and she might have witnessed indiscriminate killing and torture of others, including close members of her family. She probably knows and possibly has lived with her perpetrators. She has fled her home at least once to escape the violence, retreating either to relatives in other regions or to a camp. In the movement, she has sacrificed personal possessions, and she may have lost her home to vandalism or occupation by others. If she was able to keep her house, she is probably now sharing it with others who are homeless. Due to the economic and physical devastation, her income source has deteriorated along with her buying power and she has little or no access to health care or adequate food sources, save for the nearest nongovernmental organization (NGO). In this condition, she, like other war survivors, is more susceptible to mental distress and distrusting of past relationships; she is therefore unable to serve as a contributing member of her community.

This dismal portrayal of a war survivor's existence illustrates the comprehensive effect of communal violence. This chapter takes the discussion beyond the physical and economic impact of war to the psychological and social ramifications at the grassroots level. Here, psychosocial war damage is the loss of normal individual and interpersonal function as a result of localized violence; this includes the incapacity to attend to personal and communal needs unfettered, and the inability to sustain healthy relationships. Taking a closer look, we examine the psychological and social issues separately and then discuss their interrelationship.

Psychological Damage

At the individual level, mental illness can stem from exposure to mistreatment as either the subject or the witness, or both. A study of combat soldiers reveals four clusters of traumatic war experience that contribute to psychological trauma, including exposure to fighting, exposure to abusive violence, deprivation, and loss of meaning and control (Shay 1994, 123). Civilians living in combat zones clearly experience similar conditions. The growing number of them implies that psychological damage is becoming more pervasive. During the 1994 Rwandan civil war, for example, over 91 percent of the children experienced a death in the family[3] and a large number of women were raped, often publicly. While men still make up the majority of war-related casualties, that figure is changing as conflicts are being fought increasingly on the home front. Children and women who witness attacks on family members, or are the victims of rape or assault are often disproportionately affected by psychological trauma. The loss of family members due to war is further psychologically deleterious to women, children, and the elderly, who depend heavily on familial support.

Symptoms of mental injury resulting from exposure to extreme violence were first seriously studied in U.S. Vietnam War veterans in the 1980s. The research led to greater understanding of the spectrum of psychological reactions, culminating in post–traumatic stress disorder (PTSD). The wide-ranging symptoms include anxiety, depression, substance abuse, social withdrawal, hostility, estrangement, despair, isolation, meaninglessness, anticipation of betrayal, hypervigilance, and destroyed capacity for social trust. In PTSD specifically, the subject overresponds to stimulation of memories and often relives the original trauma (Shay 1994). Subsequent studies have examined the incidence of psychological trauma outside that of combat soldiers, including rape, incest, and physical abuse victims and adolescent Vietnamese war survivors immigrating to the United States. Nevertheless, the vast majority of the research on trauma, its symptoms, and treatment have been confined to U.S. subjects, and most of that to the combat veteran's experience of war. While it is easy to assume culture-blind responses to violence, Western connotations of trauma may be easily misconstrued in other countries; causes, symptoms and recovery processes may vary significantly from culture to culture. Furthermore, root causes of the violence, such as political repression, ethnic vendettas, or long-held territorial disputes may play a role in the psychological response to violence.

Normal psychological support, in the form of extended family, friends, elders, and religious figures, may have deteriorated along with the community's social structures, such as schools, religious institutions, and medical facilities. This loss of familiarity in routine and trust in leadership is exacerbated by estrangement following migration. Individual self-esteem may plummet as a result of such disruption, compounded by the inability to provide for oneself from the loss of human resources, economic erosion, and ruined income sources. Psychologically, this can be devastating.

In today's internal wars, the individual nature of traumatic psychological injury is potentially multiplied by the prevalence of exposure to violence. While individual incidents may be disturbing, more numerous cases can be overwhelming in a community plagued by physical and social chaos. In such conditions, the psychologically traumatized quickly become marginalized and a burden to society. This

> In a normal situation, one can get support and assistance from school, extended family, work, the state. All these are gone in war. There is nothing. You can't trust anyone. All is gone. There is no protection. The teachers, the mayors, even the family has killed.
> —*Genocide survivor in UNICEF psychological trauma training (from field notes, Rwanda, May 1995)*

was evident in Tajikistan's recent war, where many repatriating widows, devastated by the fighting and the loss of their families, could no longer contribute to productivity yet required extensive care. The communes, reeling under the disarrangement of civil war, were unable to provide for them adequately (Maynard 1993). Furthermore, the paranoia and distrust common among the mentally disturbed may influence the community mindset at a time of intense vulnerability, decreasing the odds for reintegration.

Social Damage

In war-torn societies, healthy social patterns between dissimilar groups are replaced by distrust, apprehension, and outrage, impairing community cohesion, interdependence, and mutual protection. The personal nature of current wars is all the more ruinous in communities that have had close intergroup ties, including mixed marriages, neighborhoods, business associations, church membership, and academic fellowship. Incidents of individual reprisal, group fear tactics, the threat of return to war, and political repression exacerbate the tension. Loss of leadership and human resources, due to death and migration, fractures previous social and civic institutions, reducing the ability to care for the wounded and vulnerable, educate the young, and rebuild and develop the community. Exposure to violence has destructive repercussions on democratic participation as well. Inasmuch as individuals fear for their safety, distrust others, have a limited sense of the future and tend to see the world in black and white, their ability to contribute to group decisionmaking and constructive future planning is negligible. Moreover, returning refugees and internally displaced persons may find themselves in a drastically different and hostile environment than the one they left. In the worst-case scenario, they may be completely ostracized, targeted, or abandoned.

In tension-laden communities, the initial conflictual divisions based on ethnic, religious, or political differences may subdivide into other cleavages—such as between those who remained and those who

> Unhealed severe trauma from any source destroys the unnoticed substructure of democracy, the cognitive and social capacities that enable a group of people to freely construct a cohesive narrative of their own future.   —*Jonathan Shay, 1994, p. 181.*

fled or those who receive assistance and those who do not—hindering community reintegration. In the aftermath of the most heated violence in Somalia's nomadic northern region, for instance, severe contention arose between clans with long-held roots in the region and those who had migrated more recently to the area. In such a discordant setting, community living standards deteriorate from lack of cooperation in reconstruction, mutual economic support, and demise in productivity. This results in increased dependence on outside assistance and diminished community self-esteem. Economic adversity typically contributes to scapegoating, which, in a war-torn society, may lead to a continuation of the revenge cycle. Further violence, in turn, damages remaining infrastructure, crops, and houses, which then fosters the decline in overall development, predisposing the community, and possibly the region, toward a return to war.

The psychological and social damages of war are inexorably intertwined. Poor individual psychological health erodes community stability through the exhibition of paranoia and blatant mistrust, irrational behavior, and the need for constant care. At the same time, ruined social institutions and intergroup relations further the impression of chaos, exacerbating mental vulnerability. As a result, internal warfare can have extreme deleterious effects on the psychosocial health of communities subjected to violence.

Development of the International
Response in Healing Psychosocial Wounds

Twenty-seven centuries ago in the *Iliad,* Homer wrote about soldiers' experience of war and the ensuing disastrous consequences on character. Nevertheless, our understanding of the nature and extent of war's effect on society is still far from complete. Recent international awareness of the problem in relation to contemporary conflicts has stimulated new reflection, dialogue, and programs aimed at alleviating some of the psychological and social repercussions. These are borne, in part, of the close contact between relief and development specialists and local populations in war and postwar conditions. Field-going professionals have personally witnessed the serious and potentially long-lasting consequences of violence, such as traumatized children, marginalized populations, palpable tension among former neighbors, and social comportment that disintegrates into further vengeance.

The increased international interest in psychosocial issues has led in several related directions. From one perspective, relief and development specialists are reviewing options for mitigating tension indirectly through community-based reconstruction projects. From another perspective, conflict resolution professionals—mediators, academics, NGOs, and private associations—are beginning to look at the potential for "field diplomacy."[4] In contrast to the more conventional direct methods of settling disputes involving high-level leaders in short-term cease-fire negotiations, field diplomacy features conflict managers engaging community members over root causes, for an extended period of time. And from yet another direction, psychologists are ascertaining the applicability of PTSD therapy in the Western context to civilians in Third World civil wars.

Accordingly, the multidimensional nature of complex emergencies, and of psychosocial injuries in particular, requires a multifarious approach to recovery. At a minimum, methods design for healing psychosocial wounds calls for input from public heath, psychology, sociology, and conflict studies. The implementation of resulting programs requires the expertise of relief and development professionals and specific country experts. In addition, country nationals play a critical partnership role in advising on cultural practices and implications, explaining historical roots, and pinpointing critical locations, populations, or trouble spots.[5]

Unlike physical reconstruction in these settings, however, there is little guidance in rehabilitating the psychosocial sector. Hence, the parameters need to be laid. Interestingly, psychological healing processes for traumatized combat veterans and sexual and domestic violence victims alike revolve around reestablishing a healthy relationship with others, which is the essence of social recovery. According to Shay (1994), restoring a trustworthy community has the most healing effect on PTSD sufferers. Judith Herman (1992) describes three stages of therapeutic recovery for sexual abuse and domestic violence victims: establishing safety and self-care, coming to terms with the traumatic event; and reintegrating into the community. Psychosocial recovery from intimate warfare is a similarly long, convoluted, tenuous, unmarked path complicated by international relationships, economics, and politics. However unrefined, the road presents a five-phase process, parallel to Herman's stages, leading to healthy psychosocial communities.

The Five Phases of Psychosocial Recovery

1. Establishing safety
2. Communalization and bereavement
3. Rebuilding trust and the capacity to trust
4. Reestablishing personal and social morality
5. Reintegrating and restoring democratic discourse

First and foremost to any recovery is the establishment of safety and protection. For communities in the process of receiving returning refugees and displaced populations, intergroup animosity is likely to be intense and the issue of security critical. The second phase involves communalization and bereavement. This process of sharing traumatic experiences with others and allowing a period of mourning over the losses is essential to healing. These can be done only in an atmosphere of safety. Thereafter, the individual and the community can begin rebuilding trust and the capacity to trust. In this third phase, renewing interpersonal relationships begins with restoring honor to the adversary, which has been destroyed by dehumanizing the enemy during the fighting. The fourth phase entails personal moral recovery and the reestablishment of social morality. Reconstruction of a sense of ethics reestablishes a set of socially acceptable operating rules and provides guidelines for individual behavior. The fifth and final phase involves the reintegration of all societal elements back into the community and restoration of democratic discourse. This permits future planning and development as a whole community.

This process and all of its phases are extremely complex and nebulous. There is no cathartic cure for the wounds of war; instead, methodology and responses are evolving and the capacity to recover is still unknown. Nevertheless, research into psychosocial recovery is beginning to receive greater attention, and ongoing field work reveals interesting possibilities. Current efforts in psychosocial healing cover a range of activities, many of which overlap or draw from each other. There are those designed specifically to promote psychological well-being, while others are directed toward social rehabilitation, reintegration, or reconciliation. For some, the program's focus is direct intervention wherein the main objective is healing. Others are conducted within the context of larger programs, where healing is a subcomponent of a broader undertaking and secondary to another purpose. Because of their esoteric nature, however, such delineations are theoretical, as both individuals and communities may benefit from programs in a variety of ways.

International Assistance in the
Five Phases of Psychosocial Recovery

Establishing Safety

Critical to any healing is removing the danger and replacing it with a foundation of security. In communities tormented with repeated violence, safety is the most compelling motive for action. Unstable conditions are exacerbated by the return of community members who had fled during earlier bouts of fighting. Property disputes, threats, retribution, and intimidation are common. Healing under these conditions is extremely difficult. Therefore, fundamental to recovery is a reliable sense of protection, including freedom of movement within the community, absence of personal or group threats or attacks, property security, and access to community resources.

Physical protection and security in war-torn societies are variously the tasks of peacekeeping forces, military units, local brigades, community members, and—in the case of returning migrants—the UN High Commissioner for Refugees. However, a sense of safety is frequently lacking. Individual reprisals, disappearances, and group threats undermine security, precluding a safe foundation for psychosocial or any other program development. For most psychosocial rehabilitation programs, establishing safety is not an integral part of the format. However, foreign agencies and international organizations—NGOs, UN agencies, private foundations, and bilateral aid offices—are aware that instability restricts further rehabilitation.

Communalization and Bereavement

Communalization, the act of sharing traumatic experiences, perceptions, resulting emotions, and responses with other people in a safe environment, in conjunction with a period of mourning over the losses, is a major part of the healing process. Grieving and communalization, which could require substantial time, may occur in a group setting, such as a women's organization; in an organized, public fashion, such as a symbolic burial ceremony; or informally among friends and family. The milieu is less significant than the compassion and support.

International organizations have initiated training programs on traumatic injury in war-torn societies specifically to help psychological rehabilitation. Since such programs follow Western understanding of PTSD and other forms of mental injury, communalization and bereavement are key components. A new phenomenon to most societies, the training introduces the concept of mental injury from traumatic events and encourages its early recognition and treatment. Training may include the value of grieving, causes of psychological disturbance, susceptible individuals, typical symptoms, the psychological nature of the injury, danger of prolonged neglect, activities to mitigate the negative effects, communalization, treatment routines, and the role of specific individuals in the care process. In Rwanda, several international agencies engaged in such training, aimed primarily at trauma in children, and consequently involved primary caretakers, teachers, and health professionals.

Another form of expressing the experience of crisis is through art, music, dance, and drama. Several foreign organizations have supported projects specifically intent on externalizing and sharing traumatic events through these means. Particularly popular with children's groups, these projects strive not only to activate the imagination and social awareness, but also to revitalize cultural traditions critical to healing a tormented community. Through these programs, participants engage in creative, wholesome activities that encourage them to participate and share, rather than withdraw.

Communalization in international programs also occurs through activities involved in conflict resolution. However, direct conflict intervention—attempts to settle the contentious issues and diffuse tensions, generally through mediation or negotiation—is rare at the grassroots level. Virtually nonexistent are resident conflict experts in the communities. Nevertheless, some programs potentially span several target populations. Noteworthy examples are the Nairobi Peace Initiative, which mediates conflicts throughout Africa; the Institute for Multi-Track Diplomacy, which engages different components of society in the pursuit of peaceful solutions; and sustained dialogue, a five-stage process of regular meetings aimed at problem solving. Committed to long-term solutions, all these approaches deal with the deep-seated roots of the contention and include mourning and communalization as well as later phases, such as trust development and moral recovery. Throughout their extended, though not uninterrupted, engagement with local populations, facilitators encourage participants to share and explore the experience of violation and loss. Because of their depth of involvement, these specific examples may also delve into the three succeeding phases: rebuilding trust, reestablishing a sense of morality, and reintegrating the community. Parenthetically, while organizations involved in conflict intervention do not directly address issues of protection, they usually conduct their programs in a context of relative neutrality, safety, and confidentiality.

The process of communalization and bereavement requires a significant amount of time. Since workshops and training sessions in conflict resolution skills usually span no more than several days, their formats do not engage the process, but rather emphasize the value of sharing and grieving and provide the techniques to initiate the process. Such forums are intended to develop greater understanding of the conflictual elements and improve the dispute-handling capacity of antagonistic groups. They are usually conducted by conflict resolution professionals and NGOs in a setting removed from the visible battle. Participants normally include representatives of the disputants or, at a minimum, members of the various antagonistic groups—usually professionals, intellectuals, academics, and leaders. The content of such forums may include conflict theory and analysis, presentation of the conflictual issues from various points of view, communication skills, techniques in mediation and negotiation, and exercises in viewing the conflict from the other's perspective. Some go so far as to try to establish a new paradigm of interaction. The long-term application of these learnings supports the healing properties of exchanging experiences and feelings resulting from the violence.

Critical to the discussion of communalization and bereavement is the assumption of a universal response to, and recovery process from, exposure to violence. Not enough is known yet about the cross-cultural implications of Western concepts, the transference of techniques, or even the benefits, risks, or appropriateness of discussing feelings or expressing loss in different cultures. Although many organizations endeavor to use responses and activities elicited from local participants, the spectrum among the international programs is wide. By all accounts, avoiding introducing foreign methods into a culture without consideration of ethnic and cultural differences is imperative.[6]

Heeding this, several organizations have attempted to rehabilitate and strengthen existing indigenous dispute resolution systems that may have broken down through the course of disintegrating community relations. In cultures with indigenous procedures for dealing with contention, this may involve recognizing and revitalizing the elders council, the role of the traditional peacemaker, the justice circle, the tribal court, representative committees, or the mediating role of women's organizations. Here again, communalization can play a large role in the recovery process as part of the traditional system. Revitalizing indigenous structures requires intensive investigation into local methods, cultural practices, and nuances; it also requires enlisting the support of, and empowering, groups, individuals and organizations prone to reject the violence.[7] Further, they can serve as the catalyst for revitalization by initiating and facilitating meetings, offering incentives, lending facilities or resources, and aiding protection through impartial witness. In southern Sudan, for example, international organizations played the initial role of go-between in restarting a traditional dispute settlement process, which entailed extended communalization and then provided support in the form of food, funding, transportation, and documentation.

Rebuilding Trust and the Capacity to Trust

The critical next step to a healthy psyche and interpersonal relationships is reconstructing the confidence and commitment between adversaries. Betrayal during the course of combat, particularly in today's interpersonal warfare, undermines faith and confidence in others. Further, the process of dehumanizing the opposition diminishes its power and thus respect. Restoring the adversary's humanness and honor is an essential step in recovering from psychological trauma; it also plays a critical role in reestablishing interpersonal relationships and thus community-wide interaction. Renewed trust in a war-torn society includes general belief in the good intentions of other community members, reliance on them for common services, willingness to assume a responsible role in society, and commitment to the joint future of the community.

"When 'what's right' [i.e., the concept of *thémès*] is violated in a high stakes situation in any culture regardless of the specific content ..., the body reacts the same way, with fear and rage, and the mind undergoes deep learning.   —*Jonathan Shay, 1994, p. 205.*

Relief and development projects may have trust-building attributes. Conventional reconstruction programs attempt to return the community to its prewar state and reestablish a sense of normality. They help local populations regain control over their lives, inducing a profound calming and reassuring effect. By selecting projects that require the benevolence of adversarial parties for the benefit of all, reconstruction projects can also jump-start the trust-building process. For example, in several war-torn situations, international NGOs initiated housing reconstruction projects for returning refugees and displaced persons that required the labor and even material contribution of the local population. The personal investment in the fate of the returnees resulted in their greater overall accommodation, and the gesture of goodwill on the part of the community was a large first step in restoring trust.

Reestablishing Personal and Social Morality

In war, morality and social rules are thrashed, creating a kind of social disintegration. Healing psychosocial war wounds requires reconstructing the concept of *thémès* (what is right) and reestablishing guidelines for individual behavior. Social ethics might include acceptable standards for appropriate contact and communication between each segment of the population, standards of honesty, forbidden grounds, responsibility to family and community, personal accountability, role of loyalty and obligation, and methods for handling various emotions such as anger, injustice, betrayal, envy, jealousy, etc.

As an illustration of an international program supporting moral recovery, UNICEF established peace education programs within the normal school systems of Lebanon and Rwanda. All prewar educational materials were scrutinized for biased and unethical influence and subsequently replaced with stereotype-reducing curriculums that supported moral development. Training was conducted to help teachers elicit and encourage cross-group sharing, discussion of moral principles, and appropriate, nonprejudiced behavior among students.

Holding conferences to bring warring factions together under a flag of mutual exploration is another way foreign entities can help rebuild a sense of social morality. The objective of this type of conference is to create a forum for discussion of contentious issues: to bring out various, perhaps unheard or mediating, views; to offer a safe meeting ground for cross-conflict interaction; and (ideally) to come to some agreement on proceedings. The agenda of presentations, discussions, and plenary sessions offers participants the opportunity to reevaluate their roles in the conflict, thus renewing a sense of moral obligation. International NGOs held several conferences in Rwanda, one on popular participation in national reconstruction—including rehabilitation of the psychosocial sector—and others on the deep divide that separates both the religious and ethnic communities.

Reintegrating and Restoring Democratic Discourse

A healthy society is one that accepts an amalgamation of the diverse elements of society. Though not without contention, such a community has the skills and structure with which to handle disputes peacefully. This broad inclusiveness supports participatory discussion that allows the community to make comprehensive decisions, plan for the future, and implement development strategies.

Reversing negative stereotypes requires long-term and repeated interaction between antagonistic groups—the type of exposure common in development programs. Quite a few programs conducted by international organizations are aimed at this phase, particularly those in which healing components are subelements to another rehabilitation goal. Since reintegration is the final phase and therefore an observable return to normality, the natural inclination is immediately to attempt reintegration. At the same time, many organizations expect to stimulate the preceding steps by reintegrating the warring sides.

One way of encouraging integration is through the selection of projects that benefit both sides of a mixed community and that require intergroup participation. Road reconstruction, repair of telephone lines and public utilities, and rehabilitation of shared social ministrations such as hospitals and schools are good project candidates. International organizations that intentionally employ staff representative of all sides, identify equally diverse project participants, hold joint meetings, insist on cooperative decisionmaking, and orchestrate shared management and maintenance of projects ultimately invite long-term, intergroup interaction. In-kind donations of labor and materials from all beneficiary groups further encourage cross-conflict communication and demonstrate goodwill. A mutually beneficial water project in Bosnia, for instance, stipulated bi-ethnic construction and management, as well as labor and material contribution. Similarly, "spot reconstruction," a concept devised by Intertect Relief and Reconstruction Corporation in Sri Lanka, targets villages located in low-conflict zones, often with mixed representation, in support of formal peace initiatives. By establishing programs that rejuvenate the local economy, the whole community benefits. This has the potential of drawing people back to their home areas and dissuading them from participating in the fighting. The focus of spot reconstruction is areas of minimal conflict and mixed groups, such as those containing recent returnees or urban areas with large numbers of voluntarily resettled displaced persons.

Another aspect of project selection is the use of quick impact projects (QIPs) as an incentive for greater cooperation at the community level. Usually implemented during the potentially destablizing period when refugees and internally displaced persons are returning home, QIPs provide an immediate boost to the home community through small projects with a high potential for rapid results. Through immediate return on cooperative efforts, QIPs jump-start community reintegration as well as rehabilitation. In Cambodia, for instance, QIPs in water, sanitation, agriculture, fishing, and income-generation activities significantly facilitated returnee reintegration.

International support for the revival of indigenous, nonsegregated, benevolent organizations both promotes integration and revitalizes the democratic process. These may include new or preexisting charity, civic, nongovernmental, work-related, or task-oriented groups incorporating community members across conflict lines. Foreign organizations may provide funding, resources, guidance, or project assistance. In Somalia and Rwanda, international support for interethnic women's associations exemplified cross-conflict interaction and decisionmaking. These groups not only played a large role in the psychosocial healing of the women involved, but their ensuing projects significantly contributed to country-wide rehabilitation and added vitality to the peace-building process through formal input, insistence on peaceful relations, and acceptance of a multiform society.

International organizations are recognizing the important role the media play in both splintering and reuniting societies. Hence, they are beginning to support radio stations and broadcasts that foster peaceful coexistence by airing various views on issues of rehabilitation, publicizing successful intergroup cooperation and programs rebuilding community relations, and presenting discussions on topics of civic import. Support comes through providing funding, offering material resources, providing counsel, soliciting and offering program material, and entreating public and government or authority endorsement. In Bosnia and Rwanda, organizations proposed establishing alternative radio broadcasts, to include multiethnic staffing as well as alternative information forums promoting healthy dialogue and messages of integration and peace.

A final innovative model of reintegrating and reestablishing democratic discourse is that of the African Community Initiatives Support Teams in Rwanda. Teams made up of Africans and non-Africans work within communities on local improvement initiatives such as agriculture, small enterprise, artisanry, education, cultural arts, and sports. Because they emphasize grassroots conceptualization and participation at the lowest level of society and require community contribution of labor and resources, they promote whole community interaction and decisionmaking.

Areas for Further Development in
the Five Phases of Psychosocial Healing

Because the rise in complex emergencies and the accompanying number of civilians personally affected by war has been so rapid, the experience of international organizations in psychosocial recovery is also brief. Understandably, many of these recently unveiled programs are not based on extensive research of the broader country-wide picture, specific local conditions, or other ongoing efforts in complex emergencies. In this examination of a representative handful of psychosocial healing efforts within the context of the above five-phase recovery approach, it is apparent that the bulk of international activities examined lie at the end of the spectrum. Many of these are aimed at reintegrating the adversarial groups in hopes that they will come to discuss the problematic issues, begin to redevelop intergroup trust, and thus reestablish a sense of social morality and commitment, leading both the individual and the community back to health. Very few of these organizations take into account the full spectrum of the healing process and the implications of each phase on the others. For example, the need for a secure environment is not widely considered to be a component of healing programs. Therefore, as interest in psychosocial recovery intensifies, future international assistance should expand into other possible areas. The following are illustrations of new or underutilized programs supporting the five-phase recovery.

Establishing Safety

Because international organizations are officially disengaged from the conflict, they potentially provide a unique service in the form of security and protection. As impartial parties, their presence alone usually serves as a significant pacifying force. Ideally, because they maintain strict nonpartisanship, their actions, personnel, and resources are viewed as unbiased, lending them opportunities for greater peacemaking.

Beyond improving the basic protection provided by UN peacekeeping forces, international military contingents, and the UN High Commissioner for Refugees, greater professionalization and use of resources dedicated to alternative protection programs broadens the means for the international community to provide security. New concepts and structures using civilians and nonviolent tactics for safeguarding communities are springing up worldwide. Witness and protection programs post individuals and teams in areas of particular tension, accompany individuals thought to be in particular danger, and may initiate conflict resolution efforts. These programs are underutilized and require greater sophistication and consistency, as well as coordination with other international aid elements. Further, foreign organizations, because of their reputed noninvolvement and available resources, can offer a safe meeting space for cross-conflict gatherings, individuals fearing persecution, local leadership pursuing peace initiatives or others needing sanctuary and protection.

While foreign entities can play an important tempering role in hostile environments, establishing internal sources of order and an independent capacity to provide security fulfills long-term safety needs. International assistance can increase, accelerate, refine, and routinize police force training and the development of an adequate justice system, which are critical to eradicating a culture of impunity. Finally, foreign organizations can advocate, help establish, and empower local peace committees. Made up of noncontentious, mutually respected, and diverse individuals, peace committees can help prevent community violence, mediate between contentious individuals and groups, serve as go-betweens for international agencies and the local community, support local peace initiatives, and provide incentive and support for local authorities to advocate conciliatory actions. Peace committees could have far-reaching effects on the succeeding phases.

Communalization and Bereavement

Primary to prospective programs involving psychosocial healing is the need to engage the grassroots level. The process of communalization and bereavement in particular often requires lengthy, intimate immersion from the participating foreign entities. Yet conflict resolution organizations, the groups most likely to be involved in this process, are rarely continuously occupied with local combatants themselves. Thus, the concept of field diplomacy—the long-term, resident engagement of conflict specialists in local contentions—offers great potential for improving the communalization and bereavement process. In this vein, through community-wide programs sponsored by conflict specialists, members have regular opportunities to discuss experiences and feelings, get psychological and physical support, and begin to reconcile their lives with the suffering and losses they have endured. Further, because of their particular susceptibility to psychosocial trauma, women require special attention. Rape, an extremely common wartime violence, has never been counted as a civilian casualty. Through rape counseling, special health care programs, or groups specifically catering to women's psychological needs, international organizations could facilitate the communalization and bereavement process of a significant portion of the community population.

Foreign agencies may also encourage, provide resources for, and otherwise support a public mourning period. This might include paying tribute to the losses; holding an open, symbolic bereavement ceremony; conducting a ritualistic burial for the dead; holding religious prayers; or providing a public symbol in recognition of those killed.

Such shared expression of grief can be a catalyst for individual and community psychosocial healing.

Rebuilding Trust and the Capacity to Trust

Reestablishing confidence in communities well versed in betrayal is a slow process, beginning with small, even symbolic, gestures of goodwill and gradually increasing the stakes to where material goods and even people are on the line. This aspect of psychosocial recovery obviously requires time, commitment, and patience.

Direct physical engagement in rehabilitation activities serves as a relatively safe step toward committing to the future of the community. Whereas this may be helping rebuild a health center or school, it may also entail direct contact with others through establishing vulnerable care programs for the elderly or unaccompanied children, caring for the wounded, or teaching in makeshift schools. Foreign agencies can specifically gear such projects to intergroup interaction by designating roles for people of mixed ethnic makeup and requesting tasks requiring growing levels of trust. In reconstruction projects, foreign agencies purchasing materials locally should consider explicitly buying across conflict lines, thereby establishing confidence in the manufacture, delivery, and quality of goods produced by the various groups.

Moreover, foreign organizations can establish a milieu of commitment and reliance through credit incentives and joint small enterprise programs. Accordingly, they might encourage or mandate certain kinds of interaction as a condition of funding. For example, small business startup credit may be granted more readily to those proposing cross-conflict partnership, those hiring across identity lines, or those intending to locate in shared areas, high-tension zones, or areas traditional to other groups.

Further, international agencies might offer their national program staff training in conflict resolution, workshops on specific issues such as human rights, or internal seminars on related topics such as traditional dispute resolution methods. This official in-house training broadens the skills of the participants and develops community-level understanding of the issues.

Reestablishing Personal and Social Morality

Ethics are fundamentally very personal, evolving from cultural, historical, and societal influences. Therefore, foreign organizations play more of a peripheral role in supporting and encouraging renewal of a moral climate. Providing conflict resolution training and discussion forums on rebuilding moral guidelines for government leaders lends skills and insights to be incorporated into community life. Discussion forums in which whole communities engage in debate over new rules for human conduct may also be public. Training may include managers of significant social services such as unaccompanied children's centers and educational institutes. The funding and technical assistance for rejuvenating the judicial system mentioned earlier could play a major part in reestablishing social ethics. Similarly, the potential for radio and other media to have a leading role in guiding moral recovery merits much greater advocacy by international organizations than currently exists. Besides general financial support, foreign entities could help develop programming and public interest in debates, presentations, and interactive networks on important ethical topics.

Reintegrating and Restoring Democratic Discourse

The peace committees, credit incentives, and radio programs suggested for encouraging cross-conflict interaction would contribute substantially to reintegration, fair dialogue, mutual respect, and renewal of joint participation in community life. The strongest improvement in this phase, however, might be rebuilding the community decisionmaking capacity that has been devastated in the fighting. Besides such obvious challenges as reconstruction of water systems, hospitals, roads and houses, decisions in postwar societies arise about care of the unaccompanied children, assistance to widows, burial sites for the war dead, and the opening of schools. Even more contentious are such problems as land ownership, new leadership, council membership, and political affiliations. International organizations can take advantage of the pending issues to help lay the foundation for the decisionmaking process, thereby contributing to reintegration and democratic dialogue. Accordingly, they can help establish ground rules, procedures, and methods for handling disagreements and provide guidance and facilitation during the initial discussions of common needs. Optimally, this will lead to a mutually agreeable project and process of implementation. On a larger scale, a healthy decision making process could be used as a format for rediscovering unity, discussing differences, and developing a common vision, all of which contribute to intercommunal reintegration.

Future Directions for International Assistance

The rest of this decade promises to present numerous challenges for international agencies as the number of internal wars increases, contributing to mounting estimates of psychosocial injuries. Foreign organizations should be commended for recognizing the situation and taking the initial steps toward addressing the issues. Nevertheless, the process has just begun, and the need for deeper analysis of and concerted action in psychosocial recovery is substantial. The potential benefits of psychosocial healing programs in community rehabilitation are clear. Successful grassroots activities initiated by international agencies can help strengthen community bonds, increase self-reliance, prevent further violent outbreaks, increase communication, and build an inclusive social structure. This can lead to a higher potential for civil society and democracy and pave the way for future development planning. Ultimately, such programs can support peace agreements and political rehabilitation on the national level, reinforcing the will toward peace.

Nevertheless, psychosocial rehabilitation is not yet an entirely acceptable aspect of reconstruction, and international programs are not without risks and potential pitfalls. There may be an increase in hostilities due to inadvertent competition for programs, for instance. The introduction of foreign methodologies may cause cultural barriers and disenchantment with local custom. Community members might sense a greater-than-normal level of meddling, leading to eventual backlash. Programmatic success may divert power away from local authorities who may eventually withdraw their support or even undermine progress. Outsiders entering a hostile environment may be subject to suspicion and even targeted as a perceived obstacle to the ultimate victory of one group. Especially in intractable conflicts as in Sudan and extreme violence as in Rwanda, psychosocial recovery requires extensive time, patience, and personal involvement, which in turn necessitate a prodigious commitment on the part of the international agency. This translates to long-term funding, organizational support, devotion of staff, and acceptance of personnel and programmatic hazards.

Not all risks or drawbacks can be avoided, but many can be minimized. Obviously, any favoritism or perceived favoritism toward one party could not only disrupt the program but also incite hostilities, renewing community violence. It is imperative, therefore, that all involved in communities reeling from recent violence, and particularly those dealing with the sensitive issues underlying the dispute, understand the historic, cultural, and political factors leading up to the warfare. Respect for local tradition, culture, and methodologies must underscore all relations; and, above all, care must be taken to ensure neutrality, equality, and popular participation at all levels and from all sides.

In the coming years, the international community needs to take several steps toward standardizing, consolidating, coordinating, and refining its approach to psychosocial rehabilitation and toward improving the potential for results in each of the five phases. First, the disciplines concerned with psychosocial issues should collaborate and cooperate closely. Resources, experience, and skills among practitioners in such fields as conflict resolution, humanitarian assistance, development, and the diplomatic arena should be pooled. In turn, these should draw more heavily on respective academics and invite psychologists, sociologists, and anthropologists to join the discourse. Moreover, these concerted efforts must include indigenous organizations, regional specialists, and local experts, with the goal of revitalizing traditional practices and eliciting possible activities.

Second, such collaboration should produce extensive research and studies of contemporary internal wars, their effect on psychosocial health, and dynamics in postwar society; the result should be increased understanding. This calls for concerted inquiry into such understudied areas as psychosocial trauma in intercommunal war victims; postwar social interaction; cultural implications of psychosocial injury and recovery processes; the role and impact of a third party on community hostility, specifically during the repatriation phase; tensions created by traditional relief and development assistance; and lessons learned from previous efforts at preventing, mitigating, and managing conflict at the community level.

The task of examining these issues should not be left to academics alone. They should be taken up seriously in committees and study groups made up of international organizations working in complex emergencies, including donor agencies, NGOs, consortiums, and all those within the UN Department of Humanitarian Assistance Standing Committee. Furthermore, think tanks, individuals, and related independent organizations should conduct wholehearted research on the subject at the grassroots level, funded by foundation grants and UN and government agencies. The results of these endeavors could contribute to the development of principles and standards to be integrated into organization and agency protocols and manuals, and could be developed into bilateral policy.

Third, this type of rapidly changing information must be publicized for all those working in complex emergencies. Training programs, workshops, and conferences for relief, development, human rights, military, and diplomatic personnel should cover psychosocial injury and the five phases of the rehabilitation process. Essential information for these formats should include a minimum of three subtopics. Initially, understanding the healing process requires background information on the nature of conflict, antecedents and motives of intergroup hostilities, ethnology, the pattern of deterioration in relationships, group tactics, revenge cycles, and the use and abuse of violence in power struggles. This should also include some aspects of warfare itself, including tactics, factional fighting, and power struggles.

Next, the educational aspect should incorporate specific information on psychological trauma in both children and adults such as causes, reactions to violence, symptoms, treatments, effect on community, and long-term care. Last, this area must encompass the subject of conflict resolution. It should include, for example, a brief overview of resolution, mitigation, and management techniques as well as indigenous practices and dispute resolution systems. It should also cover the process of reconciliation, forgiveness, communication, group decisionmaking, problem solving, and conventional methods of mediation, negotiation and activities aimed at tension reduction.

The fourth and final step on the road to enhancing international organizations' capacity to aid community healing is at the operational end. Here, a psychosocial sector should be added to the increasingly effective sector-based coordination system in complex emergencies. Psychosocial sectoral meetings would establish the legitimacy of and need for such programs, improve the coverage of all five phases in the international response, share methodologies and ideas, and begin to create industry standards similar to those in the health, nutrition, and shelter sectors.

Conclusion

Until recently, both warfare and humanitarian assistance were viewed as primarily problems of quantities. That is, both dealt with the management of total dead, number of casualties, morbidity and malnutrition rates, and tracts of territory gained or lost. In warfare, solutions involved increasing firepower, adjusting distribution of troops, or reconfiguring weaponry; in relief, reactions were to provide more plastic sheeting, increase the number of feeding centers, or redistribute food supplies. Increasingly, however, even the nonethereal, physical response to war on both fronts is growing more intricate and less tangible in today's complex emergencies. All the more obscure are the internal, incorporeal, psychosocial injuries. Left unattended, these wounds may continue to fester in the form of marginalized individuals and community tension, frustrating development efforts and possibly erupting again in a new surge of warfare. The international community, therefore, faces an important challenge—to understand the problem and advance methods of addressing the wounds in this era of ever increasing internal conflict. International resources should be committed to increasing understanding of the issues and providing fundamental guidelines to address them. Programmatic approaches toward each of the five phases of recovery should be strengthened and refined, and psychosocial healing should become institutionalized as a standard aspect of rehabilitation in war-torn societies.

Notes

1. There is a growing collection of terms denoting identity-based group distinctions. Gurr (1993) uses the phrase "communal groups" and defines it as "fuzzy sets" of people that make up psychological communities.
2. Civilian "victims" of conflict can be divided into three categories, according to Médecins Sans Frontières: those that are targeted as stakes in the conflict; those that are threatened by being trapped in the conflict, and vulnerable populations weakened by disruption in food and health care provision (Raisson 1995, 129).
3. From UNICEF (1995.)
4. A phrase used by Luc Reychler, professor at the University of Leuven, Belgium, and president of International Dialogue.
5. The extremely sensitive issues surrounding intergroup conflict and ensuing psychosocial injury demand absolute adherence to neutrality. The involvement of country nationals, simply by their identity, could potentially compromise the impartiality if not carefully executed.
6. For more on dispute resolution mechanisms in different cultures, see Rule (1993).
7. For more discussion on the disintegration of internal mechanisms and phases of response, see Center for Advanced Study of International Development (1991).

References

African Communities Initiatives Support Teams. 1995. "CWA-ACIST Rapport Trimestriel." Utrecht: Dutch Interchurch Aid.
Assefa, Hiskias. 1993. *Peace and Reconciliation as a Paradigm.* Nairobi: Nairobi Peace Initiative.
Center for Advanced Study of International Development. 1991. "Internal Conflicts and Their Transformation: An Interview with Dr. Kumar Rupesinghe." East Lansing: Michigan State University.
Center for Development Information and Evaluation. 1995. "Rebuilding Post-War Rwanda: The Role of the International Community." Washington, D.C.: Agency for International Development. Draft.
Cuny, Frederick C. 1989. "Spot Reconstruction: The Programming of Reconstruction and Development Assistance to Support Peace Initiatives." Dallas: Intertect Relief and Reconstruction Corporation.
Gurr, Ted Robert. 1993. *Minorities at Risk: A Global View of Ethnopolitical Conflicts.* Washington, D.C.: United States Institute of Peace Press.

Gutlove, Paula, Eileen Babbitt, Lynne Jones, and Joseph Montville. 1992. "Towards Sustainable Peace in the Balkans." Cambridge, Mass.: Balkans Peace Project.

Herman, Judith Lewis. 1992. *Trauma and Recovery.* New York: Basic Books.

Horowitz, Donald L. 1984. *Ethnic Groups in Conflict.* Berkeley: University of California Press.

International Alert. 1993. "Conflict Resolution Training in the North Caucasus and Georgia." London: International Alert.

The Kettering Foundation. 1995. "Dartmouth Conference Regional Conflicts Task Force: Tajikistan Dialogue." Washington, D.C.: Kettering Foundation.

Lederach, John Paul. 1992. "Beyond Prescription: New Lenses for Conflict Resolution Training Across Cultures." Waterloo, Ont.: Conrad Grebel College. Photocopy.

Lowrey, William O. 1995. "Sudan Case Study: Jikany-Lou Nuer Indigenous Peace Process." Washington, D.C.: United States Institute of Peace. Photocopy.

Maynard, Kimberly A. 1993. "Tajikistan: Will We Heed the Warning?" *Central Asia Monitor* 5:11–16.

Montville, Joseph. 1994. "The Healing Function in Political Conflict Resolution." In *Conflict Resolution Theory and Practice,* edited by D. Sandole and H. van der Merwe, pp. 112–126. Manchester: Manchester University Press.

Raisson, Virginia. 1995. "Civilians in the War Zones." In *Populations in Danger 1995: A Médecins Sans Frontières Report,* edited by François Jean. London: Médecins Sans Frontières.

Rule, Colin. 1993. "Questioning Dispute Resolution." *Peace Review* 5(4):407–412.

Saunders, Harold. 1990. "An Historic Challenge to Rethink How Nations Relate." In *The Psychodynamics of International Relationships,* edited by V. D. Volkan, D. A. Julius and J. V. Montville, pp. 1–30. Lexington, Mass.: Lexington Books.

Saunders, Harold. n.d. "Conflict Resolution: Enlarging the Field." Washington, D.C.: The Kettering Foundation.

Shay, Jonathan. 1994. *Achilles in Vietnam: Combat Trauma and the Undoing of Character.* New York: Atheneum.

Slaby, Andrew E. 1989. *Aftershock: Surviving the Delayed Effects of Trauma, Crisis and Loss.* New York: Villard Books.

Stein, Barry. 1991. "The Actual and Desirable Link Between Programmes of Ad Hoc Assistance to Return Movements and Long-term Development Programmes for the Local Areas Where Refugees Return." New York: UN Research Institute for Social Development.

Thomas, Lorry. 1991. *Post Traumatic Stress Disorder in Vietnamese Adolescence.* Master's thesis. San Jose State University.

UNICEF. 1995. *Rwanda Emergency Programme, Progress Report No. 1: May 1994–March 1995.* Kigali: UNICEF.

United States Mission to the United Nations. 1995. "Global Humanitarian Emergencies, 1995." New York: United States Mission.

10

Postwar Social Reconstruction in Mozambique: Reframing Children's Experiences of Trauma and Healing

Sara Gibbs

This time in Mozambique is a time of broken hearts ... but we are working now and filling our hearts with work so like this we can begin to forget, our hearts are being calmed; there is no place in our hearts for sadness and fear any more as they are filled up with work.

These words, spoken by a man then living in a RENAMO-controlled area, encapsulate the theme of this chapter. In October 1992, the signing of the peace treaty officially brought the war in Mozambique to an end. Since then, the task of both physical and social reconstruction has been, and continues to be, of paramount importance to the affected communities. I draw here on ethnographic research funded by Save the Children that was undertaken over a period of three months at the end of 1993 in the district of Milange, Zambezia province, in central-eastern Mozambique. The study focused particularly on how people were reconstructing their lives. Specifically, it attempted to establish how the disrupted psychosocial worlds of children were understood and addressed as part of the process of community and individual healing.

Currently there is widespread concern about the effect of war and displacement on children's lives. It has become the concern not only of

An earlier version of this chapter was published in *Disasters* 18 (Oxford: Blackwell, 1994), pp. 268–276.

the affected communities, but also of governments and national and international agencies. On an international level, much of the concern stems from the fact that children are assumed to be particularly susceptible to the effects of trauma—a state within the Western views of health and illness that is thought to have specific symptoms and specific cures. Yet it is debatable as to how valid and useful such a perspective is within the very different cultural context of Mozambique. Local social institutions and healers already provide both meaningful interpretations of people's suffering and particular mechanisms for managing it. Furthermore, locally it was indicated that the Western ideal of healing individuals through psychosocial processes needs to be considered in much broader terms. While social institutions such as churches, healers, and nongovernmental organizations (NGOs) have a role to play in facilitating reconstruction, that role is only part of a broader process. In particular, the actual physical work of reconstruction following return—such as the building of homes and the planting of fields—was considered by local people to be particularly crucial to the postwar healing of individuals and communities. Thus, reconstruction was conceived to arise first from individual and community actions rather than from discussions with individuals on or about the traumas of war.

In this chapter I aim to make a contribution to the improved understanding of how children in Mozambique experience "trauma" and the process of healing and reconstruction. I hope that a better appreciation of social reconstruction in communities such as those in Milange will lead to more informed policy and practice by agencies working with postwar communities. An important first step in such a process of understanding is to consider how childhood and trauma are perceived in that country, which in many ways is very different from Western perceptions. The unattributed quotes throughout this chapter are from conversations I had with people who were living or passing through the district of Milange or who were living in Mulosa refugee camp just across the border in Malawi.

Theoretical Considerations of Childhood and Trauma

While it is recognized that as a result of the war in Mozambique children have undergone the most terrible suffering; there has been relatively little research into the specific ways in which individuals and communities in Mozambique embody that suffering and address it. A number of programs have been initiated with the specific aim of helping the "traumatized" children of that country. But the majority of the work is informed by a body of literature and knowledge that has its roots in a Western European tradition. This work developed out of research during and after World War II that was designed to establish how the conditions of the war had affected children (Gibson 1989; Raundalen and Dodge 1987). Within this tradition it is commonly stated that an exposure to various identifiable "stressors" (e.g., violence, separation from parents, displacement from home) will produce specific symptoms—nightmares, bed-wetting, withdrawal, fear, and depression—all features of a "traumatized" state. Furthermore, the extent to which children are affected is said to be influenced by their "developmental" age, as Gibson indicates: "The literature on stress and within child psychology suggests that this [the developmental age of children] plays an important role in determining both their vulnerability to particular stressors and the form of their reactions" (Gibson 1989, 662).

The dominant theoretical framework that still informs our understanding of childhood maintains that children, who are perceived as vulnerable and dependent, "develop" along a predetermined path. Through the process of socialization, children pass through various required stages on the path to an independent and more "finished" state of adulthood. Yet the utility of this model of childhood, as with the medicalized model of trauma, is now increasingly being brought into question. However natural and universally valid such models may appear to those from a Western European tradition, people in Milange have an understanding of childhood and of suffering that differs significantly from this pattern. The distinctive cultural web of Mozambique, interwoven with its particular social, political, and economic threads, influences both the way the community understands and acts on the needs of its children. The problems in transporting a Western model of childhood to a country such as Mozambique is illustrated by a recent campaign display board for Save the Children, on which were the words of its founder: "The only international language in the world is a child's cry." These words appeared beside the famous black-and-white photograph taken in Vietnam in the 1970s of a screaming naked girl fleeing from a napalm bomb.

Undoubtedly in Western Europe, vulnerability is echoed in these words, and their message is a key theme underlying the construction of the child. Pia Christiensen (1994) suggests that this is because children are seen within the Western framework to be always in a dependent relationship with adults. She points to both the nuclear family and to children's legally protected status as "nonworkers" as central to this relationship of vulnerable dependency. With children known for their vulnerability, in times of great suffering such as during wars or natural disasters, they come to be portrayed, as the above example illustrates, as the archetypal victim. Such words and images are unquestionably effective in fund-raising campaigns, perhaps because "paradoxically, while we are moved by the image of a sorrowful child, we also welcome it, for it can arouse pleasurable emotions of tenderness, which in themselves confirm adult power" (Holland 1992, 148). Yet the community in Milange illustrates that this notion of the child as a victim is not as universally valid as it is cast.

Childhood in Milange

The following metaphorical tale, one that people in Milange used when speaking about children, illustrates a view of childhood different from the usual Western view:

> A child is like a banana tree ... once you plant one they will reproduce themselves, after five or six years they will grow alone—independent of their parents. Children are the same, after some years they are independent and can grow on their own. They are survivors, like the banana trees; if there is a forest fire and you go away, when you come back you can find a lot of trees burnt, but the banana trees are often alive. Their parents may be dead but they will survive, alone.

This picture of children as strong and as survivors and as actively "growing on their own" contradicts the popular Western European image and focuses conversely on the strength of children and the vulnerability of adults.

One of the most striking features to emerge from the research was that the boundaries between adulthood and childhood were very much more ambiguous than I had expected. The extraordinary situations people found themselves in during the war meant that the roles of childhood and adulthood became displaced. While the war has determined the experiences of children in the past, today it is reconstruction that is the priority in people's lives. Therefore, the roles children play today are determined not only by their past experiences but also by their present situation. The most significant point is that children actively create and re-create their roles according to the situation (Prout 1992). Neither are they seen, nor do they see themselves, as especially passive or especially vulnerable. For example, the views of Joao, a thirteen-year-old returnee, attest to the complexity of the relationship between childhood and adulthood:

> The thing I hated most about being in Malawi was that I had no garden. I had no place where I could go and uproot my own food; but now I have a field and I have filled it with sugar cane and cassava—soon I will be able to taste my own cassava again.

Joao had not only made his own fields, but when I spoke to him he had just finished making a washroom for the family. The next job he said he would do was to make a latrine (both tasks that his father might have done had he been alive), "and then I will make my own house ... when I have the energy; today I am too tired." He was still going to school in Malawi, making the ten-to-twelve-kilometer journey—each way. As such he combines a number of different roles. Not only does he take on the work, and thus part of the role of his father, but he is fulfilling both the traditional role of the child as a young producer and the more modern role of the schoolchild.

People in Milange often pointed to the way in which children were valued for their contribution to the productive work of the family. In this process the Western image of the child—in this case as a nonworker—is turned on its head. Given that survival is the priority and focus of many people's lives, it is not surprising that children are valued for their work and are described in the following way: "Children are the wealth of the man ... the more the better ... [they laughed] ... more workers." Certainly children can be seen from the age of about five or six digging in the fields. Even at play they can be seen building houses. From a very young age children are given a piece of land to prepare and plant and, as they grow older, they are expected to contribute more and more productively. Active engagement with the "ways of life" are embarked upon almost as soon as a child can wield a hoe. Yet when I questioned a father of eight children as to a comment he had just made about children as "second-class citizens" he replied:

I don't know why children are seen as second-class citizens, all I know is that they are; yet I also know that when they grow, people begin to love them ... and in time [he laughed at the thought] when they have grown to have their own riches they too will see others [indicating children with his hands] as second-class citizens.

Such a comment points to the value placed on individuals for their ability to do productive work. So while children may not be as highly valued as adults who have a greater capacity for work, they are recognized for their future potential: "A child is like an oil lamp—it illuminates your future, and for this reason it will keep you when you are old and your name will go on after you."

While the ability to work is of key importance during the present period of reconstruction, this does not mean that the value of schooling was not recognized. In fact, a number of refugee families split up, leaving the children behind in Malawi so they could continue to go to school there. Even so, people indicated that central to the process by which their lives were being reconstructed was the actual physical work of reconstruction. Even when I asked what was the most important thing allowing children to piece their lives together again, people would prioritize activities in the following way: "The most important thing we can do for children if they don't know is to show them how to work, tell them that they must work, that there is no food without work."

Thus, in summary, children do not perceive themselves, nor are they perceived, as passive, vulnerable, or being unable to work. This is not to say that they have not suffered during the war and its aftermath, only that they have suffered just as everyone else has suffered. In this respect, just as the process of suffering was deemed to be similar for adults and children, so was the process of healing through engaging in the work of building, planting, and producing.

The Heart of the Matter

Although initially the healing process appeared to be centered on productive activity for children as well as for others, and productive activity could itself be considered the main agency of healing, more formal local and national institutions played a part in assisting this process. Healing and healing ceremonies were, however, set in the context of people working to reestablish their lives.

How people embody and give meaning to their distress is significantly influenced by their particular cultural context, which indeed also affects how they identify and deal with it. In Milange, when both adults and children discussed how the war had affected them, most spoke of how their hearts had been changed. It was this embodiment of their suffering in the heart—as opposed to in the mind, a concept those more informed by a Western framework might use—that was most striking:

> It's difficult to change people's hearts, but during this time [the war] I know that people's hearts have changed. People saw things; friends killed, their sons and daughters taken ... these things that they have seen have changed their hearts.

Another said,

> I know that if a person hurts another one or kills one or becomes very angry his heart can change.

A boy who was fifteen years old when he was captured by the soldiers said:

From the time I was caught, my heart was not always in position, I was very much afraid, but when I drank that medicine [given by a 'Synanga'— a healer] I felt that pass away, the terror and fear passed away from my heart and I became like a person who doesn't worry about anything.

As indicated, the important thing now for those affected is that their hearts are "calmed." Healers can enable this settling of the heart by giving certain specific medicines to people:

For those with changed hearts they will be given medicine to restore them when they get back, the medicine has the power to change the heart to make it like a child's. ... This doesn't mean that they will act like a child only that they will have again the heart that they had as a child and that they are going to grow again from there.

Some considered that for children this healing mechanism was particularly important:

If children see such things, because their heart is not yet mature enough it will change to be something very different, something bad ... it's difficult for children. So if a child is suffering then the family—the adults and children together—must eat this food [the staple maize porridge, emsima] in which the medicine is put ... but some families just do it for the person suffering, but this isn't as good.

The nature of the treatments varies among healers and depends on the individuals and families concerned. Medicine comes in a variety of forms; it can be drunk or eaten when added to food, bathed in or given in the form of vaccinations. Whether taken by individuals alone or by whole families, the treatments were seen as something additional to the community healing ceremony that occurs when people celebrate the success of the harvest.

An elderly Synanga in Namitxitxi, part of a locality within the district of Milange, spoke about such a communal ceremony. It will happen, he said, when people celebrate the harvest and it will help them to forget about the war and settle their hearts; and children will participate in the ceremony:

You should take a young girl and a young boy, each about 16 years of age and you must take them naked to the boundaries of the village. There they must cook food and put medicine in it and also drink again some medicine. Then they must make some fire—some new fire from the earth by rubbing sticks together. When they have made it they must take it to the chief who then gives it to everyone else in the community. [They use children] because it's like if you've got fowls, you know that they are old, but if you have chicks then you know that they will grow.

> So it's the same with children. You know they will grow and establish the community. [They are naked] because they make the fire as if they are born today, it is as if they know nothing once more and like this they are starting again. [And they use fire because] it is taken into everyone's homes and it must last there right until the harvest has been reaped. Then at the end there is a great feast and after that the problem is gone. It was the same in the past when a community suffered something terrible—a great sickness or a great fear. The feast is for everyone and it will cover the problems as everyone will have so much to remember from the feast that they will all be happy.

Although everyone had suffered and everyone needed to be healed in some way, some people were affected more than others, and healers had a number of ways they could help those particularly affected. Nevertheless, it appeared that the focus of the healing process—for everyone, regardless of their individual well being—would come when the community celebrated the success of its harvest and thus "true peace." It was to this very significant point in the reconstruction and (quite literally) the rekindling of community and individual lives that people pointed.

The Church and Healing

The church also has a role to play in the process of reestablishing individuals and communities. This often appeared to be intermeshed with the role of the healers. While some people draw on both of these institutions during the process of their return and reconstruction, others indicated that they would use only one to the exclusion of the other.[1] The different ways people chose to mark their return home reveals this more clearly:

> When my son came, my son by my second wife, there was a treatment. He was given herbs and some other things to welcome him and to take the evil things away.
> When people return there is a "flower offering." They place flowers under the tree, the special ancestral tree, and there is a ceremony. Then after the first fruits, their return [home] is celebrated, they make beer and there is a great feast.
> When we returned we prayed in the church, we made no ceremonies for the ancestors as the bible is against such things, we just called out their names during the service.
> When I returned I just prayed a lot because I left here sadly and I want to stay now.

But even when speaking about the specific role of the churches and healers, people still indicated that working to physically rebuild their lives was also important, as important for children as for adults:

When we return home we are not going to have a ceremony; we will just get on and build our house and also pray for our future.

Confessions were used by the churches as an important part of the healing process, but not everyone was convinced of their value:

People do confess, but I am not sure that they can be forgiven because some of them confess and then go and do the same thing that they confessed about yesterday, today.

In another's words:

There is no need to confess because people did what they were forced to do. We won't ask them [returnees from RENAMO areas] about the war; we want only to watch to see how they will live now.

In this way, people were again indicating the importance within the healing process of simply living and working—an essential factor being the "living" proof that indeed the war was past and that people were living their lives in a good way once more. For some, however, the confessional was an important way to become reintegrated. A child soldier I spoke with felt that, in addition to the medicine he had received from a healer, the confessional had helped calm his heart:

The church made me confess in front of the whole congregation and made me tell them what had happened there. ... The congregation was very happy to have me back again and they sang songs. It was shameful [for me] to say what was happening, it was very terrible, but I had to say it ... it was important because what was happening there was very terrible, the bad things that I did there, they were the things that a person cannot do.

There is a great diversity of ways in which the different churches are dealing with people's return and reestablishment. Nevertheless, the kinds of issues they are all addressing are similar: how to interpret the meaning of the war and how to reestablish and reconstruct individual and community lives. Throughout Mozambique, the churches are recognized for their role in promoting reconciliation, yet a Protestant pastor indicated that while reconciliation was a part of their aim, the focus of the churches' work was broader than this and was to enable people to live and to work again:

The only way I know that I can help the people is to tell them the way of God, to encourage them to know God's word so they can know a new way to live. Like this we also calm people that they forget all the problems there were and forgive the people who did bad to them.

Through this process of reconciliation and forgiveness, through acknowledging and celebrating people's return, and through the system of confessions that appeared to be enabling people to put the war behind them, the churches had an active role, alongside the healers, in focusing and reaffirming the process of reconstruction and assisting children as well as adults to reconstruct their lives.

Policy Implications

In devising procedures to assist the healing work of the churches and other agencies, it is important to recognize not only the problems of transporting ideas and practices from a Western context into such a situation, but also to recognize that there may be problems in using ideas employed in one developing country in another. Although a knowledge of programs and experiences from other countries can be useful if creatively adapted, images and ideas from one country do not always transfer very well to another. A current example from Mozambique illustrates the point. In a book one agency designed to use with traumatized children, the owl is portrayed as a wise creature who is able to give good advice. In Mozambique, however, where the owl is seen as the bearer of death and destruction, the use of this symbol is clearly problematic and counterproductive. Procedures and programs, particularly for healing purposes, that involve the transfer of one cultural image to another must be devised sensitively and carefully. Such an approach, however, still focuses largely on the psychosocial healing of the individual, and this must not replace a concern for broader social and economic reconstruction. People consistently referred to the latter as the most significant factor in the remaking of their worlds.

Nonetheless, churches and healers are an important part of the healing process for both children and adults alike, particularly in combination with the work of government and other agencies involved in family-tracing programs and programs for placing orphaned children into substitute families. These programs are vitally important in that they are allowing children to be placed back in their communities, where the more multifaceted and indigenous healing process described above can take place.

Conclusion

Healing children after war is a complex process and, within a Western framework, has come to be associated with particular psychosocial symptoms of "trauma," and particular psychosocial remedies, largely centered on the individual child. Many of these ideas are set within a view that conceives of childhood as an especially vulnerable, dependent, and fragile time. It has been argued here that a Mozambican perspective on children and childhood differs from a Western one, not only in how childhood is perceived by adults, but also in how childhood is perceived by children themselves. The healing of the traumas of war, therefore, must also be considered differently, with obvious consequences for policy and practice.

It is clear that children and adults in Milange are seen as having been subject to the same traumas of war and as now being involved in the same process of reconstruction. The most significant part of this process, for both children and adults, is being actively engaged in everyday life—through building houses and planting fields. Performing these tasks is seen, in itself, as a healing process, and the involvement of other agencies, such as healers and the churches, is seen as welcome support, especially through the ceremonies they hold. For the same reason, reestablishing the local infrastructure; building roads, bridges, health posts, and hospitals; and distributing seeds and tools are of critical importance in enabling the everyday process of reconstruction to take place and to be successful in the longer term. Communities have their own cultural frameworks for understanding and addressing the distress they have suffered as a result of war. In Mozambique, the time is now for reconstruction, and the intense activity in which children and adults are engaged is part of a process of survival—a process they indicated was at the very heart of the way in which their lives were being remade.

Note

1. Both healers and churches can be found in syncretic forms. While some healers, for example, maintained that all problems and diseases are sent by the devil or his angels, some churches kept very close ties with the ancestors. Jean Comaroff's (1981) study of healing and cultural transformation in southern Africa is useful in this context, because it exposes the processes by which societies are both reproduced and transformed.

References

Christiensen, P. 1994. "Vulnerable Bodies: Cultural Meanings of Child, Body and Illness." Paper presented at Keele University's Medical Anthropology Seminar Series.

Comaroff, J. 1981. "Healing and Cultural Transformation: The Tswana of Southern Africa." *Social Science and Medicine* 15B: 367–378.

Gibson, K. 1989. "Children in Political Violence." *Social Science and Medicine* 28: 659–667.

Holland, P. 1992. *What Is a child? Popular Images of Childhood.* London: Virgo Press.

Prout, A. 1992. "Children and Childhood in the Sociology of Family." In *Studying Childhood and Medicine Use: A Multidisciplinary Approach,* edited by J. Trakas Deanna and Emilio J. Sanz. Athens: ZHTA Medical Publications.

Raundalen, M., and C. Dodge. 1987. *War, Violence and Children in Uganda.* Oxford: Oxford University Press.

Part 3

Assistance for Economic Rehabilitation

The chapters in this section deal with three important areas: the socioeconomic implications of landmines and unexploded ordnance, agricultural rehabilitation, and macroeconomic policy.

Paul Davies, in Chapter 11, suggests that there is a critical socioeconomic imperative to clear landmines and unexploded submunitions. In the past several years in Cambodia, for example, landmines have been cited as one of the biggest obstacles to the postwar reconstruction and development of the country. Davies describes the procedures and lessons learned from humanitarian interventions, including direct mine clearance, community mobilization and awareness programs, data-gathering projects, and training programs for building national institutional capacities. According to him, the direct costs of mine clearance are small compared to the enormous socioeconomic opportunity costs of not clearing the explosives, which have caused widespread land denial, leading to mass impoverishment. Davies contends that the international community must, among other things, acknowledge the long-term implications of landmines and unexploded submunitions and provide the necessary levels of assistance.

In Chapter 12, David Tardif-Douglin describes international assistance programs to rehabilitate household food production in postgenocide Rwanda. He focuses on programs that provided essential seeds and tools gratis to farmers, seed protection initiatives that distributed cereals to farmers so that they would not consume seeds as food, and plans for seed multiplication. As Tardif-Douglin shows, these initiatives were largely successful in reviving subsistence agriculture in the country. He examines the strengths and limitations of these initiatives and draws many lessons for future complex emergencies. For example, seemingly innocuous agricultural programs can rapidly become politicized in a postconflict society, where relief aid is supposed to target those perceived to be the most vulnerable. Further, governments seeking political legitimacy may not favor discontinuing the free distribution of food and inputs for short-term political benefits at the expense of longer-term welfare and incentive structures conducive to agricultural development.

In Chapter 13, James K. Boyce and Manuel Pastor, Jr. use the case of El Salvador to illustrate conflicting challenges governments face in formulating economic policy in the aftermath of civil war. On the one hand, the authors contend, resources must be mobilized to implement programs to consolidate peace—programs for demobilizing and reintegrating ex-combatants, strengthening democratic institutions, and repairing physical infrastructure. On the other hand, fiscal and monetary discipline must be exercised, particularly since civil wars generally create inflationary pressures and distort economic resource allocation. Moreover, peace building requires that long-run policy address the problem of imbalances in the distribution of income and wealth that may have produced conflict. Therefore, Boyce and Pastor suggest that in postconflict societies, the goals of macroeconomic policy cannot be simply restricted to economic stabilization and structural adjustment, but should also focus on promoting and consolidating peace. The authors conclude that in El Salvador, unless the peace process is allowed to reshape economic policy, both will fail.

11

Mines and Unexploded Ordnance in Cambodia and Laos: Understanding the Costs

Paul Davies

At least thirty-five nations are currently faced with humanitarian problems, many at the emergency level, as a result of what has been termed
"perhaps the most toxic and widespread pollution facing mankind" (U.S.
Department of State 1993). Of these, Cambodia and Laos are two of the
countries most heavily contaminated with landmines and unexploded
ordnance (UXO). Cambodia may have as many as 10 million uncleared
antipersonnel landmines, while Laos certainly has as many—and may
have many more—unexploded antipersonnel submunitions and countless larger items of UXO contaminating its remote rural areas. While the
former has been the focus of some case studies on the long-term socioeconomic implications of landmine warfare and has a much publicized
and relatively well-funded international demining program, the latter
has received scant attention and, until very recently, negligible humanitarian assistance.

The future prospects for humanitarian responses to antipersonnel
landmines and UXO in both countries will be determined by the development of donor policy in this emergent humanitarian sector. With this policy
development must come a willingness to face the long-run financial implications of such assistance programs. Such willingness can come only from a
fuller understanding by donors of the role landmine and UXO contamination played in causing profound socioeconomic stress in affected communities, generating poverty, and in impeding development activities.

Evolution of the Problem in Cambodia and Laos

In both Cambodia and Laos, the current legacy of landmines and UXO
has its roots in the Vietnam War era. In the latter, the process of contam-

241

ination, largely delivered from the air, was a direct result of the war and thus came to a halt in 1973 with the signing of the Paris peace agreements. In Cambodia, the oldest antipersonnel mines currently being cleared date from the period of the first Indochinese war in the late 1940s and early 1950s and were used by the French colonial forces. However, it was the destabilization of Southeast Asia during the 1960s and 1970s that created the conditions for the implosion of civil strife in Cambodia as well as foreign military intervention.

In the early 1970s, government forces used mines defensively to protect towns, communication and transport infrastructure, military installations, and frontline areas. While the guerrilla forces of the Khmer Rouge used mines to defend areas they controlled (in much the same way as the government forces), they also employed them as an offensive weapon to destabilize contested areas and demoralize populations not under their control. The Khmer Rouge also used mines as a means of social control. In the "liberated zones," self-contained agricultural cooperatives were established and sealed off from the outside world with mines, booby traps, and guards, creating "miles wide tracts of no-man's-land," a grim warning of the wasting of the land that continued mine warfare produces (Becker 1986, 164). Mines from these earlier periods of conflict were never systematically cleared, and the contemporary Cambodian mine problem has thus been growing for more than a generation. Even today, for the Khmer Rouge, mines remain not only a military tool, but also an instrument of terror for social and economic control over civilian populations.

Mines were also used in Cambodia by foreign military forces. The North Vietnamese used mines to protect base compounds and supply routes along the Ho Chi Minh Trail's southern sections, which ran through Cambodia. Equally, U.S. ground forces used mines to attempt to interdict the trail. U.S. forces also deployed air-dropped weapons, not only heavy bombs, but antipersonnel submunitions and mines. Cambodians, especially in the eastern areas of the country, are still dying from accidents with unexploded bombs from this period.[1]

Apart from their strategic suitability, mines were also deployed for another reason: they were cheap. In 1992, a UN mines expert suggested that the Phnom Penh regime might have as many as 4 million mines still in store. The noncommunist factions and the Khmer Rouge undoubtedly had similar stockpiles. Although the minister of defense gave an emotional speech in 1995 pledging that the newly constituted Royal Cambodian Armed Forces would stop using landmines in the continuing struggle against the Khmer Rouge, the Cambodian military is still faced with the same dilemmas: a lack of resources, limited personnel, a mobile and effective guerrilla opposition, and vast borders to protect. The one resource they still have in abundance in their depots are landmines, and reports on the ground suggest they are still being used by both sides in the continuing conflict.

Further, mines have entered the popular consciousness as much of the traditional infrastructure, including law and order, has broken down. Since mines are available and cheap, Cambodian civilians use them not only to protect their homes, livestock, fishing ponds, and boats, but also to settle disputes—a sad but pragmatic response to circumstances.

Between 1964 and 1973, neutral Laos became arguably the most heavily bombed nation on earth. Throughout those nine years, the U.S. Air Force dropped the equivalent of one B-52 planeload of bombs and bomblets every eight minutes around the clock. The bombing cost an average of $2 million a day, a total of $6.9 billion. Seen temporarily by Kennedy at the start of his presidency as the linchpin of all Southeast Asia—the domino to be defended against the Red Tide, Laos was also dragged under by the logic of the escalating conflict in Vietnam. Despite attempting diplomatic neutralization of the country, U.S. policy in Laos was essentially set by the 1961 presidential orders that authorized extensive CIA paramilitary oper-

---

Direct and Indirect Costs of Contamination by Mines and UXOs

Direct/Visible Costs

- Direct humanitarian responses to the problem: demining, community awareness education, data-gathering projects, training and support costs for creating national infrastructure
- Medical and prosthetic provision
- Skills training for those severely injured in accidents
- Income generation in heavily affected communities

Indirect/Hidden Costs

- Widespread land denial leading to mass impoverishment and increased morbidity
- Enforced risk taking producing high death and injury rates
- Significant socioeconomic opportunity costs of disabilities resulting from injury
- Psychological trauma, cultural damage, fear, and uncertainty that pervade contaminated communities
- Implications for development projects

ations. The war in Laos had essentially two theaters: the north-central Plain of Jars area and the Ho Chi Minh Trail area running down the eastern side of the Laotian panhandle.

This bombing completely devastated the civilian infrastructure in whole regions of the country, resulting in massive depopulation and perhaps the world's most intense level of unexploded ordnance contamination. It was later revealed that 80 percent of the victims of the bombing had been civilians. Twenty-three years after the air war over Laos ceased, millions of antipersonnel bomblets and other larger items of air-dropped ordnance and some land-based ammunition pose a massive humanitarian and developmental impediment to life in rural Laos.

The scale of the contamination to be found in Laos is entirely unsurprising given the volume of weapons deployed. For example, experts estimate that by 1973 some 285 million Blu-26 submunitions had been dropped on Indochina (Prokosh 1995, 7). Typically, 30 percent of all tonnage dropped in the region during the war fell on Laos, suggesting that nearly 100 million Blu-26s may have been deployed over the country (SIPRI 1978, 27). Given an estimated failure rate of 30 percent, today there may be as many as 30 million of these unexploded bomblets buried in the soil or lying on the surface.

While the mines found in Cambodia often represent military technology that is now almost obsolete except among the most impoverished armies or guerrilla groups, the antipersonnel weapons technology deployed in Laos, often for the first time, represents the first generation of many of today's and tomorrow's antipersonnel landmines and submunitions. Designed for high volume and remote delivery—from aircraft, artillery pieces, tanks or other launch platforms—these weapon systems deliberately contaminate vast tracts of land and cannot be marked or accurately recorded.

Humanitarian and Developmental Implications

In 1993, the Phnom Penh forum of nongovernmental organizations (NGOs) pronounced that "landmines are the single biggest factor hindering the development of Cambodia." In June 1995, they organized an international humanitarian conference to evaluate the socioeconomic impact of mines in the country—the first ever to be held in a mine-affected nation. Again it was noted that landmines were one of the most significant factors inhibiting the postwar reconstruction and development of Cambodia. In Laos, a similar process of rising awareness is under way, a process given enhanced impetus by the growing recognition during 1995 by the Lao government of the severity of the socioeconomic implications of UXO, and the need to prioritize clearance operations with bilateral and multilateral donors.

The highly debilitating socioeconomic, psychological, and cultural costs produced by such mine and/or UXO contamination are multifaceted and long term, as are the costs of appropriate response strategies. These communal costs, taken as a whole, typically far outstrip the more obvious personal costs to individual victims, no matter how tragic these individual cases are.

While the international community's responses to the direct costs will be detailed later, it is important to look more closely at some of the "indirect" costs.

Cambodia

Within Cambodia, the western Battambang province is one of the most heavily mine-affected provinces. But even within Battambang, only certain, geographically specific communities have significant problems with mines, and fewer still have significant accident rates. Communities may be able to coexist next to heavily mined areas with minimal accidents as long as certain conditions are met: availability of, and access to, sufficient mine-free agricultural land; adequate irrigation and access to drinking water; reliable local knowledge of existing minefields[2]; and a stable context with an absence of ongoing mine laying. Raw accident rates are thus of considerable use to humanitarian demining agencies, but only as "first-line" indicators of the relative socioeconomic pressure exerted on the communities affected. Repeated surveys have discovered that most civilian victims injured by mines in Cambodia knew they were entering areas of possible contamination prior to being injured.[3] As such, accident rates indicate communities where the socioeconomic pressures exerted by mine or UXO contamination have reduced conscious choice to such an extent, local people consider such risks to be "rational." This is the notion of enforced risk taking.

In 1992, the district leader of Rattanak Mondul suggested that some 65 percent of the highly productive agricultural land that had sustained one of the country's most prosperous centers of commercial agriculture in the mid-1960s was unusable because of landmines:

> The civilian population ... was left with two stark "choices" in order to survive, both of which involved taking enormous risks with landmines. The first of these "choices" was to clear the land of mines themselves, or employ ex-soldiers with a degree of knowledge to undertake this task for them. Understandably, most were reluctant to take on the role of deminer, and many had reservations about asking others to take these risks, even if they had the resources to buy such services locally.

Thus, most resorted to the second "option," which involves entering known mine risk areas to gather food, hunt and fish, and to cut and gather wood, bamboo, grass and other natural resources. These "substitution" activities, which before were only ever viewed as a useful (and risk free) supplement to incomes gained primarily from agriculture, became for many the only source of livelihood. (Davies 1994, 49)

Not only did landmines become the prime source of livelihood, but they also became the prime cause of accidents. Thus, there is a fundamental relationship between mine contamination in rural economies, impoverishment (and resultant loss of choice), and enforced risk taking.

With regard to enforced risk taking, new statistics gathered in 1995[4] about those injured in Battambang, Banteay-Meanchay, and Kompong Thom provinces for the period June-September 1995 reveal that some 37 percent of civilian males and some 53 percent of females were injured while engaged in these types of substitution activities.[5] These activities do not include farming, during which nearly a quarter of all male accidents occurred. Further, information from Battambang clearly indicates the existence of seasonal factors with accident rates. Rates rise steadily from January, when the rice crop is harvested, until March/April; they decrease as field preparation, planting, and transplanting take over in the wet season, beginning in June. In areas like Rattanak Mondul, people are not farming their own fields, but there is seasonal work available to them as day laborers in mine-free areas. Thus, the percentages quoted above on accidents that are likely to have arisen as a result of enforced risk taking are occurring during a period when seasonal alternative sources of income generation are maximized in the local economy.

In terms of age, the new data confirm that 76.3 percent of the victims are young adults, with the highest incidence coming from the nineteen to twenty-five age group. When this is added to the low incidence of female victims (6 percent of total data, 18.4 percent of total data for civilians), it becomes clear that the demographic implications of mine accidents, as previously thought, are far worse than firsthand impressions of the raw data would suggest. Projections in 1995 suggest that long-standing estimates of 300 mine incidents a month are accurate and may even be conservative—the true figure may be as many as 500 a month.[6] However, these accidents are coming disproportionately from the young male adult population—a sector of the population already underrepresented because of Cambodia's recent history, and consisting of no more than 15 percent of the overall population. This clearly relates to the gendered division of working responsibilities in the rural economy and the relative risks involved.[7]

Another area of great interest that emerges from these new statistics is the relationship between UXO and the young. Children under eighteen make up 21 percent of the victims from these new statistics in all three provinces. "In Kompong Thom, 64% of children's accidents involved UXO in a province where UXO accidents make up 25.2% of the total … (similar patterns emerge in Battambang and Banteay-Meanchay). … For all three provinces combined, children account for 63.8% of UXO accidents, but only 13.8% of mine accidents"(Moyes 1995, 3). These patterns emerge as a result of children playing with unexploded ordnance, which—as in Laos—is often found lying on the surface rather than buried in the ground as with mines. Such unessential "adventurist" risk taking, especially among children, is prevalent in both Cambodia and Laos where the warrior is revered and martial ethos is predominant. Fortunately, the unessential nature of this risk taking means it may well be possible to have a significant impact on such behavior through community awareness education campaigns.

Laos

The prime humanitarian problem in Laos today comes from small, tennis ball–sized antipersonnel submunitions, which both lie on the surface and are buried in the soil. In effect, these bomblets have become de facto antipersonnel mines in terms of the stress they put on the community. Not only do they result in accidents (which due to the heavy metal content and design intentions—to kill rather than injure—lead to a far higher death rate than in the mine-affected nations), but they also produce land denial, which directly results in widespread poverty and food insecurity. The majority of villages surveyed in Moung Pek and Moung Kham districts of Xieng Khouang report several months of acute food insecurity each year, a situation that never existed before the war. Harder to quantify, but real nonetheless, is the general climate of fear that pervades every interaction with the environment in these areas. Even fields which have been used for years can suddenly yield a deadly bomblet when the time comes to cultivate.

The humanitarian situation is intensified by the ubiquitous nature of the contamination. In Cambodia, the minefields are geographically specific and have definite boundaries (once identified), but in Laos, nowhere on the Plain can be said to be a truly "safe area." Bomblets have been found by clearance teams in the center of Phonsavan, the provincial capital; they have also appeared outside the airport terminal and buried in the runway of the town's airport (areas that have been under constant use for nearly twenty years) and in the packed earth floors of schoolrooms. Even when severely corroded by years of weathering, bomblets are unlikely to function like a pressure-initiated land-mine, because they usually require a sharp blow.[8] However, such blows are often caused by traditional farming techniques—in particular, the use of the Lao hoe, or when children discover and throw bomblets against trees. There is also a significant threat from larger bombs; any construction or rehabilitation work—especially along the primary road network (heavily targeted in the war)—runs the risk of encountering unexploded bombs.

It is clear even at this stage that accident rates in Xieng Khouang, while unacceptably high and disproportionately affecting children, are not likely to compare with severely mine-affected areas like Rattanak Mondul, Cambodia. Nevertheless, in terms of "hidden impacts," UXO has a profound and debilitating impact on rural life. Survey work in the Moung Pek district of Xieng Khouang between October 1994 and February 1995 revealed that only 7 percent of villages could report no UXO in the areas surrounding the village, while 47 percent reported severe contamination and 46 percent moderate contamination; 34 percent of villages had fields surrounding the village that could not be cultivated due to fear of UXO, and 18 percent reported that the presence of UXO inhibited the development of irrigation systems—development work which often the villagers themselves could complete with no external assistance required. Fifteen percent of villages reported areas of contamination so severe they would not even graze their animals in them, while 3 percent had difficulty accessing drinking water due to UXO contamination.

Interventions of the International Community

Development and Growth of Interventions

In Cambodia, the international community started to respond to the mine issue only when it suspected that without some sort of demining response, the UN peace process for Cambodia during the 1991–1993 period might not be able to function. The demining mandate given the UN by the peace agreements was purely to establish a local demining capacity to facilitate UN purposes and to create a body of trained personnel on the ground, rather than to establish an infrastructure that could sustain the long-term responses that were necessary to meet the country's ongoing technical need in this sector—that was soon to be acknowledged as essential to reconstruct Cambodia's war-shattered economy. In reality, the demining—or rather training for demining—that the UN did in Cambodia had little impact on the ability of the broader UN mission to function. But the Cambodian Mine Action Centre (CMAC), the national demining agency, emerged out of the mission. Although donor pledges fell below the operating budget of $20 million for the first two-year cycle, which finished in November 1995, CMAC still employs over 1,500 Cambodian staff, 92 percent of whom are directly employed in field demining operations.[9] Its projected five-year operating budget is forecast at $37.9 million, a quarter of which will ultimately come from the Royal Cambodian Government, leaving just under $30 million to come from the international community in straightforward donor funding, over and above the gifts in kind of personnel, who serve as technical advisors, seconded from various UN member states.[10]

The initial shape of the international response was in part determined by the relatively recent development of the notion of mine clearance and UXO eradication as a legitimate concern of the humanitarian community. In the early 1990s, demining was seen as a technical component to be "bolted on" to rehabilitation, reconstruction, and development programs, rather than as an independent humanitarian priority in its own right. Alternatively, demining was seen as a useful emergency intervention, securing residential land for returning refugees in heavily mined communes, or simply seeking to reduce death and accident rates. Until 1990, this area had also been entirely viewed as a military domain, a notion that, even now, is changing only slowly. Over time, donors have come to understand the long-term nature of the problem and the need to develop effective local institutions to continue to deliver these services long after expatriates have withdrawn from the program. It became clear that, if for no other reason than the costs of mounting these projects, the short-term "relief" outputs of the programs could never justify the expenditure relative to other humanitarian interventions. However, the development of sustainable, high-quality, local capacity would in the long run justify the funding commitment.

NGOs have evolved from mere technical service providers to more rounded humanitarian agencies interested in mines and UXO as a development issue in the broadest sense. They have developed multimedia community education programs—by using video, dance, drama, puppetry, posters, and more formal instructional sessions—operating first in relief mode (rapid, emergency dissemination of information) but gradually evolving into a development mode that seeks to engage and involve the target communities in constructing and sustaining their own education programs. NGOs have also acted as facilitators in the villages rather than as disseminators of predetermined messages. They have developed data-gathering teams and village agents and integrated these elements of their operations into their clearance responses, thus giving a community-responsive and community-based reality to their operations. As a result, the demining NGOs in Cambodia have grown and played a crucial part in developing the whole concept of humanitarian action in this sector.

In Laos, the international community has yet to provide substantial assistance, although matters changed dramatically over the course of 1995. The Mines Advisory Group (MAG) project has been the first systematic, professional humanitarian response to the problem of clearance and community awareness, and its data-gathering work has also been the first systematic attempt to study the broader impacts of contamination. By mid-summer 1995, following a visit to the project in February 1995 by the minister of labor and social welfare (the lead ministry for UXO issues in Laos), a Lao government trust fund, with assistance and support from the UN Development Programme (UNDP) Laos, had been established to mobilize and channel international funding and to coordinate humanitarian responses to UXO in the country. At the start of 1996, the trust fund had some $2.5 million pledged to it, with more expected over the course of the year.[11] From the trust fund, it is also hoped that a UXO cell will be developed within the Ministry of Labour and Social Welfare as the first step on the road to creating a Lao national infrastructure—perhaps loosely based on CMAC in Cambodia—with an operational clearance capacity.

In Laos, UNDP's stewardship of the idea of developing such a trust fund has had huge implications, not least UNDP's firm understanding that long-term meaningful response must be based on thorough research and clear understanding of the problem(s). They have thus commissioned a nationwide UXO socioeconomic impact survey to identify the nature of the stress imposed by UXO, determine its developmental and humanitarian meaning, and identify priority areas for further clearance operations. Only when this basis has been established can a meaningful appeal for finance be launched and plans developed to build an appropriate national infrastructure to sustain a long-term response to the challenges posed by UXO in rural Laos.

Specific Components

It may be useful to focus a little more sharply on some of the actual ground activities.

Training.   Because training is the key to developing sustainable indigenous demining capacity, training facilities were established early on by the international community in Cambodia. Currently, local deminers all receive their initial training at the central CMAC training school, which was developed with the resources established during the UN peace process in Cambodia (1991–1993).[12] Initial training courses lasting less than a month are then reinforced by on-the-job training and work experience in a supervised environment. MAG, for example, gives its graduates of the CMAC school further technical training and maintains close working relationships between its deminers and its expatriate Explosive Ordnance Disposal (EOD) experts, who work closely with them in the minefield. To create sustainable demining capacity in Cambodia, the training given to local deminers needs to ensure not only technical excellence, but also a fuller range of skills needed to sustain the operation in the long term, when it is no longer financially viable or appropriate for expatriates to have leadership roles.

It became clear that existing personnel within the teams were not sufficiently qualified to become the EOD counterparts. Nearly all the existing deminers, with the exception of the female deminers, are former military personnel. Often conscripted into the army at young ages from poor rural communities with little access to formal education, these deminers lack the education and, in many instances, ability to rise to the higher levels of management on the EOD side of the operation. Responding to this reality, MAG has identified and recruited individuals whose educational achievements and natural ability should prove sufficient to reach the standards of an EOD counterpart of an expatriate specialist. Thus, these individuals are expected to become site location managers who, once they have completed their basic time with the clearance teams, will then shadow the expatriate specialists for several months. They will receive both theoretical and on-the-job training, taking over responsibilities related to radio communication, stores and equipment, control of explosives, liaison, and management. As their proficiency increases so will their responsibilities. The eventual management structure would then run from the expatriate senior specialist (ultimately based out of Phnom Penh), to site location managers, to supervisors, to deminers.

Survey. Technical survey is the fundamental starting point for planning the operational side of any large-scale demining program. Initial surveys in Cambodia were concerned more with the repatriation of refugees from Thailand, seeking to identify mine-free areas for residential and farming purposes, than with the planning of a national demining response. However, the survey process once started should always be something of an ongoing exercise during the medium-term period. Information on mined areas was (and is) gathered from a variety of sources, including the military and resistance factions, local authorities, and accident data, where available. Once identified as potentially mined, all such minefields then have to be verified as such. Information gathered early on in the Cambodia operation (1992–1993) is still being verified by CMAC survey teams today. Survey is also an ongoing part of NGO operations in Cambodia.

Prioritization and tasking. Once areas have been verified, the minefield can be integrated as part of the national priorities plan. Such priorities are based on a number of basic humanitarian and developmental criteria. On this basis, CMAC has tasked its demining resources, following the example of the demining NGOs operating in Cambodia, all of whom have access to the information held on a central database within CMAC. However, actual locations worked may be a function of other considerations. In Cambodia, CMAC and the other demining agencies have to be constantly aware of security considerations and such factors as the weather in determining which locations can be worked.

Given the limited demining resources available, even in a relatively well-funded country like Cambodia, it is imperative that prioritization be taken seriously if outputs are to be maximized for the communities affected, and for the society as a whole. One of the weaknesses at the national level appears to be a lack of integration between the minefield location information held on the CMAC database and more general social and economic data. Only by integrating the two can meaningful national priorities and work plans be established. For example, Cambodia's 10 million mines have been estimated as taking perhaps as many as 250 years to clear completely. Certainly, the country has a long-term requirement for quality humanitarian clearance capacity. However, perhaps as many as 40 percent of Cambodia's landmines are tied up in the K5 border minefield, laid by the Vietnamese in 1984 around the western and northern frontier. These mines are in areas that are heavily forested and sparsely populated, with well-known safe paths through the minefields on cross-border routes.[13] In fact, the whole K5 belt could be safely marked off and ignored—for several generations—leaving humanitarian deminers with just 60 percent of the mines to worry about. And so the prioritization process should go on, until a manageable task list of humanitarian priority sites is developed. It is not the volume of mines and UXO contaminating any given context that is significant, nor even the areas contaminated, but rather the humanitarian, developmental, social, economic, and cultural implications of the contamination.

For humanitarian clearance operations in Laos, the ubiquitous nature of the ordnance poses several dilemmas. Fundamentally, clearance operations have to be even more carefully prioritized to ensure that the communal benefits, both in terms of reduction in accident rates and in terms of facilitating development and a restoration of prosperity, are maximized. Only effective integration with the local community through data gathering and social analysis can really achieve this. At a national level, macroeconomic planning and socioeconomic information have to be amalgamated to produce a priorities plan; the first stage in this process will be a nationwide UXO socioeconomic impacts survey.

Marking. Minefields identified during the survey process, but accorded a lower priority, are marked and left until they can be cleared. CMAC and the NGOs engaged in marking such areas of lower priority ensure that local people are informed of the limits of such minefields.

Clearance. The actual mechanics of minefield clearance in Cambodia are relatively straightforward. Despite the constant search for technological quick fixes in the area of humanitarian demining, none has been found that can achieve the humanitarian requirement of 100 percent clearance of areas prioritized. There are several different types of mechanical systems and equipment available, but these have all been developed by the military to enable minefields to be breached (broken through) during warfare, a process that does not require 100 percent clearance of the minefield as a whole. Currently, such equipment cannot, of itself, replace the work of the manual deminer on the ground.

The basic method employed is for the minefield perimeters to be established and marked. The minefield is then cleared in an orderly fashion with a mine detector; clearance progresses up one-meter-wide lanes that are spaced so that deminers working in one lane would not be injured if colleagues in the adjacent lane had an accident. In areas where combat has taken place, the scrap metal content of the ground is high, which makes clearance painstakingly slow. Once a metal reading is recorded, the detector operator retires a safe distance, and a colleague uses a prod to locate the item. It is critical that deminers wear protective clothing and ballistic helmets and visors, equipment that has proven itself effective in minimizing injuries should an accident occur. If the item is found to be a mine, an explosive charge is placed and the mine destroyed in situ. Risks are reduced to the minimum by adhering to a "no handling" policy. At the end of the clearance operation, the area cleared is not only mine free but also metal free.

UXO clearance teams in Laos have split their limited resources into two components: instrument-led clearance tasks and a "roving team" response. The roving team concept was introduced following analysis of the initial results of the data gathering team. Work in Moung Pek district revealed that children playing with UXOs lying on the surface accounted for some 44 percent of deaths and injuries from UXO. Therefore, it was important to clear such ordnance swiftly. With relatively few resources, it would be possible to have a high impact in the immediate environment of the villages. Clearly, this does not produce cleared land, but the physical reduction in child injury rates and the psychological value for parents of creating a safer environment more than justify the response, and underscore the need for flexibility in planning and implementing such programs. With just four Lao technicians and one expatriate EOD expert, the roving team visited forty-six separate locations and destroyed some 2,988 bomblets and 2,188 other items of UXO over a period of ten months.

Data gathering.   The lack of reliable baseline data on accidents has been rectified by the establishment of a data-gathering program. Other humanitarian agencies had in the past collected information on mine-related issues, but these were nearly always conducted to meet the narrow needs of their own programs. As late as December 1994, there was no widespread, comprehensive, and reliable data-gathering program in operation in Cambodia, nor any standardization of data-collection categories or methodologies. CMAC lacked the resources and personnel to implement such a program. With support from UNICEF, MAG-Cambodia's community awareness team was able to initiate such a data-gathering program, becoming operational in Battambang province in December 1994, in Kompong Thom in April 1995, and in Banteay-Meanchay the following June.

There are plans to expand the project to include all mine-affected provinces by the end of 1996. Although such information on accident rates, locations of accidents, the social breakdown of victims by age and sex, and activity at the time of injury is of vital importance in assisting the process of prioritization, social analysis of the existing data categories is required to draw out the full meaning of the data, as described above. Once this has been done, further socioeconomic research can be conducted to bring greater understanding of the humanitarian and developmental implications of landmine and UXO contamination in the affected communities.

Although such a process might seem extremely academic, it actually has very practical applications for the development of clearance and community awareness operations in countries such as Cambodia. For example, the new statistics from the data-gathering program reveal that among civilian males, "adventurist risk taking" may also play a part in causing accidents.[14] A remarkable 19 percent of all male victims were injured by UXO in an environment where humanitarians have traditionally regarded the problem as one of landmine contamination. Accordingly, CMAC has recently acknowledged the need for more community awareness in its new five-year plan.

Community mobilization and education.   Given the time required to clear even the top priority sites in Cambodia, it became clear early on that it was necessary to mount community mine awareness education programs, designed to allow communities to live more safely in areas of landmine or UXO contamination. The approach revolves around creating a truly indigenous organization and also improving the community responsiveness to the prioritization process. It is clear that a shift in emphasis is required from one of information dissemination to information sharing and facilitation of dialogue about mines, UXO, and awareness messages among the villagers themselves so that they develop far more ownership of the mine awareness program.

In the MAG program, different groups of representatives from each village will be taught how to deliver several basic mine awareness messages and how to facilitate participation themselves within their own groups. These representatives will decide on what the curriculum will be in their area and how they will pass these messages on in the long term. The program has subsequently expanded to include a schools program, training instruction in the Battambang teacher training college, and a series of data-gathering teams. MAG has since been working with CMAC on developing a national mine awareness curriculum for use in Cambodia's primary schools, and is assisting the national agency as it develops a village-based program on a national level.

This style of community mobilization is expected to increase a community's knowledge of the dangers of mines and how to best avoid them —the mine information will be more locally relevant and will be taken up by the community itself; to change the behavior and attitude of a community by encouraging people to look for their own alternatives, which can be implemented themselves or by an outside agency; and to make programs more integrated in their approach by improving the quality of the information that is given to the clearance teams and thus improving the humanitarian aspect of demining.

Lessons from Southeast Asia

The following are seen to be the most important generalized lessons that have come out of the responses by the international community in implementing humanitarian programs designed to address the implications of large-scale landmine and UXO contamination in Cambodia and Laos. This emergent area of international humanitarian action has much to consider—especially from the Cambodian context—that may have broad relevance in developing these initiatives in other contaminated nations, particularly those in the developing South.

1. *It is vital that to work efficiently in the short to medium term, those directing humanitarian demining and UXO eradication programs fully*

understand the different types of socioeconomic stress caused in the affected communities by the contamination. This will enable workers to effectively plan the training, equipping, tasking, and deployment of local clearance capacity and to ensure maximum benefits for the society as a whole in the shortest possible time. These benefits can be evaluated in terms of reductions in death and injury rates, but also in terms of enhancing communal recovery in the postconflict period and in allowing development to take place. Only through such qualitative understanding of communal benefits can sense (and hope) emerge from sheer volumes of mines and UXO at large. Clearly, if conducted properly, such a process will ensure that those communities most impoverished by contamination will be targeted first. Equally, those developmental tasks most impeded by contamination can be identified and facilitated by tasking the clearance resources that are developed—perhaps specifically to meet these task needs.

2. *A full understanding of the contamination levels affecting the community and the socioeconomic stress the contamination produces can come only through baseline survey and data-gathering activities, combined with suitable mapping and information collation and retrieval systems.* Such information systems should be developed centrally and should be readily accessible to all humanitarian clearance and awareness operators in the country context. The information provided is essential in targeting demining and community education resources in the first instance, and beyond that in delivering a broader range of rehabilitative measures to the affected communities. With some exceptions, preoperational survey missions have focused purely on technical aspects of the problem—for example, where is the ordnance? Broader questions include: Where is the ordnance that really impacts the community? Which types of ordnance cause the community most problems? How does this ordnance impact the community and what are their coping mechanisms, if any? These questions have never really been satisfactorily addressed at the planning stage. The result has been that responses have evolved in an ad hoc fashion, as a result of working on the ground. The late realization of a need for an integrated EOD response in Cambodia, over and above a simple mine clearance capacity, clearly illustrates this problem.

In practice, of course, humanitarian clearance agencies have not made, nor should they expect to make, prioritization decisions in vacuo. Other humanitarian agencies and local authorities will always have to be consulted, and their development and operational plans will have to be included in the prioritization equation. Effective information sharing between those planning reconstruction and development initiatives, including international agencies and governmental bodies in the country, should be established and institutionalized. The commissioning of the

UXO Socio-Economic Impacts Survey by UNDP in Laos is a welcome sign that such planning processes are being taken seriously. Although to some extent after the fact, it may be useful for such a survey to be commissioned in Cambodia as well.

3. *A full understanding of the broader socioeconomic implications of and profiles of stress created by mine and UXO contamination is of vital importance to planning humanitarian responses that go beyond the clearance and awareness initiatives.* For example:

a. Understanding that mine victims in Cambodia are often the poorest of the poor—those with no choices will take risks with mines—might help medical agencies overcome fears about selectively targeting "relief health" programs to mine victims. It was clear from the studies conducted in Battambang that once admitted to hospitals, mine victims, because of their preexisting poverty, were highly unlikely to be able to cope with the personal burden of financing the drugs and painkillers needed for their recovery. Understanding that mine injuries disproportionately drain hospital resources will help those developing national medical infrastructures plan for the additional resources required in each location and encourage them to try to redress situations such as those existing in Battambang, where the sick are expected to pay for their own treatment because of the lack of resources available at the provincial level.

b. By understanding the socioeconomic profiles of the injured, those planning prosthetics programs can ensure that their projects are an integrated part of a broader social policy—one aimed at creating an infrastructure that provides after-care services. This will ensure that the immediate high impact of providing prosthetics is sustained in the long term and dovetailed into skills training and income generation programs that radically improve the economic position of those injured. There can be no more disheartening image for the prosthetists than to see that restored mobility allows a return to enforced risk taking in an economic environment that has not changed.

c. Understanding that 82 percent of the disabled population in Battambang in 1992 had been "artificially manufactured" by landmines will help those planning social welfare programs. It also demonstrates the huge human burden and social opportunity costs of these perfect weapons of social attrition.

d. Since clearance operations take a long time to work through all the high-priority tasks, measures should be planned to provide alternative sources of income generation in entire communities badly impacted by landmines or UXO. Where conditions of enforced risk taking are evident, emergency humanitarian action is essential. Such programs are now being run in the severely mine-affected areas of SW Battambang by NGOs, including World Vision International. Such measures as a mat-weaving initiative rely on importing materials to the areas and establishing marketing arrangements that will provide a baseline income sufficient to liberate local people from enforced risk taking.

4. *It follows that technical resources without humanitarian (management) expertise are doomed to have negligible value in countries as indiscriminately and comprehensively contaminated as Cambodia and Laos.* Personnel selected to establish international clearance and community awareness programs need to be drawn both from individuals with technical understanding (usually ex-military—although increasingly there is a pool of expatriate technicians with practical experience in implementing humanitarian clearance operations) *and* from individuals with suitable humanitarian management experience. However, there are currently very few such individuals, and in the medium term, personnel with sound groundings in relief and development operations will find their skills easily transferable into this area of humanitarian action.

5. *Although each country context should be thoroughly investigated at the start of any national program, donors should plan to fund integrated programs aimed at creating technical capacity suitable to deal with the full range of explosive ordnance disposal tasks, rather than focusing purely on the more straightforward task of landmine clearance.* Cambodia is well known for its landmine burden, but it also has a significant problem with UXOs. For instance, during July-September 1995, MAG Cambodia destroyed a total of just thirty-four landmines, but some 541 items of UXO. Of the 12,634 items of explosive ordnance destroyed in Cambodia since MAG operations began just over three years ago, the majority have been UXOs and a specific UXO rapid response capacity has been developed to respond to this need. Laos is also now becoming known for its problem with air-dropped submunitions, but it also has a problem with land-based ordnance and landmines. Realizing the need for an integrated approach will have clear implications for training, trainers, and equipment needed to develop appropriate local capacity.

6. *Community awareness education programs should be considered a vital component of any response to severe mine and UXO contamination.* As noted, clearance resources are unlikely to be able to reach all the top priorities in the short term, and such communities need to be involved in

a process to identify ways they can learn to live more safely in their contaminated environments. Such approaches should adopt multi-media presentations that enliven the messages and communication methodologies that seek to get away from dull and formal lecturing. In some circumstances, a relief-style program may be appropriate in which, after a period of field research and testing, those implementing the program and their local staff disseminate information to a target population (such as in a refugee repatriation situation). In other contexts, such as contemporary Cambodia, participative methods may be more effective, whereby those operating the programs act as facilitators and engage local people in constructing their own community awareness programs and give them ownership of the responsibility of communicating these messages and keeping them alive in their communities. Such an approach allows the programs to be tailored to the individual needs of each location or village.

7. *Training programs for clearance operatives should be funded and implemented only if they are clearly dovetailed into plans for establishing a sustainable local infrastructure for those trained to work within.* While this might sound like a statement of the obvious, many examples show that it is not. Humanitarian responses in this sector are necessarily long term, and although local governments can and should be expected to shoulder an increasing share of the costs involved, donors should be prepared to fund such initiatives from long-term development resources rather than viewing such operations as being short-term emergency relief operations. (However, in some circumstances such relief-oriented approaches to jump-start a national program or to facilitate specific relief operations should obviously not be precluded.)

The establishment of well-trained and well-equipped local technical capacity without a local management hierarchy and effective logistical support systems will clearly be of limited value. Local people with levels of skill and education appropriate to managing such institutions have to be identified and recruited from the start. Since they should have a full understanding of their humanitarian mission and its developmental importance, they should have practical experience in clearance and/or community awareness operations at the village level. Such management training should allow local leaders to effectively represent their national program to the international donor community.

8. *Vulnerable groups who have directly suffered as a result of landmine or UXO contamination should be employed in the integrated clearance and awareness programs.* This can include (where possible and practical) amputee deminers and female deminers, but attempts should

also be made to select deminers from heavily contaminated communities, especially those where enforced risk taking exists. The motivation of all such individuals is likely to be high, and their inclusion can add a valuable social dimension to the program. The inclusion of women helps break down the image that mine and UXO eradication is a military- (i.e., male-) dominated affair, and shows it instead to be a humanitarian endeavor. In Cambodia, it should not be forgotten that nearly all the trained deminers currently working in the humanitarian sector are former military personnel, many of whom actually laid the mines they are now clearing.

9. *Last, where private organizations are contracted to provide demining services with humanitarian funding from the international community, great care should be taken to ensure that they are not associated with interests involved in the manufacture of landmines.* Again this should be self-evident, and some donors, such as the European Union, operate under strict guidelines in this regard. Although not a situation experienced in either Cambodia or Laos, there are sadly too many examples of such companies receiving funding from humanitarian bodies in other country contexts. It should also be noted that while there are many commercial clearance companies that operate to high standards in the nations of the developing South, few if any have the humanitarian understanding to independently plan and implement the types of integrated community-based responses described above.

Conclusion

Divergent experiences in Cambodia and Laos in the past few years are overall far less important than the areas of commonality. While the technical, humanitarian, and developmental issues posed by the differing types of ordnance in each country at first seems to suggest different sets of problems, on closer inspection, the similarities start to emerge. In both cases, contamination has caused, and continues to cause, enormous human suffering. In both cases, contamination causes poverty, creates a demand for relief programs and inhibits development. In both cases local people and their governments face long-term struggles with the debilitating legacies of the massive and indiscriminate use of these weapons of mass destruction in slow motion.

If the case histories of Cambodia and Laos tell us anything, it is that as a class of weapon, antipersonnel landmines and antipersonnel submunitions apparently cannot be put to "responsible" military use. International humanitarian law is quite clear on this. The customary principle of proportionality imposes a positive obligation on combatants to consider the possible impact on civilians of any attack or military strategy, and demands that the combatants seek to minimize such effects on civilians. If impacts are likely to be disproportionate in relation to the concrete and direct military advantage anticipated, the attack must be called off (or, by extension, the technology abandoned). Once the full long-term costs to communities in the affected nations are documented and exposed, it is almost unthinkable to suggest that such costs could ever be outweighed by any short-term military utility derived from the deployment of such weapons.

Sadly, the insights shared from Cambodia and Laos are by no means unique. These multifaceted and profound long-term humanitarian and developmental problems will exist to some extent in every one of the thirty-five or so mine- and UXO-contaminated nations that exist today. It is also not entirely accidental that most of these nations are located in the poor and underdeveloped South, and the weapons systems causing such debilitating effects have almost always been produced by the rich nations of the developed North. In this light, it is even less acceptable that the humanitarian funds available to respond to clearing up these nonbiodegradable remnants of conflict are still so minute when compared to the size and effects of the problem.

The cost of clearing the current worldwide burden of 100 million antipersonnel mines is already estimated at some $33 billion. The UN trust fund set up in New York for mine-clearance assistance in November 1994, after much lobbying by NGO/PVOs and intergovernmental organizations, held its first conference in July 1995. However, only one-third of the hoped-for budget of $75 million was pledged by member states.

If member states refuse to acknowledge the full humanitarian and developmental consequences of antipersonnel mines, and of UXO that have similar effects in postconflict situations, then they should—as a minimum—face the humanitarian arguments for a ban on these weapons more honestly. However, there seems little evidence that they are prepared to do this either. In September and October 1995, the 1980 Inhumane Weapons Convention and its protocol on landmines was reviewed in Vienna. Delegates were unable to agree even on a new protocol, let alone entertain the humanitarian arguments for a total ban. As one NGO observer noted, "The conference was designed to update international humanitarian law in order to protect civilians. However, governments on the whole seemed more interested in protecting their own weapons systems." Without such a ban, the devastation wrought upon Cambodia and Laos will continue to occur with every fresh conflict.

Notes

The views and opinions expressed here are the author's own, and do not necessarily express or imply those of the Mines Advisory Group, which has been operational in Cambodia since October 1992 and in Laos since May 1994.

1. In other areas, such as the central province of Kompong Thom, MAG has discovered a significant problem with unexploded antipersonnel submunitions, again predominantly the Blu-26 bomblet.

2. In the absence of professional humanitarian demining capacity, with operating minefield survey and marking capacity, local people build up mental maps of mine-contaminated areas by means of collective memory of where others have been injured or killed. However, in Cambodia, demining groups have labored for months only to clear a handful of mines in vast areas that the community had been denying themselves on the basis of just one accident. Accordingly, it is critical to consider the socioeconomic value to the community of the land being cleared rather than merely a number count of items destroyed. Destruction of an old ammunition dump might produce huge mine destruction rates but have minimal communal value.

3. The focus of my research in Cambodia in 1992–1993, presented in the book *War of the Mines*, was Rattanak Mondul district in the extreme southwest of Battambang province. The book was one of the first studies attempting to document the full socioeconomic impacts of landmine warfare.

4. Data gathering by the Mines Awareness Group.

5. Cutting wood, fishing, cutting grass, traveling in known mined areas, and collecting food.

6. Some sense of the scale of this underrecording has now started to emerge. For example, in 1992, Battambang provincial hospital had records on 164 mine cases admitted. Results from the MAG's data-gathering work have revealed that there were 183 mine accidents in Battambang during April-May 1995 alone. Clearly, accident rates are not likely to have escalated to such an extent.

7. Data from the three provinces indicate that average death rates of those having accidents with mines or UXO are 10.7 percent for women, 24.5 percent for civilian men and 32.2 percent for children (Moyes 1995). This again suggests that the gendered division of working responsibilities may also lead to women being injured in less remote areas and thus having better survival prospects.

8. Although they do become progressively less stable, causing difficulties when they are cleared.

9. However, there does seem to be uncertainty as the future of CMAC's funding past April 1996.

10. The sum of $30 million for CMAC over five years represents extraordinary value for the money. This budget requirement should be contrasted with the $88,782,000 allocated by the UN for vehicles during the two short years of the peace process period (1991–1993), or the $10,585,100 for generators, or even the $2,496,000 for contractual services (laundry, dry cleaning, tailoring, and hair-cutting services for contingent personnel).

11. Initial funding support to the project came from the Mennonite Central Committee, which had long been concerned about the burden of UXO in Laos. MAG also started to receive bilateral grants for its work in Laos, most notably from the British Overseas Development Agency, and has been able to greatly expand its integrated clearance, awareness, and data-gathering operations in

Xieng Khouang as a result. Other donors such as SIDA have expressed an interest in funding both the MAG project and the trust fund, and the European Union is planning a technical assessment mission during the first half of 1996.

12. The establishment of a training school to produce a regular flow of trained technicians every month is being planned for 1996 in Laos.

13. Ironically, minefields in these areas might be the only thing that prevent total environmental degradation at the hands of Thai gem miners and timber contractors, whose concessions, signed with the Khmer Rouge, are destroying great swathes of Cambodia's virgin forests.

14. Consists both of playing with UXO, moving UXO, and extracting explosives for fishing.

References

Becker, Elizabeth. 1986. *When the War Was Over: Cambodia Revolution and the Voices of Its People.* New York: Simon and Schuster.

Davies, Paul. 1994. *War of the Mines: Cambodia, Landmines and the Impoverishment of a Nation.* London: Pluto Press.

Moyes, Richard. 1995. "Preliminary Analysis of Mine Accident Report Data From Battambang, Kompong Thom and Banteay-Meanchay Provinces, Cambodia 1995." Cockermouth, England: Mines Advisory Group.

Prokosh, Eric. 1995. *The Technology of Killing.* London: Zed Books.

SIPRI (Stockholm International Peace Research Institute). 1978. *Anti-Personnel Weapons.* Internal report.

U.S. Department of State. 1993. *Hidden Killers: The Global Problem with Uncleared Landmines—A Report on International Demining.* Washington, D.C.: U.S. Department of State. Bureau of Political-Military Affairs.

12

Rehabilitating Household Food Production After War: The Rwandan Experience

David Tardif-Douglin

The purpose of this chapter is to examine relief and development agency efforts to rehabilitate household food production after the 1994 war and genocide in Rwanda. Review of the Rwandan experience provides lessons for future interventions aimed at rapidly reestablishing livelihoods and improving food security of large agricultural populations in other war-torn societies. The Rwandan case adds two particularly difficult dimensions to rehabilitation, however. First, the most fundamental institutions underlying social and economic life, except the most autarkic and self-sufficient, were destroyed by the genocide. This makes any intervention fraught with risk both for the short- and long-term stability of the society coming out of crisis. Second, Rwandan agricultural households were already facing substantial food insecurity before the crisis. In such a context it is not clear what rehabilitation, narrowly defined, achieves over the longer term. The Rwandan experience thus provides the extreme case, in which agricultural rehabilitation—generally considered neutral—can take on political dimensions, and where rehabilitation is clearly not enough.

The chapter begins with a brief description of Rwanda and key aspects of its agriculture before and immediately after the crisis. This allows the reader to decide the extent to which programs in Rwanda are transferable to countries having dissimilar agriculture systems. The next section reviews first-phase rehabilitation activities of the international community: provision of seeds and tools to farmers, food aid to ensure that seeds are not consumed before planting, and local multiplication of adapted seed. This is followed by an assessment of the problems and prospects, success, failures, and omissions of interventions aimed at reestablishing food security. The concluding section gleans those lessons that are most generalizable for other war-torn societies as they emerge from crisis.

Background

Rwanda is a small, mountainous, landlocked, and extremely densely populated country in Central Africa whose history has been marked by ethnic violence. It is bordered on the south by Burundi, which shares a similarly troubled and violent history. Its neighbor to the west is the Kivu region of Zaire. The Kivu has a large "ethnic" Rwandan population. To the north is Uganda, which also has a Kinywarwanda-speaking population (both Hutu and Tutsi-related Hima or Ankole). On the east is Tanzania, whose northwestern region has traditionally been an area of Rwandan migration. The mountainous terrain of Rwanda is partly responsible for its unique settlement patterns, in which families or households live in individual homesteads on hillsides or *collines* rather than in villages. Cool climates and few tropical diseases make much of Rwanda highly habitable. High, well-distributed rainfall, and good soils, especially in the volcanic regions, have permitted the sustenance of large populations.

Before the 1990 civil war intensified and degenerated into genocide and mass migration (between April and July 1994), more than nine in ten of the Rwandan population of nearly 8 million lived on farms, making Rwanda a highly agrarian society with a very small urban population.[1] Population density before the genocide was very high and population pressure severe. According to the 1991 census, the ethnic makeup of Rwanda before the war was roughly 90 percent Hutu, 8 percent Tutsi, and less than 1 percent Twa (an aboriginal group).[2] The postwar composition is unknown. The Hutu are believed to have migrated into the region nearly a thousand years ago and found the Twa already there. The Tutsi began to appear in the region 400 years later (fifteenth century) and were assimilated by the Hutu. The former took on the language and incorporated traditions and cults of the latter and lived in proximity to them. Clear ethnic distinctions existed, but clan affiliation, which cut across ethnic lines, seems to have been more important in precolonial times. Gradually, Tutsi military rule and administration were established over the Hutu and Twa.

The Rwandan economy is based on the largely rain-fed agricultural production of small, semisubsistence, and increasingly fragmented farms. It has few natural resources to exploit other than its ecotourism potential, and it has a small uncompetitive industrial sector. The production of coffee and tea, however, is very well suited to the small farms, steep slopes, and cool climates of Rwanda, and has ensured access to foreign exchange over the years. Nonetheless, Rwanda is extremely poor and faces the stark prospect of an even poorer future because of the juxtaposition of rapid population growth (in spite of the large number of people killed) with continued reliance on semisubsistence agriculture.

Agriculture, the mainstay of the economy, had been experiencing a growing crisis well before the war. While population has grown at the extremely high rate of 3 percent a year, agricultural technology has progressed very little. Consequently, per capita production of food has been declining (see Figure 12.1). The population density in 1994 was approximately 466 persons per square kilometer of arable land. Farm sizes were declining and were on average smaller than one hectare by 1994. Agricultural productivity continued to decline as near-continuous use of farmland with little use of fertilizer led to soil exhaustion and erosion. Rwandan farmers were acutely aware of population pressure, the limits to traditional solutions such as fallowing, and the high cost of modern solutions such as fertilizers. Out-migration, used frequently in the past as the solution of last resort, was becoming less tenable as populations (and resentment of immigrants) in neighboring countries were growing.

The intensification of civil war in April 1994 affected agricultural production. Precise figures are impossible to obtain. Nonetheless, the government of Rwanda and a UN Food and Agricultural Organization/World Food Programme (FAO/WFP) assessment estimated the

Figure 12.1
Daily Food Production Per Capita

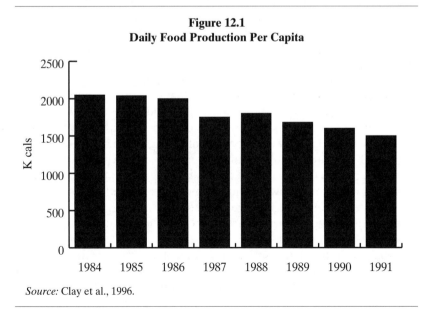

Source: Clay et al., 1996.

devastating effect of war and genocide. By the time the fighting had ended, large tracts of farmland had been abandoned, the coffee harvest had declined by half,[3] more than 80 percent of the cattle population had been lost, and four-fifths of all small ruminants had disappeared. Much of the equipment and material for household-based enterprises had been destroyed or looted, and rural infrastructure was heavily damaged. An FAO/WFP assessment concluded that the 1994B season crop, which should have been harvested in August-September, yielded only about 45 percent of 1993B levels.[4] Further, the government estimated hundreds of hectares of natural high-elevation forests had been damaged by displaced persons. Support systems for agriculture were almost completely destroyed. In the aftermath of the war, only two out of sixty researchers with the national agriculture research system remained in the country. None of the nine research stations and labs remained operational. The services of the Ministry of Agriculture—central administration, agriculture extension, and regional agriculture units—also suffered extensive losses.

Renewed fighting, massacres, and large-scale population displacements began in April, the planting period for Rwanda's second agricultural season. Consequently, many crops were not planted or, if planted, not tended during the critical first months of growth. What was planted in March-April should have been harvested in June-August, which is precisely when more than one-quarter of the prewar population had fled the country into asylum or had gone to camps for internally displaced persons (IDPs). Much of the harvest rotted in the field. This was especially so of the legumes (beans and peas) and the grains (sorghum and maize). The perennial crops (bananas, sweet potatoes, and cassava) were less affected, although some crop deterioration and loss occurred. This is important to understand because of their importance in the Rwandan diet. Export crops, primarily coffee and tea, were neglected during the war. Coffee harvest begins in March-April, and more than three-quarters of annual production is harvested between April and July. This production pattern agrees with reports that much of the 1994 coffee crop was lost. Tea, primarily a large plantation crop, was even more severely damaged, but the direct effect of lost tea production on the food security of small-scale farmers, few of whom grow it, was limited.

The condition of agriculture immediately after the war and genocide was one of generalized scarcity and food insecurity caused by lost food production and lost cash income. It is not clear what percentage of the population had been absent from their homes for protracted periods during the war, but many farms were abandoned for a month or more during a critical period in the agriculture cycle. This meant that many farmers lost some of their seeds and inputs for agricultural production. Coffee growers, nearly half of all farmers, experienced substantial losses in cash income. Furthermore, most components of the marketing system—merchants, vehicles, market administration, etc.—were destroyed. Without some assistance, rural people faced serious deprivation.[5] More than an estimated 150,000 metric tons of imported grains and pulses were needed to cover the consumption needs of the affected populations through the end of 1994.[6] Overall estimates of food aid requirements for Rwanda in 1995 were an additional 116,000 metric tons, valued at $66.9 million.[7]

Key Areas of International Assistance

Many interventions were made by the twenty-five or so agencies involved in agriculture rehabilitation. Besides the key programs discussed at greater length below, interventions included assistance in harvesting and transporting crops; rehabilitation of livestock; livestock vaccination campaigns; reforestation programs focusing on agroforestry; market garden production with farmer groups; and credit for women's agriculture and marketing cooperatives. Several UN and other relief agencies also provided logistical support to the Ministry of Agriculture and local agriculture associations, generally in conjunction with their own programs.

The principal nationwide interventions aimed at affecting agricultural production and food security were seeds and tools programs, programs of seed protection, and seed multiplication initiatives, including the Seeds of Hope Initiative. These programs were carried out largely by nongovernmental organizations (NGOs) and international organizations with the funding of bilateral and multilateral donors. Some relief agencies contributed sizable amounts of their own funds to agricultural rehabilitation. NGOs were usually the key implementing agencies. Among them (and international organizations) the most important were CARE, Catholic Relief Services (CRS), International Committee of the Red Cross (ICRC), Action Nord-Sud, Lutheran World Federation, Trocaire, and World Vision. The FAO, WFP, and UNICEF were the most active UN organizations. The United States, European Union, Germany, Belgium, the Netherlands, and the World Bank provided most of the funds for agriculture rehabilitation programs. Their support has been channeled (and tracked) through the United Nations Appeals Processes and the UN Development Programme (UNDP) Round Table Conference for Rwandan Reconstruction. The Consolidated Appeals processes for the Rwandan crisis began with the July 1994 Appeal, and culminated in a large, comprehensive Appeal in January 1995, which included key UN agencies and some international organizations and NGOs. The 1995 Appeal included about $54 million in programs aimed specifically at first-stage rehabilitation of the rural economy. Most of the funding for the programs reviewed below was channeled through the UN Appeal. During the Round Table Conference, donors pledged $79 million for long-term rehabilitation of agriculture and the rural economy, of which only 4 percent had been disbursed by May 1995 (see Table 12.1). Of the donors pledging funds specifically to agriculture and the rural economy through the Round Table, only Belgium and the UK had made any disbursements. Some donors included in their Round Table pledges funds they had provided through the 1995 Appeal, but overall, uniformity or standardization in cross-referencing rehabilitation funds between the Appeal and the Round Table was lacking.

Determining the immediate needs of the rural population was clearly one of the most urgent priorities facing the government and relief agencies as they attempted to reestablish some degree of food security in the countryside. Several nationwide assessments had important impacts on the level and nature of interventions. While the most comprehensive assessments of crop and food supply situations were the WFP/FAO missions,[8] many larger, more experienced NGOs undertook assessments in their areas of intervention. Nonetheless, some initial interventions in agriculture and the rural economy were made with little but impressionistic and anecdotal information of the situation on the ground.

Table 12.1   Principal Round Table Donors for Rehabilitation of Agriculture and Rural Economy (US$ millions)

Donors	Pledged	Committed	Disbursed
International Fund for Agricultural Development	30.4	25.4	0
European Union	16.9	0	0
African Development Bank	14.1	7.1	0
Germany	10.2	6.3	0
Spain	3.5	0	0
Belgium	2.7	2.7	2.7
FAO	0.8	0	0
United Kingdom	0.6	0.6	0.6
Total	79.2	42.1	3.3

Source: "Situation des engagements du PRRRSE," Round Table tracking document produced by Government of Rwanda, Ministry of Plan, May 16, 1995.

Seeds and Tools Programs

Immediate rehabilitation of household agricultural production to achieve food security was the primary emphasis in the rural sector. The provision of seeds and tools began as early as May 1994 in parts of the country that had come under Rwanda Patriotic Front control and had gained some stability and security. With the end of the war the international community faced the prospect of providing massive amounts of food aid to many farm families whose livelihoods had been disrupted. To avoid this, relief agencies turned their attention to helping farmers restart their production. Speed was of the essence because there was little time between the end of fighting and the beginning of planting for the subsequent agricultural season. Agriculture agencies realized farmers were going to need assistance. The FAO had requested funds for seeds and tools programs in the July UN Consolidated Appeals. Nevertheless, no one could predict when the crisis would be over and access possible.

> Seeds programs can be considered political.
>
> *—Official of relief agency, New York*
>
> We generally did not target food aid for fear of creating conflict. Targeting requires greater political will than we were able to bring to bear on the situation. Everyone was "vulnerable."
>
> *—Representative of UN agency, Kigali*

Initial distribution of seeds and tools was ad hoc; various relief agencies, using their own funds or soliciting funds from donors, provided seeds and tools as and where they deemed necessary. NGOs providing other services in an area often undertook to provide agriculture inputs in the same area. The complexity of procurement varied from local seed purchase to solicitation of international bids for farm tools.

Starting in August 1994, FAO and the Ministry of Agriculture provided a degree of coordination and coherence through a series of weekly meetings. The principal relief agencies participating in agriculture rehabilitation attended these meetings, which focused on ensuring regional coverage.[9] By the time the weekly meetings began, some NGOs had already begun to distribute packages of seeds and tools. Thus, an initial objective of coordination was to find out who was working where and to direct new agencies to regions that were not being served. Another objective was to define the target population, that is, those farmers most needing assistance. WFP also participated in these meetings to ensure coordination between food aid, food for seed protection, and the seeds and tools.

Seeds and tools programs were initially conceived for returning refugees and IDPs but became general in scope. This change in emphasis was prompted by the realization that many survivors who had never left their homes or had been away briefly had also lost their productive inputs and tools and were in need of assistance. Targeting was a popular theme, especially in program proposals and documents. In practice, most agencies distributed to all households in their region of intervention, often on a first-come-first-served basis. Targeting was considered neither feasible, cost-effective, nor politically advisable in the already highly polarized and tense situation in much of the countryside.[10] Local authorities at *commune* and *secteur* (administrative subdivisions) levels were asked to draw up lists of farm households in their jurisdiction. These lists were used for distribution. Depending on availability, each household on the list received a "package" of bean, sorghum, maize, and vegetable seeds and one or two hoes. This was done for two seasons (1995A/B). In the first season of distribution, packages were generally undifferentiated. In the second season, types and quantities were more closely tailored to the needs and growing conditions of farmers.

For most agencies, distribution for the first season (1995A) was rushed. Consequently, seeds provided were not carefully screened for adaptability, quality, diseases, or pests. Furthermore, regional variation in crop mixes and crop varieties was not effectively taken into account; packages did not vary substantially from region to region. Most agencies had no more than one month between the cessation of hostilities and the beginning of the planting period to procure, ship, prepare, and distribute the agriculture packages. This, of course, raises the issue of advance planning and prepositioning. The FAO and other specialized agriculture agencies must have known that massive rehabilitation assistance would be needed after the war. It is not clear, however, what they had done to ensure that the process of rehabilitation would be expedited once the opportunity for intervention presented itself.

Many start-up difficulties of the first season had been solved by the time a new push was made to distribute agriculture rehabilitation packages for the second season (1995B). By this time, regional coverage was better; through the weekly meetings cochaired by FAO and the Ministry of Agriculture, uncovered regions were identified and coverage ensured. In fact, it appears that regions initially believed not to need assistance, much of Ruhengeri, for example, were nonetheless provided seeds and tools. More households were covered during the second season; estimates of coverage are 80 percent. The seeds provided were better adapted, and quantities of seeds were better tailored to the needs of the many regions and agricultural microclimates of Rwanda.

By May 1995, agencies and the government were debating the merits of general versus targeted distribution for the subsequent season (1996A). One view was that distribution should target returnees and designated vulnerable groups, such as widows and child heads of households, if distribution should occur at all. Some individuals felt strongly that assistance for food agriculture rehabilitation should be reduced or ended. A CRS list of criteria for targeting attests to the difficulty deter-

---

Catholic Relief Services Seeds and Tools Program

Catholic Relief Services (CRS) is a highly experienced NGO with extensive knowledge of Rwanda and Rwandan agriculture. Most of CRS's involvement in rehabilitation in Rwanda has been in conjunction with Caritas Internationalis and with the local Catholic church.

The agency had been working in Rwanda before the crisis, and was among the first to undertake agriculture rehabilitation projects after the war. Between July 1994 and July 1995, CRS, through Caritas and the Catholic dioceses, provided nearly 1,150 metric tons of vegetable seeds and 96,000 hoes to 98,600 farm households in Butare and Gitarama in the south of the country. Lists of households in each of the dioceses in which CRS was working were drawn up. These lists served as the basis for distribution of seeds and tools.

Because of its food pipeline (largely dependent on USAID Food for Peace funding or provision of food), CRS was also able smoothly to combine seed protection packages with its seeds and tools distributions. As discussed below, this also enabled CRS to be more liberal in its definition of seed protection and provide much larger rations than most other agencies.

CRS staff were actively involved in weekly coordination meetings cochaired by the FAO and Ministry of Agriculture during the early phases of agricultural rehabilitation. The agency proposes to continue free distribution into a third season.

—Catholic Relief Services Situation Reports, July 1994–August 1995.

mining who should receive assistance. Qualifying as vulnerable and therefore the target group for continued distribution of seeds and tools were households

- Having less than 60–70 areas of cultivable land
- Having no cattle
- Having a known unstable situation
- Not having produced in the last season
- Headed by widows or widowers[11]

Most Rwandan households would likely meet one of these criteria, making the list too expansive and of limited use for targeting.

During two seasons, more than 10,000 metric tons of bean and maize seeds, 700,000 hoes, and vegetable and other seeds were distributed to 690,000 households.[12] The estimated coverage (50 percent in season 1995A, 80 percent in season 1995B)[13] raises two issues. The first concerns the target population to whom these figures refer. When the first season distribution began, many individuals were only beginning to return to their land from internal or external displacement. The population should have been more settled by the second season distribution. Nonetheless, the target population (individuals on their own farmland or squatting on others') must have been exceedingly variable. Furthermore, according to interviews with field staff of NGOs and other relief agencies, seeds and tools packages were provided according to *commune* and *secteur* lists drawn up by local officials. It is not clear whether the percentages refer to listed households or to all households in the region. A rapid reconnaissance interview with farmers in regions where distributions were made suggested most had received assistance, but coverage was not complete. We were not able to find out the extent to which lists presented by *commune* and *secteur* leaders were fair and inclusive.

The other issue, in many ways more fundamental, was the relationship between programs and needs. As mentioned above, the seeds and tools programs were initially designed with refugees and IDPs as the primary target. This was based on the assumption that they lost all their productive inputs—seeds, hoes, machetes. The extraordinarily high tensions within the communities that forced relief agencies to remove machetes from the "packages" suggested that only general distribution to all available farmers would be acceptable. In fact, many farmers who were on their land at the time of distribution had also felt it necessary to abandon their homes at some point in the fighting, or had their tools stolen or destroyed. Seed supply, especially, could have been short. These factors provided the rationale to distribute to all comers on a first-come-first-served basis. The problem is that some farmers who did not receive seeds or tools resumed farming just the same. Figuring out the extent to which the supply of seeds and tools matched the need is very difficult. Furthermore, it is possible that the greatest value was in showing concern to the war-affected population and in recapitalizing to some extent small farms.

Food Distribution for Seed Protection

Along with the distribution of seeds and tools, relief agencies provided food aid for "seed protection." As the name implies, this was done on the

---

CARE International

CARE was working in Rwandan agriculture when the civil war intensified. It resumed emergency and rehabilitation programs in July 1994, when the war ended.

After having distributed seeds and tools in five of Rwanda's ten prefectures, CARE initiated a survey to determine the success of its program. Key criteria were the quality and appropriateness of the seeds and tools provided, and the effect of the program on the communities served. The survey of nearly 2,000 randomly selected households was conducted in CARE's areas of intervention in the east, center, and southwest, and focused on results of season B (February 1995) assistance. According to the survey report, 1 percent of the target population was surveyed.

The results were: (a) between 90 and 95 percent of the target population had received seeds and tools packages; (b) households in some prefectures receiving sorghum and bean seeds too late for (optimal) planting; (c) the majority of the population in some areas consumed more than half the bean seeds they received; (d) in other areas most recipients of sorghum seed consumed more than half of what they received; and (e) 70 percent of households received at least one hoe.

Reasons most frequently cited for not receiving agricultural inputs were:
- Exclusion from distribution lists
- Absence when lists were drawn up
- Insufficient quantities
- Unfair distribution

—*Greer, Heather, and Abby Maxman. "CARE International in Rwanda's Seeds & Tools Survey Report in Byumba, Gikongoro, Gitarama, Kibungo, and Kigali," CARE International in Rwanda (Kigali, May 1995).*

premise that providing substantial amounts of food aid to protect more expensive selected seed for planting was worthwhile. When farmers were given seeds and agricultural implements, they were given food rations for a few weeks. Not all agencies stuck to the three-week seed protection program; some chose to provide food aid to farmers for three months, until beans and some sweet potatoes were harvested. CRS, for example, felt strongly that seed protection needed to continue until harvest, not just until seeds were planted. In most regions, food aid for seed protection was distributed for both agricultural seasons.

The lead agencies, WFP, CRS, and ICRC, had their own food pipelines and coordinated with the Ministry of Agriculture and other relief agencies to ensure food distribution to farm households. Seed protection food distribution was carried out while general distribution was made. So it is not clear how effective the seed protection programs were. Their advantage was that food could be given directly to the same households receiving seeds. The results of CARE's survey suggest that despite the seed protection programs, substantial numbers of farm households may have eaten the seed they received. Whether this was out of extreme need or because farmers chose to plant their own seed is not clear. Sorghum seed, especially, was extremely likely to be consumed rather than planted.

How much food was distributed to farm households as seed protection versus general food aid is unclear. In the January 1995 Appeal, WFP requested $32.9 million specifically for seed protection and other agriculture support programs. According to WFP Kigali staff, no seed protection "packages" were distributed in the north, considered relatively unaffected or to have rebounded quickly from the war. WFP and its implementing partners distributed seed protection food rations to 200,000 farm households in the first season (6,000 metric tons of commodities) and 300,000 in the second season. By WFP accounts, seed protection programs were more targeted in the second season than they had been in the first.

Seed Multiplication

An important concern to agriculturalists was the possibility that Rwanda's crops may have lost much of their genetic diversity through destruction of varieties adapted to local conditions. Practically, farmers reestablishing their production needed appropriate, clean, and easily available seeds. Seeds provided in the first season of assistance came largely from outside Rwanda, usually from Uganda and Burundi, but in some cases from outside the region. Germination rates, adaptability to soils, and resistance to diseases were poor. Agriculturalists realized that rapid multiplication of known and tested seeds would be a more effective way to provide adapted seeds to farmers with insufficient stocks of their own.

In February 1995, several research and technical agencies,[14] relief and development agencies, Belgium's Seeds Service Project, and the Rwandan agricultural research system (ISAR) met to coordinate activities to reestablish a national seed program. The International Agriculture Research Centers (IARCs), through the Seeds of Hope Initiative, were to focus on the provision of "foundation stock"— that is, seeds that provide the input for the multiplication process. The Seeds Service Project was to provide the basic seed to be multiplied, which would be done largely by NGOs in collaboration with ISAR research stations.

The Seeds of Hope Initiative led to several activities: the multiplication of potato seed in Uganda through a regional potato research consortium; the contracting of Cargill Tanzania to multiply maize varieties grown in Rwanda; and the multiplication of regionally adapted "basic" seed for sorghum and bean for final multiplication and distribution within Rwanda. More than 18 tons of potato seed and 148 tons of maize seed were to be transported to Rwanda for further multiplication and distribution by the third quarter of 1995. The IARCs were asked by the government, NGOs, and the FAO to focus quickly on in-country research, multiplication and capacity building. In their absence, it is largely NGOs that are helping with multiplication and rudimentary testing of seeds for distribution. World Vision, the most active of the NGOs, is operating multiplication fields in four ISAR field stations. In addition, CRS/Caritas Internationalis is engaged in a program of sweet potato and cassava multiplication with diocesan organizations and farmer associations. CRS provides the basic inputs—seedstock, pesticides, and fertilizer—through the diocese, and purchases multiplied seed from the farmers for onward distribution.

Intervention Shortfalls

Along with the successes, some weaknesses of international assistance for agriculture rehabilitation in Rwanda have been pointed out. This section focuses on issues of omission and of unintended effects that could affect medium- to long-term reestablishment of household food security. These include the possible dependency effects of continued general distribution of seeds, tools and food aid; the issue of land rights; neglect of export crops; ignorance of market effects; and ignorance of the deep effects of genocide.

World Vision International

World Vision International is an experienced and very large relief and development NGO, but with limited experience in prewar Rwanda. Because of large grants and impressive agriculture capacity, however, World Vision quickly became a major player in agriculture rehabilitation.

It was an important provider of seeds and tools packages, called Agpaks, in the center, north, and southwest regions of Rwanda. Agpaks were distributed for two cropping seasons beginning in September 1994. World Vision's most unique role in agriculture rehabilitation was in rebuilding national seed multiplication capacity. Other agencies undertook programs to rapidly multiply seeds for onward distribution, but none went so far as World Vision in its involvement with the government.

Under the conditions of a Memorandum of Understanding with the government, World Vision undertook the rehabilitation of seed multiplication in some of the largely abandoned research stations of Rwanda's respected agricultural research center (Institut des Sciences Agronomiques du Rwanda [ISAR]). World Vision agreed to pay the salaries of some technical staff, extension agents, and researchers until the government could assume them.

At the seed multiplication fields in northwest Rwanda, which had been the site of a donor-funded potato research center, World Vision has taken over operations, pays salaries, and is focusing on mutiplying potato and maize seed, key crops for the region. The seed from these fields, some of it coming through the International Agriculture Research Centers "Seeds of Hope" partners, is distributed to farmers' associations or individual farmers who then multiply further and sell (in principle) 80 percent of the seed back to World Vision for onward distribution.

The Seeds of Hope "consortium" has asked World Vision to coordinate formal training for Rwandan seed multipliers (researchers and technicians) in collaboration with the much-diminished ISAR.

—*World Vision Situation Reports, July 1994–August 1995*

One important issue that is not unique to the Rwandan case, but is underscored by it, is dependency. Clearly the devastation experienced by Rwandan farm households at one point precluded much self-help. With time, however, farmers gained greater ability to improve their own situation. Relief and development agencies faced the dilemma of deciding when to cut off assistance or at least phase it out. However, by their very nature—mandate, culture, funding, etc.—relief agencies find this difficult to do. An example of this difficulty is the definition of vulnerable households in Rwanda according to CRS. Nonetheless, for longer-term development of agriculture, farmers must as quickly as possible resort to the sum of their own initiatives as "managed" through a combination of market and cooperative or public action. Relief agencies needed to decide what constituted realistic cutoff points for free distribution for entire communities rather than for individual households. After the initial emergency distribution, community-based assistance (not free distribution of food aid or agricultural implements) that aimed at strengthening the capacity of entire communities to help the most vulnerable would be preferable to distribution of aid at the household level.

Not moving quickly to eliminate free distribution creates dependency, an especially sobering prospect for Rwanda given the reputation for hard work and productivity of Rwandan farmers. In May 1995, after two distributions of seeds and tools, some Rwandan officials of agencies involved in agriculture rehabilitation were actively trying to stop free general distribution, which they insisted was eroding incentives and creating dependency among farmers. The flip side of dependency is waste. If more is given than needed to rehabilitate productivity of farm households, scarce resources are being wasted. This was (rightly) not an overriding concern in the early period (first distribution) of rehabilitation; but it should have become an increasingly important issue during subsequent distributions.

Property rights are clearly an important and explosive issue in contemporary Rwanda. Competing claims on land, especially, threaten political progress and improvements among ethnic groups. The government is on record supporting the Arusha accords, which do not recognize land claims of the "old caseload" refugees/returnees who were away from their land for more than ten years. It is the government's responsibility to protect the rights of "new caseload" refugees to the land they abandoned temporarily. Nevertheless, the international community must also avoid even the appearance of supporting counterclaims. This becomes a thorny issue when squatters (old caseload refugees who returned) are provided with seeds and tools. This tacit approval of their land use rights, however temporary, can exacerbate tensions between old and new caseload returnees. It is not clear how or whether relief and development agencies attempted to consider this issue in designing programs or in their decisions about continuing or ending distribution.

The neglect of export crops, especially coffee, which is produced almost exclusively on small farms, represents an important missed opportunity. The agencies traditionally involved in supporting the development of export crops have been slow to move (World Bank, European Union) or uninvolved (French). We have mentioned above that it was perfectly normal, and even desirable, to emphasize food agriculture first. Nonetheless, NGOs that would have liked to do something to help harvest coffee or rehabilitate production or the marketing chain felt constrained from doing so out of concern that export crops were not part of their mandate and that any intervention in the sector should be left to agencies with more experience in that sector.[15]

Ensuring fair market access for coffee growers (and farmers picking coffee from abandoned fields) would have been the most efficient and effective means to remonetize the rural economy. Ironically, while little was done to reconstruct the coffee marketing and processing system (some farmers were getting far less than the official 300 FRW/kg), relief agencies were rushing to develop projects to inject funds into the rural economy. Well-timed and well-placed assistance to the coffee sector would have had important financial and psychological effects at both the household and the national level. The financial effects are self-evident. Psychologically, farmers and government officials alike would have felt that their destiny was largely in their own hands.

Rwandan agriculture was in crisis even before the war. This was in large part due to structural problems, including land scarcity and soil depletion and erosion, and partly due to external shocks—the precipitous fall in world coffee prices from 1989 to 1993. However, agricultural policies that reduced the choice of farmers and relied on civil servants to dictate to farmers what was best also had a role in the crisis. Such an approach to agriculture policy needs to be rethought. It is not apparent, however, that any agency has taken the opportunity that rehabilitation affords to help the new government rethink agriculture policy. Many aspects of previous agriculture policy reflected paternalistic attitudes of the government toward farmers. Policies on crop choice and land tenancy, for example, stressed subordination of individual objectives to national ones. For example, coffee-growing households could not freely stop producing coffee even if their own calculations suggested it was unprofitable. According to policymakers, the need for foreign exchange outweighed the need for individual households to be profitable. Similarly, land sales were restricted. Farmers having farms smaller than a minimum size were not allowed to sell their land. This was ostensibly to protect farm households from falling further into poverty, but it also took decisionmaking away from farmers. These and other aspects of Rwanda's agriculture policy need to be reviewed by the new government with help from the international community. The new government is considering greater control over how agricultural land is used. For example, Ministry of Agriculture officials are considering insisting that farmers with land well suited to coffee production grow coffee or vacate the land. Greater freedom of crop choice by farmers, not less, is more likely to lead to solutions to Rwanda's agriculture crisis. International intervention aimed at the rehabilitation and ultimate development of Rwandan agriculture should urgently engage the government in such policy debate.

Conclusion

Given the lack of statistically sound baseline data, measuring the impact of seeds and tools programs, let alone the interventions that would affect production more indirectly (seed protection and seed multiplication), is not possible definitively. This is not surprising given the devastation. It is almost a truism to point out that the data-gathering and processing capacity of the state was destroyed by the war and has not effectively been rebuilt.

Ideally, to assess the impact and effectiveness of agriculture rehabilitation programs fully, it is first necessary to understand the need. However, lacking good information about the most basic aspects of the rural population after the war, even this is not completely clear. With returnees, the need for agricultural tools and seeds appeared clearest, which is one reason the seeds and tools programs were initially designed for them. Sometimes, however, returnees had left behind caches of tools and favorite seeds before departing. Conversely, some farmers who had never left their homes or had left only briefly had their belongings looted. Knowing what percentage lost their productive capacity, or how many farmers would have been completely unable to farm their fields without seeds and tools programs, is almost impossible. The process by which seeds were lost—eaten or lost (rotted) in the fields—is completely understandable. However, it is not evident what might have happened to the lost agricultural tools unless they were carried away to countries of asylum to be sold or used there. Many relief agencies were operating with little more than anecdotal or impressionistic information about the needs of individual households; much of the information simply did not exist.

Also, impact on aggregate agricultural production depends on the extent to which rehabilitation programs actually met needs: the extent to which farm households planted at all or planted more than otherwise. As mentioned above, however, measurement of this is compounded by the poor information about the level of need. Since targeting was considered by many agencies to be inadvisable, it is certain that households that did not need free tools and seeds to begin farming received packages nonetheless. So, from a purely sectoral perspective, the program was less than maximally effective. Political imperatives forced a certain level of impact ineffectiveness on the seeds and tools program, supposedly because without paying attention to the political realities, the whole program (along with other interventions) would have been put at risk. Thus, in a case such as Rwanda, lacking nearly all the information upon which assessments of impact and effectiveness can be based, evaluations must rely on the intuition and logic of careful, trained observers who are knowledgeable of the sector in question.

The short-run effect of agriculture interventions by the international community was positive. The increase in the supply of seed and tools reduced the cost of their procurement and very likely increased the acreage planted. In-country seed multiplication, independent of outside foundation stock, or with the Seeds of Hope Initiative, further contributed to the supply of seeds and, more important, to the supply of adapted seeds. Similarly, the volume of increased production from seed protection food aid can only be surmised. The medium- and long-term impacts, however, are much less certain, fraught as they are with the pitfalls of dependency and the sense of entitlement fostered by extended free distribution of inputs.

Lessons Learned and Recommendations

- In complex emergencies, even apparently innocuous agriculture rehabilitation programs can be political. To avoid serious political repercussions, it may be necessary to accept some programmatic inefficiency by delaying targeting initially. The reluctance of relief agencies' field representatives to enforce targeting—that is, giving seeds, tools and food only to the most vulnerable—reflected an understanding of political tensions. Some field staff realized that during the early phases of rehabilitation, further division of Rwandans according to degrees of vulnerability was dangerous. Because of this, field staff appear to have passively resisted unwarranted pressure from home offices and donors to target more aggressively. The latter did not understand the tense political climate in which distribution was made, or were more responsive to home country pressure for efficiency. NGO home offices and donors should consider more carefully the legitimate concerns of field staff about their perceptions of cost efficiency–political expediency trade-offs.

- For governments seeking legitimacy, continuation of programs of general, free distribution of seeds, food, and tools is popular and difficult to end. Yet for longer-term welfare and reestablishment of incentive structures conducive to development, such programs must be ended as soon as there is a minimal restoration of productive capacity. The implication of Rwandan NGO and UN staff who suggested termination of free distribution was that the government (and possibly relief agencies) perceived short-term political benefit in continuing distribution past the point of usefulness. This sort of calculus is natural and valuable up to a point. However, at some stage the political benefits are likely to be outweighed by the economic and psychological (morale) costs. These staff intuitively (and with anecdotal information) realized the high cost of continuation: dependency and erosion of incentives. The international community must also realize the need of Rwandans to quickly, if painfully, begin to solve their problems themselves.

- Interventions should draw more completely on existing information to ensure that proposed actions are firmly grounded in the best available information, are necessary, and are sufficient. Field staff of one NGO explicitly stated that seeds and tools programs were designed in the home office with very little participation from the field. Such disregard for field opinion is assumedly based on a belief in greater programmatic transferability than may be possible. For interventions in developing countries, and Africa in particular, it may also be predicated on a sense that there is little or no useful information to be gained from the field. Whatever the reasons, underutilizing existing resources leads to such errors as a large U.S. NGO providing vegetable seed in inappropriately large quantities.

- The primary objective of agricultural rehabilitation programs should be to ensure food security for the medium term and, ultimately, to establish the base for progress to longer-term food security. Food aid is a better tool for short-term food security. If seeds and tools programs are looked to for solutions to short-term food shortages, they are likely to be rushed and lead to inconsistencies and medium-term costs that will erode their impact.

Notes

1. The population of the largest city and the capital, Kigali, was slightly more than 300,000. The next largest town had a little more than 30,000 residents.

2. The remaining 1 percent were expatriates, largely from neighboring countries, residing in Rwanda. Preindependence estimates of ethnic composition

were 85 percent Hutu, 14 percent Tutsi, and 1 percent Twa. See Government of Rwanda (1993).

3. The lost earnings from coffee alone are staggering. Had the coffee harvest occurred as normal, the 30,000 tons of coffee likely to have been exported would have earned three times as much as in 1993, up to $92 million more than the normal annual earnings, owing to exceptionally high world prices for coffee.

4. Total area of 1994B was similar to 1993B, but estimated output in 1994B was 60 percent of 1993B. Only 75 percent of output was harvested, which suggests that only 45 percent of 1993B levels was available for consumption in 1994B. See FAO/WFP (1995).

5. See FAO (1995).

6. See UN Department of Humanitarian Affairs (1995, vol 1).

7. See UN Department of Humanitarian Assistance, *International Humanitarian Assistance to Rwanda and Burundi.*

8. The first WFP/FAO mission was conducted October 29–November 21, and the second February 9–23, 1995.

9. Interview with Wilmer Collette, FAO Representative, Kigali, Rwanda, May 1995.

10. One NGO, World Vision, insists that it did target the most vulnerable populations; however, it appears that targeting was by region, not household.

11. Catholic Relief Services–Rwanda Program, "Sitrep #53," August 31, 1995, Kigali, Rwanda.

12. See FAO (1995).

13. Interview with Mr. Roome, CARE official, Kigali, Rwanda, May 1995.

14. To include the International Agriculture Research Centers (IARCs) CIP, CIAT, CIMMYT, ICRISAT, as well as the FAO and the World Bank.

15. Based on field interviews in Kigali, Rwanda, and phone interviews from Washington, D.C.

References

CARE. 1994. *CARE International in Rwanda—Rwanda Disaster Operations Project: Final Report.* Kigali: CARE.

CIAT. 1994. "Rwanda Civil War Disrupts Key African Food Program." *CIAT International* 13:1–2.

Clay, D., F. Byiringiro, J. Kangasniemi, T. Reardon, B. Sibomana, D. Tardif-Douglin, and L. Uwamariya. 1996. *Promoting Food Security in Rwanda Through Sustainable Agricultural Productivity: Meeting the Challenges of Population Pressure, Land Degradation and Poverty.* East Lansing: Michigan State University.

Economist Intelligence Unit. 1994a. *Country Profile: Rwanda, Burundi.* London: Economist Intelligence Unit. Photocopy.

Economist Intelligence Unit. 1994b. *Country Report: Uganda, Rwanda, Burundi.* London: Economist Intelligence Unit. Photocopy.

FAO (UN Food and Agricultural Organization). 1995. *République du Rwanda: Diagnostique et propositions d'actions prioritaires pour la réhabilitation et la relance du secteur agricole.* Rome: FAO.

FAO/WFP (UN Food and Agricultural Organization/World Food Programme). 1995. *FAO/WFP Crop and Food Supply Assessment Mission to Rwanda.* Rome: FAO.

Government of Rwanda. 1993. *Recensement général de la population et de l'habitat au 15 août 1991*. Kigali: Government of Rwanda.

Government of Rwanda. Ministry of Plan. 1995a. S*ituation des engagements du PRRRSE*. Kigali: Ministry of Plan.

Government of Rwanda. 1995b. *Programme of National Reconciliation and Socio-Economic Rehabilitation and Recovery*. Kigali: Government of Rwanda. Photocopy.

Government of Rwanda. 1995c. *Policy Declaration of the Rwandese Government on the Occasion of the Round Table Conference Held in Geneva on 17–18 January 1995*. Kigali: Government of Rwanda. Photocopy.

Pottier, Johan, and John Wilding. 1994. *Food Security and Agricultural Rehabilitation in Post-War Rwanda*. Save the Children/UK. Photocopy.

UN Department of Humanitarian Affairs. 1995. *UN Consolidated Inter-Agency Appeal for Persons Affected by the Crisis in Rwanda: January-December 1995*. Vols. 1 and 2. New York: UN Department of Humanitarian Affairs.

U.S. Committee for Refugees. 1994. *Selected Chronology of the Rwanda Crisis, April 5, 1994 to September 30, 1994*. Washington, D.C.: US Committee for Refugees.

Vassall-Adams, Guy. 1994. *Rwanda: An Agenda for International Action*. London: Oxfam Publications.

World Bank. 1995. *Rwandese Republic Emergency Recovery Project Technical Annex*. Report No. T-6483-RW. Washington, D.C.: World Bank. Photocopy.

13

Macroeconomic Policy and Peace Building in El Salvador

James K. Boyce and Manuel Pastor, Jr.

The transition from civil war to peace poses formidable challenges for economic policy. During the postconflictual transition, the goals of economic policy cannot be limited to macroeconomic stabilization and conventional structural adjustment but should also promote the adjustment toward peace. In a world where civil conflict is tragically widespread, the postwar experience of El Salvador offers valuable lessons.

The interdependence of peace and development in El Salvador is widely recognized. A failure to achieve broad improvements in living standards would fuel social tensions and heighten the risk of renewed war—and a return to war would shatter hopes for economic revival. Yet there has been little systematic discussion of how economic policy should be reshaped in the special circumstances of a country emerging from civil war. In El Salvador, the government and the international financial institutions (IFIs) have pursued essentially the same macroeconomic stabilization and structural adjustment policies they would have followed had the country never been at war, partly because of a belief that if the peace process were allowed to interfere with economic policy, both might fail. We maintain, in contrast, that *unless* the peace process is allowed to reshape economic policy, both will fail.

Three broad sets of economic issues arise in the adjustment toward peace. The first concerns the problem of financing the immediate costs of peace, including the establishment of new democratic institutions, the reintegration of ex-combatants into civilian life, and the repair of physical infrastructure. The mobilization of resources for the peace process is a political problem as well as a financial one. External actors must deploy appropriate conditionalities if their aid is to support the momentum of the peace process and "crowd in" domestic resources for peace-related needs.

The second set of issues concerns the need for macroeconomic stability. Civil wars often generate underlying inflationary pressures, sometimes relieved by the presence of external aid to the government at war, as well as the distortion of economic resource allocation. Given the demands of peace building outlined above, it is tempting to consider a simple expansion of demand to buoy the economy and keep all domestic actors (temporarily) satisfied. But because this risks macroeconomic crisis in the future, adjusting countries need to maintain some degree of fiscal discipline even as they seek to finance the requirements of peace.

The third set of issues concerns the longer-term interrelationships among economic growth, income distribution, and peace. Civil wars often arise from a perceived imbalance of income and wealth; unless this is corrected, the seeds for war are sown once again. Fortunately, recent research suggests that ameliorating inequity can actually produce better economic policy and faster economic growth. Convincing economic policymakers that promoting equality is a reasonable recipe for reactivating the economy and promoting peace is a critical task for international financial institutions. One way to do this is to stress the positive impacts of investment in human and natural capital as well as physical capital. Recognizing that economic policy does not emerge from a technocratic vaccuum, policymakers also need to consider the political economy of (or political constituencies for) improved equity. In this light, democratization—in the broad sense of movement toward a more equitable distribution of power—can improve the functioning of both the state and the market and remains a key component of economic policy. Naturally, these issues are not unique to countries emerging from civil war. But the postconflictual setting presents them in exceptionally stark relief.

In this chapter, we consider these issues of finance, macroeconomic stability, and equity in the context of El Salavador. While we search for generalizable lessons from the Salvadoran experience, we also stress at least one unique feature of this case: Because El Salvador wound up "exporting" so many of its people during the period of conflict, it now has a foreign exchange bonanza of remittances that, if properly used, can ease its transition. A key policy issue for El Salvador, we suggest, is evaluating whether both this source of foreign exchange and external assistance are indeed being used to support peace, equity, and growth in the most effective manner.

The chapter proceeds as follows. Section 2 sketches the context for economic policy in postwar El Salvador, including a brief history of both the political aspects of the peace process and recent macroeconomic performance. Section 3 discusses the short-run issues of financing the costs of peace in the current circumstances. Section 4 considers the longer-term policy issues of equity and growth and argues strongly for seeing the complementarity of both imperatives. Section 5 offers some concluding observations.

Ending the War in El Salvador:
The Peace Accords and Macroeconomic Policy

The Peace Accords and the Political Setting

The war in El Salvador had many losers, but no clear victors. The peace accords brokered by the United Nations and signed at Chapultepec, Mexico, in January 1992 were born of a military stalemate. The twelve-year civil war, which claimed some 75,000 lives, had brought neither the government nor the guerrillas of the Farabundo Martí Front for National Liberation (FMLN) the prospect of a decisive victory. Both sides agreed to major concessions, to be implemented in phased steps in the ensuing months. The government agreed to recognize the FMLN as a legitimate political party; to disband its paramilitary police forces and replace them with a new, politically neutral police force; to purge the armed forces of those responsible for human rights abuses; to reform the judiciary and establish new democratic institutions; and to transfer land to ex-combatants and supporters of the FMLN. In return, the guerrillas agreed to lay down their arms and contend for power via free elections.

Under the timetable established in the accords, each side agreed to implement a series of measures tied to complementary actions by the other. The implementation process was beset by a number of delays, however. While these delays were sometimes blamed on financial constraints, the real reasons were generally political; basically, the process of conflict and negotiation did not end with the signing of the accords. For example, the purge of the army officer corps occurred only after substantial delays and required strong international pressure. A particularly serious threat to the peace process came in October 1992, when the FMLN halted its phased disarmament in response to lack of progress in the land transfer program; this dispute culminated in a further UN-brokered agreement designed to expedite the transfer of lands. The establishment of a new National Civil Police (PNC) was also subject to numerous delays. The dismantling of the former police force, originally slated for the end of 1993, was not completed until January 1995.

Still the peace process had its positive moments. One landmark was the March 1994 elections, in which the government party, ARENA, won the presidency, the largest share of seats in the Legislative Assembly, and the vast majority of municipal elections; the FMLN, participating in elections for the first time, finished second in the presidential race and won a number of assembly seats. Although the elections were marred by incomplete voter registration and polling irregularities, the voting process was peaceful and the outcome was regarded as reasonably fair by most observers.[1] Given El Salvador's flawed electoral history and the bitter feelings of ex-combatants, this was a truly impressive step toward the consolidation of civil society.

One key component of the accords was the establishment of a land transfer program, itself a partial recognition of the role that inequality of land ownership had played in triggering the Salvadoran civil war. We say "partial," however, because the program did not seek to further widespread land reform but rather, under the October 1992 supplemental agreement, provided for voluntary land transfers to ex-combatants on both sides and to peasant supporters of the FMLN in the former conflictive zones. As de Soto and del Castillo (1994b, 11) observe, "The land transfer program was certainly not an attempt at land reform or a mechanism for income redistribution as such, but rather the main venue in the Agreement through which ex-combatants and supporters of the FMLN would be reintegrated into the productive life of the country." In short, the program was a sort of "land-for-arms" exchange, with landowners to be compensated at "market prices." The fulfillment of even this limited aim has proven problematic, however: The transfer program is now far behind schedule; agricultural credit and technical assistance have not been readily available; the current macroeconomic environment is very unfavorable to agriculture; and the recipients are saddled with debts for land acquisition they are unlikely to be able to repay.

Failures to fulfill the expectations of demobilized ex-combatants have had serious implications for public security. Ex-combatants are widely cited as a factor in the country's recent crime wave. Moreover, protests by ex-combatants periodically threaten to rekindle organized violence. In January 1995, for example, ex-soldiers occupied the Legislative Assembly and other government buildings in San Salvador for two days, taking hundreds of hostages and blocking key highways. The weekly journal *Proceso* commented: "The actions taken by the demobilized soldiers demonstrate the extremes to which desperate people, without jobs or a future, can resort" (Center for Information, Documentation and Research Support 1995).

The Peace Accords and the Macroeconomic Setting

The peace accords have been implemented against the backdrop of a surprisingly healthy macroeconomy (see Table 13.1). The war itself likely created macroeconomic difficulties—the early 1980s saw negative economic growth and plummeting investment ratios—but the war-related causes of these outcomes are hard to distinguish from the impacts of deteriorating terms of trade in this period as well as the generalized economic crisis that confronted most of Latin America.

Table 13.1 Macroeconomic Performance in El Salvador, 1982–1994

	1982	1983	1984	1985	1986	1987	1988	1989	1990	1991	1992	1993	1994
GDP growth (annual %)	-5.6	0.8	2.3	2.0	0.6	2.7	1.6	1.1	3.4	3.5	5.3	5.1	5.5
Inflation (Dec.–Dec. %)	13.4	15.3	9.4	31.9	30.3	19.6	18.2	23.5	19.3	9.8	20.0	12.1	8.9
Investment (as % of GDP)													
Private	6.5	7.0	7.6	8.7	10.6	10.7	9.5	9.8	9.5	10.9	12.3	12.9	13.7
Public	6.1	4.6	3.9	3.3	2.5	2.9	3.1	3.5	2.3	2.5	3.6	3.6	3.4
Real currency value (1980 = 100)	115.2	128.9	140.4	172.6	120.8	142.6	164.2	184.1	160.9	156.9	166.4	186.7	203.3
International trade (U.S. $ millions)													
Exports	700	758	726	679	778	590	611	498	580	588	597	732	NA
Imports	(800)	(832)	(914)	(895)	(902)	(939)	(967)	(1,090)	(1,180)	(1,294)	(1,559)	(1,767)	NA
Trade balance	(100)	(74)	(189)	(216)	(124)	(349)	(356)	(592)	(600)	(706)	(961)	(1,035)	NA
Current account	(120)	(148)	(189)	(189)	(17)	(68)	(129)	(330)	(235)	(213)	(195)	(118)	NA
Trade Balance (as % of GDP)	-2.8	-2.1	-4.9	-5.3	-3.0	-7.8	-7.6	-11.9	-11.2	-12.1	-15.1	-13.6	NA
Current account (as % of GDP)	-3.4	-4.1	-4.9	-4.6	-0.4	-1.5	-2.8	-6.7	-4.4	-3.6	-3.1	-1.6	NA
Reserves less gold (U.S. $ millions)	109	160	166	180	170	186	162	266	415	287	422	536	NA

Sources: IMF (1995), World Bank (1994c), and author estimates.

What is less difficult to determine is the cause of inflation through the 1980s. The Salvadoran economy is quite typical of small, export-reliant developing countries: The availability of foreign exchange is a key factor limiting industrial output (through its effect on intermediate imports) and the resulting changes in the exchange rate are often passed through to prices. This implies that depreciation to regain competitiveness can often trigger inflationary spirals, particularly if fiscal discipline is lax. The country was able to avoid such depreciation through most of the early 1980s due to external assistance from both the United States and the International Monetary Fund (IMF). In 1984–1985, however, a newly elected Christian Democratic government decided to loosen the fiscal purse strings, partly to mobilize more military resources and partly to quell social pressures via the expansion of public employment. This gave a domestic impetus to inflation and, in 1986, the U.S. Agency for International Development (USAID) persuaded the government to adopt a typical "orthodox" economic package combining fiscal restraint and currency depreciation. Inflation hovered above 30 percent in both 1985 and the "adjustment" year of 1986, low by Latin American standards but a record high for the country's post–World War II history.

The negative experience with depreciation-cum-inflation led the government to subsequently pursue a strategy largely based on stabilizing the exchange rate. For most developing countries, such a strategy would be infeasible, but El Salvador had the advantage of massive flows of external resources. Through most of the 1980s, this consisted largely of official transfers to support the government; growing throughout the period, however, were worker remittances sent by those who had fled the conflict and were working in the United States and elsewhere. These remittances were often sent through unofficial channels, partly because of unfavorable official exchange rates; so although such flows helped poorer citizens maintain their standard of living through purchases in the black market, direct foreign exchange relief for the government was not as forthcoming. The government of Alfredo Cristiani, taking power in 1989, decided to tackle this issue by setting a single exchange rate to eliminate the black market incentive and by opening up currency exchange shops to channel and better capture incoming dollars. These policies were effective: By 1993, remittances had risen to 108 percent of exports (from 41 percent in 1989); by 1994, remittances stood at nearly 10 percent of GDP, more than double the volume of official external assistance (see Table 13.2).

The resulting foreign exchange bonanza has propped up the *colón* and helped keep inflation in check. Growth has been relatively strong,

Table 13.2   Macroeconomic Significance of Family Remittances, 1984–1994

Year	Remittances (US $ millions)	Remittances as a % of exports	Remittances as a % of net transfers	Remittances as a % of GDP
1984	121.0	16.7	38.4	2.6
1985	101.9	14.7	31.9	1.8
1986	134.5	17.8	35.0	3.4
1987	168.7	28.5	29.4	3.6
1988	194.0	31.9	38.1	3.5
1989	203.7	41.0	39.2	3.5
1990	322.1	55.4	56.6	5.9
1991	518.0	88.1	94.6	6.8
1992	686.0	114.7	91.7	8.1
1993	789.0	107.8	89.4	8.1
1994	870.0	104.7	NA	9.7

Source: Excerpted from Boyce (1996, Table 4.3)); based on data provided by the Fundación Salvadoreña para el Desarrollo Económico y Social and Banco Central de Reserva de El Salvador.

posting above 5 percent annually from 1992 on, partly because of the ability to run large trade deficits. The key, as we have suggested, is a strong *colón* that, because of the currency inflow, is now twice as strong against the dollar as it was at the beginning of the Salvadoran conflict. A second factor has been the recuperation in private investment since the beginning of earnest peace negotiations, with a rise by over 4 percent of GDP between 1990 and 1994.

This macroeconomic scenario suggests at least two key themes. First, peace has been good for the Salvadoran economy; it has brought a resurgence of confidence and investment and created a healthy burst of growth. This indicates that peace and economic stability are complementary objectives; the task of policymakers is to intertwine them successfully. The second theme is more cautionary: Aside from peace, the other dynamic driving the Salvadoran economy forward is a potentially unstable currency, which may help inflation and sustain short-run growth but can threaten long-run export competitiveness. Economic policy should therefore be focused on both adequately financing the peace accords and lowering the real value of the currency; as we will see, the government of El Salvador has tended to lean in the opposite direction.

The Peace Accords, the Economy, and International Financial Institutions

The Chapultepec accords were hailed as a "negotiated revolution" by Alvaro de Soto, who mediated the peace talks on behalf of the Secretary-General of the United Nations (Golden 1992; Karl 1992). Neither the negotiation nor the revolution ended, however, with the signing of the accords. The peace agreement stopped the shooting, but the conflicts that rent El Salvador's social fabric continue to be fought by other means. In such a context, the policies of external actors can strengthen, or weaken, the political resolve of both sides to implement the accords and consolidate the peace.

Economists and the international financial institutions they staff are generally ill prepared to operate in this sort of setting. Contemporary economic theory typically takes for granted the basic underpinnings of an economy, including a well-defined and socially accepted distribution of property or "initial endowments," a legal system to enforce property rights and contracts, and a state able to perform necessary economic tasks not fulfilled by markets, such as the provision of public goods. All these preconditions are compromised or shattered by civil war, if indeed they existed before it—and they do not spring forth spontaneously upon the signing of a peace agreement. Rather, they must be built gradually in a process regarded as legitimate by all parties to the conflict. Unfortunately, conventional economic theory has little to say about how this crucial process of institutional change is to be accomplished.

International financial institutions such as the World Bank, the IMF, and the InterAmerican Development Bank (IDB) cannot so readily ignore these core issues of political economy. Yet these agencies historically have sought to distance themselves from such "political" issues, straying as little as possible from the familiar economic terrain in which they can claim technocratic expertise. In El Salvador, this has contributed to a lamentable lack of coordination between economic policy and the peace process. The IFIs have continued recommending their usual economic policies, including budget discipline and trade liberalization. They have missed, we would suggest, the unique opportunity provided by El Salvador's relative abundance of foreign exchange to use economic policy to also address the more fundamental issues of equity, institution building, and citizen access.

Institutionally, the disconnection between economic policy and peace building has been manifested in the division of labor between the Bretton Woods institutions (the World Bank and the IMF) and the United Nations: Economic policy has been the province of the former, the peace process the province of the latter. Writing in the March 1994 issue of *Foreign Policy,* Alvaro de Soto and Graciana del Castillo depict the resulting situation by means of a metaphor: El Salvador is a patient on the operating table "with the left and right sides of his body separated by a curtain and unrelated surgery being performed on each side."[2] Sketching policies that can overcome this disconnection and better build the peace is the central focus of this chapter; to do this, we begin by sketching out the conflicts between economic policy and social consolidation that have occurred in El Salvador's recent history.

Stabilization During a Postconflictual Transition

Economic Stabilization Versus Political Stabilization: Is There a Trade-off?

Contemporary macroeconomic policy distinguishes between short-run stabilization and medium-to-long-run adjustment. Stabilization involves primarily fiscal and monetary policy; in the division of labor among the IFIs, this is mainly the province of the IMF. Adjustment refers to policies designed to alter the structure of the economy, including the relative sizes of the public and private sectors and of the tradable and nontradable sectors; this is mainly the province of the World Bank and the regional development banks. In this section, we concentrate mainly on short-run stablization issues.

Short-run economic policy during a postconflictual transition faces potentially conflicting challenges. On the one hand, economic discipline is probably necessary in order to recuperate the domestic economy. On the other hand, political stabilization requires the successful implementation of the measures negotiated in any peace agreement; this in turn requires adequate funding for programs mandated by the accords and a continuing commitment by both sides to the ongoing peace process. Economic stabilization and political stabilization are both necessary for pushing the society back onto a path of long-run economic growth: Both raging inflation and raging social conflict each have the potential to dampen private investment and impede recovery. Thus, economic policy cannot be judged with regard to its "soundness" without looking at the conflicts and trade-offs between political and economic stabilization.

Adjustment efforts in El Salvador have been largely guided by what John Williamson has termed the "Washington Consensus," an informal agreement among policymakers in U.S. agencies, international financial institutions, and Latin American capitals that government deficits should be small, exchange rates competitive, and trade and investment flows deregulated (Williamson 1990). In El Salvador, the IMF stabilization agreements of 1990–1991 and 1992–1993, the World Bank structural adjustment packages of 1990–1991 and 1993–1994, and the thrust of U.S. aid conditionality have all pushed economic policy in this general direction. El Salvador has received somewhat special treatment in that the IFIs have demonstrated a relatively high degree of tolerance for relatively large fiscal deficits during the war. Moreover, the usual focus on promoting exports through depreciation has been largely thwarted by the continuing upward pressure on the exchange rate due to external aid and remittances; indeed, as noted earlier, Salvadoran authorities seem to have shifted to what is an emerging Latin American consensus on the need for a stable exchange rate, in the manner of the recent inflation-fighting experiments in Mexico and Argentina; and the government has even discussed the notion of adopting a currency board arrangement that would take both exchange rate and monetary policy out of the hands of elected officials.

Despite these divergences, Salvadoran economic policy has generally been consistent with traditional stabilization approaches, and its emerging longer-term economic strategy has included the trade liberalization and domestic deregulation components of the "Washington Consensus." This package of policies may not be entirely appropriate for postconflict economies. While fiscal discipline is usually to be applauded, there is a large intermediate terrain between rigid adherence to the macroeconomic targets on the one hand, and profligate deficit financing expenditures on the other, particularly if the deficit is connected to the building of peace and not the waging of war. Analogous to the familiar trade-off between inflation and unemployment depicted in macroeconomics textbooks, there may exist a trade-off between the size of the government budget deficit on the one hand and the social tensions arising from inadequate peace expenditures on the other. This situation is depicted in Figure 13.1; the figure is backward-bending to indicate the possibility, often viewed as probable by IFIs, that beyond some point the net effect of increased government budget deficits may be to fuel social tensions, for example, by sparking hyperinflation.

One crucial issue, of course, is exactly where on this curve we are; another is whether policy priorities can induce shifts in the curve (i.e., create a better set of trade-offs such that lower social tensions are consistent with more modest budget deficits). On the first issue, IFI officials have often seemed to believe that we are on the AB portion of the curve, suggesting that a relaxation of budget deficit targets would jeopardize macroeconomic stability and ultimately endanger the peace process itself. Hence, IFI officials have stressed the need to finance peace expenditures by increasing tax revenues, shifting government expenditure, and tapping external resources rather than running large deficits.

Figure 13.1
The Trade-off Between Deficits and Social Tension

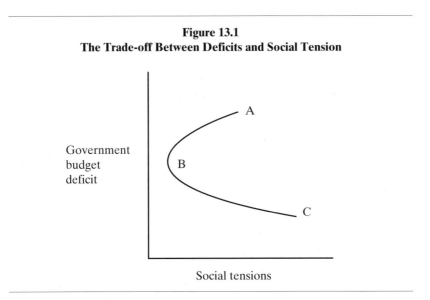

Government
budget
deficit

Social tensions

Those responsible for the peace consolidation component of the postconflict transition have often argued, however, that this is a very perilous moment in El Salvador's history and one that requires some relaxation of the budget constraint in order to better fund peace-related programs; in short, this view suggests that we are safely in BC territory, in which rising deficits might cause some minor macroeconomic disruption but still wind up having a positive net impact on social stability. For example, an August 1993 study, "Economic Consequences of Peace in El Salvador," undertaken by the secretariat of the UN's Economic Commission for Latin America and the Caribbean, concluded:

> It might be necessary to explore the possibility, should the situation arise, of slightly extending the deadline for reducing inflation or of pursuing trade liberalization less vigorously. Within limits, setting more flexible quantitative goals for the stabilization programme might be an acceptable sacrifice, since it would secure the higher goal of ensuring the governability of a society that has, for years, been in the throes of a disastrous civil war. (CEPAL 1993, 12)

Since determining where we are on the curve is difficult—the factors behind the trade-off rely not just on actual macroeconomic outcomes but also on the ability of political actors to mobilize against negative economic effects—one strategy that both sides could potentially agree on is a shift leftward of the curve, such that any given deficit is consistent with a lower level of social tension (or, alternatively, that tension reduction could be achieved with a lesser level of deficit spending). In this case, the argument would be not about aggregate expenditure ceilings but rather about government fiscal priorities; indeed, IFI officials have suggested that overall spending limits in El Salvador are not as tightly binding as they might be given the presence of U.S. and other external aid (see Figure 13.2). Attempts to use IFI influence to improve the trade-off—to promote "deficit-neutral" shifts in revenues and spending designed to increase funding for the peace accords—might be labeled "peace conditionality." The crucial issue is whether the IFIs have built such priorities into the usual forms of conditional assistance extended on macroeconomic issues.

Peace Conditionality in El Salvador

In El Salvador, the government has often sought to shift the costs of various peace-related programs onto the external assistance agencies. External assistance, although substantial, has not been sufficient, leaving domestic authorities three options: (1) accept shortfalls in the funding of peace-related programs; (2) run a larger budget deficit; and/or (3) in-

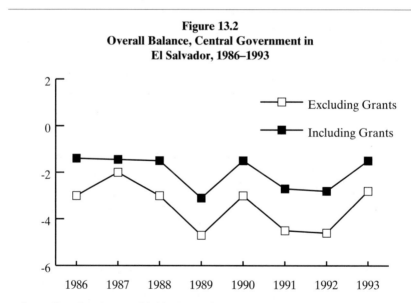

Figure 13.2
Overall Balance, Central Government in
El Salvador, 1986–1993

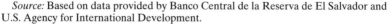

Source: Based on data provided by Banco Central de la Reserva de El Salvador and U.S. Agency for International Development.

crease domestic resource mobilization by shifting government expenditure from other uses and/or increasing tax revenues. Option (1) is problematic: This remains a fragile peace and the accords were, if anything, overly limited in their fiscal demands, since they do not fully get at the longer-term distributional issues that triggered the war in the first place. Option (2) is only moderately viable: While there is some limited room for easing the budget deficit targets, excessive relaxation would indeed prove costly in terms of macroeconomic stability and it is, at any rate, largely ruled out by the IFIs. We are left therefore with option (3): Unfortunately, the government has made only limited progress on resource mobilization and expenditure shifting, and the IFIs have been of little help on this issue, as they themselves have largely failed to apply a new sort of conditionality oriented not simply toward macroeconomic stabilization but also toward the building of peace.

Such a new "peace conditionality" would stress the need to raise tax revenues, particularly from the wealthy, and to reduce military and other nonessential expenditures. In El Salvador, however, progress on the tax front has been less than spectacular. Figure 13.3 illustrates the fall in the tax coefficient from the 1977 prewar peak of 15.7 percent of GDP to a low of 7.6 percent of GDP in 1989. In 1989, the government introduced an overhaul of the tax system, including the elimination of export taxes (in part to counter the disincentive effect introduced by an increasingly overvalued colón), elimination of the tax on net worth, reduction of the top income tax rate, and the creation of a value-added tax. Although these measures, as well as the improvement of auditing mechanisms, managed to raise the tax coefficent by nearly two points in the succeeding years, the World Bank (1994b, 182) reports that total government revenue in 1992, at less than 10 percent of GNP, was the lowest of any middle-income country in the world. Moreover, the shift toward reliance on a value-added tax may have eased revenue collection, but it made the tax system more regressive, and this worked against any desire to use tax policy to redress distributional inequities.

On the spending side, military expenditure is the most obvious candidate for budget cuts to free more domestic resources for programs mandated by the peace accords, particularly since the IMF reports that "in the Western Hemisphere, El Salvador allocated the largest share of total [government] spending for defense (16 percent) in 1992, and the smallest share for social security and welfare (3 percent)" (Abdallah 1995, 77). But while Salvadoran military spending has declined since the war, it continues to absorb a substantial amount of scarce government resources. The share of Salvadoran GDP devoted to the military in 1993 was 1.7 percent, according to the

Figure 13.3
Tax Coefficient in El Salvador,
1977–1994

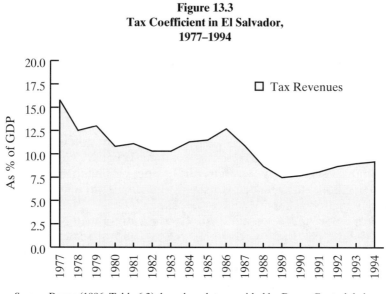

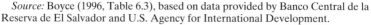

Source: Boyce (1996, Table 6.3), based on data provided by Banco Central de la
Reserva de El Salvador and U.S. Agency for International Development.

IMF (1994, 45).[3] This compares unfavorably with the 0.5 percent for
health and 1.6 percent for education (see Table 13.3), and remains far
above its prewar level of 0.7 percent of GDP.

The scale of military spending has not, however, been a significant
source of conflict between the IFIs and the government of El Salvador.
Interviews with IFI officials suggest a sort of benign neglect. The IMF
has traditionally tended to focus on aggregate government expenditure
rather than its composition, leaving the details to adjusting governments;
it chose not to alter its approach despite the special circumstances of a
war-torn country.[4] A World Bank official closely involved with El Salvador policy stated that the Bank "never discussed explicitly" the issue
of defense expenditure, arguing that the issue lies outside the Bank's
mandate and competence. In a personal interview, an IDB official suggested that donor pressure on the Cristiani government would have
been counterproductive: "There are political realities. The Peace Accords were delayed by Cristiani's problems with the military. I have no
doubt that he would have liked to cut their budget more, but those guys
are powerful. Had Cristiani not been able to postpone the sacking of 100
top military officers, the peace process might be in shambles now."

Table 13.3   IMF Estimates of Central Government Expenditures on the Military, Education, and Health, 1989–1993 (as % of GDP)

	1989	*1990*	*1991*	*1992*	*1993*
Military	3.7	3.0	2.6	2.2	1.7
Education	1.8	1.6	1.5	1.5	1.6
Health	0.8	0.8	0.8	0.8	0.5

Source: IMF (1994, pp. 26, 45).

What about the United States, the principal financier of the Salvadoran military during the war? Following the signing of the peace accords, U.S. military aid was scaled down to $23 million in 1992.[5] While cutbacks in U.S. military aid were accompanied by substantial U.S. funding for peace accords programs, initial conditionalities with regard to progress on peace-related issues (such as land transfers) were not as strong as they might have been, partly because, in the words of one official, "*we ourselves* didn't have the political will." The efficacy of recent U.S. pressures on the government has also been limited by the lack of support from the IFIs. While the World Bank, IDB, and USAID have negotiated cross-conditionality on macroeconomic issues, they have not done so with respect to implementation of the peace accords. According to a senior USAID official, "The IFIs have steadfastly refused to talk about military expenditure targets in El Salvador. They say: 'This is political conditionality, and we are apolitical organizations. We cannot include budgeting sufficient funds for the PNC or land transfer in our conditions. The U.S. government can do that because it has a political agenda, but we don't.'"

The reluctance of the IFIs to venture into the terrain of expenditure shifting in El Salvador is not entirely consistent with the public posture of these institutions.[6] An April 1991 communiqué of the IMF's Development Committee raised "the need to re-examine the possible reallocation of public expenditure, including excessive military expenditures, to increase their impact on poverty reduction."[7] In the same year, at the joint World Bank/IMF annual meeting, the IMF managing director, Michel Camdessus, announced that military budgets are "a proper subject for our attention" and characterized this as "just an extension and intensification of our traditional work to help countries improve their macroeconomic policies."[8] To this end the IMF staff has produced several research papers examining data on military spending and its economic impact. According to former IMF economic counselor Jacques Polak, the IMF in a few cases "has exercised pressure to reduce military expenditures as part of a program of fiscal adjustment."[9]

Similar expressions of official concern have been heard at the IDB, where the new emphasis on social sectors in recent years has led to heightened awareness of the constraints posed by excessive military spending (Griffith-Jones et al. 1993). The failure of the IFIs to raise effectively these issues in El Salvador suggests that the emerging consensus against military spending is yet to be widely affirmed at the operational level.[10] Peace conditionality, in short, has not been practiced with great success in El Salvador.

Peace Conditionality and Governance

Political economy analysis suggests that policy change occurs when external or internal constituencies can recognize their own interests, organize collectively, and pressure for reform. If the IFIs remain unwilling to directly impose peace conditionality in the programs they sponsor, they can at least contribute more directly to the domestic conditions for peace consolidation by promoting *governance* reforms that encourage democracy and allow the populace a larger role in the determination of economic policy; this would create a sort of "back door" route to encourage a more progressive tax system and less regressive expenditures.

While governance issues, including the legal framework, judicial reform, and the strengthening of democratic institutions, were once viewed as outside the purview of the IFIs, IMF Managing Director Camdessus, speaking in June 1994, included "good governance—that is, publicly accountable and participatory government that serves the interests of all of society rather than sectional interests" as a crucial ingredient in the "recipe for success" in structural adjustment and economic development (*IMF Survey* 1994, 209).

Similar pronouncements have been heard from the World Bank, including a 1994 publication titled *Governance,* whose glossy cover featured the terms *legal framework, military expenditures, accountability, participation, judicial reform,* and *human rights* (World Bank 1994a). Yet the practice of the IFIs in El Salvador has fallen far short of the pronouncements: In their own project lending, the IFIs have contributed nothing to the various high-priority programs mandated by the peace accords, nor have they deployed formal conditionality or informal policy dialogue to support these programs indirectly.[11]

The record of the United States on governance issues is more positive but still mixed. As early as 1991, the United States included in its Economic Support Fund (ESF) program measures to strengthen democratic institutions, especially the judiciary. According to USAID officials, "The combination of conditionality and provision of resources through project assistance increased the allocation of public expenditures to democratic institutions" (Belt and Lardé 1994, 7). In 1993–1994, the United States held up deliveries of police vehicles and equipment until the Salvadoran government agreed to remove the controversial former head of the National Police's narcotics unit from his position as deputy director of the new civilian police force.

In the case of the land transfer program, the U.S. position has been less strong. The administrative impediments to land transfers—such as the need to ensure that all back taxes on the land have been paid, or that all joint owners (some of whom cannot be traced) sign the various transfer documents—could be removed, for example by presidential decree. Moreover, the land could be transferred as an outright gift, rather than saddling the new owners with a debt for its purchase. The Salvadoran government has been politically unwilling to take these steps, partly because authorities remain uneasy about tithing land to individuals who were on the other side of a civil war. The United States, the main funder of the land transfer program, has chosen not to pressure the government to be more forthcoming; the result has been a land transfer program that, in the words of a USAID memorandum, is "doomed to failure because, quite simply, it is designed to fail."[12]

The leverage of the United States over the peace process has diminished with time. The Salvadoran economy was, at one time, extremely dependent on U.S. transfers to remain afloat. However, the rise of remittances has given the government an independent source of "unconditional" foreign exchange; indeed, one key policy issue between the United States and the Salvadoran government is the latter's desire for the former to continue to permit Salvadoran immigrants to reside in the North and send remittances South. It is, however, not too late to change strategies and exercise what influence remains to truly promote peace; this will require, however, a more unified and committed voice on the part of the IFIs and the United States.

Peace Conditionality: Too Loose or Too Strong?

During a postconflictual transition, there often seems to be a conflict between economic and political stabilization. The former requires budget discipline, the latter perhaps a loosening of the purse strings. In El Salvador, external assistance has dropped off and the government has little choice but to run a tight fiscal ship. With this as background, increases in domestic tax collection and shifts in budget priorities are necessary to consolidate peace in the short run. Not surprisingly, a government still smarting from the wounds of war is not eager to do all that would be necessary to incorporate its former enemies and the sectors they represent; the government also must carefully downsize a bloated and politically powerful military sector.

While the support of the international community has played a crucial role in the Salvadoran peace process, international actors could help the process along at this stage by exercising a more active "peace conditionality." The conditionalities of major aid donors—in particular, the international financial institutions—for the most part were not deployed in support of such objectives as the reallocation of government spending from the military to the new democratic institutions, or the timely implementation of such key programs as the creation of the PNC and land transfer. In this sense, then, the IFIs have impeded the consolidation of peace by being both "too tight"—failing to recognize the need to move up the deficit-tension trade-off—and "too loose"—not insisting more forcefully on the reallocation of domestic resources in return for external assistance. With the first few years of postconflict transition now shakily in hand, observers can only hope that the IFIs will find the proper mix with regard to long-term aid, the topic of our next section.

Growth, Distribution, and the Consolidation of Peace

Long-run economic policy after a civil war must promote not only economic adjustment but also a process of political adjustment: the consolidation of peace. In such a context, distributional equity cannot be relegated to a lower priority than economic growth. This is partly because inequity is often a cause of domestic conflict; this is particularly true in the Salvadoran case where massive inequities in the distribution of land are viewed by many observers as a significant factor behind the revolutionary challenge to Salvadoran authorities through the 1980s.

Unfortunately, both the war and the recent Salvadoran adjustment program have likely worsened the distribution of income in that country. Real income levels at the end of 1993 were still 20 percent below those of 1978 (USAID/ESDAT 1993), and the fragmentary evidence suggests that social inequity and poverty continue to worsen. The percentage of the population living in poverty and extreme poverty, for example, grew from 51 percent in 1980 to 56 percent in 1990, while the share of income accruing to the wealthiest 10 percent of all households rose from 31 percent to over 38 percent between 1977 and 1990–1991.[13] There is, furthermore, consensus across the political spectrum that fundamental inequality in access to land is the principal source of endemic poverty for the 73 percent of the Salvadoran population living outside the San Salvador metropolitan area and defined by USAID as rural (USAID 1994). This underlying structural factor will not be eliminated by the limited land transfer program for ex-combatants, and the general distributional difficulties will be only moderately affected by the macroeconomic policies touched on above; what is needed instead is deep institutional and economic reform.

Both the Salvadoran government and the IFIs still have the time to elevate the cause of equity and engage in these deep reforms. The intellectual ammunition for this peaceful "war on poverty and inequality" has been provided by a recent wave of studies linking improved equality with faster economic growth; the policy mechanisms to do this concentrate on a positive complementarity between investments in human, natural, and physical capital. What may be lacking, as in the case of short-run "peace conditionality," is the political will.

Growth and Equity Revisited

Recent years have seen a quiet revolution in economists' understanding of the relationship between growth and equity. For many years the dominant view was that there was a "great trade-off" between these objectives; policies to improve distributional equity would exact a price via lower growth. A revisionist view popularized in the 1970s by World Bank president Robert McNamara, among others, held that "growth with equity" was possible if the income increments from growth could be directed disproportionately to the poor. In the 1990s, fresh empirical and theoretical work has advanced a third and strikingly different proposition: Equity not only is compatible with growth, but positively promotes it.

On the basis of a cross-sectional study of more than forty countries over the quarter century from 1960 to 1985, Rodrik (1994) concludes that the countries with more equal distributions of land and income experienced more rapid growth. In an analysis with clear relevance to El Salvador, Alesina and Perotti (1993) suggest and establish that a key link in the causal chain from equity to growth is political stability. Similar results on the positive impact of equity on growth are obtained in Persson and Tabellini (1994) for both a long-run historical panel of nine industrialized countries and a postwar cross-section of fifty-six countries.

Birdsall and Sabot (1994) likewise find that countries with lower income inequality tend to have higher growth, arguing that an important equity-to-growth link is investment in basic education. This echoes Rodrik's 1994 result that primary school enrollment—a rough indicator of equity in the allocation of human capital investment—had strong positive effects on growth. Again, the analysis is quite relevant to El Salvador. Whereas public expenditure on education in "medium human development" countries rose from 2.5 percent of GNP in 1960 to 4.7 percent in 1990, in El Salvador it declined over the same period from 2.3 percent of GNP to 1.8 percent (UNDP 1994, 158).[14]

A further strand in the recent literature focuses on how inequality can impede growth in the presence of financial market imperfections. In these theoretical models, the poor are blocked from undertaking high-growth activities by their inability to afford the initial setup costs, and because of imperfect financial markets they are unable to borrow for this purpose. Plausible examples include not only investment in physical capital but also investment in education. Hence, policies to redistribute income and wealth, as well as policies to reduce imperfections in credit markets, can enhance growth.[15]

It is still early to speak of a new consensus on growth and equity in development economics. But signs of an impending shift are evident. In *The East Asian Miracle,* the World Bank's (1993) widely publicized study of the economic performance of the "high-performing Asian economies," great importance is attached to the role of widespread primary education in laying the foundation for growth. Other dimensions of distributional equity also feature in the analysis. Equity is recognized as a source of political legitimacy (p. 158); land reform in Taiwan is held to have advanced both land productivity and political stability (p. 161); successful land reform in China, Japan, Korea, and Taiwan "helped to lay the foundation for rapid, shared growth" (p. 169); and the failure of the Philippines to share this success is attributed to the fact that "Philippine policy making has historically been captive to vested interests that have shaped economic policy to protect and enhance their privileged position, often to the detriment of national well-being" (p. 169). Despite these insights, however, *The East Asian Miracle* for the most part echoes the McNamara-era view that growth with equity is merely possible, stopping short of the recognition that equity actually promotes growth. Indeed, the legacy of the old trade-off mentality is still apparent in that the successful combination of rapid growth with equity is regarded as "the essence of the miracle" (World Bank 1993, 8), rather than as the logical, unmiraculous result of causal links from equity to growth.

In November 1994, a delegation from the government of El Salvador visited the World Bank and IMF in Washington, lunched with the principal author of *The East Asian Miracle,* and carried multiple copies of the book back to El Salvador. It remains to be seen whether Salvadoran policymakers will build on the vital lessons of the East Asian experience regarding the importance of equity—notably in land distribution and education—for economic development.

Investment in Natural, Human, and Physical Capital

Any long-run strategy to link together equity and growth must center on investment. Investment in physical capital—the plant and equipment with which labor transforms raw materials—has long been recognized as a basic precondition for economic growth. However, investment in human capital—the health and education of the labor force—is now widely agreed to be of comparable or perhaps even greater importance.[16] In El Salvador, there is considerable scope for greater public and private investment in both physical and human capital. As a share of GDP, El Salvador's gross domestic investment is among the lowest in Latin America. It also has the lowest primary school enrollment ratio of any country in the Western Hemisphere with the exception of Haiti (UNDP 1994, 156–157).

Despite the recent concerns about "sustainable development," investment in natural capital—that is, in the renewel of sources of raw materials and in less deleterious methods to dispose of by-products of economic activity—has yet to receive comparable attention from policymakers. Soil erosion and the depletion and degradation of water supplies are critical environmental problems in many countries; El Salvador faces them in extreme forms (Acevedo, Barry, and Rosa 1995). While appropriate human interventions such as soil conservation and integrated pest management can slow and even reverse these processes, many of the returns to such investments accrue to society in general rather than simply to the investor. In the absence of social mechanisms to correct this classic externality problem, there will be systematic underinvestment in soil conservation, water quality protection, and other types of natural capital.

Investments in natural, human, and physical capital are highly complementary; that is, one type of investment can enhance the scale and productivity of the others. For example, investment in the human capital of the poor can lead to greater investment in natural capital by several routes: by reducing their need to degrade the environment for immediate survival; by improving their ability to combat environmental degradation; and by diffusing knowledge of the relationships between economic activity and the environment (Segura and Boyce 1994). Moreover, greater equality of wealth and power can be expected to result in lower rates of environmental degradation, by lowering the discount rates of the poor and by enhancing the ability of the less powerful to resist the imposition of external costs on them by the more powerful (Boyce 1994). El Salvador offers striking examples of the effects of political and economic inequalities on natural capital, ranging from the environmental damages inflicted by the war itself to the current threat to San Salvador's aquifer from attempts to urbanize disputed lands at the adjacent El Espino coffee cooperative (Barraza 1994).

Getting "There" from "Here"

What sort of policies could promote investment, enhance equity, and maintain macroeconomic discipline? In the larger report (Boyce 1996) from which this chapter draws, we argue that El Salvador's remittance-driven foreign exchange bonanza has created a unique opportunity for economic policymakers: Since the country can "afford" currency depreciation—and indeed needs it to better promote nontraditional exports—the country can actually run a larger government deficit and encourage faster economic growth. We should stress that we do not believe in excessive deficits; as noted earlier, priority shifts with regard to taxation and spending are also necessary, particularly with regard to increasing the progressivity of the tax system, raising overall tax collection, reducing military expenditures in favor of peace-related projects, and encouraging spending on primary education. To ensure that any temporary deficit "pays off" in the long run, we argue that any increased spending should focus on public investment in human and natural capital along the lines sketched above; we also argue that private investment should also be heavily encouraged and suggest that it would, in fact, be lifted by improvements in equity and social stability.

This short-term macroeconomic strategy should be accompanied by microeconomic or institutional policies that directly target improving equity. Aside from shifts in fiscal and investment priorities, we suggest that the IFIs and the Salvadoran government work together to enhance agrarian reform beyond the simple granting of land to ex-combatants, to create employment guarantee programs for the rural poor (oriented toward infrastructure projects so as to build physical capital complements to private investment), to develop programs of microlending and microenterprise development, to use privatization revenues to generate or subsidize projects with direct positive impacts on the poor, and to encourage community-based organizations and development projects. We also suggest selected interventions in the tradable goods sectors, particularly to help the exporters who have been recently hurt by the overvalued currency.

We also argue that a necessary complement to our economic policy is continued political reform. In El Salvador, as elsewhere, a central element of the structural adjustment programs backed by the IFIs has been the "modernization" of the state. In practice, this has primarily meant efforts to trim the size of the state by privatizing state-owned enterprises and eliminating certain agencies and functions, coupled with attempts to increase the efficiency of what remains. But while efficiency improvements may create the economic "space" to address equity, only *democratization*—both in the broad sense of promoting a more equitable distribution of power and in the narrow sense of strengthening democratic institutions such as free elections, the protection of human rights, and the administration of justice—can create the political space to ensure that equity will remain a top concern.

This focus on democracy may seem odd for those concerned about promoting economic health. Economic theory frequently separates state and market; in addition, numerous authors have suggested that democracy can derail development if the "median voter" is poor and hence resents and resists measures that can improve the conditions for capitalist growth. Some have therefore argued for "technocratic insulation"—defined in *The East Asian Miracle* as the ability to formulate and implement policy "with a minimum of lobbying for special favors from politicians and interest groups" (World Bank 1993, 167).

But more recent studies have suggested that democratic structures are actually consistent with improvements in private investment and economic performance, partly because they enhance political stability and help guarantee that technocrats in fact pursue the public interest (see Pastor and Hilt 1993; Pastor and Sung 1995). In El Salvador, democratic accountability is critical, particularly since successful economic policy in El Salvador will require the interventions outlined above and citizen access and oversight will be necessary to reduce rent seeking and other unproductive behavior. Moreover, in the wake of a negotiated settlement to a civil war, the essence of which is the creation of checks and balances on the exercise of power, technocratic insulation is not a real possibility.[17]

For El Salvador, then, the task is combining growth, equity, and democracy. While this may seem a difficult balancing act, we should recall two things: First, if the recent research is right, these imperatives may actually be mutually reinforcing rather than contradictory. Second, this is a country that has already been able to achieve a negotiated peace after a bitter civil war; perhaps a "Salvadoran miracle" on the economic and political front could point the way for other postconflictual transitions.

Conclusion

While the Salvadoran experience has unique features, including the presence of relatively abundant supplies of foreign exchange, it offers clear lessons for other postconflictual transitions. As in El Salvador, a ne-

gotiated conclusion to a civil war inevitably poses the short-run problems of securing the financial and political preconditions for implementation of the peace accords. Countries must therefore weigh the need to
achieve macroeconomic balance against the desire to sufficiently fund
postconflict peace programs. Priorities need to shift both to make budget
room for postconflict initiatives and to diminish the fiscal, and hence political, influence of the military. To help these processes along, international financial institutions should insist on "peace conditionality." Unfortunately, in El Salvador, too little has been done on this front.

Over the long run, the consolidation of peace in countries emerging
from civil war often hinges on the forging of a more equitable distribution of wealth and power. Both peace and growth can benefit from equity improvement, that is, improved balance in the distribution of income and wealth; enhanced investment in human, natural, and physical
capital; and increased democratization to achieve balance in the distribution of power. Economic policy during the postconflictual transition
therefore must aim to secure not only stabilization and growth but also
equity and the consolidation of peace. Policies that fail to build on the
powerful complementarities among these objectives will ultimately fail
to achieve any of them. While this may seem a tall task for the countries
themselves and the funding institutions, the charge for both peacemak-
ers and economic policymakers can be no less.

Notes

This paper draws on the authors' research for the Adjustment Toward
Peace (ATP) project commissioned by the United Nations Development Programme in El Salvador. We are especially grateful to our colleagues on the ATP
research team: Carlos Acevedo, Deborah Barry, Michael E. Conroy, Colin
Danby, Eva Paus, Herman Rosa, Alexander Segovia, and Elisabeth J. Wood. In
addition, we benefited from the suggestions of the members of the project advisory board: Michael E. Conroy, Victor Bulmer-Thomas, Hector Dada, Keith
Griffin, Gabriel Siri, and Lance Taylor. Responsibility for the views expressed
here rests with the authors alone and should not be attributed to the United Nations or any of its member agencies.

1. The Secretary-General of the United Nations reported that "the elections were held under generally acceptable conditions, without any major acts of
violence, although serious flaws regarding organization and transparency were
detected" (United Nations Security Council 1994, 2–3).

2. For a more general analysis of coordination problems between the UN
and Bretton Woods institutions, see Childers and Urquhart (1994, 77–87).

3. Different sources provide conflicting data on defense expenditures.
Compared to the IMF data reported in the text, government budget data generally show somewhat lower defense expenditures and somewhat higher education
and health expenditures.

4. The government's November 1991 Letter of Intent to the IMF did include a commitment to reduce military spending from 22 percent of recurrent expenditure in 1991 to 20 percent in 1992 (IMF 1991a, 58). This provision does not appear to reflect an IMF initiative, however.

5. The United States provided over $1 billion of military assistance during the 1980s (Congressional Research Service 1989, 26). This figure includes only direct support via the Military Assistance Program, Foreign Military Sales Program, and International Military Education and Training Program.

6. For reviews of the debate regarding appropriate IFI policy on military expenditures, see Ball (1992) and Kan (1993).

7. IMF (1991b), cited by Polak (1991, 52).

8. Quoted by Ball (1993, 2).

9. IMF papers on military spending include Hewitt (1991), Bayoumi, Hewitt, and Schiff (1993), and Happe and Wakeman-Linn (1994).

10. The gap between official pronouncements and the operational level may be due in part to the muted way Bretton Woods officials seek to raise the issue of military expenditures. A December 1991 memorandum codifying World Bank policy called on Bank staff to "raise issues of unproductive expenditures where they are significant, as part of its policy dialogue and public expenditure reviews, rather than to impose conditionality related to military expenditures" (World Bank 1991, 2).

11. A noteworthy exception is a proposed $20 million IDB loan to El Salvador to support judicial reform. Such a loan would, in effect, expand the notion of "infrastructure" considered appropriate for IDB lending beyond the traditional foci on physical works and human capital investment to include the strengthening of democratic institutions.

12. The latter quote appears in a May 1994 USAID memorandum titled "Land: The Impossible Dream."

13. The shifts in poverty and extreme poverty come from CEPAL (1993, 7), while the changes in household distribution are detailed in Gregory (1992). Gregory believes the distributional shift is overstated, particularly in the lower deciles (which we are not reporting here), because of significant underreporting of income. While the reallocation upward may be less than that reported in the text, it is likely to have still been substantial.

14. The composition of public expenditure on education is also important. Birdsall and Sabot (1994, 4) observe that in Latin America as a whole, the ratio of total public expenditure on education to GDP has been similar to that in East Asia, but that the share allocated to basic (as opposed to higher) education has been notably lower. They attribute this to pressure from high-income families "to channel subsidies to higher education where their children will be the beneficiaries."

15. See, for example, Galor and Zeira (1993). Danby (1995) discusses credit market imperfections in El Salvador.

16. *The East Asian Miracle* (World Bank 1993, 52), for example, concludes that "primary education is by far the largest single contributor to the HPAEs' [high-performing Asian economies] predicted growth rates." See also Rodrik (1994, 15–22).

17. This can be contrasted to the situation facing an occupation government installed by external powers after an international conflict, as in postwar Korea and Japan.

References

Abdallah, K. W. 1995. "*GFS Yearbook* Highlights Trends in Fiscal Balance, Military Spending," *IMF Survey* 24(5):76–77.

Acevedo, Carlos, Deborah Barry, and Herman Rosa. 1995. "El Salvador's Agricultural Sector: Macroeconomic Policy, Agrarian Change, and the Environment," *World Development* 23 (12): 2153–2172.

Alesina, Alberto, and Roberto Perotti. 1993. "Income Distribution, Political Instability, and Investment." Working Paper No. 4486. Cambridge, Mass.: National Bureau of Economic Research.

Ball, Nicole. 1992. *Pressing for Peace: Can Aid Induce Reform?* Policy Essay No. 6. Washington, D.C.: Overseas Development Council.

Ball, Nicole. 1993. "Development Aid for Military Reform: A Pathway to Peace." Policy Focus Paper No. 6. Washington, D.C.: Overseas Development Council.

Barraza, Beatriz. 1994. "El conflicto por El Espino: Dónde está el estado?" *Prisma Boletín* No. 7.

Bayoumi, T., D. Hewitt, and J. Schiff. 1993. "Economic Consequences of Lower Military Spending: Some Simulation Results." Fiscal Affairs Department and Research Department, Working Paper 93/17. Washington, D.C.: International Monetary Fund.

Belt, J., and A. Lardé. 1994. "El Salvador: Transition Towards Peace and Participatory Development." USAID/El Salvador. Mimeo.

Birdsall, Nancy, and Richard Sabot. 1994. "Inequality as a Constraint on Growth in Latin America." *Development Policy: Newsletter on Policy Research.* Office of the Chief Economist. Washington, D.C.: Inter-American Development Bank.

Boyce, James K. 1994. "Inequality as a Cause of Environmental Degradation." *Ecological Economics* 11:169–178.

Boyce, James K. (ed.). 1996. *Economic Policy for Building Peace: The Lessons of El Salvador.* Boulder: Lynne Rienner Publishers.

Center for Information, Documentation and Research Support. 1995. "Editorial: Demobilized Soldiers Mobilize." *Proceso* 647 (February 1).

CEPAL (Comisión Económica para América Latina y el Caribe). 1993. *La economía salvadoreña en el proceso de consolidación de la paz.* LC/MEX/R.414/Rev.1. Mexico City: CEPAL.

Childers, Erskine, and Brian Urquhart. 1994. *Renewing the United Nations System.* Uppsala: Dag Hammarskjold Foundation; New York: Ford Foundation.

Congressional Research Service. 1989. *El Salvador, 1979–1989: A Briefing Book on U.S. Aid and the Situation in El Salvador.* Congressional Research Service, Foreign Affairs and National Defense Division. Washington, D.C.: Library of Congress.

Danby, Colin. 1995. "Challenges and Opportunities in El Salvador's Financial Sector," *World Development* 23 (12):2133–2152.

De Soto, Alvaro, and Graciana del Castillo. 1994a. "Obstacles to Peacebuilding." *Foreign Policy* (Spring):69–83.

De Soto, Alvaro, and Graciana del Castillo. 1994b. "El Salvador: Still Not a Success Story." New York: Office of the Secretary-General of the United Nations. Mimeo.

Galor, O., and J. Zeira. 1993. "Income Distribution and Macroeconomics." *Review of Economic Studies* 60:35–52.

Golden, T. 1992. "The Salvadorans Make Peace in a 'Negotiated Revolution'." *New York Times,* January 5, 1992, p. E3.

Gregory, P. 1992. "Income Distribution in El Salvador." Report for USAID/El Salvador under contract No. 519-0177-C-00-203-00.

Griffith-Jones, S., H. Singer, A. Puyana, and C. Stevens. 1993. *Assessment of the IDB Lending Programme, 1979–92.* Brighton, Sussex: Institute of Development Studies.

Happe, N., and J. Wakeman-Linn. 1994. "Military Expenditure and Arms Trade: Alternative Data Sources." Policy Development and Review Department. Washington, D.C.: International Monetary Fund.

Hewitt, D. P. 1991. "Military Expenditure: International Comparison of Trends." IMF Fiscal Affairs Department, Working Paper 91/54. Washington, D.C.: IMF.

IMF (International Monetary Fund). 1991a. *El Salvador. Staff Report for the 1991 Article IV Consultation and Request for Stand-By Arrangement.* Washington, D.C.: IMF.

IMF. 1991b. "The Fund and Poverty Issues: A Progress Report." *Development Issues, Presentations to the 39th Meeting of the Development Committee.* Development Committee Pamphlet No. 26, pp. 29–34. Washington, D.C.: IMF.

IMF. 1994. *El Salvador: Recent Economic Developments.* Staff Country Report No. 94/10. Washington, D.C.: IMF.

IMF. 1995. *International Financial Statistics, September 1995.* CD-ROM version. Washington, D.C.: IMF.

IMF Survey. 1994. "IMF Helps Developing Countries Achieve Sustainable Growth." *IMF Survey* (June 27):208–210.

Kan, S. A. 1993. "Military Expenditures by Developing Countries: Foreign Aid Policy Issues." Washington, D.C.: Congressional Research Service, Library of Congress.

Karl, T. L. 1992. "El Salvador's Negotiated Revolution." *Foreign Affairs* 71 (2):147–164.

Pastor, Manuel, Jr., and Eric Hilt. 1993. "Private Investment and Democracy in Latin America." *World Development* 21 (4):489–507.

Pastor, Manuel, Jr., and Jae Ho Sung. 1995. "Private Investment and Democracy in the Developing World." *Journal of Economic Issues* 29 (1):223–243.

Polak, Jacques. 1991. "The Changing Nature of IMF Conditionality." Essays in International Finance No. 184, Princeton University.

Persson, T., and G. Tabellini. 1994. "Is Inequality Harmful for Growth?" *American Economic Review* 84 (3):600–621.

Rodrik, Dani. 1994. "King Kong Meets Godzilla: The World Bank and *The East Asian Miracle.*" In *Miracle or Design: Lessons from the East Asian Experience,* edited by A. Fishlow, pp. 13–53. Washington, D.C.: Overseas Development Council.

Segura, Olman, and James K. Boyce. 1994. "Investing in Natural and Human Capital in Developing Countries." In *Investing in Natural Capital: The Ecological Economics Approach to Sustainability,* edited by A. Jansson, pp. 470–489. Washington, D.C.: Island Press.

Taylor, L. 1993. "Stabilization, Adjustment, and Reform." In *The Rocky Road to Reform: Adjustment, Income Distribution and Growth in the Developing World,* edited by L. Taylor. Cambridge: MIT Press.

UNDP (United Nations Development Programme). 1994. *Human Development Report 1994.* New York: Oxford University Press.

United Nations Security Council. 1994. "Report of the Secretary-General on the United Nations Observer Mission in El Salvador." S/1994/561, May 11. New York: United Nations.

USAID. 1994. "Concept Paper: Equitable Rural Economic Growth Activity," USAID/El Salvador.

USAID/ESDAT. 1993. "El Salvador: Selected Economic Data," ESDAT: LAC/DPP.

Williamson, J. 1990. "The Progress of Policy Reform in Latin America." In *Latin American Adjustment: How Much Has Happened,* edited by J. Williamson. Washington, D.C.: Institute for International Economics.

World Bank. 1991. "Bank Work on Military Expenditure." Internal management note (circulated under the title "Military Expenditure," Sec. M91-1563, and subsequently incorporated into Operational Directive 2.00, Annex B, December 6).

World Bank. 1993. *The East Asian Miracle: Economic Growth and Public Policy.* Oxford: Oxford University Press.

World Bank. 1994a. *Governance: The World Bank's Experience.* Washington, D.C.: World Bank.

World Bank. 1994b. *World Development Report 1994.* New York: Oxford University Press.

World Bank. 1994c. *World Data 1994: World Bank Indicators on CD-ROM.* Washington, D.C.: World Bank.

About the Authors

Krishna Kumar is the sector team leader for humanitarian assistance and democracy in the Center for Development Information and Evaluation of the U.S. Agency for International Development (USAID). He represented USAID in the multidonor Evaluation of Emergency Assistance to Rwanda and was the principal author of "Rebuilding Post–War Rwanda." He is now directing evaluation series of political rehabilitation in war-torn societies. Dr. Kumar has written or edited eight books, as well as numerous monographs, reports, and articles in professional journals.

Nicole Ball is director of the Program on Enhancing Security and Development at the Overseas Development Council in Washington, D.C. Her publications include *Security and Economy in the Third World* and *Pressing for Peace: Can Aid Induce Reform?*

James K. Boyce is professor and chair of the Department of Economics at the University of Massachusetts, Amherst. He is editor of *Economic Policy for Building Peace: The Lessons of El Salvador* and author of *The Philippines: The Political Economy of Growth and Impoverishment in the Marcos Era.*

Charles T. Call is a 1995–1996 Peace Scholar of the U.S. Institute of Peace, an affiliate of the MacArthur Consortium on International Peace and Cooperation, and a Ph.D. candidate in political science at Stanford University. He is author of *Clear and Present Danger: The U.S. Military and the War on Drugs in the Andes,* as well as articles on military and police aspects of inter-American relations.

John M. Cohen is an Institute Fellow at the Harvard Institute for International Development. He has served as a Peace Corps lawyer for the government of Ethiopia (1964–1966), a lecturer in political science at Haile Selassie I University (1971–1973), and a consultant to aid agencies, most notably USAID and SIDA (1974–1995). He has also taught at Cornell University (1974–1978) and Harvard University (1978–1995).

Paul Davies is Southeast Asia desk officer of the Mines Awareness Group, a British NGO specializing in humanitarian demining and community awareness education programs. He is author of *War of the Mines: Cambodia, Landmines and the Impoverishment of a Nation,* a study of the socioeconomic impact of landmines in Cambodia.

Sara Gibbs is a research associate at the International NGO Training and Research Centre (INTRAC) in Oxford, UK, and currently heading the NGO Sector Analysis Programme that provides NGOs with an ongoing analysis of key strategic trends in the context of a rapidly changing NGO environment. Recent consultancy work has included field research into psychosocial issues in Cambodia as a part of the UN Study on the Impact of Armed Conflict on Children.

Rafael López-Pintor is a professor in the Department of Sociology of the Universidad Autónoma in Madrid. He holds a Ph.D. in political science from the University of North Carolina, Chapel Hill and a doctoral degree in law from the Universidad Complutense of Madrid, and has been an electoral consultant to the United Nations Secretariat since 1989.

Joanna Macrae is a research fellow in the Relief and Disasters Policy Programme at the Overseas Development Institute in London. She is coeditor, with Anthony Zwi, of *War and Hunger: Rethinking International Approaches to Complex Emergencies.*

Peter M. Manikas is currently senior fellow at the International Human Rights Law Institute of De Paul University's College of Law. He has served as a consultant to the National Democratic Institute for International Affairs and has worked in West Africa, Pakistan, and Bangladesh on judicial administration, the protection of human rights, and election law reform. He is also coauthor of *The Law of the International Criminal Tribunal for the Former Yugoslavia.*

Kimberly A. Maynard is a consultant in humanitarian assistance, with particular expertise in complex emergencies. Both practitioner and researcher, she specializes in coordination and strategy, the role of foreign militaries, conflict mitigation at the grass roots, policy development, and reintegration of forced migrants. Currently, she is conducting research on the interrelationship between relief assistance and violent conflict in civil wars.

Manuel Pastor, Jr. is associate professor of economics at Occidental College and director of Occidental's International and Public Affairs Center. Among his published works on Latin American development are *The International Monetary Fund and Latin America: Economic Stabilization and Class Conflict* and *Inflation, Stabilization, and Debt: Macroeconomic Experiments in Peru and Bolivia.*

William Stanley is assistant professor of political science at the University of New Mexico. He has published a number of articles and reports on the demilitarization of policing in El Salvador and is author of *The Protection Racket State: Military Extortion, Elite Politics, and Civil War in El Salvador.*

Barry N. Stein is professor of political science at Michigan State University. His publications include three coedited volumes of reports and case studies: *Repatriation Under Conflict in Central America; Repatriation During Conflict in Africa and Asia;* and *Refugee Repatriation During Conflict: A New Conventional Wisdom.*

David Tardif-Douglin is currently a staff agricultural economist with Development Alternatives, Inc. (DAI). He recently served as assistant team leader, economist, and country specialist for a multidonor evaluation of humanitarian assistance to Rwanda. His previous experience includes forty-two months in Rwanda as an adviser to the government of Rwanda on agricultural and rural policy.

Index

About the Book

With civil wars and internal violence on the rise over the past two decades, bilateral donor agencies, intergovernmental organizations, and NGOs have been playing an increasingly critical role in rehabilitation efforts once an acute conflict is over. In this process, it has become clear that the traditional aid focus on the economic sector, though essential, is not sufficient; the political and social institutions of war-torn societies must also be reconstructed.

This collection addresses three questions fundamental to international aid to war-torn societies: What are the sectors that require assistance to promote political stability and economic growth? What lessons can be learned from past experience? And how, together with the leadership of the affected societies, can more effective policies and programs be designed and implemented?

Drawing on case studies, the authors focus particularly on issues of food security, health services, human rights, military demobilization, resettlement, and reconciliation at the local level.